Lawfare and the Ovaherero and Nama Pursuit of Restorative Justice, 1918–2018

The Fairleigh Dickinson University Press Series in Law, Culture, and the Humanities

Series Editor: Caroline Joan "Kay" S. Picart, M.Phil. (Cantab), Ph.D., J.D., Esquire Attorney at Law; Adjunct Professor, FAMU College of Law; former English & HUM professor, FSU

The Fairleigh Dickinson University Press Series in Law, Culture, and the Humanities publishes scholarly works in which the field of Law intersects with, among others, Film, Criminology, Sociology, Communication, Critical/Cultural Studies, Literature, History, Philosophy, and the Humanities.

Publications

Marouf A. Hasian Jr., *Lawfare and the Ovaherero and Nama Pursuit of Restorative Justice, 1918–2018* (2019)
George Pate, *Enter the Undead Author: Intellectual Property, the Ideology of Authorship, and Performance Practices since the 1960s* (2019)
Victor Li, *Nixon in New York: How Wall Street Helped Richard Nixon Win the White House* (2017)
Marouf A. Hasian, Jr., *Kafkaesque Laws, Nisour Square, and the Trials of the Former Blackwater Guards* (2017)
Michaela Stockey-Bridge, *The Lure of Hope: On the Transnational Surrogacy Trials from Australia to India* (2017)
Ted Laros, *Literature and the Law in South Africa, 1910–2010: The Long Walk to Artistic Freedom* (2017)
Peter Robson and Johnny Rodger, *The Spaces of Justice: The Architecture of the Scottish Court* (2017)
Doran Larson, *Witness in the Era of Mass Incarceration: Discovering the Ethical Prison* (2017)
Raymond J. McKoski, *Judges in Street Clothes: Acting Ethically Off-the-Bench* (2017)
H. Lowell Brown, *The American Constitutional Tradition: Colonial Charters, Covenants, and Revolutionary State Constitutions 1578–1786* (2017)
Arua Oko Omaka, *The Biafran Humanitarian Crisis, 1967–1970: International Human Rights and Joint Church Aid* (2016)
Marouf A. Hasian, Jr., *Representing Ebola: Culture, Law, and Public Discourse about the 2013–2015 West Africa Ebola Outbreak* (2016)
Jacqueline O'Connor, *Law and Sexuality in Tennessee Williams's America* (2016)
Caroline Joan "Kay" S. Picart, Michael Hviid Jacobsen, and Cecil E. Greek, *Framing Law and Crime: An Interdisciplinary Anthology* (2016)
Caroline Joan "Kay" S. Picart, *Law In and As Culture: Intellectual Property, Minority Rights, and the Rights of Indigenous Peoples* (2016)

On the Web at http://www.fdu.edu/fdupress

Lawfare and the Ovaherero and Nama Pursuit of Restorative Justice, 1918–2018

Marouf A. Hasian, Jr.

FAIRLEIGH DICKINSON UNIVERSITY PRESS
Vancouver • Madison • Teaneck • Wroxton

Published by Fairleigh Dickinson University Press
Copublished by The Rowman & Littlefield Publishing Group, Inc.
4501 Forbes Boulevard, Suite 200, Lanham, Maryland 20706
www.rowman.com

6 Tinworth Street, London SE11 5AL

Fairleigh Dickinson University Press gratefully acknowledges the support received for scholarly publishing from the Friends of FDU Press.

British Library Cataloguing in Publication Information Available

Library of Congress Cataloging-in-Publication Data Available

ISBN 978-1-68393-188-1 (cloth)
ISBN 978-1-68393-189-8 (electronic)

Contents

Acknowledgments

I want to begin by thanking the Dean of the College of Humanities at the University of Utah, Stuart Culver. My Department of Communication, the College of Humanities, and the University of Utah provided me with sabbatical support during the Fall of 2018 that allowed me to focus most of my attention on writing and revising this book. I would also like to thank Jake Jensen, our Associate Dean for Research in the College of Humanities. Although we approach our research from very different methodological angles, his support for the humanities—as well as his promotion of all of our research in our college—is commendable.

I would also like to extend my thanks to my colleagues in the Department of Communication (who are often a little confused about how someone who is supposed to be in the woods of Oregon on sabbatical could spend so much time in front of computers screens in his department office). Danielle Endres, our former department chair, has helped me every step of the way as I worked on this text, and she, and my colleague Kent Ono, share a common interest in the "decolonial turn" within communication studies.

In many ways I feel that I am also intellectually indebted to the work of scholars I have never met, but admire. Larissa Forster's work on Namibian Studies, indigenous voices, repatriation guidelines, etc. has been very influential. I have never met Jürgen Zimmerer, and yet his work on globalizing genocide studies is inspiring.

I would also like to thank Myra Washington for this manuscript who made sure I included relevant material from interdisciplinary sources on decolonizing studies. I will also thank Marek Muller for the time we spent discussing issues of animality and humanity.

Last, but certainly not least, I have to thank James Gifford, Caroline Picart, and Zachary Nycum for the help that I received from them on many, many occasions.

ONE

Introduction

Colonial Unknowing, Lawfare, and Transgenerational Calls for Ovaherero and Nama Reparations

During the first decades of the twenty-first century representatives of Ovaherero and Nama communities in the African state of Namibia and their allies have participated in protracted societal, legal, and mediated battles with the Federal Republic of Germany. Hoping to gain redress for what the Ovaherero call "*Otjitiro Otjindjandja*"—many people died in one place[1] —these activists and their supporters sought to tell the world about the horrors that took place when German settlers and soldiers, between 1904 and 1908, annihilated tens of thousands of Ovaherero and Nama in "German South West Africa" (GSWA). Many journalists, working for mainstream or alternative presses, now comment on this "forgotten" genocide or "holocaust,"[2] but I will be arguing in this book that few realize that this is not the first time that global audiences have heard about this violent colonial war or calls for reparations. With the passage of time, generational interest in remembering these GSWA horrors has waxed and waned, and in many ways these twenty-first-century Namibian advocates are carrying on the consciousness-raising traditions of their predecessors.

Given all of these concerted consciousness-raising efforts to garner support for Ovaherero and Nama reparations, why do so many resist the "decolonizing" efforts of indigenous activists, postcolonial scholars, critical genocide scholars, and investigative journals who write and talk about the "Namibian genocide"? Surely, part of the answer to that type of question has something to do with the recent rise of the Far Right in Germany, whose members seek to "rehabilitate" the German Empire at the same time that they glorify German colonization.[3] Yet what about the moderates in the Bundestag, the German federal parliament, who have also resisted calling the GSWA violence genocidal in nature? Why isn't more support for Namibian activists coming from the ranks of European communities who recognize other modern or colonial genocides?

Some, like Reinhart Kössler, have tried to explain some of this reticence by pointing out how "contradictory interpretations" of German South West African colonial wars and different "fields of knowledge" and "divergent practices of commemoration" have all contributed to the "gross differences" that exist between indigenous activist remembrances of the Namibian genocide and the views of German speakers living in Namibia.[4] As Kössler would note in a review of the work of Larissa Förster,

> Again, the differences between narratives can be traced to different ways that people acquire and transmit knowledge about what happened in the region commonly known as the Waterberg [the site of a colonial battle that took place on August 11, 1904]. . . . For their sources of knowledge German speakers largely draw upon and invoke German publications from the period shortly after the events that include official accounts. . . . Herero, on the other hand, generally rely on orally transmitted information, including praise songs of the localities concerned, as well as family histories and generally accounts by elderly people handed down by their parents and grandparents.[5]

Professor Kössler called these contradictory "memory-landscapes," and he explained that some of the key social agents involved in controversies about the GSWA wars were "farmers in the rich environs of the Waterberg," who "limit their knowledge to the area of commercial farming," where both epistemic and topographical boundaries were informally set that end "abruptly at the boundary of the former Herero reserve."[6] Kössler—who elsewhere had written dozens of articles on the Namibian genocide—contends here that taking seriously the claims that are embedded in Ovaherero oral histories and elderly reminisces would "undercut the claims of superior knowledge still maintained by certain vociferous German-speaking hobby-historians based in the Waterberg region."[7]

Does all of this imply that the unwillingness of so many in Germany or Namibia to discuss colonial atrocities has to do with colonial nostalgia, national amnesia, or some other malady? How should readers and interdisciplinary scholars assess these competing ways of conceptualizing claims about some Namibian genocide that may have been perpetrated more than a century ago? Is this a case of lack of remembrance, forgetfulness, or refusal to master what some academics call "difficult" colonial heritages?[8]

While some activists, law students,[9] interdisciplinary scholars, journalists,[10] and bloggers[11] have called the GSWA atrocities that were committed by the German soldiers the *Schutztruppe*, the "forgotten genocide," I will be arguing in this book that calling this forgetting or cultural amnesia only gets at some of the ambivalence, the contradictions, and the complexities of the dominant and dissident rhetorics that were produced since the battle of Ohamakari, the Ovaherero name for what the German speakers in Namibia call Waterberg.[12]

Many of those who argued so vehemently about whether colonial-settler activities in German South West Africa could be characterized as a "genocide" could hardly be characterized as uncaring or disinterested stakeholders in these disputes who didn't remember their own histories—they simply had difficulty accepting the viewpoints of others who had used different historicizing and commemorative practices. They viewed their own positions and their own research as knowledge-based, while they treated the viewpoints of the others as muddled, incoherent, lacking in facticity, or politically motivated.

I will be arguing that critical interdisciplinary scholars who review this period need to think of how we scholars and readers can reconceptualize situations where there are almost willful forgettings, colonial nostalgias, and what Manu Vimalassery, Juliana Hu Pegues and Alyosha Goldstein called the "colonial unknowing."[13] These authors explained that this colonial unknowing was not a matter of collective amnesia or an act of omission, but was instead a type of ignorance that was related to "disavowals" of or active attempts at concealing pasts so that some could avoid "culpability."[14] Vimalassery, Pegues, and Goldstein argued that if critics were willing to take seriously critical indigeneity studies in the same way that they analyzed colonial settler rhetorics then they might come to understand how the investigation of "colonial unknowing" was a particular type of "agnosia," or the study of ignorance. These authors called upon their readers to see why many resisted decolonization efforts, failed to follow UN sanctioned protocols that protected indigenous communities, and were unwilling to ruminate about how colonial settler archives produced *both knowledge and ignorance*.[15]

In this book I will be extending the work of Vimalessery, Pegues, and Goldstein; and I will be trying to explain to readers just why so many participants in elite and public disputes about the Ovaherero and Nama genocide are engaged in an activity that is related to what Benedict Anderson called "remembering to forget."[16] An even better descriptor for this malady might be what Ann Stoler once described as "colonial aphasia." Using her own extensions of Michel Foucault's genealogical works, Stoler observed,

> Colonial histories possess unruly qualities. Sometimes they remain safely sequestered on the distant fringes of national narratives where they have long been deemed to belong. Sometimes they transgress the propriety rules of historiographical decorum, trample manicured gar-

> dens, uproot precious plants, or ignore trespass and zoning ordinances. . . . [T]his phenomenon, "colonial aphasia" . . . is to emphasis both loss of access and active dissociation. In aphasia, an occlusion of knowledge is the issue. It is not a matter of ignorance or absence. Aphasia is dismembering, a difficulty speaking, a difficulty generating a vocabulary that associates appropriate words and concepts with appropriate things.[17]

This notion of colonial aphasia, I contend, is an apt way of describing how so many have such a difficult time representing, or (mis)representing, the activities of the colonizers and the colonized following the 1904–1908 Ovaherero/Nama–German War. Applying Professor Stoler's work on colonial aphasia is also a helpful way of conceptualizing the communicative and ideological difficulties that so many generations after 1908 have had with indigenous requests for apologies and other acts of restorative justice for colonial or imperial wrongdoing.

Few understand that the colonization of GSWA was not just some peaceful, incremental expansion of empty regions that were not occupied or developed by "pastoral" African communities who did not stake out any claims to sovereignty or ownership, but was instead a hotly contested space and place where many ethnic communities and many different groups of colonizers—British, German, Afrikaner, and so on—battled for control. As Melber Henning would note, this was a place where the Nama (Khoi-khoi) and the Ovaherero and other indigenous communities quarreled over scarce resources, and when the German settlers and soldiers came, extreme violence had to be used in order subjugate hundreds of thousands who resisted dispossession.[18]

When European colonizers arrived in this south west part of Africa, they did not see this as a land occupied by fellow human beings who possessed similar rights and needs, but as a place filled with nonhumans who were living on underdeveloped lands. One German woman who came to settle GSWA left us this typical account in the archives: "What do we know about the past of this country. Thousands of years of deepest ignorance passed over it. People, living until the present day like animals, dwelt in the grasslands and mountain nooks. They lived and perished without realising any sense of life."[19] This all assumed that the colonizers—with their railroads, their mining needs, their building of wharfs, and their laws controlling the mobility of indigenous communities were the knowledgeable ones that nature intended to feel that "sense of life." The colonial usages of divide and conquer, informal strategies of rule—that allowed a few Nama and Ovaherero leaders to be awarded pensions of 2,000 German marks a year—helped legitimate the movement of entire indigenous communities to "fixed areas in order to restrict their mobility and to improve colonial administrative control."[20] Over the course of a few decades, tens of thousands of Ovaherero and Nama would die, "reserves" were established, and during the later South African apartheid years, these same reserves would be reterritorialized as "traditional homelands."[21] Given these painful colonial or imperial pasts, we can readily understand why so many who live in former colonial-settler states, or who know about other genocides, have difficulty finding the grammars that are needed to decolonize this aphasia.

This particular book helps explain the rhetorical and historical dynamics of all of this knowing and "colonial unknowing" in many generational contexts, and it allows readers to get a glimpse of how overtime opinions, prejudices, conjectures, and other figurations became incontrovertible "archival facts" or "primary" sources for so many who would participate in debates over the Namibian genocide and related controversies. This will not be the type of social science book that tries to separate out rhetoric from reality, myth from fact, but rather a critical, humanistic book that puts on display the repetitive usage of the same rhetorical texts or visualities over and over again, to the point where arguers forget about the constitutive production and origination of these colonial "facts." My interest will not be in the discovery of some absolute "true" history of German South West Africa, but rather what Foucauldians call the "truth effects" of these half-forgotten origins and usages.

More specifically, I will be showing readers in this book the ways that colonial and imperial legal arguments were crafted and deployed by both the colonized and the colonizers as they tried to marshal together various nineteenth- and twentieth-century legal arguments about human rights, "native policy," domestic German law, European informal and formal rules of empire, international laws, and so on, to justify various ways of apportioning lands and rights in what used to be called "German South West Africa."

Henning Melber has argued that the capitalists, settlers, administrators, soldiers and others who came to establish a colony in German South West Africa used a "pretended humanitarianism" to cover their willingness to use violence to dispossess local African populations, and he has speculated that the "majority" of governor Theodor Leutwein's officers may have agreed with those settlers who were willing to use "terrorist methods, aimed at the complete subjugation of the African population—even at the risk of genocide."[22]

This type of argument might appeal to those who support twenty-first-century Namibian reparations efforts, but is it a fair way of writing and talking about colonial laws or the ideological views of the colonial setters or soldiers who boarded ships to come and protect the German farmers and their families? Is it even fair to use the term "genocide"—a word that wasn't coined and popularized before World War II—to material conditions in a place like German South West Africa? Given the famous 1884–1885 Berlin Conference, and The Hague Conference of 1899—weren't there any international laws in place that could be used by anti-imperialists, indigenous rhetors, and others who might object to some

German colonial interpretations of domestic German law or international law? Besides, given the fact that these events took place more than a century ago, isn't there a statute of limitations on this type of retrospective analysis that should prevent activists, critical scholars, and others from rummaging through colonial archives as they produce their own revisionist histories or (post)colonial memories?

By providing readers with critical genealogical studies of the legal and moral arguments about colonial atrocities and "reparations" that have circulated between 1885 and 2019, I will work on providing provisional, tentative answers to these types of questions. I want to provide readers with broad, detailed, and "critical" overviews of the synchronic (across the same time period) and diachronic (across time) arguments that been deployed by different generations who oftentimes had ambivalent feelings about the near annihilation of the Ovaherero and the Nama.

In portions of this book I will be decoding some of the mutable, operative logics that were used by both the colonized and the colonizers in all of this disputation over colonial atrocities that have migrated across time; and in other parts of the book I will be putting on display some of the very rhetorical texts or pictorials that would reappear and be used when Ovaherero litigants filed cases in U.S. federal courts in 2001 and when the Ovaherero and Nama worked together in the filing of different lawsuits in 2017.

One of the most contentious arguments that I will be making in this book is that it is not the lack of formalistic understanding of America's Alien Tort Statute (ATS), or U.S. jurisdictional rules, that is the primary reason that advocates have difficulties in these situation, but rather that they oftentimes face those who consciously, or unconsciously disagree with the Overaherero and Nama about the "merits" of their case. It will be my contention that critical genealogical studies of GSWA colonial affairs, as well as comparative studies of generational remembrances of these affairs, have a great deal to tell us about the lingering discursive power of all sorts of colonial knowing and unknowing.

I will also be explaining how the absence of political will—as well as the strategic use of legal argumentation—hindered the efforts of Namibian activists who tried, between 2001 and 2019, to use lawfare—the politicization of the law—to get the U.S. federal court system to intervene in these German-Namibian debates about GSWA atrocities.

The chapters of this book are organized in some unconventional ways because each chapter is trying to provide readers with needed, but slightly different information, on some of the rhetorical and historical origins of the varied strands of argumentation that appeared in both legal materials in these Namibian reparations cases as well as the commentaries on these cases that appeared in various public venues. In some cases I will be taking micro looks at specific court texts but at other times I will be taking macro views of how those texts are applied in these disputes over colonial genocidal affairs or reparations.

Each chapter also focuses on the rhetorical invention of key facts and laws that were (mis)remembered, ignored, or redeployed by generations who were not always sure what to do with those "unruly" colonial histories (Stoler) or those Namibian "memory-landscapes" (Kössler) that were used by those who sympathized with German settler colonial suppressions of "rebellion" or who viewed all of this colonial violence as genocidal in nature.

Readers may be familiar with some of the Holocaust consciousness-raising efforts of academics, universities, videographers like Stephen Spielberg, places like Yad Vashem in Israel or the United States Holocaust Memorial Museum (USHMM), but relatively few may be aware of the contentious nature of "colonial genocide" studies in general or the Namibian "holocaust" in particular.[23] Even fewer may realize that each year more and more litigants are trying to use the jurisdiction of the U.S.'s Alien Tort Statute to argue that that either America's laws or the "law of nations" provide remedies for various alleged human rights violations or colonial atrocities.

The very topic of the role that the rule of law and courts have played in condoning, or critiquing, particular colonial genocides or imperial atrocities has long fascinated diverse scholarly communities and public audiences. Jodi Byrd, in her trenchant critiques of the American governmental structures that were put in place by populists like President Andrew Jackson, has explained how legislative acts and judicial precedents were once used to grant sovereignty, as well as create dependency, as the Chickasaw and Choctaw Nations were removed to territories west of the Mississippi river.[24] She was convinced that these types of American acts become a part of the structural features of "colonial logics" that justified "theft of Indigenous lands and death for Indigenous peoples."[25] Haidy Geismar, writing about settler-colonial property relations in Aotearoa/New Zealand, would write about how an "expanded genealogy" of applications of European property laws in the colonies, as well as the usage of "alternative genealogies," would show how some of New Zealand's laws were used by the "policing of government of rights" that impacted whether or not empowered communities would recognize indigenous entitlement.[26] Alyosha Goldstein, in a study of agrarian domestication, dispossession, and commerce, opined that oftentimes jurisprudential principles were used to provide "evidentiary logics that weigh against adjudicating systemic culpability" of former settler colonial states, even in cases where researchers could find "entangle histories of racial and colonial dispossession."[27] No wonder that Mahmood Mamdani would similarly comment on the need to decolonize various historical and contemporary settler colonial rhetorics, especially in situations when one cared about the "makeup of postgenocide" societies.[28]

In many interdisciplinary studies—critical genocide studies, settler colonial studies, postcolonial studies, political geography, Third World Approaches to International Law (TWAIL) critical sociology, and so forth—these politicized ways of selectively (mis)remembering colonial atrocities are said to be in need of "decolonization."

This book invites readers to see the many tangled threads of argument that would be woven by various generations who read or heard about alleged German South West African genocidal acts that may have been committed sometime between 1893 (at the colonial battle of Hornkranz) and 1915, when the Union Defence Force invaded GSWA during the Great War. Some who have visited the extant academic archives in Namibia or Germany have concluded violent GSWA colonial battles between German soldiers and Ovaherero or Nama "tribes" never met international thresholds that warranted the "g" (genocide) label, while others have been just as adamant that those who refuse to characterize this as a genocide or holocaust are performing acts of denialism or revisionism.

The traditional "historical" features of this genocidal disputation in GSWA contexts are well known and have been chronicled in many other books or journal articles—by Helmut Bley, Horst Drechsler, Jan-Bart Gewald, Hull, Jürgen Zimmerer, and many others—but some of us are just beginning to study the jurisprudential features of these complex German-Namibian relationships and colonial memory wars. Before November of 2015, for example, neither the Namibian government nor the Federal Republic of Germany were willing to engage in protracted deliberations about how best to master these difficult GSWA pasts, and when they did decide to tackle these issues they tried to exclude Ovaherero and Nama activists from many of these diplomatic conversations. Characterizing colonial violence remembrance as "bilateral" diplomatic matters empowered a few privileged officials in Germany and Namibia who tried to control the shape of the master narratives that would be used in these twenty-first-century conversations about such topics as the public acknowledgment of the genocide, the jurisdictional reach of the ATS, Germany's "sovereign immunity," or the differences that might exist between German "moral" and "legal" culpability for what happened at places like Ohamakari/Waterberg.

While many Germany negotiators characterize these GSWA topics as "political" or "social" relational matters reparations advocates counter by focusing on the "legal" aspects of this "Namibian genocide."[29] Not surprisingly, given my above comments on German and Namibian reticence, there would be those who wanted to dismiss some of these Ovaherero and Nama lawsuits when they were filed in U.S. federal district courts. In 2018, for example, Jeffrey Harris, a lawyer for Germany, appeared before U.S. judge Laura Swain in Manhattan, New York, and he asserted that her court "should abstain from this case under the political question doctrine and let the bilateral negotiations" between Germany and Namibia "proceed."[30]

Excluded Ovaherero and Nama activists—perhaps sensing that these empowered German and Namibian negotiators would be using truncated colonial GSWA histories to avoid discussing legal restitution—became members of many different reparations movements. These movements had members who were asking for much more than German contrition or the provision of a few million Euros in German development aid. Ovaherero and Nama activists who traveled to America produced their own counterhistories or countermemories about what happened between 1904 and 1908, when thousands of *Schutztruppe* (German protection forces) arrived on South West African shores so that they protect German settlers and other colonizers.[31] Using arguments that would sound familiar to readers who might be acquainted with the way that Raphael Lemkin once wrote about "cultural" as well as "biological" and "physical" genocide,[32] the Ovaherero and Nama advocates use interviews, journals, books, documentaries to get across the message that those living in postcolonial nations cannot, and should not, avert their gaze and avoid mastering these difficult settler colonial pasts.

Unlike other traditional academic books that try to provide objective, empirical evidence of "what happened" during these colonial or imperial periods,[33] my primary interest is in explaining to readers *how rhetorical histories are used and abused* to try and advance contentious arguments about colonial genocides in general and the GSWA atrocities in particular. I extend the work of Friedrich Nietzsche, Michel Foucault,[34] Ann Stoler, and many others who are interested in the perspectival study of the power/knowledge/discourse dimensions of colonial and postcolonial disputation. Readers of this book are going to be presented with illustrations of how empowered and disempowered communities, across time and across geopolitical spaces, have left us indeterminate archival materials about GSWA. These rhetorical fragments have been reassembled in many different constellations of meaning, including assemblages that allow for what Elizabeth Baer has called the "genocidal gaze."[35]

Some who rummage through these (post)colonial archives are not trying to help the cause of the Ovaherero or Nama activists, because they have their own motivations. Amateur historians who represent German-speaking communities in Namibia may be revisiting the archives so that they can try and restore the honor of the German soldiers and settlers who fought off the armed Herero and Nama "rebels" between 1904 and 1908. Others who read the same GSWA histories, or who visit German or Namibian archives, are looking for textual or visual evidence that puts on display the consequential damage that came when German leaders and their followers sought to kill, or expel, all of these "rebels" and their families from what they regarded as a "German" colony.[36]

At this point in my introduction I should note that I respectfully disagree with those who might argue that the Ovaherero and Nama advocates are the only parties involved in lawfare, or the "politicizing" of legal venues. It will be my contention that *all colonial and postcolonial texts*—regardless of how they frame "what happened" in GSWA between the 1880s and 1915—have the potential to become the signifying devices that are used in all sorts of territorializing, deterritorializing, and reterritorializing efforts.[37] For example, standard historical works that characterize Ohamakari/Waterberg as a "battle" that is was just part of a typical colonial "war"—without mentioning genocide—are producing texts that could be used by those who disapprove of genocidal labeling. Absence, as well as presence, matters in this disputation.

Decolonizers and postcolonial critics who support Ovaherero and Nama calls for reparations oftentimes come across permutations of these old pro-colonial arguments that appeared in colonial texts and visualities in twenty-first-century conversations. These older ideological fragments become parts of "ideological drifts"[38] that can be recirculated by those who wish to debunk the notion that Germany should apologize for 1904–1908 GSWA activities. The archives—that traditional researchers might treat as the objective, apolitical repositories of traditional German histories—can be conceptualized as those contested places and spaces that become entangled in Namibian-German disputation. These archival materials are some of the places that store information that help colonizers attribute "finality to conquest and dispossession."[39]

Instead of bemoaning the "politicization" of the GSWA archives by the Namibian activists, I will be arguing that a more "critical" approach to these reparations disputes recognizes the inherent ideological nature of all attempts to selectively remember colonial or imperial acts. Regardless of which "mutable historicity" social agents employ, they are all producing, or reproducing, discourse/power/knowledge formations, especially in "lawfare" contexts.

I am obviously not the first scholar to notice the attraction of lawfare for those who seek restorative justice for colonial grievances. As Jean Comaroff and John Comaroff would note,

> With the growing heterodoxy of the twenty-first-century polity, legal instruments *appear* to offer a ready means of commensuration: a repertoire of more or less standardized terms and practices that permit the negotiation of values, beliefs, ideas, and interests across otherwise-impermeable lines of cleavage. . . . Under these conditions [neoliberal privatization of former state functions], in which the threat of disorder seems everywhere immanent, everywhere proportional to the retraction of the state, civil law presents itself as a more or less effective weapon of the weak, the strong, and everyone in between.[40]

Legal forums, in other words, can theoretically become the spaces and places for disputation that allows for the presentation of arguments by many different motivated rhetors, including judges, lawyers, plaintiffs, defense attorneys, and others who use legalese to advance contestable claims.

With each passing day more and more bloggers and users of the World Wide Web are learning about Ovaherero and Nama legal maneuvers. As Reinhart Kössler has noted in his analysis of what he calls Namibian "mnemoscapes," the study of what happened more than hundred years ago in German South West Africa has "much to tell us about postcolonial relationships and related intercultural communication."[41] Jan-Bart Gewald would similarly argue in an essay on the "Herero genocide" that after the passing of the "physical resistance" competing "memories may continue to inform and justify political action long after the events that spawned them receded into the past."[42]

One's subject position, and one's political views, regarding restorative justice claims for past wrongs, often influences how one will argue about the legitimacy of the Herero and Nama redress claims. Here are some of the key research questions that will guide my critical analyses in this book:

1. How have transgenerational audiences, over the last century, characterized the colonial violence that took place in GSWA during the thirty-one years of German colonial rule?
2. What type of historical, cultural, and legal evidence do interdisciplinary scholars have that the "suppression" of the Herero-Nama "rebellion" of 1904–1908 involved any loss of recognizable international human rights for indigenous communities in this part of the world?
3. How have changing cultural perceptions influenced the ways that various colonial archival materials have been used, and abused, by those who now debate about Ovaherero or Nama reparations?
4. Do twenty-first-century U.S. courtrooms provide the best avenues for social change in Namibia as Ovaherero and Nama litigants file their reparations suits in American legal venues?
5. Should worries about setting precedents for other colonial reparations cases impact the ways that we characterize Ovaherero and Nama legal claims for restorative justice?

There will be many other subtopics and sub-issues that I will be tackling in this book, but these might be viewed as the five major overarching claims that will guide the ways that I approach all of this colonial warfare and postcolonial lawfare.

In the next subsection I provide readers with a basic overview of some of the lawfare questions that help contextualize the Herero and Nama filings in U.S. courts.

CONTEXTUALIZING OVAHERERO AND NAMA REPARATIONS CLAIMS AND ACTIVISTS USE OF LAWFARE

Is it any coincidence that some of the very same social agents in Germany, Namibia, or elsewhere who view the 1904–1908 GSWA battles as genocidal in nature are also some of the strongest supporters of the filing of Ovaherero and Nama reparations claims in American courtrooms? As Karie Morgan has argued, although some of the lawsuits seeking compensation for the "Herero genocide" often fail to "yield legal accountability, and payment of reparations," they serve as "a powerful mobilizing tool inside and outside of Namibia."[43] Readers may of course wonder if these colonial reparations lawsuits should be used for those mobilizing purposes, and this will a topic that I will revisit in the last chapter of this book.

One of the obvious issues that I will need to address in this book is whether the entangled German colonial histories and Namibian public remembrances of GSWA violence *should* have anything to do with U.S. courtrooms. I need to evaluate whether Judge Laura Taylor Swain was fair when she argued, in March of 2019, that Germany should be "immune" from claims by descendants of the Ovaherero and the Nama "tribes."[44] As Amanda Ottaway would note several weeks later, for those in Namibia who view themselves as "victims of a little-known genocide," they were having to take a "long journey to justice."[45]

While most lawyers and other commentators who focused on the legalistic features of these reparations cases wanted to write about the lack of jurisdiction to hear any substantive due process claims of the Ovaherero and Nama, other pundits wanted to comment on how these litigants were facing some of the very same historical and political hurdles that confronted other potential litigants. After all, many academics or laypersons can think of other colonial incidents—from the British occupation of Ireland to the Japanese occupation of Korea—that could serve the needs of other advocates who may want to form related reparations movements.[46]

Does that mean that America's Alien Tort Claims Act of 1789 should be *selectively used* by foreigners who want to combat "genocide denialism" at the same time that they seek legal compensation for historical "takings?" Are twenty-first-century judges, who have to interpret twenty-first-century precedents, unwilling to treat reparations for colonial genocides in the same way that other judges once treated Holocaust reparations claims?

As I will explain in more detail in chapter 7, some of the reparations efforts that received a great deal of international media attention would be led by the late Ovaherero Paramount Chief Kuaima Riruako, who would be one of the plaintiffs who filed a September 2001 lawsuit for Herero reparations in the district court of the U.S. District of Columbia.

Some sixteen years later, different filings were presented by Riruako's successor, Vekuii Rukoro and Chief David Fredericks of the Nama Traditional Authorities Association. Supporters of these litigants, like the Association of the Ovaherero Genocide in the U.S.A. Inc., have helped document how the GSWA violated "international law, crimes against humanity, genocide, slavery and forced labor."[47]

Supporters of Ovaherero and Nama reparations efforts are constantly referencing earlier post–World War II restitution efforts, and readers may be familiar with the voluntary payments by the West German government to former Holocaust victims, or they may know about the late 1980s payments to former Japanese-American internees. However, these reparations cases,[48] until recently, have rarely been viewed as examples of lawfare.

The Ovaherero and Nama plaintiffs in these reparations lawsuits argue that they have suffered in unique ways because the "Namibian genocide" is one of the few colonial atrocities that can be documented through the use of rhetorical texts like the infamous *Vernichtungsbefehl* ("annihilation order") that was delivered by a German lieutenant general by the name of Lothar von Trotha after the battle of Ohamakari/Waterberg. Reparations advocates opine that the near extermination of the Ovaherero and Nama is also different from many other violent affair because it was discussed openly—by Kaiser Wilhelm's administrators, by the German general staff, by parliamentarians in the Reichstag, by citizens in saloons, and by settlers in African colonies.

For those who are skeptical of these reparations claims, this may seem like a half-forgotten incident of colonial "warfare" that has little to do with New York jurisdictional matters or presentist American, German, or Namibian needs. As one scholar noted, unless you are familiar with the politics, and the back stories, of these reparations claims it is easy to forget about the lingering consequences of a colonial war that was followed by the passage of "Native ordinances" that took away what little lands indigenous tribes had. "The consequences," argues Reinhart Kössler," are "readily evident" when one sees the former lands owned by the Ovaherero that were settled by those who now patrol "neatly fenced-in farms." The "apparent emptiness" of today lands and territories, Kössler goes on to explain, is not only due to an "arid climate," but also to a "radical reorganizing of the spatial and socio-economic orders on the basis" of a "genocide" that "laid the groundwork" for this "societal set up."[49]

Genocide scholars are not the only social agents who are familiar with some of these academic histories and public memories, and some today put up blog sites that underscore the point that the descendants of German colonial settlers have fared well over the years.[50]

To be fair, many German-speaking Namibians are bothered by the massive income disparities that exist in their country, and they work with the Namibian government to try and find viable solutions to these issues. They also support the efforts of representatives of impoverished Ovaherero and Nama who are demanding that they get some type of monetary compensation that will help them "buy back" some of these lands. In some cases those who have been excluded from bilateral negotiations between German and Namibian diplomats point to the provisions of the U.N. Declaration of the Rights of Indigenous Peoples so that they can defend their right to participate in some bilateral decision making.[51]

These issues divide the ranks of the German-speaking Namibians who don't always agree about how best to remember, or forget, some of Namibia's or Germany's difficult heritage, and critical scholars need to find theories and methods that help them render visible what others sought to obscure.

PERSPECTIVAL, CRITICAL GENEALOGICAL APPROACHES AND THE STUDY OF "LAWFARE" IN OVAHERERO AND NAMA REPARATIONS CONTEXTS

I have been influenced by an eclectic group of writers—critical genocide scholars, "third world" writers in law schools, post-colonial critics, Nietzscheans and Foucauldians—who suggest that comparative studies of genocidal and other colonial claims provide heuristic ways of studying the strategic usages of archival colonial histories. Readers will notice that at times I will be following Professor Ann Stoler's admonition that we try to read "along the grain" so that we can get a textured sense of the governmentalities and mentalities of the colonizers. At other times I will be reading "against the grain," and I will be following Edward Said's suggestion that we attend to subaltern views and produce what he called "contrapuntal" readings of imperial texts.[52]

When I study colonial or imperial reparations disputes, I am not looking for the correct interpretation of some domestic law or international humanitarian law that might provide the Archimedean measuring tool that will help readers determine whether a particular colonial event or "atrocity" ought to be characterized as a "genocide." What interests me are the claims that advanced by many different communities of arguers who are motivated to debate about whether a particular colonial war or horrific imperial event warrants genocidal labeling.

I therefore follow the lead of critics like Michel Foucault, Edward Said, Gayatri Spivak, Lorenzo Veracini,[53] Jürgen Zimmerer, and other scholars who study the role that discourse plays in historical and contemporary (post)colonial disputation. At the same time, I align myself with those members of the Third World Approaches to International Law (TWAIL) community, like law professor Antony Angie, who study international humanitarian laws in ways that provide "alternative histories—

histories of resistance to colonial powers, history from the vantage point of the peoples who were subjected to international law."[54]

Given the multi-layered nature of reparations debates, it makes sense that those who want to untangle some of the argumentative threads that go into the weaving of these tapestries of postcolonial argumentation about reparations take into account the contingent, the indeterminate, and the ideological nature of reparations disputation.

These argumentative threads can be studied in many diverse ways, but given the legal, diplomatic, and public attention that has been lavished on the Ovaherero and Nama filings of legal cases in U.S. courts, it makes sense that critical genealogists pay attention to some of the persuasive power of lawfare. We need to find perspectival ways of tracing some of the sources of the legal arguments have been used in legislative forums, executive corridors of power, and judicial courtrooms to advance a host of competing arguments about colonial reparations.

The use of these critical genealogical approaches helps readers appreciate the ironies that come when we find that during 1896, when many German officers used the term "reparations," they were trying to explain why "rebelling" indigenous forces had to hand over even more lands and cattle to the German "colony" as compensation for the damage that the "rebels" had allegedly caused![55]

This type of strategic usage of colonial wordsmithing reminds scholars and readers that there many different types of symbolic realms and material conditions that impact the resonance of select colonial *epistemes* that are formed by different generations.[56]

Writers of legal treatises, journalists, military diarists, and even authors of colonial adventure books helped with the constitutive production of what I will be calling "public archives" that augmented the more elite traditional archives that were used to discover "primary" sources on these colonial histories. All of this memorialization and monumentalization of the victorious *Schutztruppe* spilled over from the pages of texts into the streets, where the colonizers and the colonized were expected to pay their respects to the soldiers who died defending the colonial settlers.

The constant and repetitive circulation and recirculation of these types of words and deeds are what will occupy my attention in the following chapters as I provide readers with critical genealogical analyses, and my decoding of legal texts and public rhetorics has sensitized me to ways that material colonial conditions impacted particular framings of colonial and postcolonial situations. For example, how one reacted to Ovaherero and Nama calls for reparations during the South African apartheid years could be influenced by one how expressed their feelings about the Lüderitz and Windhoek statues, the graveyard markers, and the naming of the streets that dotted Namibian landscapes and mnemoscapes.

Were manicured European gravesites to be viewed as honorable markers of noble deeds, where German soldiers gave their lives to stop the raids of African "savages," or were these the symbolic markers that might appeal to Namibian genocide "denialists" or reactionaries, who also opposed the use of legal forums for the provision of any kind for Ovaherero or Nama reparations?

As various generations outside of Germany debated about whether certain events in GSWA could be characterized as a "battle" or as an "atrocity" they had to face an embarrassing fact. As Jan-Bart Gewald has noted, given the "gravity of the Herero genocide, it seems remarkable that the only published account of it in English until the 1970s was the Blue Book."[57]

As noted above, Ovaherero and Nama communities had their own oral histories and traditions, but the arguments and genres that appeared in those materials looked nothing like the claims about colonial violence that appeared in some Euro-centric texts.

In this book I want to illustrate how colonial and postcolonial *lawfare has been used by all participants* in these generational debates to help or hurt the cause of ethnic groups like the Ovaherero and Nama who try to seek symbolic or material redress for events that happened during imperial or colonial times.[58]

DIPLOMATIC BOUNDARY WORK, ACKNOWLEDGMENTS, AND SELECT RESPONSES TO CALLS FOR OVAHERERO AND NAMA REPARATIONS

Readers can readily understand why nation-states that are linked to former empires—French, British, Japanese, Ottoman, and the like—might not be in any rush to provide heartfelt apologies or other forms of redress that might have attendant *realpolitik* costs. As Christian Matthias Schlaga, the German ambassador to Namibia, explained to journalists for Al Jazeera, "[W]e do not talk about reparations."[59] German officials are willing to talk about their "special relationship" with Namibia, their developmental aid plans, their on-going negotiations with Namibian ministers, but they are unwilling to talk about financial reparations or legal redress for what happened in GSWA during the colonizing years.

Until the mid-1990s only a few Africanists and other specialists in colonial studies had more than a passing familiarity with these genocidal allegations outside of Namibia, and when diplomats visited this region they were not always sure what to make of reparations requests. When German President Roman Herzog visited Namibia in 1998, he was asked to meet with groups of Ovaherero who wanted to talk with him about what happened in German South West Africa after 1904. A media savvy Kuaima Riruako prepared for Herzog's visit by sending a document on reparations to UN delegates, members of the German embassy in Windhoek, the International Court of Justice at The Hague, and German newspapers.[60] Instead of attending a dialogue session with the Herero, Herzog visited with other Namibian communities, and he characterized the Herero-German war as something that was "not in good order" that created a "burden on the conscience of every German" who was aware of Germany's "history."[61] This ambiguous commentary was not mistaken for any major state apology or German admission of guilt for past colonial wrongs.

These types of general diplomatic answers may have satisfied some Germans and German-speaking Namibians who wanted bygones to be bygones, so that "reconciliation" would replace "tribalism," but the presentation of these vague colonial references by German governmental officials or settlers' descendants did not dissuade legions of academics, public activists, and lay persons who started to recirculate mainstream and alternative press accounts of what would be called the "Namibian genocide" or the "Kaiser's Holocaust."[62] Afro-Germans, who sometimes felt as though they were caught between epistemic worlds, oftentimes joined the ranks of those who campaigned for Ovaherero or Nama reparations.[63]

A confluence of other factors converged to revitalize interest in studying what were once deemed to be an obscure colonial or imperial topic that were reserved for specialists. All of this was further complicated when Holocaust experts started to debate with genocide experts about the uniqueness of the Judeocide and the strengths and weaknesses of "critical genocide" studies that were cited by reparations advocates.[64]

By 2004, on the centennial of the battle of Ohamakari/Waterberg, studies of "Germany's forgotten genocide" proliferated. Now audiences were hearing about real and feigned apologies, the need to repatriate skulls and other human remains (see chapter 9), the quest for monetary reparations, and the potential redistribution of Namibian lands. The power of the internet could be harnessed so that all sorts of public communities could join the ranks of German parliamentarians, academics, and activists who were becoming increasing vocal as they articulated their restorative justice demands.

Talk of Ovaherero or Nama "rights" became a part of these ongoing conversations when those who tried to meet with Hertzog realized that German diplomats were going to assiduously avoid commenting on reparations. Over time it seemed as though almost every time that a leading Herero or Nama representative commented on either the 2001 or 2017 U.S. lawsuits this became yet another mediated event that would be covered by some investigative journalist.

This mass-mediated coverage of these reparations lawsuits provided one more opportunity for publics to talk and write about that Herero-German "war" or "genocide." Colonial photographs, that once appeared in the old 1918 British Blue Book or in German dairies (see chapter 4), have been copied and digitalized, and they are used to adorn many activist blogging websites. These were pictures of people who "looked like walking skeletons with no flesh," noted Utijua Muinjangue, one of the members of the Herero Genocide Committee.[65] Comments like this appear on YouTube, Facebook, Twitter, and other mass media outlets.

However, those same colonial photographs can be read by all sorts of interpretative communities in complementary or contradictory ways. If we use what Elizabeth Baer has called the "imperial gaze,"[66] instead of the "genocidal gaze," are we rendering invisible some of the ravages many half-forgotten European colonial wars?

Many representatives of the Ovaherero and Nama who are interviewed by global presses can talk about how the "historical record" shows that some one hundred thousand Africans lost their lives between 1904 and 1908, and these historical materials are then linked to larger claims that are made about the parallels that can be found between the grievances of Jews after the Holocaust and Namibian reparations claims. My close reading of many judicial opinions filed by U.S. federal judges will show that very few American jurists see these same parallels, and when they do, they feel that those topics have more to do with "political" questions than "legal" issues (see chapters 7 and 9).

Differing public and legal views regarding past events, presentist needs, and future plans for Namibia thus become entangled in what German scholars and interdisciplinary writers call a complex "politics of memory,"[67] which brings together a host of epistemological, ontological, and axiological claims.

One taboo issue that I will be exploring in this book is the question of whether the use of expressions of regret or contrition are *used to stave off more demanding calls* for costly reparations or land redistribution. In 2016—after more a century of transgenerational advocacy—the daily newspaper *Frankfurter Rundschau* reported that for the first time an official government document of the Federal Republic of Germany referred to the massacres that had taken place in German South West Africa in the early twentieth century as "genocide." Kate Brady, who interviewed some members of the Left Party's faction in the German Parliament, characterized this as evidence that the "German government has fundamentally changed its assessment of the atrocities committed by German soldiers in what is now Namibia."[68]

Yet where is there any evidence that this acknowledgment has led to the payment of reparations, equitable land redistribution, or financial assistance for the descendants of those who were massacred or enslaved during the GSWA years?

Until fairly recently German authorities had steadfastly argued that these GSWA "historical events' could only be classified as "genocide" if they were committed after the implementation of the UN Convention of 1951, implying that the colonial atrocities that were committed during the German colonization years couldn't be characterized as genocidal in nature. When German legislators became involved in debates about the recognition of the Armenian genocide in the Bundestag (Germany's lower house of parliament), the conspicuous absence of discussions of their own colonial genocidal histories was palpable.

How, after all, could German parliamentarians reclassify the massacre of the Armenians during the Ottoman empire years as genocidal and not do the same for atrocities that were committed in some of their own overseas colonies?[69]

Many observers who supported the Ovaherero and Nama reparations efforts hoped that the 2016 announcements by the spokespersons for the Federal Republic of Germany would open, and not close doors. Would this be the beginning of (post)colonial mastering of difficult pasts? Would acknowledgment lead to repatriation of human remains, reparations, and other forms of legal redress?

In 2017, those who gathered outside of a Southern District of New York courtroom talked to reporters about everything from the need to return indigenous skulls that were found in a nearby natural museum to the colonial purchase of particular buildings of New York.[70] Clearly these reparations disputes involved more than just technical legal disputation about jurisdiction or subject matter jurisdiction.

The access to mainstream journalistic outlets and other media venues helped the cause of reparations activists who were aware that winning legal lawsuits against German defendants involved uphill political battles. Many supporters of the Ovaherero and Nama reparations initiatives used the filing of the U.S. lawsuits as pedagogical tools to teach millions of readers and listeners who may not have known about these Namibian requests for legal redress. The *Washington Post,* for example, contained an August 2018 article that quoted Rukoro—one of the 2017 claimants—in a short essay that showed how "Europe" was "struggling" to "atone for its colonial evils."[71] Readers were told that in 1904, German Lieutenant-General Lothar von Trotha told his soldiers that "every Herero, without or without rifles, with or without cattle, will be shot" if they stayed in "German" territory.[72]

This discursive fragment from von Trotha has appeared in countless articles over the last century, but now it was being recirculated in mainstream Western news outlets. The author of the *Washington Post* piece, Ishaan Tharoor, supplied his readers with this short synthesis of that literature:

> The violence and indignity did not end there. Moved by the racist eugenics of the time, German authorities shipped thousands of skulls and other body parts of the aboriginal dead back to Europe. The specimens were subjected to studies that formed the basis for now-discredited theories of European racial superiority. Many of the skulls belonged to tribesmen left to die in squalid concentration camps in the desert; their bodies were beheaded. In some instances, according to a 2011

> article in *Der Spiegel,* widows were ordered to use shards of glass to scrape the flesh off their husbands' heads so as to better prepare the skulls for transport.[73]

Rhetorical fragments about reparations were linked to comments about repatriation of human remains, German racial science, aboriginal rights, concentration camps, and images and remarks about the packaging of skulls that originally appeared in a 1907 book written by a German soldier.

All of this thanatopolitical horror that appeared in a major American newspaper seemed to be deployed in ways that invited readers to ask this question: Who could possibly question the fact that these historical events that took place in German South West Africa during colonial times constituted a "genocide"?

Ishaan Tharoor did not single out the Germans as the only colonizers who were slaughtering indigenous populations or were "hoarding the body parts of slain natives," and he mentioned how "myriad museums, clinics and universities in Europe still house remains of colonized peoples."[74] This was a brief, but fair, summary of some of the issues that were raised when readers reviewed the dark colonial histories that were associated with these particular African geopolitical spaces and places.

Permutations of these arguments appeared in some of the legal materials that were submitted to judge Laura Taylor Swain's court in *Rukoro et al. v. Federal Republic of Germany,* the official name for that 2017 Ovaherero and Nama court case. In one portion of the amended class action lawsuit complaint that circulated on the World Wide Web after February of 2018 lawyers for the law firm McCallion & Associates, argued that "defendant's property-based violations, which it interwove with its crimes against humanity, were also, independent of the genocide, violations of international law."[75] While parts of the ninety-six-page amended complaint covered formalistic types of jurisdictional arguments, other portions were much more emotive and extra-judicial in nature, where authors of this text discussed the lives that were lost after the battle of Ohamakari/Waterberg. Readers were told about the suffering of women and children found near desert water holes and the agonies experienced by those Herero and Nama who survived the war, only to be placed in five major German concentration camps.

As I will note in more detail in chapter 9, legal writers who cobbled together the 2018 amended complaint for the Ovaherero and Nama litigants were trying to take some lessons from their previous failures to convince U.S. judges that they had the jurisdiction to hear these complaints. Between 2001 and 2007, myriad problems with sovereign immunity and personal jurisdiction had scuttled previous Herero attempts at obtaining legal redress in American courtrooms, but this time around the lawyers for the claimants included Nama representatives, and these legal advocates did a much better job of trying to pass jurisdictional hurdles.

In fascinating ways, twenty-first-century arguers who are concerned about the genocidal nature of GSWA activities seem to be recycling some of the claims that appeared in European media outlets when Reichstag members debated about what to do with their colony in German South West Africa between 1900 and 1914.

SOME OF THE KEY POLITICAL AND ACADEMIC ISSUES THAT BECOME ENTANGLED IN OVAHERERO AND NAMA REPARATIONS DEBATES

Although some academics complain when their colleagues become involved in politics and social justice activism, others contend that the inclusion of academic voices facilitates, rather than debilitates, both scholarship and legal decision making, especially in restorative justice contexts. As Mark Osiel would note in his pathbreaking work on various constructed memories, legal judgment, and distorted histories, academics were some of the social agents who handed over materials to prosecutors. Osiel observed how academic materials that were deployed in this instrumentalist type of litigation were nevertheless used to further the cause of those who seek "social solidarity."[76]

Not all academics were that interested in social solidarity, and they used their archival research that was conducted in Germany or Namibia to help with advance our understanding of the "genocide thesis," or the "continuity thesis," or the possible existence of some new German "*Sonderweg*" (special path). Would studies of colonial genocides end up revising histories in ways that challenged the "uniqueness" of the Holocaust? Were some scholars who specialized in studies of the Ovaherero and Nama atrocities trying to find links between what happened in GSWA and the rise of the Nazis? Were authors of texts on these subjects alleging that German colonialism was somehow worse than French assimilationist practices or British "informal" empire building?

If we review several fragmentary parts of the Ovaherero and Nama amended class action complaint of 2018, we would find implicit or explicit references to academic arguments about the continuity "thesis" or related concepts. On page 5 of the 2018 amended complaint, readers find this allegation:

> Germany's express written policy to exterminate the Ovaherero and Nama indigenous peoples in southwestern African during the 1904–1908 period was Germany's first genocide of the twentieth century. In many ways, Germany's genocidal policies and practices toward the Ovaherero and Nama peoples, including the use of mass extermination, concentration camps and mistreatment of a targeted population

as a "sub-human" group, was a precursor to Germany's later effort to exterminate European Jewry.[77]

If critical scholars parse these words, they will find that the authors of this amended complaint don't mind calling this a genocide as they intervene in these labeling debates. Then there is the matter of how this fragment is also used to advance the argument that the German concentration camps that were put in place after Ohamakari/Waterberg were intended for "mass extermination." Add to this the complications that come when these legal writers are trying to follow the precedents that were provided by previous reparations cases when the West Germans paid Jewish survivors of the Holocaust.

Are these the type of legitimate questions that ought to concern America's lawyers, judges, or lay persons? Why should U.S. citizens be concerned about what happened in a part of Africa during imperial periods that may have only tangential links to any U.S. geopolitical interests or matters of legal "concern"?

One of the intriguing features of the 2017 filing of the Herero and Nama lawsuits had to do with the portion of the complaint that averred that activists for these communities should not be left out of bilateral negotiations.[78] Journalists began to report that *Rukoro et al. v. Federal Republic of Germany* was a case that involved the use of scholarly research on GSWA histories that would supplement the more jurisdictional arguments that appeared in these legal texts.[79]

By the fall of 2018 Judge Laura Taylor Swain had already been presented with a host of legalistic arguments about "Germany's sovereignty" and the supposed impoverished nature of the plaintiffs' "legal theory" of jurisdiction, but the Paramount Chief of the Herero, Vekuii Rukoro, wanted to comment about some of the evidence that had been collected by generations of academics. For example, Rukoro talked to the press about the ready availability of public copies of the October 2, 1904, proclamation order that was circulated by General Lothar von Trotha.[80]

Several scholars who are familiar with Ovaherero and Nama claims note the "entangled" nature of Namibian histories, public memories, historiography, and legal claims in these situations,[81] and a critical review of these linkages shows how these are matters that involve everything from bodies to buildings to disputes over the purchasing of "stolen" lands. As Katharina Schramm argued in 2016, elite and public debates about postcolonial redress after colonizing years oftentimes involve "historical fault lines, collective memories, material relations and contemporary affiliations."[82] Talk about indigenous rights, land redistribution in Africa, and even "migrating" colonial archives became a part of what Henning Melber called the negotiation of "a Namibian-German past in the present."[83]

Some of the very buildings that were once used by Germans anthropologists, eugenicists, and ethnologists to store collections of thousands of skulls, skeletons, and other human remains are now serving as sites for "decolonization" of minds. These spaces and places have been turned by European students and concerned professors into public and academic forums where visitors to websites can learn about the "provenances" that track the histories behind skulls and skeletal remains that were taken from those who died in places like the Shark Island concentration camp. The postcolonial work of scholars like Jan-Bart Gewald, Larissa Forster, Henning Melber, Reinhart Kössler, and Jürgen Zimmerer traverses that mythic line between "politics" and "scholarship" as these experts complement the efforts of those who send petitions to German parliamentarians who debate about Herero and Nama grievances.

This has created situations were transcontinental alliances have been formed that bring together activists from a variety of countries. For example, Ovaherero and Nama advocates now appear in documentaries and other videos that educate publics about the filing of lawsuits, the evidencing of the GSWA genocide, and the topological changes that are taking place in places like Berlin, Hamburg, and Strasbourg because of the public pressure that has been brought to bear by students allied with Afro-German activists. We are now witnessing the tearing down of monuments and street signs that were once dedicated to the military officers who once carried out the annihilation of the Ovaherero and Nama.[84] And all of this public consciousness-raising is happening outside of courtroom walls at the same time that many law students keep track of what is happening within American courtrooms.

In many ways it could be argued that all of this renascent public and legal interest in what David Olusoga and Casper Erichsen called the "Kaiser's Holocaust"[85] represents the culmination of many generations of consciousness-raising efforts, where intrigued journalists and laypersons are heartened by the prospect of seeing academics join the ranks of those who want to educate publics about Germany's forgotten genocide.

Will all of this activity end up helping, or hurting, the cause of the impoverished Namibians who are asking for help as they try to buy back lands that were taken from indigenous communities during German colonization periods?

CONCLUSION

Pessimists might point out that at the same time that we are now hearing monthly—if not weekly—calls for Ovaherero and Nama reparations, American judges in U.S. courts seem to be signaling that they may never get to the "merits" of these reparations cases. Legal experts have noticed that with the passage of time American federal judges have been more hesitant to interpret the Alien Tort Claims Act (ATCA) in elastic ways that might aid the cause of Namibian litigants. Jeremy Sarkin and Carly Fowler are aware of this hesitancy, but they take the position that while "it is by no means certain that reparations *will* ever be paid by Germany to the Herero, the fact remains that reparations *should* be paid".[86]

It is an open question whether most American jurists, or Western publics, share these sentiments. Note, for example, the general reluctance to actually apply some of the principles that come from UN declarations of indigenous rights. J. Kēhaulani Kauanui has remarked that it was telling that in 2007, when the UN General Assembly adopted the Declaration of the Rights of Indigenous Peoples, the declaration was met by a vote of 143 in favor and 4 against. The "four nations that voted against the declaration," Kauanui noted, were Australia, Canada, New Zealand, and the United States.[87] She surmised that these four nations refused to adopt the declaration because they were worried that claims that had to do with the full rights of self-determination "could empower indigenous peoples to disrupt the contiguous landmass of these nation-states."[88]

Germany's responses to Ovaherero and Namibian reparations requests may simply represent the general reluctance to grapple with the lingering effects of settler colonialism. In spite of mounting public pressure, German chancellors and other German governmental representatives, as well as Namibian officials, have stayed the course. Some seventeen years ago Sidney Harring, writing in the *West Virginia Law Review*, argued that the Germans and Namibians needed to keep in mind the patterns of "violent land seizures in Zimbabwe" as various parties discussed "the need for effective land reforms."[89] This implied that legal wrangling in courtrooms or negotiated settlements were better than having frustrated postcolonial communities engage in physical violence.

Have any of this changed since 2002?

Critics of empire still occasionally hear talk about the beneficence of German rule, and how the traditional archives contain materials that chronicled how German settlers risked much by buying parched lands from the Herero as they developed the central regions of German South West Africa. Here the stories that are told are not about German atrocities but the beastly practices of rebellions Africans who murdered hundreds of farmers and workers who were trying to build coast towns or inland communities.[90] It is said that before the Germans arrived, Namibia was simply a vast wasteland occupied by African communities who had migrated from the North or from the South as they tended their herds of cattle. Photographs taken from German photo albums are circulated by German speakers in Namibia and others that show the blasting of rocks for railways, the building of hospitals for "natives," missionary outposts, and other markings of "civilizing" missions. In the name of "context" pro-imperialists focus on the German "enlightenment" that would be dispensed by colonizers as skeptics of Herero reparations efforts express puzzlement at the international public reception of genocidal claims that are now circulating by critics of empire.

Some observers are also skeptical of the motives of those who did not file complaints in Namibian courts or German courts or in international criminal courts. Were the plaintiffs simply going after the proverbial "deep pockets" when they filed in U.S. courtrooms, or did they genuinely believe that they had legitimate claims that needed to be addressed in the few forums that were willing to potentially hear their grievances?[91] Why didn't these Ovaherero and Nama reparations cases include the grievances of the Damara or the San or other marginalized communities in Namibia whose ancestors were also victims of horrific colonial violence?

This book will try to provide tentative answers to these types of queries, and the perspectival approaches that are adopted in each chapter are used to flesh out the myriad historical and contemporary issues regarding reparations claims that swirl around the 2001 and 2017 filings of those Ovaherero and Nama claims in U.S. courts.

The first four chapters of this book will show how, before World War II, most of the histories that were written about German South West Africa and housed in various archives were written by soldiers or administrators or settlers who had a vested interest in defending German rights as they colonized Africa. Today interdisciplinary scholars call these settler colonial discourses, and for a time all sorts of novels, travelogues, and even shipping brochures circulated hagiographic accounts of the *Schutztruppe* maintaining the peace in GSWA to pave the way for future German and European settlement of this region.[92]

The last five chapters of the book show readers some of the post–World War II hurdles that were placed in the paths of Ovaherero and Nama advocates who had to cope with both colonial and apartheid legacies. Each of these chapters provides readers with genealogical critiques that render visible many of the discursive origins of settler and indigenous arguments that would be used for generations as various transcontinental communities listened to various calls for genocidal acknowledgments, expressions of regret, apologies, repatriation of remains, and reparations.

NOTES

1. See Karie L. Morgan, "Remembering the Nation-State: Hereros' Pursuit of Restorative Justice," *Time & Society* 21, no. 1 (2012): 21–38. Morgan's work builds on Desmond Tutu's commentaries on restorative justice. See Desmond Tutu, *No Future Without Forgiveness* (New York: Doubleday, 1999).

2. Olusoga and Erichsen, *The Kaiser's Holocaust*. See also Rich Tenorio, "Genocide of African Tribes Was Germany's Dress Rehearsal, Says Scholar," *The Times of Israel*, last modified August 9, 2018, https://www.timesofisrael.com/genocide-of-african-tribes-was-germanys-holocaust-dress-rehearsal-says-scholar/.

3. See *France 24* staff, "100 Years On, German Far Right Seeks to Rehabilitate Empire," *France 24,* last modified October 26, 2018, https://www.france24.com/en/20181026-100-years-german-far-right-seeks-rehabilitate-empire.

4. Reinhart Kössler, "Review: *Postkoloniale Erinnerungslandschaften. Wie Deutsche und Herero in Namibia des Kriegs von 1904 gedenken,*" *Africa Spectrum* 2 (2010): 129–132, 129.

5. Ibid., 130.

6. Ibid.

7. Ibid.

8. See, for example, Shu-Mei Huang, *Difficult Heritage in Nation Building: South Korea and Post-Conflict Japanese Colonial Occupation Architecture* (New York: Palgrave Macmillan, 2018); Ronald Niezen, "Speaking for the Dead: The Memorial Politics of Genocide in Namibia and Germany," *International Journal of Heritage Studies* 24, issue 5 (2018): 547–567.

9. Colleen Devine, "The Forgotten Genocide: Jurisdiction in *Rukoro v. Federal Republic of Germany,*" *Michigan Journal of International Law* 40 (2018), http://www.mjilonline.org/the-forgotten-genocide-jurisdiction-in-rukoro-v-federal-republic-of-germany/.

10. David Olusoga and Casper W. Erichsen, *The Kaiser's Holocaust: Germany's Forgotten Genocide* (London: Farber and Farber, 2010).

11. See Aisling C. Walsh, "The Forgotten Genocide: Herero and Nama, 1904, Part One," *Stop Genocide Now,* last modified December 13, 2018, https://stopgenocidenow.org/2018/10/22/forgotten-genocide-herero-nama-1904-part-1/.

12. Given the multi-vocal nature of some terminology, I will sometimes be using several different terms to reference the same communities. For example, most of the time when I write about the Ovaherero ethnic community, I will use the term "Ovaherero," but at other times, when academic journals or military texts or journalistic outlets or other publications use the term "Herero," I will use that designation. I will also be using the terms "Ohamakari" and "Hamakari" interchangeably to refer to the same August 1904 battle between the German forces of Lieutenant General Lothar von Trotha and the Herero men, women, and children who were camped near the Waterberg Plateau before the attacks. German speakers call this the battle of Waterberg.

13. Manu Vimalassery, Juliana Hu Pegues, and Alyosha Goldstein, "Introduction: On Colonial Unknowing," *Theory and Event* 19, no. 4 (2016): https://muse.jhu.edu/article/633283. Vimalassery, Pegues, and Goldstein cite the work of Stoler on aphasia, and at times they also discuss related colonial and postcolonial maladies.

14. Ibid., paragraph 1.

15. Ibid., paragraphs 1–8.

16. See Craig Calhoun, "Nation and Imagination: How Benedict Anderson Revolutionized Political Theory," ABC.net, last modified May 9, 2017, https://www.abc.net.au/religion/nation-and-imagination-how-benedict-anderson-revolutionized-poli/10095810.

17. Ann Laura Stoler, "Colonial Aphasia: Race and Disabled Histories in France," *Public Culture* 23, no. 1 (2011): 121, 124.

18. Henning Melber, "Namibia: The German Roots of Apartheid," *Race & Class* 27, no. 1 (1985): 63–77.

19. Ibid., 68.

20. Ibid., 70.

21. Ibid.

22. Ibid., 67, 72.

23. To provide just one example of how some members of World Wide Web communities link together Holocaust grammars with colonial genocide lexicons, see *Genocide Watch* Staff, "Video: Namibian Tribal Governments Sue Germany for Holocaust Reparations," *Genocide Watch,* last modified August 5, 2018, http://www.genocidewatch.com/single-post/2018/08/05/VIDEO-Namibian-Tribal-Governments-Sue-Germany-for-Holocaust-Reparations.

24. Jodi A. Byrd, "'Variations under Domestication": Indigeneity and the Subject of Dispossession," *Social Text* 36, no. 2 (June 2018): 123–141. See also Michael Paul Rogin, *Fathers and Children: Andrew Jackson and the Subjugation of the American Indian* (New York: Alfred A. Knopf, 1975); Rennard Strickland, "Genocide-at-Law: An Historic and Contemporary View of the Native American Experience," *University of Kansas Law Review* 34 (Summer 1986): 713–55.

25. Byrd, "Variations under Domestication," 125.

26. Haidy Gesmar, "Resisting Settler-Colonial Property Relations? The WAI 262 Claim and Resort in Aotearoa New Zealand," *Settler Colonial Studies* 3, no. 2 (2013): 230–43.

27. Alyosha Goldstein, "The Ground Not Given: Colonial Disposition of Land, Race, and Hunger," *Social Text* 36, no. 2 (June 2018): 83–106, 89.

28. Mahmood Mamdani, "Settler Colonialism: Then and Now," *Critical Inquiry* 41 (Spring 2015): 596–614, 614.

29. See Reinhart Kössler and Henning Melber, "Namibian Genocide Victims' Remains Are Home. But Germany Still Has Work to Do," *The Conversation*, last modified September 4, 2018, https://theconversation.com/namibian-genocide-victims-remains-are-home-but-germany-still-has-work-to-do-102655.

30. Jeffrey Harris, quoted in Brendan Pierson, "Germany Urges U.S. Court to Dismiss Lawsuit over Namibian Genocide," Reuters, last modified July 31, 2018, paragraph 2, https://www.reuters.com/article/us-namibia-genocide-germany/germany-urges-u-s-court-to-dismiss-lawsuit-over-namibian-genocide-idUSKBN1KL2KH?il=0.

31. For more on the role that counter memories play in debates about colonial apologies and colonial atrocities see Tom Bentley, *Empires of Remorse: Narrative, Postcolonialism and Apologies for Colonial Atrocity* (New York: Routledge, 2016).

32. For a helpful overview of Raphael Lemkin's views on "cultural" genocide that also provides a critique of Herero genocidal claims, see A. Dirk Moses, "Chapter 1: Raphael Lemkin, Culture, and the Concept of Genocide," in *The Oxford Handbook of Genocide Studies*, edited by Donald Bloxham and A. Dirk Moses (Oxford: Oxford University Press, 2010), 19–41.

33. For rare examples of the type of more "critical" books that share affinities with the way that I view this Herero and Nama disputation, see Reinhart Kössler, *Namibia and Germany: Negotiation the Past* (Windhoek: University of Namibia Press, 2015); Jürgen Zimmerer and Joachim Zeller, *Genocide in German South-West Africa: The Colonial War of 1904–08 in Namibia and Its Aftermath* (2008: Monmouth: Merlin, 2016). Some of these texts use variants of approaches that straddle the lines between orthodox, modernist approaches and postmodernist, post-structural, or postcolonial approaches, but many of the arguments of these authors would resonate with members of TWAIL or critical indigenous studies communities.

34. Michel Foucault, *Surveiller et Punir. Naissance de la prison* (Paris: NRF Éditions Gallimard, 1975).

35. Elizabeth R. Baer, *The Genocidal Gaze: From German South West Africa to the Third Reich* (Detroit: Wayne State University Press, 2017).

36. See, for example, the materials that have been collected in the National Archives of Namibia. I am also referencing the formation of more "public archives" that are assembled by investigative journalists and others that do not directly cite traditional archival sources.

37. For a trenchant critique of some of this lawfare—especially in the area of contracts and property rights—see Steven Press, *Rogue Empires: Contracts and Conmen in Europe's Scramble for Africa* (Cambridge: Harvard University Press, 2017).

38. For more on "ideological drifts," especially in legal contexts, see Jack M. Balkin, "Ideological Drift and the Struggle over Meaning," *Connecticut Law Review* 25 (1993): 869–91; David E. Pozen, "Transparency's Ideological Drift," *The Yale Law Journal* 128 (2018): 100–165.

39. Vimalassery, Pegues, and Goldstein, "Introduction: On Colonial Unknowing," paragraph 1.

40. Jean Comaroff and John L. Comaroff, "Law and Disorder in the Postcolony: An Introduction," in *Law and Disorder in the Postcolony*, edited by Jean Comaroff and John L. Comaroff (Chicago: University of Chicago Press, 2006), 332–33.

41. Reinhart Kössler, "Entangled History and Politics: Negotiating the Past between Namibia and Germany," *Journal of Contemporary African* Studies, 26, no. 3 (July 2008): 313–39, 313.

42. Jan-Bart Gewald, "Herero Genocide in the Twentieth Century: Politics and Memory," in *Rethinking Resistance: Revolt and Violence in African History*, edited by Jon Abbink, Mirjam de Bruijin, and Klaas van Walraven (Boston: Brill, 2003), 279–304, 304.

43. Morgan, "Remembering Against the Nation State," 28.

44. Laura Taylor Swain, quoted in Jonathan Stempel, "Lawsuit against Germany over Namibian Genocide Is Dismissed in New York," Reuters, last modified March 6, 2019, paragraph 2, https://www.reuters.com/article/us-namibia-genocide-germany/lawsuit-against-germany-over-namibian-genocide-is-dismissed-in-new-york-idUSKCN1QN2SQ.

45. Amanda Ottaway, "For Victims of a Little-Known Genocide, A Long Journey to Justice," Courthouse News Service, last modified March 20, 2019, https://www.courthousenews.com/for-victims-of-a-little-known-genocide-a-long-journey-to-justice/.

46. See, for example, Hyonhee Shin, "Thousands of Koreans Sue Government over Wartime Labor at Japanese Firms," Reuters, last modified December 19, 2018, https://www.reuters.com/article/us-japan-forcedlabour-southkorea/thousand-koreans-sue-government-over-wartime-labor-at-japan-firms-idUSKCN1OJ0F7; Boaventura de Sousa Santos, "The Age of Pardon or the Age of Aggression?" *Critical Legal Thinking*, last modified April 12, 2019, http://criticallegalthinking.com/2019/04/12/the-age-of-pardon-or-the-age-of-aggression/.

47. Morgan, "Remembering Against the Nation State," 28.

48. See Rhoda E. Howard-Hassmann, "Getting to Reparations: Japanese Americans and African Americans," *Social Forces* 83, no. 2 (December 2004): 823–40.

49. Kössler, "Entangled History," 315.

50. Some sources estimate that somewhere between twenty thousand and twenty-five thousand German descendants of German colonizers are now living in Namibia. Materials in the rest of my chapters will show that there are vast disagreements about just how much land these German speakers control in today's Namibia.

51. Henning Melber, "Genocide Matters—Negotiating A Namibian-German Past in the Present," *Wiener Zeitschrift Für kritische Afrikastudien* 17, no. 33 (2017): 1–24, 14.

52. See George M. Wilson, "Edward Said on Contrapuntal Reading," *Philosophy and Literature* 18, no. 2 (October 1994): 265–73.

53. See Lorenzo Veracini, "Decolonizing Setter Colonialism: Kill the Setter in Him and Save the Man," *American Indian Culture and Research Journal* 41, no. 1 (2017): 1–18.

54. Antony Anghie, *Imperialism, Sovereignty and the Making of International Law* (Cambridge, UK: Cambridge University Press, 2005).

55. Horst Drechsler, *Let Us Die Fighting: The Struggle of the Herero and Nama against German Imperialism* (1884–1915) (London: Zed Books, 1980), 99–101.

56. Michel Foucault once defined a "*dispositif*" as an "apparatus," and he argued that what he meant by that term were the heterogeneous ensembles of discourses, philosophic ideas, institutions, architectural forms, laws, administration measures, philanthropic propositions, and so forth that were used to decide what could or could not be said about key controversies. Foucault used the word "element" to describe some of the rhetorical fragments that went into the production of any large, sedimented *dispositif* that one could find in places like archives. See Matti Peltonen, "From Discourse to '*Dispositif*': Michael Foucault's Two Histories," *Historical Reflections* 30, no. 2 (Summer 2004): 205–19, 213–14.

57. Gewald, "Herero Genocide," 294.

58. I share the views of those who contend that some of Foucault's perspectival work serves as a type of "anti-method" that was used to critique some of the scientism

of more positivistic approaches to linguistic power. See Larry Shiner, "Reading Foucault: Anti-Method and the Genealogy of Power Knowledge," *History and Theory* 21, no. 3 (October 1982): 382–98. Here I need to admit that I disagree with those theorists who argue that a major shift took place when Foucault moved way from talking about "archaeology" and toward "genealogy." I see little concrete evidence that this altered the ways that he discussed many of the rhetorical features of his biopolitical and thanatopolitical topics.

59. Christian Matthias Schlaga, quoted in Al Jazeera staff, "Namibia Tribes Lodge Case Against Germany over Genocide," Al Jazeera, last modified March 16, 2017, paragraph 7, https://www.aljazeera.com/news/2017/03/namibia-tribes-lodge-case-germany-genocide-170316162133276.html.

60. Morgan, "Remembering Against the Nation State," 28.

61. Ibid., 28.

62. Olusoga and Erichsen, *The Kaiser's Holocaust*.

63. See Henning Melber and Reinhart Kössler, "Germany Is Backpedaling on Calling Its Century-Old Namibian Genocide a Genocide," *Quartz*, last modified January 13, 2018, https://qz.com/africa/1178317/namibia-genocide-germany-is-trying-to-protect-itself-from-a-widening-legal-liabilities/.

64. See, for example, Kirsten Dyck, "Situating the Herero Genocide and the Holocaust among European Colonial Genocides," *Przegla, DZachodni* 1 (2014): 153–72, https://iz.poznan.pl/plik,pobierz,921,39ff75735dbab2a13c53d6c2d9886a08/41-10-KIRSTEN-DYCK.pdf.

65. Utijua Muinjangue, quoted in Al Jazeera staff, "Namibia Tribes Lodge Case." paragraph 7.

66. Baer, *The Genocidal Gaze*.

67. The phrase "politics of memory" is also used by some who worry about the "politicization" of memory in today's debates about Herero and reparations for alleged colonial genocidal acts. See David Bargueño, "Cash For Genocide?: The Politics of Memory in the Herero Case for Reparations," *Holocaust and Genocide Studies* 26, no. 3 (December 2012): 394–424.

68. Kate Brady, "Germany Official Refers to Herero Massacre as Genocide," *Deutsche Welle*, last modified July 13, 2016, paragraph 4, https://www.dw.com/en/germany-officially-refers-to-herero-massacre-as-genocide/a-19396892.

69. Ibid., paragraphs 5–6.

70. See, for example, Lynsey Chutel, "The Remains of the Victims of Germany's First Genocide Are in the American Natural History Museum," *Quartz*, last modified September 16, 2017, https://qz.com/africa/1078660/namibia-genocide-natural-history-museum-has-remains-of-victims-of-germanys-genocide-in-africa/.

71. Ishaan Tharoor, "Europe Struggles to Atone for Its Colonial Evils," *The Washington Post*, last modified August 30, 2018, https://www.washingtonpost.com/world/2018/08/30/europe-struggles-atone-its-colonial-evils/?utm_term=.a3d23af35785.

72. Ibid., paragraph 3.

73. Ibid., paragraphs 4–5.

74. Ibid., paragraph 6.

75. Daniel Steinmann, "Reparations Claimants Leverage German State Property in New York to Establish District Court's Sovereign Jurisdiction," *Namibian Economist*, February 18, 2018, paragraph 6, https://economist.com.na/32789/headlines/reparations-claimants-leverage-german-state-property-in-new-york-to-establish-district-courts-sovereign-jurisdiction/.

76. Mark J. Osiel, "Ever Again: Legal Remembrance of Administrative Massacre," *University of Pennsylvania Law Review* 144 (1995): 463–704, 479.

77. See amended complaint by the plaintiffs, *Rukoro et al. v. Federal Republic of Germany*, Case Number 1.17-cv-00062, New York Southern District Court, 2018, 5.

78. Jens-Uwe Guettel, "The SPD Should Return to Its Anticolonial Roots," *The Jacobin Magazine*, August 2018, paragraph 1, https://www.jacobinmag.com/2018/08/spd-namibia-herero-nama-genocide-colonialism.

79. For a helpful overview of some of the formalistic legal arguments in Ovaherero and Nama reparations case, see Andreas Buser, "German Genocide in Namibia before U.S. Courts," *Võlkerrechtsblog,* last modified January 11, 2017, http://voelkerrechtsblog.org/german-genocide-in-namibia-before-u-s-courts/.

80. See *Namibian Sun* staff, "We Have von Trotha's Extermination Order—Rukoro," *The Namibian Sun,* last modified January 16, 2018, https://www.namibiansun.com/news/we-have-von-trothas-extermination-order-rukoro2018-01-16.

81. See, for example, Melber, "Genocide Matters," and Reinhart Kössler's work on Namibian and German memories.

82. Katharina Schramm, "Casts, Bones and DNA, Interrogating the Relationship between Science and Postcolonial Indigeneity in Contemporary South Africa," *Anthropology Southern Africa* 39, no. 2 (June 2016): 1–14.

83. Melber, "Genocide Matters."

84. For an informative overview of some of this activism see Elise Pape, "Postcolonial Debates in Germany—An Overview," *African Sociological Review* 21, no. 2 (2017): 2–14.

85. Olusoga and Erichsen, *The Kaiser's Holocaust.*

86. Sarkin and Fowler, "Reparations for Historical Human Rights Violations," 360. Emphasis in the original.

87. J. Kēhaulani Kauanui, "Colonialism in Equality: Hawaiian Sovereignty and the Question of U.S. Civil Rights," *South Atlantic Quarterly* 10, No. 4 (Fall 2008): 835–50. 647.

88. Ibid., 647.

89. Sidney L. Harring, "Germany Reparations to the Herero Nation: An Assertion of Herero Nationhood in the Path of Namibian Development?" *West Virginia Law Review* 104 (2002): 393–417, 395.

90. For a short critique of some of these narratives see Bill Nasson, "The Beasts of Berlin," *South African Journal of Science* 107 nos. 3/4 (March/April 2011): 1–2.

91. For an excellent discussion of the selective nature of some of the choices that were made regarding venues before this filing of Ovaherero and Nama claims see Bargueño, "Cash for Genocide?" This critique is primarily focused on discussing some of the strengths and weaknesses of the first Herero case that was filed in 2001.

92. See Volker Langbehn, editor, *German Colonialism, Visual Culture, and Modern Memory* (New York: Routledge, 2010): David Ciarlo, *Advertising Empire: Race and Visual Culture in Imperial Germany* (Cambridge: Harvard University Press, 2011); Willeke Sandler, *Empire in the Heimat: Colonialism and Public Culture in the Third Reich* (New York: Oxford University Press, 2018).

TWO

Heroic and Tragic Tales of Colonial Deeds in German South West Africa, 1884 to 1908

When lawyers for the Ovaherero and Nama communities filed their case, *Rukoro et al. v. Germany et al.* (2017) in an American courtroom, this raised a number of intriguing questions. Why had they taken so long to file their claims? Why weren't these litigants suing German-speaking descendants in Namibian courtrooms? Given the fact that "South West Africa" was once captured by the British shouldn't these types of colonial genocide cases be filed in South African legal forums? Why should American judges be using U.S. taxpayers' money to hear about Namibian genocidal claims? Were former colonizers protected from these types of cases by juridical concepts like "sovereign immunity"? If U.S. judges ever got to the point where they heard the merits of this case could they fairly conclude that a genocide had indeed taken place, and that Ovaherero and Nama litigants, like the Holocaust victims before them, deserved some form of equitable redress?

Those who review the legal and historical arguments that are presented in some of the 2017 court filings by the Ovaherero and Nama litigants focus most of their attention on jurisdictional or "political" question issues. A typical response to these filings was presented in a helpful summary by Felicia Stephan in 2018:

> The case brought by representatives of the Nama and Ovaherero people against Germany faces several legal challenges and will most likely not succeed. It has, however, achieved worldwide media coverage and will at least raise sympathy for the cause. It might also increase pressure on the German government by NGOs and German parliamentary groups and might lead to an inclusion of Nama and Ovaherero repre-

> sentatives in the negotiation process concerning reconciliation between Germany and Namibia.[1]

Stephan seemed to be joining the ranks of those who believed that these claimants and their lawyers might run into insurmountable jurisdictional hurdles as they tried to garner the attention of American jurists.

Yet given the growing societal support for these types of reparations lawsuits it may be prudent at this point in time to have scholars and others ask about the ideological usages, as well as the historical origins, of the "evidence" that is cited in these Namibian reparations cases. As Renisa Mawani argued in her essay, "Law's Archive," historical and legal archives are sites that derive meanings, authority, and legitimacy in ways that obscure their "original violence" and their "ongoing force."[2] Professor Mawani goes on to argue that studies of law's archive have to involve more than just a "politics of truth" or a "grammatology," for the "actions of colonial, postcolonial, and liberal democratic states aimed at killing, wounding, and destroying their racial, subaltern, and indigenous enemies are often recorded and authorized as legitimate and necessary violence justified in the name of law."[3]

From a critical genealogical standpoint, what archival materials about "German South West Africa" get reappropiated by these litigants, and what imperial histories are elided in these court filings? These types of questions are important to raise, for as Renisa Mawani noted, where "violence is excessive or clearly illegitimate, records may be destroyed or concealed as secrets of the state."[4] This is especially the case in studies of German colonial laws, given that Henning Melber has argued that during the GSWA days there was no "appeasement policy" that was used in this part of Africa once sufficient numbers of troops arrived to back up Theodor Leutwein's "divide and conquer" governmental policies.[5]

Litigants who want to win these reparations cases about colonial violence will have to be armed with historical ammunition that will help them answer these types of questions:

- Were the Ovaherero and Nama communities ever deemed to be "sovereign" powers who owned personal or real property under customary laws during colonial times, and is there evidence that the German colonizers "took" or "stole" this property?
- What might lead Anglo-American judges to conclude that all sorts of colonial or imperial property cases, torts claims, human rights grievances, or criminal cases were justiciable?
- What types of counterhistories or countermemories have been produced by German-speaking Namibians and others who contest the Ovaherero and Nama genocidal claims, and what impact will these alternative historical readings have on reparations litigation?[6]

In order for readers to be able to fairly assess whether the Ovaherero and Nama ethnic communities deserve apologies, reparations, or other forms of equitable redress, they first need to be presented with evidence of the conflicting interpretations of historical materials that were left by Herero and Nama survivors, German settlers, *Schutztruppe* forces, colonial civil administrators, and those in Berlin who cabled their orders to those who suppressed the "Native" rebellions between 1904 and 1908.

One helpful theoretical schema that could be of use to critical scholars who study contested memories is Michael Rothberg's work on the differences that exist between "multidirectional" memory and "competititve" memory formations.[7] Given the fact that the Ovaherero and Nama claimants are constantly drawing parallels between the "Kaiser's Holocaust" and the World War II Holocaust, it makes sense to take advantage of a conceptual framework that allows us to juxtapose different genocidal memory formations.

Michael Rothberg contends that societies today have to find ways of coping with all sorts of "multidirectional" and "competitive" memories. One of Rothberg's essays opens up with this set of queries and commentaries:

> What happens when different histories of extreme violence confront each other in the public sphere? Does the remembrance of one event erase others from view? When memories of colonialism, occupation, slavery, and the Holocaust bump up against one another in contemporary multi-cultural societies, must a competition of victims ensue? . . . I argue against a logic of competitive memory based on the zero-sum game, which has dominated many popular and scholarly approaches to public remembrance. . . . I argue that collective memories of seemingly distinct histories—such as those of slavery, the Holocaust, and colonialism—are not so easily separable from one another.[8]

Rothberg contends that problems arise when communities engage in "memory wars" that invite listeners or readers to choose which particular genocide deserves more attention than others. He calls this "competitive" memory work, and he contrasts these nonproductive activities with what he characterizes as more productive "multi-directional" work. For example, if the Ovaherero and Nama discuss the Judeocide in ways that would raise consciousness *about both* the atrocities committed during German colonizing years and the Holocaust—without turning this into a type of victimage contest—then that would be example of what Rothberg views as constructive, multidirectional memory work.

Although Rothberg has explicitly critiqued some of the Foucauldian ways of viewing collective memories and Foucauldians' comparative historiographic work, there is no reason why those critics interested in perspectival, post-Nietzschean work can't place these approaches in productive tension as they try to review archival recollections of "what happened" in GSWA between 1884 and 1908. Given that Renisa Mawani has recently argued that "colonial-legal laboratories" were once places where "racial labor hierarchies, rules of order and regimes of violence were projected, implemented," and "disputed,"[9] isn't it possible that all of our archives contain shards of elite and public fragments that come from multidirectional and competitive memory formations?

Michael Rothberg may be overly optimistic when he provides readers with examples of how writers can reconcile some colonial and Holocaust histories, but his notion of multi-directional memories helps explain why some Holocaust scholars support the inclusion of colonial genocide studies—including the Ovaherero/Nama genocide—in the expanding canons of genocidal studies.

In this particular chapter I want to extend Rothberg's work on competitive and multidirectional memories at the same time that I provide readers with an understanding of the various indeterminate historical artifacts that have been left in the archives by Ovaherero, Nama, German-speaking, and other communities who have written about what happened in GSWA.

The competitive or multidirections histories or public memories that are catalogued in archives in places like Namibia or Germany serve as reservoirs of symbolic meaning for historians, cultural anthropologists, and many other interdisciplinary scholars who have noticed that familiar story lines reappear as various pieces of "parchment papers" (Foucault) are scribbled over and copied again and again.[10]

It is important to revisit these older colonial archives because those who visit them will find evidence that some of those who have deposited materials in these imperial or colonial archives were well aware that future generations were going to be analyzing how particular colonial adminstrators or soldiers or indigenous warriors justified what they did between 1884 and 1908. Even those who did not write down their thoughts nevertheless shared perspectives that were oftentimes recorded by others in songs or folklore. The letters and other messages that were exchanged between German Major Theodor Leutwein and Herero Chief Samuel Maherero have become the stuff of legend.[11]

At times, in the name of coexistence and naked self-interest, some Ovaherero and Nama leaders accepted the German colonial hierarchies and plans for land distribution when it suited their needs. However, at other times, when these leaders of indigenous communities realized that they were being pushed onto reservations, deported, or marginalized in other ways they started to push back against imperial expansionist plans for the Germanization of territorialized places like "Hereroland."

Some of these territorial and representational contests took place before the 1904 Herero war with the Germans, but other rhetorical conflicts were waged when words and photographs were used to try and contextualize what happened during and after the "battle" of Hamakari/Waterberg.

It will be my contention that the use of (post)colonial or other critical readings of many of these older texts and photographs reveals that the attempted crafting of some single, linear, "history" of "what happened" in German South West Africa between 1884 and 1908 will always be self-serving and will always leave out other competitive or multidirectional histories or public memories. This is because those who fought colonial wars, the Ovambo indigenous communities in the North who stayed out of the fighting, writers in the British "Cape colony," military chronicles in Berlin, and many others left us polyvalent chronicles of these activities.

Remembrances of 1904–1908 battles could be placed in different heroic or tragic frames, and the "truth effects" of these chronicles depending on one's subject position, ethnicity, gender, social status, tribal allegiance, or nationality. In what Reinhart Kössler calls "entangled" imperial histories "the festering issue of genocide committeed by the German colonial army in what was then called German South West Africa" involved confrontations with "construction of ownership of history, which in turn is related to competing claims of possessing some truth" about what happened long ago.[12] This involves disputation about what constitutes a colonial "fact" as well as debates about the best way to interpret those historical facts.

These contentious and partial colonial histories, and these contested postcolonial public memories, are epistemic assemblages that do not speak for themselves. Any placement of these contentious histories or memories in a single historical grid, or any dominant constellation of symbolic meaning, is inevitably going to leave out some "other" representations, especially during traumatic times. As Susan O'Donnell and David Perley have noted, Indigenous and non-Indigenous communities who are interested in decolonization care about reconciliation, but they also recognized that oftentimes these conflicts involve resource extraction debates and the attempted settling of "the land question."[13]

I agree with Jürgen Zimmerer when he writes about how researchers need to do some "archaeological" digging, so that critical scholars who use comparative approaches can get at the "structural similarities" and the "direct references" that link colonial pasts to postcolonial presents.[14] This is especially the case in reparations contexts, where litigants must show that they have legal standing, that they have sustained particular traumas and other injuries, and that named defendants have engaged in reprehensible and culpable behavior.

Lawyers producing case briefs for aggrieved twentieth-century or twenty-first-century parties must necessarily be selective in their choice of facts, interpretative frame, and the other rhetorical "elements" that Michel Foucault once argued were used to produce a *dispositif* (see chapter 1), but these attorneys are not the only social agents who cherry-pick the colonial facts that go into the constitutive production of legal histories.[15]

Jurists, scholars, and others may not like having to talk about the selective nature of all chronicling of historical events, and agonizing choices have to be made about how to write about the authenticity of materials, the motivations of those who placed colonial materials in particular archives, or the relevance of materials that are not cited in these genocidal disputes.

Those lawyers and advocates who wish to put former colonizers "on trial" have to confront the conflictual nature of not only the interpretation of evidence *but the rhetorical production of this evidencing*. This involves a dynamic process of producing both archival presence and absence. As Ann Laura Stoler argued in 2018,

> Michel-Rolph Trouillot once noted that silences occur at four critical moments: the moment of fact creation (the making of sources), the movement of fact assembly (the making of archives), the movment of fact retrieval (the making of narratives) and the moment of retrospective signifance (the making of history) . . . . archives are sites of power and processes of inscription.[16]

I would ask that readers keep these constitutive moves in mind as they review the multidirectional or competitive histories that have been produced by motivated social actors who debate about what happened in GSWA between 1885 and 1908.

I will have more to say about colonial archival retrieval and knowledge production when I get to the chapters on the 2001 and the 2017 legal cases filed in American courts (chapters 7 and 9), but for now I want to stress that it matters a great deal who gets to chronicle the events that are placed into emploted histories that filled with colonial heroes and tragic events. We shall see in this chapter that we have been bequeathed conflicting accounts of who started the 1904 Herero "rebellion" as well as myriad numbers of perspectives on the waging of these colonial battles by German soldiers, Ovaherero warriors, and Nama fighters.

Until followers of Jan-Bart Gewald's revisionist histories had their say in many academic circles during the late 1980s and early 1990s, it was often taken for granted that it was the Ovaherero who started the 1904 German-Herero war. Before that period there was less scholarly agreement about who owed "protectorate" lands in GSWA, especially after so many treaties were signed, so many colonial promises were made, and so many "German" deeds were filed.

Some of the most intriguing colonial issues that would be raised by contemporaries during the GSWA years had to do with the issue of who was actually committing "atrocities" and acting in barbarous ways. It was not always easy for Europeans to admit that Ovaherero or Nama leaders sometimes acted in chivalrous ways, but more than few writers in the early 1900s referenced how Samuel Maherero, after the rebellion began in January of 1904, made a point of letting it be known that he spared German women and children, and that his warriors would not be targeting British subjects.[17] Those who wanted to configure the Ovaherero or Nama as anti-colonial heroes could deploy tragic frames, of rhetorical analyses that highlighted what happened when indigenous communities lost their lands, their personal property, their cultures, and their dignity.

Obviously this was not the way that some Prussian militarists and their supporters contextualized "German" affairs in GSWA. In their martial telling of the tale the only responsible leaders of the Ovaherero and the Nama were the ones who turned in their arms, scouted for the German protection troops, or left the colony. German officers viewed themselves as honorable soldiers when they hanged the leaders of the rebellion and spared the lives of those who were willing to live under German formal and informal rules and regulations.

As I will explain in more detail below, monuments and memorials would be put up across GSWA commorating the acts of the soldiers who fought disease and enemies as they protected the settlers. Books were written by German officials who commented on the alleged mutilation of settler bodies during Ovaherero or Nama raids, and it was almost obligatory that these German chroniclers reference the barbarity of their enemies who were oftentimes dehumanized in these accounts. In 1909, Lothar von Trotha, writing in *Der Deutschen Zeitung*, looked back on his leadership during the 1904–1908 war; and he argued that the suppression of these rebellions could not be waged "according to the laws of the Geneva Convention."[18] In theory, those European laws of war and Geneva regulations were intended to benefit civilized soldiers and they did not apply when small numbers of European troops faced hordes of uncivilized African warriors.

How many German social agents living during these GSWA years shared von Trotha's views? Is it possible that many settlers—long before 1904—dreamed of a GSWA bereft of any free Africans? How many were willing to write about the need to protect "Native" "rights" and how many ridiculed those idealistic notions?

Other chapters of this book will cover how Social Democrats in the Reichstag (chapter 3), or how the British viewed some of these GSWA affairs (chapter 4), but in this particular chapter I want to lay the groundwork for the following chapters by showing the fact creation, the various archiving, the narrativizing, and the crafting of "history" (Stoler) that took place between 1884 and 1908. These colonial accounts could be (re)organized in ways that produced some of the less threatening multidirectional memories that Michael Rothberg alluded to, but they could also be reassembled into exclusionary colonial and postcolonial metanarratives that silenced the voices of indigenous "Others." As Jodi Byrd and Michael Rothberg pointed out in a 2011 coauthored essay, logics of colonialism could be used to "erase indigenous perspectives completely, especially within the juridical exercises of colonialist power that deploy and constrain sovereignty as justification for land dispossession."[19]

Although some twenty-first-century writers like to argue that annihilationist sentiments only manifested themselves *after* the 1904 battle of Waterberg, and colonial settler ideologies had to be radicalized before massacres occurred, I want to suggest that many of the missionaries, soldiers, traders, settlers, and colonial administrators who arrived in GSWA between the 1880s and 1903 did not hesitate to write and talk about a time when those German settlers living GSWA would no longer have to worry about any armed Africans or large tribes of "Natives" living in their midst. Today's scholars are fond of citing textual materials that are used to document the existence of assimilationist sentiments, but they underestimate the persuasive power, and the pervasiveness, or these and other exclusionary colonial rhetorics.

Granted, from the time of the mythic "founding" of this German "protectorate" or "colony" there were always some who were willing to live as guests or European migrants among empowered indigenous African communities, but there were also many others who had other plans. More than a few seemed to harbor more sinister, more brutal, and more annihilationist ways of thinking about the lands or personal rights of the indigenous "other."

Competitive narratives were produced by those German colonizers who disagreed amongst themselves about whether adminstrators, traders, or settlers had to at least acknowledge some minimal form of African sovereignty or indigenous ownership of lands.[20]

THE MYTHIC "FOUNDING" OF GERMAN SOUTH WEST AFRICA AND THE SIGNING OF "PROTECTIVE" TREATIES

Interdisciplinary scholars who wrote about the Namibian genocide before Ovaherero and Nama litigants filed their twenty-first-century lawsuits spent decades arguing about the nineteenth-century mindsets of the traders from South Africa, the Rhenish missionaries, and the first German civil servants who traveled to the "wild" frontiers of what was then called "Damaraland" or "Hereroland." When only a few hundred Germans were living among hundreds of thousands of Africans it made sense to those back in Germany that the civil administrators sent to GSWA had to create the impression that they were going to follow the guidelines for the protection of "Natives" that were set out in texts that came out of the 1884–1885 Conference of Berlin. One section of the General Act for the Berlin Conference outlined how German rulers were supposed to oversee the "preservation of the native tribes, the suppression of slavery and the slave trade, and the protection of religious freedom."[21]

Could this "preservation" take place without recognizing indigenous title to the lands that would be occupied by European colonial settlers?

Several years after the Berlin Conference German delegates to Hague Conferences signed agreements that were supposed govern the conduct of warfighting and the treatment of prisoners captured on battlefields. Respect for the laws of war, however, focused on the social agency of empowered Europeans, and this was supposed to provide one more indication of the civilized nature of European colonial or imperial expansionism.

Those scholars who belong to Third World Approaches to International Law (TWAIL) movements, or related critical disciplines or subdisciplines, can be forgiven for wondering if all of this wordsmithing was simply a ruse that allowed outnumbered colonizers to gain time before their populations eventually backed the funding of colonial troops that were needed to help with dispossession of most, or all indigenous lands that would be transferred over to the German settlers. Given the ambiguous nature of the colonial archival materials will we ever truly know just how many settlers pretended to believe in the need to respect indigenous rights as they anticipated the days when sufficient colonial force could be exerted to help with the "annihilation" of the Herero? When the Herero and Nama learned about the plans for the confiscation of all of their cattle and their placement on "reserves," was this something that led to expected violence? Or did this colonial violence spontaneously escalate or radicalize, and if so, when did this happen?[22] Did anyone during these colonial years even contemplate the possibility that the Ovaherero or Nama needed to survive, and that they should be compensated for their losses, before they were placed in places like "reservations" or "camps"?

Most social scientists or humanists who study German colonization in Africa seem to take the view that relatively few colonizers, before 1904, were annihilationists. As the story goes all of this began when Heinrich Vogelsang, an employee of a trader by the name of Adolf Lüderitz, traveled to a bay called Angra Pequeña so that he could hastily sign as many treaties as possible with local tribal leaders. Otto von Bismarck, during and after the Berlin Conference, often remarked that the German flag followed colonial trade, and this was put to the test by entrepreneurs like Vogelsang and Lüderitz.

Stories were told about how Vogelsang and Lüderitz, aided by a missionary by the name of Bam, proceeded to get the signatures of Nama leaders like Joseph Fredericks, who in May of 1883 supposedly traded away indigenous rights to Angra Pequeña and the surrounding areas. Writers disagree about the equitable nature of this trading, but capitalists who wanted believed in the legitimacy of European ways of viewing contracts, property rights, and imperial governmentalities in imperial realms could argue that it made sense for Fredricks to be deemed the "owner" of these lands who could transfer that ownership over to the

Germans for 100 pounds sterling and two hundred rifles. David Olusoga and Casper Erichsen—who clearly did not sympathize with this German reterritorialization of indigenous lands—would later note that as "Joseph signed he could not possibly have realized that this sale of a small patch of desert around a desolate harbor would set in train the complete take-over of south-Western African by European colonialists and disaster for his people."[23]

Critical scholars who critiqued the signing of these German "protection" agreements would note that acknowledging their legitimacy, or their legality, depended on ignoring indigenous ways of conceptualizing communal land ownership or generational transference of property. Many of the treaties that were negotiated by Vogelsang for Lüderitz were said to have been written in strategically ambiguous ways, that allowed indigenous signers to believe that they were being treated as empowered leaders of egalitarian nations who retained sovereign rights to lands that would later be "rented" to the Europeans. In theory, during the early colonizing years, the German traders who traveled to these regions would stay out of indigenous African affairs, they would bring their trade goods, and they would ask permission before they trekked across Herero or Nama lands. Some—perhaps a minority—refused to call these "German" lands during the 1880s or before 1893.[24]

The Germans who wrote about these "protective" treaties in their private correspondence seemed to be candid about the instrumentalist nature of their quest for agreements that allowed for the German purchase, or the seizure of lands or safe passage in return for "protecting" one indigenous tribe from another indigenous tribe. European divide and conquer strategies thus included the archiving of tales of cattle raiding between the Ovaherero and Nama that were configured as "wars" by the Europeans. All of these colonial stories were used to rationalize the supposed need for German settlements in GSWA.

Legal class action complaints that were filed in U.S. courts by the Ovaherero in 2001 would later document the extractive nature of some of this German colonization (see chapter 7), but if readers review the military archives of the Germans they will find that many of those back in Berlin were skeptical that these indigenous or "protectorate" lands could ever be colonized in productive ways that would help the German empire. For decades it seemed as though German speculators and other investors lost money before the discovery of diamond mines in GSWA. However, inspite of these financial losses, many Germans joined colonial societies and more than a few hoped that the "protectorate" would eventually become a "colony."

Many Germans living in the European metropoles during the early 1880s weren't even sure that they wanted overseas colonies on the peripheries of empire, and Bismarck shared the views of those who thought that commercial success was a prerequisite for colonial viability. He, and other Germans, had to be persuaded that diplomats or troops were actually needed to protect Lüderitz's interest.

Lüderitz eventually had to travel to Berlin so that he could get consular protection for his employees and the few settlers in the region. When he was approached by this famous trader, Otto von Bismarck replied, "Sovereignty over this country now lies either with the Negro [*sic*] prince concerned, or with Lüderitz, but not the Reich."[25]

This feigned respect for any "prince," or indigenous rights for Africans, did not last when Ovaherero or Nama or other indigenous communities realized that it was just a matter of time before most, or all, of their cattle and lands would be seized by the Germans.

A few scholars have recently argued that some Germans may have believed that the British were the real owners of Angra Pequeña, and that in spite of the signing of the Berlin Act they expected British ships to arrive on the scene. Given the signing of different international treaties—and the *realpolitik* abrogation of those agreements—German diplomats had to be wary of the activities of British rivals who already controlled the nearby Cape Colony and Walvis Bay. At any time during the 1880s these British rivals might come forward with evidence of prior claims to these same South West African regions. If this happened, then precious German monies might be wasted on Lüderitz's gambles.

Bismarck would soon be talked into abandoning his usual anti-colonial stance. First of all, public pressure started to be brought by German colonial societies like the *Deutsche Kolonialverein* and other supporters of German expansionist schemes. Second, Lüderitz had some unfortunate financial setbacks, and he announced that he was going to have to sell his holdings in this part of the world. In order to prevent perceived British encroachment, Germany was forced to buy out Lüderitz and this newly minted entity—that included nine hundred miles of coastline footholds between the Orange River and Portuguese Angola—which became some of the first places that led to the mapping of the colonial empire of Kaiser Wilhelm's Second Reich.

After Bismarck's interventionism, fewer and fewer missionaries, civil administrators, or other chroniclers of these events mentioned indigenous rights or those African "princes" as they embraced the idea that these lands were now a part of a mappable German "protectorate" or "colony." These discursive shifts set the stage for what was to come.

Chroniclers of these events noted that Bismarck appointed the first Imperial Commissioner, Heinrich Göring, so that he could travel to this new colony and sign many more treaties in the name of the Fatherland.[26] Heinrich Göring would be remembered in the annals of German colonial histories as the father of the Nazi leader Hermann Göring. Those who wrote about the "continuity" thesis that I mentioned in chapter 1 could use familial connections like this to make broader claims about how what happened in GSWA during colonial wars provided the experiments in governance that led inexorably to the Nazi Holocaust.[27]

The pro-colonial German expansionists who had to listen to the stories that were told about Heinrich Göring and his treaties were caught in a bind. On the one hand, if they listened to some of the Rhenish missionaries, and if they pretended to respect some of the provisions of the Berlin Act, this might lead to the legitimation and the preservation of indigenous rights and religious practices. This would slow down the pace of Germanization of lands, and it might create the impression that they respected what they viewed as pagan, uncivilized, and unproductive ways of using lands that should be farmed.

On the other hand, if the German expansionists wished to create the impression that under doctrines like "*terra nullius*" they themselves had land rights, that needed to be respected.

By arguing that they were developing "empty" lands between 1885 and 1904, they could ignore those who harped on "Native rights."

The rhetoric about "buying" indigenous lands seemed to provide a compromising way out of this bind. Instead of dwelling on the need to protect "Native" rights German administrators, soldiers, and European investors could use their economic power to "purchase" lands from the Ovaherero and Nama. Buying the lands, or seizing the lands from Africans who violated European laws or colonial codes, could be configured as legitimate activities that had nothing to do with illegal dispossession.

Like other European colonizers the pro-imperial Germans had to find tribal leaders who were willing to go against the grain, who disrespected tribal ways of viewing the lands, and were willing to personally profit from following European ways of conceptualizing property rights. Samuel Maherero, for example, received 2,000 marks per year after 1896 when he signd a treaty that allowed Governor Leutwein to place a border between German settlements and indigenous lands that "ran through the middle of Hereroland."[28] This would provide an example of what postcolonial and post-structural critics would call the "reterritorializing" of GSWA.

This framing of settler colonial activities and indigenous sales of land made sense to German occupiers of more and more portions of Hereroland or "Damaraland," but it made little sense to those members of indigenous tribes who believed in more communal ways of treating these same lands.

The movement of indigenous herds of animals created potential problems for those who wanted to "buy" land, set up borders, and stabilize these property rights, but German colonizers could argue that once cattle set foot on particular lands that meant that those lands automatically belonged to the Ovaherero leaders who owned the cattle.[29] That individualistic way of conceptualizing land ownership helped German traders, adminstrators, and settlers who now sought to identify a few indigenous "captains" and pay them well for pasture lands that extended to Rehoboth and the Kuiseb River in the South, and included the Waterberg, Otavi and Grootfontein regions in the north.

The inevitable cultural traumas that came with land disputation, major population dislocations, and colonial power disparities impacted the lives of hundreds of thousands of Africans who were living in GSWA before the outbreak of the 1904–1908 war.[30] This also impacted how indigenous communities later recorded in their oral histories their memories of these foreign incursions.

Rhenish missionaries tried to educate diplomats about what life was like in the German protectorate, but it was perhaps inevitable that misunderstandings would arise when German imperialists acted as if the "protectorate" or the "colony" was already an extension of Germany itself. Civil administrators had little trouble convincing the *Schutztruppe* or German settlers that Germany laws—and not African societal practices—ought to govern colonial affairs. Yet as readers might imagine, those German laws could be interpreted in ways that helped the German imperial expansionists.

The existence of these varied and contentious ways of viewing land ownership confused some of the colonized and the colonizers. During the early years of German colonization, some members of indigenous communities could make fun of German pretensions and they could display their own powers. For example, Imperial Commissioner Heinrich Göring had to make a hasty exit from the colony in order to save his life when he offended the sensibilities of local communities. In 1885, he had bought an old mission building, and Göring proceeded to try and build an extension to that edifice that involved building over an older Herero grave site. Angered that their ancestors had been disturbed, in 1888 Göring was summoned to Okahandja, one of the key meeting places for the Ovaherero, and he found himself standing in a room full of some hundred angry Herero. They proceeded to tell him that they were going to nullify their "protection" treaty with Germany and that they were dismissing him. Fearing for his life, the Imperial Commission got on a ship and sailed back to Germany.[31]

Ovaerero and Nama chroniclers could take pride in telling the tale of Göring's escape, and they respected the activism of those who would not tolerate this abuse of the Ovaherero dead. Generations of indigenous narrators would use their oral histories to explain how German interlopers mistreated the African living—and the dead.[32] In the middle of one of the battles that would later be fought between German soldiers and the Nama, the Nama leader Hendrik Witbooi died from a shrapnel wound. Fearing that his body would be exhumed by Germany soldiers, Witbooi's men drove their cattle over his remains in order to conceal his unmarked grave.[33]

At the same time, the arrival of Maxim guns, artillery, and hundreds of German soldiers helped remind the German settlers that they would not longer be embarrassed by those types of affronts.

While some academics have lampooned Heinrich Göring's efforts and have argued that his mission failed, others contend that this overlooked the contributions that he made to the Second Reich. Defenders of his actions noted that Göring had signed treaties that helped legitimate German land claims.

Göring kept meticulous records of his treaty negotiations and the specific contents of some of his "protection" treaties now (re)appear in academic textbooks—and in the complaints of twenty-first-century litigants. Many Europeans who review Göring's efforts could argue that by the end of 1886 the Germans had managed to obtain "legal title" for the legal possession of most, if not all, of the lands that would be characterized as "German" South West Africa.[34]

European theories about imperial geography, anthropology, entropy, eugenics, ethnographical classification, zoology, and racial degeneration were carried abroad, in ideological drifts, by those who traveled to GSWA after Göring's departure. Many in Berlin, and some in the colonies, participated in debates about what Friedrich Ratzel called *Lebensraum,* or "living space." In *Der Lebensraum* Ratzel had argued that there were many differences that existed between "those populations" that "failed" and those that could "grow" during colonization periods. His particular stories about racial degeneration or regeneration focused on geographic power and environmental influences.

In theory, those who agreed with Ratzel might note how advanced populations were those that avoided the failures of the "groups that were torn apart, "lawless," and poor.[35] Elsewhere Ratzel, in his 1891 *Anthropogeographie,* claimed that the races that were "dying out" were the ones that were "inferior," communities who exposed their weaknesses when they came in "contact with culture."[36] When Ratzel wrote about GSWA he optimistically noted how this particular colony would provide the lands that were needed for successful German settlement.[37]

Some colonial administrators in GSWA wrote as if they too had studied geography, ethnology, anthropology, and other subjects, as they made key decisions in the German colonies. One of the first governors of GSWA, who was known for his efficacious "divide and rule" strategies, candidly explained in his memoirs why some Europeans had misplaced views regarding the goals of German expansionism:

> The final aim of each and every colonisation is—stripped of all its idealist and humanitarian accessories—finally just a simply business. The colonised race does not intend to bring the possible expected fortune to the indigenous population of the country to be colonised. Instead it is in the first instance looking for its own advantage. . . . With respect to the way of colonization, there is consequently basically one

> guiding principle, namely the one which leads most safely towards the aspired business.[38]

The circulation of these types of attitudes helps explain how the Ovaherero and Nama "captains" might be paid thousands of German marks annually just before their "tribes" were slaughtered, placed in camps, then reserves, and then treated as necessitous, but dangerous, labor pools.

The colonizing arguments that appeared in textual fragments from writers like Ratzel or Leutwein obviously looked nothing like the oral histories of the Nama and Ovaherero, or the mission reports that were authored by those who tried to record how indigenous communities felt about their own social identities, their cattle, and their lands.

The existence of contradictory ways of viewing land ownership must have frustrated those who were looking for orderly "German" transfers of land rights. That said, both the colonized and the colonizers understood the pragmatic role that guns, ammunition, and relational power placed in GSWA. In 1889 Missionary Brincker of the Rhenish Mission wrote,

> Only power counts here; it takes the place of right. If the riches of the country are to be utilized, a European Administration must be established so that every case of arrogance on the part of the Natives, and damage to the interests of the settlers can be punished. Under such protection the Natives would again develop their important raising of cattle. Every European enterprise would be secure, and the work of the Mission would prosper.[39]

This type of assimilationist way of viewing colonial relationships assumed that the "Natives" should be living in segregated, orderly places that afforded them the chance to continue raising cattle. The formation of this "European administration" would remedy the apparent chaos that Brincker must have felt he was witnessing when he traveled to places where armed Ovaherero and Nama and other indigenous groups were carrying out cattle raids. This administraton would later be called the "German colonial enterprise" by both researchers and lawyers.

Brincker's almost Nietzschean way of viewing GSWA affairs did not dwell on the power of signed treaties, and he did not treat the "Natives" as potential equals. After looking around at the power of those who should have been listening to their missionary betters, Brincker became convinced that he knew exactly what the German colony needed to reduce Native hautiness—four hundred more *Schutztruppe* and eight cannons.[40]

Critical genealogical reviews of the settler discourses that were produced during these periods in GSWA reveal the temporary, suasory power of these assimilationist rhetorics, what Helmut Walser Smith characterized as the ideological features of "accommodationist racism." Smith catalogued some of the constellations of meanings that were assembled together in this particular colonial *dispositif*:

> a Lamarckian emphasis on the ability of environment to influence genetic make-up, on the necessity of slow, patient cultural training on the diffusion of white civilization, and on the resultant homogeneity of mankind. The accommodationist position did not preclude colonial violence, but instead, it situated colonial violence in a narrative of progress. But it also envisioned a point of harmony, where violence was no longer part of the racial encounter or part of the epic clash of civilizations, superior with inferior.[41]

Unlike the annihilationist rhetorics and ideologies that were produced by those who wanted to openly defend the wiping out of lesser "sub-human" "beasts," this German accommodationist assemblage had much in common with the British "conciliatory" rhetorics that were produced by Aboriginal Protection Societies or other Europeans interested in protecting "Natives."[42]

Notice the potential attraction of this accomodationist racial position for those who were living in places where only a few dozen *Schutztruppe* were patrolling coastal towns like Lüderitz. Rhenish missionaries might be attracted to some of its tenets, in that accomodationism allowed for the redemption of African souls and the conversation of heathens. Accommodationist ideologies might appeal to European farmers who could use their whips to dispense "paternal" learning to their inferior laborers. Colonial administrators who deployed assimilationist or accommodationist rhetorics could defend the orderly and incremental dispossession of indigenous cattle and lands. Permutations of these same accommodationist rhetorical frames could later be used to rationalize the formation of "reserves" or camps for those who needed to be segregated for their own good.

During times of peace these accomodationist variants of colonial racist rhetorics appeared to resonate with German civil servants, *Schutztruppe*, and settlers who needed indigenous labor or cattle, but during times of war it was not hard to *rationalize the move away from this accommodationism and toward acceptance of more annihilationist ideologies*. Scholars would later write about the hardening of colonial hearts, the increased popularity of extermination rhetorics and the radicalization of military solutions. Helene von Falkenhausen, in her memoirs, had chapters that explained how her family had lived in peace with indigenous communities after arriving at the Swakopmund port in 1893, but by 1907 she would write about how Herero women physically attacked her, and how other Africans killed her husband and two other settlers near Otjihaenena.[43]

A perusal of the elite and public colonial archives shows that during the 1880s and 1890s heated disagreements took place between those who adhered to either assimilationist or annihilationist ways of viewing colonial theories and practices. Manifestations of these complex debates included deliberations about where to place the Ovaherero and Nama on mythic Social Darwinian rungs, the testing of ethnological and race science claims, the education of the "Natives," and even the "humanity" of indigenous African neighbors. It was not unusual to read European essays or books that were written by those who averred that the Herero were good workers and ought to be saved, while the Khoikhoi, (the Nama, or "Hottentots)" could be treated as lazy, troublesome, or "dying" races.

Neo-Lamarckian views made little sense to the biological determinists and militarists who simply wanted to wipe out inferior races, but the accommodationist views seemed to be validated when it appeared that even "nature" conspired to help with the education or control of the Ovaherero and Nama pastoral populations. When a dreaded disease, known as rinderpest, destroyed herds of cattle that were not vaccinated in 1897, this decimated the cattle holdings of the indigenous pastorial communities. This forced the Ovaherero to leave behind their pastoral ways. In order to survive many participated in the German colonial capitalist system that aided the cause of colonial settler expansionism. The destruction of indigenous societies could be configured within assimiliationist tragic frames as something that was to be regretted, but inevitable.

Is it possible that all this dispossession and disease, which threatened to unravel Ovaherero societies, helped embolden more than a few European colonizers who dared dream of a German South West Africa that had fewer "Natives" to worry about? As the Germans interceded in internecine wars that were fought between the Ovaherero and the Nama, the unthinkable became thinkable. Perhaps, just perhaps, the arrival of thousands of new settlers, and the use of more "docile" indigenous labor from other places like the British Cape Colony, obviated the need to put up with those who "rebelled" against their German betters.

Annihilationists often left archival traces of the fury and frustration that they felt when sentimental missionaries or farmers or administrators catered to the needs of the Africans. Karl Dove, writing in 1903, left us these prescient remarks:

> I express my fears here and the future will prove me right that the system of administration [in South West Africa] so beloved in Berlin shall one day bring us a bloody *Kaffir* [Nama] rebellion and that there is only one means to prevent such a rebellion and that is the adoption of the native policy which has been practiced by the Boers in relation to the Kaffirs from the beginning.[44]

These would be the types of ideological fragments that would drift across time and be picked up by apartheid generations (see chapters 5 and 6).

Lawyers, working on twenty-first-century claimants' briefs had to be circumspect in the ways that they later referenced this type of assimiliationist colonial commentary. On the one hand, the existence of these assimiliationist rhetorics indicated that many European missionaries and settlers realized that the indigenous African communities owned their land and could "sell" it to willing German buyers. Yet, on the other hand, the circulation of these assimilationalist discourses could mean that not all settlers were actually annihiliationists, and this could have potentially undermined the efforts of Namibian activists and litigants who wanted to use this lawfare to help prove the facticity of the Ovaherero and Nama genocide.

THE DISCURSIVE MOVES AWAY FROM ASSIMILATIONIST COLONIAL LEXICONS AND TOWARD THE EMBRACE OF MORE ANNIHILATIONIST RHETORICS

George Steinmetz has argued that at some key point in time many whites living in GSWA appeared to have stopped believing in the feasibility and wisdom of enforcing what he called "Native policy"—a legal instantiation of accommodationist principles.[45] While some have argued that the radicalization of these rhetorics can be traced to what happened at Hamakari/Waterberg in 1904, I would argue that the ideological seeds for this shift were planted much earlier.

I am convinced that these seeds germinated when confident settlers welcomed the arrival of hundreds of German troops to the colony. Kurt von François, who grew tired of negotiating and corresponding with Nama leaders, in 1893 led a small force of heavily armed German protection forces to a place called Hoornkrans. At this mountain stronghold German troops killed dozens of followers of Hendrik Witbooi, and this infuriated many members of indigenous communities who felt that the signing of treaties meant that they would be protected from these types of military engagements.

It could be argued that the march on Hoornkrans—that could only take place after the sending of more German troops—signaled the move away from official acceptance of accomodationist principles. Now, it would be military officers like Kurt von François who made most major decisions that impacted GSWA affairs. It would be the leaders of the *Schutztruppe,* and not *Reichskommisars* like Dr. Heinrich Ernst Göring, who were the real powers governing the colony.

The granting of these types of martial powers by superiors back in Berlin came at a precipitous moment in time, when more than a few were starting to believe that the presence of von François's troops signaled the beginning of the "end" of Herero and Nama hegemony. After Hoornkrans, Kurt von François asked for more troops; and merchants, missionaries, and indigenous populations soon learned that military leaders monopolized much of the power in GSWA. Those in the colony watched as Kurt von François and his troops, in the name of military necessities, carried out deadly raids, banished some African leaders, and then condemned to death, without trial, "outlaws" who were deemed existential threats to the German colony. As soon as von François started to curtail shipments of guns and munitions into the colony, he strengthened the hand of those who no longer had reason to worry about either the preservation of "Native" rights or the future of the colony.

The leaders of the Herero and Nama forces must have realized that the presence of von François and his troops might herald the arrival of many thousands of armed German settlers who were intent on taking even more African lands. For years Hendrik Witbooi kept a famous diary that has served as one of the best sources of information on indigenous responses to German colonization, and what happened at Hoornskrans served as a warning to thousands of Africans who soon learned that their signed treaties were not going to be respected. A wise but disheartened Witbooi sent a letter to John Cleverly, the British magistrate at Walvis Bay, imploring the British to help protect his tribe's sovereignty:

> The Germans are encroaching on my land, and are now threatening to destroy me with war. . . some rulers surrendered to German Protection and are today bitterly sorry for they have not seen any of the beautiful promises kept. The German told them he would protect them against mighty invaders threatening to take our land by force, without permission from the chiefs. But from what I hear and see of the man, it now appears the German himself is . . . doing exactly what he said we would be protected from. . . . German officials told my officials how they had beaten the men in a disgraceful and brutal manner, as the dumb and ignorant creatures they think us.[46]

Regardless of whether the Europeans were using accomodationist or annihilationist rationales to justify their dispossessions, it seemed obvious to Africans like Witbooi that they were going to be regarded as inferior beings whose rights could be trampled at will.

The constant circulation of all these colonial variants of European property laws and racist ideologies created a *dispositif* that contributed to the dehumanization and the dispossession of the Ovaherero and the Nama. These European racializations of colonial relationships varied only in qualitative intensity, and the use of select assimilationist or annihilationist grammars only signaled *the speed at which colonizers wished to carryout out displacements* and dispossession. Assimilationists wanted to witness the slow, non-violent transfers of land and populations, while the annihilationists saw no reason why violence ought not be used to speed up the inevitable.

For more than a decade Hendrik Witbooi and some other Nama tribal leaders would trust Germans like Governor Theodor Leutwein, and they would send their warriors to help Leutwein when the Germans requested scouts or fighters for the battles that had to be fought with the Ovaherero. The archives contain pictures of Leutwein and his soldiers or administrators toasting Witbooi and his second in command, creating the impression that these were allies.

In some of the claimants' briefs that were filed in American courts in 2001 and 2017, Theodor Leutwein is cited as one of von Trotha's critics, someone who respected the rights of the Herero and Nama (see chapters 7 and 9), but a more critical look at his words and his deeds supports the positions of the scholars who have argued that his governorship aided the cause of those who were also intent on reducing Ovaherero power through expropriation of indigenous resources.[47] Leutwein, after all, could not fathom the idea that German soldiers and settlers would one day pack up and leave these lands and return to Europe. Nor was he willing to see a minority of Europeans occupying tiny slivers of land and having to pay taxes to African lessors of land.

At first glance it might appear that Governor Leutwein's arrival meant the return of respect for Ovaherero and Nama sovereignty, but his policies led to the loss of more and more indigenous lands. He helped plan out future "reservations" for indigenous populations and he earned the reputation of an administrator who stopped outright contractual thievery of cattle by unscrupulous traders. However, he also called for more troops who patrolled "protectorate" or "German" lands and he acted in ways that helped with the Germanization of these African lands.[48]

The arrival of more troops and more German settlers, as well as the disempowerment of the Ovaherero and Nama, brought chaos to a colony that was already suffering from deteriorating ethnic relations. A review of German legal records and other texts shows the chronicling of cases where indigenous women were raped with impunity by the colonizers.[49] In the decades before the 1904 uprising, African laborers were beaten, and indigenous pastoralists who were used to moving their grazing cattle ran up against barbed wire and settler fences. It dawned on the Witbooi and the other Nama that Leutwein and the German settlers may have been using talk of Herero threats as a way of deflecting attention away from German colonial misbehavior.

Yet it would be the Ovaherero, and not the Nama, who were blamed for starting what Europeans would call the "rebellion" of 1904. Regardless of who started the war, critics now know that Herero combatants, led by Paramount Chief Samuel Maherero, left Okahandja and started to attack isolated German farms and homesteads. German contemporary accounts noted that within a matter of days, 123 Europeans died at the hands of the "rebels."[50] As Professor Benjamin Madley would later write in 2005, the initial "Herero attacks on 267 German farms and businesses provoked war fever and inspired murderous rhetoric among both colonial and metropole Germans."[51]

German authors filled small libraries with books on the "atrocities" that were committed by the Ovaherero and other indigenous fighters who were depicted as having threatened German farmers and their families. It would be these shards of memory that would be used and reused over the next century to convey the idea that German settlers, soldiers, and missionaries were carrying out their civilizing missions in GSWA by suppressing rebellions.

Confident Germans who watched the unloading of ships filled with troops were sure that the Ovaherero would be quickly defeated. As one chief engineer of the Otavi Construction Company reported, "everyone here [in GSWA] believes that the uprising will be smashed ruthlessly and a *tabula rasa* created."[52] A policy of "*Vernichtung*," or annihilation, seemed to be adopted by those who wanted to wipe the slate clean and finally clear the "German" lands of indigenous existential threats.

Some of those who chronicled these events noted how the Herero attackers targeted those Germans whom they suspected of having committed rape or murder. These "rebels" also attacked the traders who had taken lands in payment for real or imagined debts.[53]

Missionaries and others who tried to recontextualize the carnage helped produce counternarratives and multidirectional memories that mentioned the land disputes and the arrogance of the colonizers, but many of the German journalists who reported on the Ovaherero rebellion for audiences in the metropole produced popular texts that contained lurid stories about the Herero mutilation of hundreds of Germans settlers or traders in GSWA (see chapter 3).

Critics of the 1904 war might focus on the loss of civilian lives, but the soldiers and others who witnessed the brutality of this totalizing warfare oftentimes underscored the social agency of the Ovaherero women who taunted the German troops who tried to track them down and surround their kraals. At the battle at Onganjira on April 9, 1904, the battle lines between the German and the Ovaherero fighters were so close that it was said that one could hear the war chants of the Herero women. They sang, "To whom belongs Hereroland? To us belongs Hereroland! To us belongs Hereroland!"[54]

German efforts at trying to deterritorialize Hereroland were met by indigenous efforts at reterritorialization.

German writers oftentimes argued that Ovaherero ignorance and African savagery forced the hand of reluctant German warriors who now had to use violence to quell the rebellion. It was said that Governor Leutwein did his best to maintain German control of these lands, but impatient superiors back in Berlin were embarrassed by some of the early victories of the Ovaherero. The German General Staff decided to replace Theodor Leutwein with General Lothar von Trotha—a man who had participated in brutal and repressive colonial campaigns in China and in German East Africa.

Von Trotha, who traveled to GSWA during the summer of 1904, eventually witnessed the arrival of tens of thousands of *Schutztruppe*, and with them came Krupp guns and the machinery of modern warfare.

I would argue that at this point in time—if not in 1893 after Hoornkrans—most German colonizers joined the chorus of those who had little interest in talking or writing about the preservation of "Native" rights in "Hereroland." Back in Germany a government geologist, Doctor Hartmann, may have represented the views of many when he argued that "the final solution *[Endlösung]* to the native question can only be to break the power of the natives totally and for all time."[55] Regardless of whether we call this politicide, or an example of Raphael Lemkin's "cultural genocide," this represented the abandonment of many imperial pretenses.

As the tide of battle turned during 1904, many of the Ovaherero, along with their families and their cattle, retreated to Hamakari, a place the Germans called Waterberg, and some missionaries and other sympathetic writers commented on how the Ovaherero once again assumed that they were going to have to negotiate a peace with the Germans. The tens of thousands who huddled around campfires near the Waterberg plateau perhaps anticipated that they would be punished for their transgressions before being allowed back into "Hereroland."

This was not to be. General von Trotha joined those settlers and administrators who had no interest in the preservation of treaties that were signed with brutal "savages" who purportedly committed unforgivable acts. The Ovaherero had armed themselves, had dared to attack their superiors, and had acted as if they were the equals of the Germans. They apparently did not understand either the laws of nature, or the martial codes that governed colonial relationships during wartime.

Von Trotha, in other words, could be configured by archivists and other chroniclers as someone who had little interest in carrying out accommodationist policies. Those who wanted to treat him as an iconic, condensation symbol for annihilationist principles could dwell on his popularity with many of his officers, and the way that he seemed to assume that GSWA was as a part of the *Helmut*, the German homeland.

Researchers who focus on von Trotha's social agency, and his intentionalities, often turn their attention to what happened at Waterberg, and they dutifully record how von Trotha commanded ninety-six officers who brought along soldiers who carried 1,488 rifles. It did not hurt that the *Schutztruppe* arrived at the plateau with thirty artillery pieces and twelve Maxim machine guns. It was estimated that the German forces were facing somewhere between five thousand and six thousand mounted Herero who were armed with breechloading rifles.[56] Those who wrote about coming genocidal activities noted that between fifty thousand and sixty thousand other Herero women, men, and children traveled with these Herero fighters.

Like many "small wars" that were fought in places like the Congo Free State, "French Algiers," "Spanish Morocco" or the Sudan, Hamakari/Waterberg was more of a slaughter than a battle. For two days the Ovaherero fighters did their best to protect their women, children, and cattle as machine gun bullets and artillery shells were fired in their direction.

Countless numbers were killed before the survivors fled and started to perish in inhospitable deserts. One author would note, "Seldom in history has an entire nation been hoarded together to meet the horrors of that devastating a battle as was the case with the Herero people at the Waterberg Mountains."[57] A veteran soldier who served in this war would later have a final chapter in his war memoir that would be titled "The End of the Herero People."[58]

Those who later circulated heroic tales of these conflicts noted how, after spending several months on the outskirts of the desert, the German troops who chased the Ovaherero were exhausted, feverish, and in a sad state. Yet their victims were in much worse shape, and some archival records contained countless examples of rhetorical fragments that were left by those who now took for granted that the future of the colony depended on the wiping out of rebel forces.

Those who led the *Schutztruppe* wanted to make sure that the Ovaherero realized that they were now considered to be rebels, trespassing on German lands, and the colonizers hoped that this would have a major deterrent effect. They warned entire bystanding indigenous populations—including the Ovambo in the Northern regions—about what would happen if they joined the ranks of Ovaherero leaders who were already condemned to death for their mutiliation of Germans. On October 2, 1904, Lieutenant General von Trotha would read out these infamous words that have reappeared in several legal documents:

> I, the great general of the German soldiers, send this letter to the Herero people. Hereros are no longer German subjects. They have murdered, stolen, and have cut off the ears and noses and other limbs on wounded German soldiers and now refuse from cowardice to fight further. I tell the people that everyone who surrenders one of the captains at one of my stations as a prisoner receives 1,000 marks. Whoever brings Samuel Maharero receives 5,000 marks. The Herero people must now leave the land. If the people do not do this, then I shall compel them to do so with the great tube [cannon]. Within the German borders every Herero with or without a rifle, with or without cattle, shall be shot. I will take care of no more women or children but drive them back to their people or shoot at them. These are my words to the Herero people.[59]

These words did not appear in the pages of the official German General Staff archival materials that meticulously tracked and preserved the correspondence that von Trotha maintained with his superiors in Berlin, but somehow some of the German Social Democrats who later argued about these events in the *Riechstag* got hold of a copy of the order and discussed it during parliamentary debates. Translations of these same words appeared in both 2001 and 2017 legal complaints.

Various chroniclers of these events tell us that at a place called Osombo zoWindimbe, after hanging several captured Herero men in front of women and children, Lieutenant General von Trotha gave copies of his proclamation to some of the surviving Ovaherero. He told them to show these copies of his "proclamation" order to the other "rebels" in order to deter them from carrying out any future attacks on the colonial settlers.

The vast majority of twentieth-century and twenty-first-century essayists who write on the Ovaherero and Nama genocide mention or quote from this October 1904 order. For those lawyers who want to hold up Raphael Lemkin's definitions of genocide as the litmus test, it is von Trotha's proclamation that is oftentimes said to provide that legal "smoking gun," one of the clearest examples of the existence of annihilationist sentiments or genocidal "intent."

In his correspondence with his superiors in Berlin, Lieutenant General von Trotha often blamed those who used humanitarian, assimilationist strategies for the displays of weakness that he was convinced led to the Herero rebellion. Two days after he read that proclamation at Osombo zoWindimbe, von Trotha explained that the "uprising is and remains the beginning of a race struggle, which I foresaw as early as 1897 in my reports to the Imperial Chancellor."[60]

In order to help buttress their lawfare cases against the Second Reich—and the later Federal Republic of Germany—many twenty-first-century plaintiffs' lawyers join the ranks of the interdisciplinary scholars who provide rhetorical analyses of von Trotha's correspondence with those in Berlin, including General Alfred von Schlieffen, the chief of the German General Staff. It mattered a great deal that von Schlieffen agreed with von Trotha's approach, and on November 23, 1904, von Schlieffen sent this message to Chancellor Bernhard von Bülow: "One can agree with his [von Trotha's] plan of annihilating the whole people or driving them from the land. The possibility of whites living peacefully together with blacks after what has happened is very slight unless at first the blacks are reduced to forced labor, a sort of slavery."[61] Von Schlieffen went on to note that these types of race wars could only be ended "by the complete annihilation or complete subjugation of one of the parties."[62]

Von Bülow's supporters seemed to have wanted to see subjugation instead of annihilation, and Germany's chancellor asked von Trotha to restrain some of his troops. Von Schlieffen tried to placate an angry von Trotha by reminding the lieutenant general that Kaiser Wilhelm II has "not forbidden you to shoot the Hereros," but only that the "possibility of showing mercy is to be restored."[63]

Critical rhetorical analyses of these types of martial exchanges indicates that von Schlieffen was well aware that German colonizers were going to have to make agonizing choices when they were faced with having to choose between annihilationist or accommodatist ways of viewing indigenous dispossession. This general's commentaries on impending "race wars" spoke volumes about the paradigmatic shifts in the direction of accepting annihilationist solutions to rebellious situations.

As I will explain in more detail in other chapters, the archival chronicling of the exchanges between von Schlieffen and von Trotha have been used to impugn the motives of the colonizers living in GSWA as well as the German General Staff, Kaiser Wilhelm, and those in the metropole who did not stop the carnage on the peripheries of empire.[64] All of this would later be configured as epistemic fragments that were part of a massive German colonial "enterprise."

This is also of interest to critical genocide scholars who argue with other researchers about whether this violence needs to be labeled a typical colonial "war" or an atypical "genocide." Those critical scholars who keep track of contested colonial ideologies—what George Steinmetz called the "parallelograms of force"—are also interested in studying competing representations of what happened at Hamakari/Waterberg, especially after the Germans refused to negotiate with the Ovaherero populations. Most note that the *Schutztruppe* encircled the Herero "nation" with thousands of troops, but questions remain about whether their officers were trying to encourage the Ovaherero to flee to eastern deserts.

THE VARIED RESPONSES OF THE SCHUTZTRUPPE AND THE LOCAL GERMAN SETTLERS TO OHAMAKARI/WATERBERG AND VON TROTHA'S ORDERS

For more than a century, missionaries, soldiers, military strategists, settlers, and others have quarreled about how to frame what happened during and after the battle of Ohamakari/Waterberg. While some observers adopt more structuralist or functionalist ways of explaining the carnage, other researchers don't mind using more intentionalist frames of analysis as they study the mindsets of individual perpetrators, bystanders, or victims in these wartime situations. Intentionalists, for example, are convinced that authors of incriminating texts, like von Trotha, meant exactly what they said, and that this provides the requisite genocidal "intent" that shows that he, and like-minded Germans living in the colony, violated international customary laws of war. Other intentionalist approaches are used by trained legal experts to find the necessary evidence that was needed to document portions of domestic German criminal, property, torts, and other legal cases.

It would be a mistake, however, to argue that all German administrators, soldiers or officers joined von Trotha and spoke in one collective, monolithic colonizing voice. On March 28, 1904, after witnessing alleged Ovaherero brutalities, Bernhard von Bülow sent Governor Leutwein an order to stop the hunting down of the Hereros. Von Bülow apparently worried that European diplomats might view the German suppression of the Herero rebellion as an illegitimate affair that involved revenge killings. European could accept the idea that the suppression of the Herero rebellion was an internal, domestic affair, but it had to be waged in ways that did not violate the laws of humanity. Von Bülow exhorted von Trotha to see to it that no violation "against humanity and against Herero soldiers, unable to defend themselves, and against women and children, be countenanced."[65] Yet for years the African "rebels" would be hunted down by the colonizers, and as late at 1915 British and South African Defence forces were finding camps and prisons that housed indigenous prisoners.

Despite these orders from the metropole, German soldiers on the peripheries of empire spent several months carrying out the indiscriminate killing of unarmed Herero men, women, and children. We do not know exactly how many died between August of 1904 and January of 1905. One German private, Adolf Fischer, wrote that whoever "took part in the chase through the Sandveld [desert] lost his belief in righteousness on Earth."[66] The Ovaherero who lost their lives were pushed into the deserts in the eastern parts of GSWA, and this set the stage for later arguments about whether that pushing constituted any violations of contemporary laws or war or the carrying out of culpable colonial "atrocities."

Some German officers, like Ludwig von Estorff, argued that they were genuinely horrified by the orders that they were given, and von Estorff wrote that he tried to change von Trotha's mind about the handing out of brutal orders. Another officer, Major Stulman, who fought at Hamakari/Waterberg, recorded that he received an order not to take any Ovaherero prisoners. Stulman would write, "We had been explicitly told beforehand that what we were dealing with was the extermination of the whole tribe, nothing living was to be spared."[67]

Some of those who later objected to the filing of Ovaherero and Nama lawsuits would join those who denied that an African "holocaust" had taken place, and they would argue that von Trotha was merely giving orders that served *as threats.* It was said that only a few rogue soldiers did the bayoneting, and that many German soldiers simply fired warning shots over the heads of indigenous women and children.

For a host of understable patriotic reasons future generations of German-speaking Namibians did not want to view this as any unique example of a German "*Sonderweg*" [special path] that could be used to impugn the motives of the *Schutztruppe* that colonists believed had miraculously saved their colony. That said, there is no shortage of evidence that can be found in many dozens of memoirs and books written by German soldiers that tell other tragic tales that point to an example of what Hannah Arendt called "administrative mass murder."[68]

Many of these writers produced intentionalist or functionalist accounts of the Ovaherero "rebellion" that deflected attention away from the colonizing process itself. For example, in a typical essay that was written in the *Deutsche Kolonialzeitung* in the summer of 1904, it was said that the "cause of the Herero war was not sporadic misdeeds perpetrated by single individuals and officials; it was Herero hatred of hardening German control of the land and their desire to shake off these shackles."[69]

Some who argued about the causes of war combined natural with supernatural explanations for why the rebellion happened. Talk of problematic credit regulation, the reduction of "Native" lands, or the failure to send over an adequate number of troops could be tethered to commentary on the swiftness of the attacks that shocked unprepared colonizers. Dr. Stuebel, director of the *Kolonialabteilung* of the German Foreign Office from 1900 to 1905, opined that the rebellion could be viewed as just another naturally occurring event, like a cloudburst or an urban fire. The war could be configured as having started when German settlers faced an outburst of primitive animosity that led to "an unfortunate act of God."[70]

Was it possible that Africans did not understand that this land belonged to God's soldiers on earth?

Dozens of books would be authored by German soldiers and officers who wrote about the poisoning of wells, the bones found in deserts, and the pained looks that they faced when soldiers tracked down those who survived the battle of Waterberg.[71] In the official pages *of Die Kämpfe der deutschen Truppen in Südwestafrika,* the two-volume official record of the war published by the German General Staff in Berlin, it was said that many could hear "the death rattle of the dying and the furious scrams of madness" that "faded away in the sublime silence of infinitude."[72]

When word about the slaughter at Hamakari/Waterberg reached European shores, many recalled what happened at Hoornkrans, and German militarists worried that these types of rebellions were going to present chronic military problems. A combination of arguments about Christian charity, the need for future laborers, and imperial perceptions abroad led to the formation of new plans. Chancellor von Bülow, who worried that the von Trotha's extermination order might "demolish Germany's reputation among civilized nationas and indulge foreign agitation," worked to convince Kaiser Wilhelm that perhaps von Trotha's annihilation order needed to be rescinded. On December 8, 1904, the Kaiser finally agreed that von Trotha was to "treat mercifully those Herero who voluntarily surrendered."[73]

As I will note in the next chapter, the word "*Konzentrationslager,*" or concentration camps, entered the lexicons of German imperial grammotological formations when von Bülow also ordered that camps be established for the "temporary housing and substance of the Herero people."[74] The *Berliner Zeitung* published a leader on January 7, 1905, titled, "Trotha, the Annihilator" ("*Trotha, der Vernichter*"), and the author of this article criticized von Trotha's announcement to the settlers' council in Windhoek that "the annihilation of the rebellious tribes is the objective of all military operations."[75]

For the next several years, a running rhetorical battle took place between those who attacked and those who defended the decisions that were made by von Trotha and others who supported the use of harsh and brutal methods for suppression of colonial rebellions. Maximilian Bayer was one of the most outspoken of the German officers who served under von Trotha, and he had this to say in his *Der Krieg*:

> In times of peace we do not have to bother whether or not a few thousands of Hottentots [Nama] wander around in a vast territory such as South West Africa. We don't have to exterminate them because they are absolutely useless for the cultural development. Nature itself will achieve that task. . . . The day will come when the Hottentots will disappear, but not to the detriment of mankind, because they are only born robbers and thieves, nothing else.[76]

Yet what did one do with the Ovaherero, who were supposed to provide indigenous labor for colonizers, but had rebelled before they were joined by the Nama? Did Germans have to wait for nature to take its course with the Ovaherero or other indigenous communities, or could the Germans need to act eugenically and efficiently, and help speed things along?

All sorts of religious, scientific, political, militaristic, and legal rationales could be used to justify the annihilation or dispossession of the losers in this particular savage war of peace.

Today, when twenty-first-century lawyers try to calibrate the costs of various "takings" during genocidal wars, they focus on the loss of indigenous cattle and lands, but during the first decade of the twentieth century, it *was German losses that were mentioned* in conversations about the future of GSWA. The writers who prepared the official histories of the 1904–1908 war would note that during this war some 689 members of the *Schutztruppe* died of diseases, 676 were killed in action, and 76 were recorded as missing.[77]

With victories on the battlefield came control of the archives, and the Ovaherero and Nama who lost the 1904–1908 war lost their lands, their guns, their political power, and much more. Colonial administrators in GSWA started to pass measures that tried to ensure that the Ovaherero and Nama communities could never be viewed as "nations" that threatened the Germany colony. A member of the *Kolonialabteilung* would note on December 26, 1905, that an ordinance was passed that dictated that all tribal lands were withdrawn from "rebelling" Natives, and all the lands that were confiscated by the colonial government would be handed over to the German settlers who could make the best use of these lands.[78] Indigenous populations had to bow before Europeans and they were forbidden from riding horses.[79]

The few remaining Ovaherero and Nama who had been granted mercy could now live in labor camps. Within a few years some moved to reservations that were adjacent to white settlements. Conquered Africans who had survived Hamakari/Waterberg would now provide the colonial labor that was needed to rebuild a war-torn GSWA.

To make sure that the thousands of indigenous survivors did not go back to their old pastoral ways, rigid "pass" laws were put in place that allowed for inspections by any white person. The Ovaherero and Nama were prohibited from keeping any large cattle herds. They could own goats, and they could request permission for other related activities, but the indigenous workers had become "serfs" who now worked for white settlers.[80]

Meanwhile, back in Germany, it was noted that Kaiser Wilhelm presented von Trotha with medals. German relatives received letters from GSWA settlers or soldiers who praised von Trotha's pragmatic brand of colonialism.

Many of the soldiers and settlers who left memoirs in the colonial achives lionized the efforts of the heroic *Schutztruppe* who protected the German settlers. In 1912, for example, almost everyone in Windhoek turned out to hear the German governor dedicate a massive Rider Statue to the *Schutztruppe*, and he proclaimed "to the world that we are and will remain masters here."[81] A few years later this very same governor had to witness the surrender of the colony to invading British and Union of South Africa military forces during World War I (see chapter 4).

We have archival records that indicate that with the passage of time more than a few Germans involved in these colonial affairs sought to recontextualize some of the extreme measures that were taken by the annihilationists. For example, in the memoirs that he wrote long after the signing of the Treaty of Versailles, von Bülow painted this texual picture of von Trotha: "In order to deal more quickly with the Herero, he suggested driving them with their women and children into a waterless desert, where they would have had to face a certain and painful death."[82] By 1934 the former German chancellor wanted to distance himself from allegations of colonial atrocities.

CONCLUSION

As noted above, those who fought against the Ovaherero and Nama soon found themselves involved in discursive battles that allowed them to leave shards of archival histories and memories that would be picked up by future generations who had their own presentist needs. Some of the very same words that sounded patriotic and were informed by the ethnological and military sciences during the early 1900s could be reappropiated by future generations who wanted to talk and write about colonial genocide, Herero and Nama reparations, and other forms of redress.

Readers might be able to predict some of the arguments that conventional scholars—and "autodidactic historians" (Reinhart Kössler)[83] —use to try to deny the existence of what mainstream writers and bloggers call the Herero/Nama genocide or "Kaiser's Holocaust." A few deniers or revisionists, for example, have argued that one's close textual reading of von Trotha's proclamation does not necessarily mean that one would be forced conclude that this had anything to do with any colonial "atrocity" or potential violations of Hague Conference provisions. Perhaps he, and others who shared his views, were using annihilationist grammars in metaphorical ways, in the same way that Prussian militarists used similar terms when they defeated the French forces in 1871. These denialists or revisionists would ask their audiences: Isn't it common for aggressive combatants to always say they want to wipe out their enemies?

A few chroniclers speculated that what happened after the battle of Hamakari/Waterberg involved a case of *Tropenkoller,* or colonial madness, where a single rogue general simply went too far.[84] In order to counter claims that any of this constituted some master colonial plan of German administrators it is argued that a few soldiers spontaneously chased Ovaherero families into deserts. In theory, what we were witnessing was not some systematic, large-scale massacre that served as a precursor to the Holocaust, but rather a much more disorderly, chaotic, and unorganized situation where *ad hoc* and haphazard decisions were being made on the fly. Instead of recording triumphal victories one finds that these type of accounts focused on the suffering of German soldiers who were on the brink of defeat.

These types of denialist or revisionist arguments could be used by those who wished to undermine the "truth effects" (Foucault) of what they called the "genocide thesis." Apologists for empire, or supporters of the *Schutztruppe,* could ask this: Why don't those seeking reparations or Namibian land distribution pay any attention to the benefits that came from the building of railroads, the bringing of missions, the building of wharfs, and the "development" of the colony? Is it too much to ask that observers interested in "context" also take into account the mindsets of those who rescinded von Trotha's annihilation order?

This type of pro-colonial advocacy tries to shift the burden of proof in these academic or pseudo-academic debates so that supporters of Ovaherero and Nama activitism now have to show that von Trotha's views were shared by his officers, soldiers, the settlers in places like Windhoek, or his superiors in Berlin.

Other participants in these debates argue about what does, or does not, constitute a genocide, and they try to control the trajectory of these debates by presenting a definition taken from Raphael Lemkin or some UN Genocide conference and then use that particular definition to argue deductively that the 1904–1908 war should not be viewed as the "first" of the twentieth-century genocides. These deductive approaches are used to form a very high legal bar that places hurdles in front of those who seek acknowledgments or reparations. Professor James Crawford, who was interviewed by the BBC in September of 2001, would argue that "there was no prohibition on genocide at the beginning of the twentieth century" and at that time the "the term genocide hadn't been invented."[85]

This statement—which circulated at the time of the filing of the first Ovaherero lawsuit—echoed the remarks of many German officials who also used this same type of reasoning. What many conveniently leave out are discussions of the rows of books that were written by those who once used the term "atrocity" in place of the term "genocide," and who complained that colonial atrocities violated nineteenth-century and twentieth-century domestic or international laws.

While some scholars, like Jan-Bart Gewald, have tried to intervene in some of these historical or legal debates by arguing that it would be the carelessness of German Lieutenant Zürn that triggered the violence that led to the beginning of the 1904 war, others want to comment on how other colonial acts need to also be taken into account in conversations about potential violations of nineteeth- and early-twentieth-century international laws. Rachel Anderson, in a law review article published in 2005, tried to make the case for genocidal redress, but even she was forced to conclude that it "is widely supposed that the genocidal wars waged by colonial administrators against indigenous peoples or nations before 1948 did not violate rules of international law."[86]

Is it possible that many of today's skeptics—who don't like the arguments presented by members of Ovaherero and Nama reparations movements—are using some of the very same types of arguments that individuals like von Trotha used when he alleged that his 'war" with the Herero was not governed by European conventions or treaties?

Many other chapters in this book will underscore the point that transglobal reparations activists, in the name of solidarity, have tried to overcome what they view as prejudicial ways of reading the archives, signed treaties, and customary international humanitary laws (IHL). Instead of using post–World War II definitions of genocides, they go back and review some of the same genealogical materials that I presented in this chapter so that they can argue that von Trotha's troops—and the banks that funded them or the ships that carried them—may have violated the Hague Convention of 1899 or "customary law" at the time.[87]

In the next chapter, I provide a complementary portion of the book that explains how some Social Democrats in the German parliament reacted to allegations of atrocities during 1907 election campaigns.

NOTES

1. Felicia Stephan, "The First Genocide of the 20th Century before a Domestic Court," *Võlkerrechtsblog*, May 28, 2018, paragraph 18, https://voelkerrechtsblog.org/the-first-genocide-of-the-20th-century-before-a-domestic-court/.
2. Renisa Mawani, "Law's Archive," *Annual Review of Law and Social Science* 8 (2012): 337–65, 337.
3. Ibid., 357.
4. Ibid.
5. Henning Melber, "Namibia: The German Roots of Apartheid," *Race & Class* 27, no. 1 (1985): 63–77, 71.
6. For an excellent discussion of the historical arguments that have been marshalled by some of these German-speaking Namibians, see Reinhart Kössler, "Facing Postcolonial Entanglement and the Challenge of Responsibility," in *Reconciliation, Civil Society, and the Politics of Memory*, edited by Birgit Schwelling (Bielefeld: Verlag, 2012), 277–312.
7. For a basic introduction to Rothberg's theoretical schema see Michael Rothberg, *Multidirectional Memory: Remembering the Holocaust in the Age of Decolonization* (Stanford: Stanford University Press, 2009).
8. Michael Rothberg, "From Gaza to Warsaw, Mapping Multidirectional Memory," *Criticism* 53, no. 4 (Fall 2011): 523–48, 523–24.
9. Renisa Mawani, *Across Oceans of Law: The Komagata Maru and Jurisdiction in Time of Empire* (Durham: Duke University Press, 2018), 22.
10. See Marlene Manoff, "Theories of the Archive from Across the Disciplines," *Portal: Libraries and the Academy* 4, no. 1 (January 2004): 9–25.
11. See Jan-Bart Gewald, *Herero Heroes: A Socio-Political History of the Herero of Namibia, 1890–1923* (Athens: Ohio University Press, 1999).
12. Reinhart Kössler, "Entangled History and Politics: Negotiating the Past Between Namibia and Germany," *Journal of Contemporary African Studies* 26, no. 4 (2008): 313–39, 313.
13. Susan O'Donnell and David Perley, "Toward a Sociology of the Reconciliation of Conflicting Desires," *Canadian Review of Sociology* 53, no. 4 (November 2016): 474–81, 477.
14. Jürgen Zimmerer, "Colonialism and the Holocaust—Toward an Archaeology of Genocide," *Development Dialogue* 50 (2008): 95–124. Zimmerer is looking at the personnel relationships, the structures, and the ideologies that could be used to link colonial genocides to the Holocaust, and I am convinced that this type of archaeological investigations can be used in many other comparative settings. In this chapter my interest is in outlining some of the evidence, and arguments, that would be produced between 1904 and 1908 that would then be picked up, and reappropriated by those who participated in transgenerational debates about reparations and other forms of redress during the 21st century.
15. See Tilman Dedering, "The German-Herero War of 1904: Revisionism of Genocide or Imaginary Historiography?" *Journal of South African Studies* 19, no. 1 (1993): 80–88.
16. Ann Laura Stoler, "On Archiving as Dissensus," *Comparative Studies of South Asia, Africa and the Middle East* 38, no. 1 (2918): 43–56, 48–49.
17. This is a historical point that became a part of many twentieth-century and twenty-first-century memoryscapes. See, for example, Donald G. McNeil, Jr., "Its Past on Its Sleeve, Tribe Seeks Bonn's Apology," *The New York Times*, last modified May 31, 1998, https://www.nytimes.com/1998/05/31/world/its-past-on-its-sleeve-tribe-seeks-bonn-s-apology.html.
18. Lothar von Trotha, quoted in Gerhardus Pool, *Maharero* (Windhoek: Mibagus, 1990), 293; Benjamin Madley, "From Africa to Auschwitz: How German South West Africa Incubated Ideas and Methods Adopted and Developed by the Nazis in Eastern Europe," *European History Quarterly* 35, no. 3 (2005): 429–64, 444.

19. Jodi A. Byrd and Michael Rothberg, "Introduction: Between Subalternity and Indigeneity," *Interventions* 13, no. 1 (2011): 1–12, 3.

20. For an excellent overview of settler colonial activities in this region that helps provide some insight into how settlers viewed their own land rights, see Guido G. Weigend, "German Settlement Patters in Namibia," *Geographical Review* 75, no. 2 (April 1985): 156–59.

21. David Olusoga and Casper Erichsen. *The Kaiser's Holocaust: Germany's Forgotten Genocide and the Colonial Roots of Nation* (London: Faber and Faber, 2010), 341.

22. For an example of a writer who is convinced that there was no genocidal intent to annihilate the Ovaherero before late August or September of 1904, see Matthias Häußler, "From Destruction to Extermination: Genocial Escalation in Germany's War against the Herero, 1904," *Journal of Namibian Studies* 10 (2011): 55–81.

23. Ibid., 30.

24. Before thousands of *Schutztruppe* arrived on GSWA shores, it made perfect sense that German journalists or lawyers or diplomats would write about "Native" ownership of Hereroland. This reflected the Kaiserreich's ambivalence about paying for the expanding overseas colonies and the need to protect them with large numbers of German troops. Prussia, after all, had just recently defeated France, and some Germans who were worried about population density looked to the continental "East"—Poland, and so on—when they contemplated the future growth of Kaiser Wilhelm's Second Reich.

25. Ibid., 33.

26. Ibid., 28–42.

27. For a critique of the use of familial and other ways of evidencing these various continuity theses, see Max Woxland, *Lebensraum in Context: A Challenge to the Southwest Africa to Auschwitz Continuity Thesis* (Waltham, MA: Brandeis University, 2013).

28. Ibid., 7.

29. Heinrich Vedder, *South West Africa in Early Times: Being the Story of South West Africa Up to the Date of Maherero's Death in 1890* (New York: Oxford University Press, 1938), 406.

30. See Jon M. Bridgman, *The Revolt of the Hereros* (Berkeley: Unversity of California Press, 1981).

31. Olusoga and Erichsen, *The Kaiser's Holocaust*, 53.

32. For examples of these studies and critiques of indigenous Namibian oral histories and public memories of the "Herero-German" War and the aftermath, see Jan-Bart Gewald, "The Road of the Man Called Love and the Sack of Sero: The Herero-German War and the Export of Herero Labour to the South African Rand," *Journal of African History* 40, no. 1 (1999): 21–40; Memory Biwa, *"Weaving the Past with Threads of Memory": Narratives and Commemorations of the Colonial War in Southern Namibia* (Cape Town: University of Western Cape, 2012).

33. Ibid., 187.

34. Willhelm Schüssler, *Adolf Lüderitz* (Bremen: Carl Schunemann Verlag, 1936), 209.

35. Madley, "From Africa to Auschwitz," 433.

36. Ibid.

37. Ibid.

38. Governor Theodor Leutwein, quoted in Henning, "Namibia: The German Roots," 69.

39. Paul von Rohrbach, *Deutsche Kolonialwirtschaft* (Berlin-Schöneberg: Buchvert der Hilfe, 1907) I, 230–31, quoted in Arnold Valentin Wallenkampf, *The Herero Rebellion in South West Africa, 1904–1906* (Los Angeles: University of California, Los Angeles, 1969).

40. Ibid.

41. Hermut Walser Smith, "The Logic of Colonial Violence: Germany in Southwest Africa (1904–1907), The United States in the Philippines (1899–1902)," in *German and*

American Nationalism: A Comparative Perspective, edited by Hartmann Lehmann (Oxford: Berg, 1999), 205–31, 226–27.

42. For a critique of some of these conciliatory, assimiliationist and annihilationist rhetorics in Tasmanian contexts, see Benjamin Madley, "From Terror to Genocide: Britains Tasmanian Penal Colony and Australia's History Wars," *Journal of British Studies* 47, no. 1 (January 2008): 77–106.

43. Helene von Falkenhausen, *Ansiederschicksale, Elf Jahre in Deutsch-Südwestafrika 1893–1904* (Berlin: Dietrich Reimer Verlag, 1907), 217; Woxland, *Lebensraum in Context,* 14.

44. Karl Dove, *Deutsch-Südwest-Afrika* (Berlin: Wilhelm Süsserott, 1903), 188, cited in Wallenkampf, *The Herero Rebellion,* 62–63. John Galbraith would provide an explanation for this "Boer" way of thinking about indigenous disposition. He argued that the Boers believed that "their divinely ordained superiority" justified "slaughter of the Natives and the seizure of their lands." John S. Galbraith, *Reluctant Empire* (Berkeley: University of California Press, 1963), 39.

45. George Steinmetz, "From 'Native Policy' to Extermination: German Southwest Africa, 1904, in Comparative Perspective," *University of Michigan's Theory and Research in Comparative Social Analysis* (Los Angeles: University of California, 2005), https://escholarship.org/uc/item/11z1k021.

46. Olusoga and Erichsen. *The Kaiser's Holocaust,* 65.

47. See, for example, Jan-Bart Gewald's critiques of Leutwein's motivations and actions. Jan-Bart Gewald, *Herero Heroes.*

48. For a critique of the times when Theodor Leutwein tried to appeal to settler communities in GSWA, see Zimmerer, "Colonialism and the Holocaust."

49. See Krista O'Donnell, "Poisonous Women: Sexual Danger, Illicit Violence, and Domestic Work in German Southern Africa, 1904–1915," *Journal of Women's History* 11, No. 3 (Autumn 1999): 32–54.

50. Madley, "From Africa to Auschwitz," 440. Lieutenant Kurt Schwabe, in his appendix I, lists the names of the German citizens who were killed by the Herero between 1904 and 1907. See Kurt Schwabe, *Der Krieg in Deutsch-Sudwestafrika, 1904–1906* (Berlin: C. A. Weller, 1907).

51. Madley, "From Africa to Auschwitz," 440.

52. Horst Drechsler, *Südwestafrica unter Deutscher Kolonialherrschaft* (Berlin: Akademie-Verlag, 1966), 169; Madley, "From Africa to Auschwitz," 440. For other background reading on some of these GSWA histories see John H. Wellington, *South West Africa and its Human Issues* (Oxford: Oxford University Press, 1967); Israel Goldblatt, *History of South West Africa* (Capetown: Juta and Company, 1971); Helmut Bley, *South West Africa Under German Rule,* translated by Hugh Ridley (Evanston: Northwestern University Press, 1971); Peter Katjavivi, *A History of Resistance in Namibia* (Paris: Unesco Press 1988).

53. Gewald, *Herero Heroes.*

54. Paul Rohrbach, quoted in Wallenkampf, *The Herero Rebellion.*

55. Madley, "From Africa to Auschwitz," 440.

56. See George Steinmetz, "The First Genocide of the 20th Century and Its Postcolonial Afterlives: Germany and the Namibian Ovaherero," *The Journal of the International Insitute* 12, no. 2 (Winter, 2005), https://quod.lib.umich.edu/j/jii/4750978.0012.201/—first-genocide-of-the-20th-century-and-its-postcolonial?rgn=main;view=fulltext.

57. J. P. Van S. Bruwer, *South West Afrika: The Disputed Land* (Beperk: Nasionale Boekhandel, 1966), 75.

58. Schwabe, *Der Krieg,* 300; Madley, "From Africa to Auschwitz," 440.

59. August Bebel, quoted in Wallenkampf, *The Herero Rebellion.*

60. Lothar von Trotha, quoted in Olusoga and Erichsen, *The Kaiser's Holocaust,* 151.

61. Jon M. Bridgman, *The Revolt of the Hereros* (Berkeley: University of California Press,1981), 130; Smith, "The Logic of Colonial Violence," 210.

62. Bridgman, *The Revolt of the Herero,* 130.

63. Von Schlieffen, quoted in Olusoga and Erichsen, *The Kaiser's Holocaust,* 158.

64. The discursive fragments that are taken from a massive annihilationist *dispositif* that was co-produced by militarists like von Trotha and his superiors in Berlin are used in utilitarian ways to provide claimants' lawyers with evidence of that requisite "intent" that might aid the Ovaheroro and Nama litigants as they construct their *prima facie* postcolonial reparations cases.

65. Von Bülow, quoted in Wallenkampf, *The Herero Rebellion*, 348.

66. Adolf Fischer, quoted in Olusoga and Erichsen, *The Kaiser's Holocaust*, 146–47.

67. Major Shuhlman, quoted in Olusoga and Erichsen, *The Kaiser's Holocaust*, 147.

68. For a critique of Arendt's links between colonial violence and future European administrative mass murder see Yehouda Shenhav, "Beyond 'Instrumental Rationality': Lord Cromer and the Imperial Roots of Eichmann's Bureaucracy," *Journal of Genocide Studies* 15, no. 4 (2013): 379–99.

69. Material from *Deutsche Kolonialzeitung*, quoted in Wallenkampf, *The Herero Rebellion*, 209.

70. Oskar Stuebel, quoted in Wallenkampf, *The Herero Rebellion*, 4.

71. For typical examples of these soldiers' accounts see Maximilian Bayer, *Der Krieg in Südwestafrika* (Berlin, Engelmann, 1905); Conrad Rust, *Krieg und Frieden im Heerolande* (Leipzig: L. A. Kittler, 1905); Maximilian Bayer, *Mit dem Hauptquartier in Südwestafrika* (Berlin: Wollenbüttel Melchlor, Historischer Verlag, 1909).

72. Steinmetz, "From 'Native Policy' to Extermination," 4.

73. Olusoga and Erichsen, *The Kaiser's Holocaust*, 158.

74. Von Bülow, quoted in Madley, "From Africa Auschwitz," 446. Von Bülow's worries about international perceptions were justified. For example, the *Cape Times* approvingly cited the words that appeared in the Berliner *Vossische Zeitung* when the latter observed that "General von Trotha's methods of conducting the campaign have brought discredit upon Germany in the eyes of civilization." *Cape Times*, August 21, 1905, quoted in Wallenkampf, *The Herero Rebellion*.

75. See also Maximilian Bayer, *Der Krieg*, 23, 25.

76. Ibid., 10–11.

77. The German General Staff, *Die Kämpfe der deutschen Truppen in Südwestafrika* (Berlin: E.S. Mittler, 1907) II, 335.

78. Speech by Hohenlohe-Langenburg, representing the German Imperial Colonial Department, the *Kolonialabteilung*, March 23, 1906, quoted in Wallenkampf, *The Herero Rebellion*.

79. Zimmerer, "Colonialism and the Holocaust."

80. Wallenkampf, *The Herero Rebellion*.

81. Kössler, "Facing Postcolonial Entanglement," 284.

82. Bernhard Fürst von Bülow, *Denkwürdigkeiten* (Berlin: Verlag-Ullstein, 1934), II, 21.

83. Kossler, "Entangled History," 325.

84. Steinmetz, "From Native Policy," 15.

85. James Crawford, quoted in BBC News staff, "German Bank Accused of Genocide," BBC News, September 25, 2001, http://news.bbc.co.uk/2/hi/business/1561463.stm.

86. Rachel Anderson, "Redressing Colonial Genocide under International Law: The Hereros' Cause of Action against Germany," *California Law Review* 95 (2005): 1155–90, 1155.

87. See, for example, Jeremy Sarkin and Carly K. Fowler,"Reparations for Historical Human Rights Violations: The International and Historical Dimensions of the Alien Torts Claims Act Genocide Case of the Herero of Namibia," *Human Rights Review* 9 (2008): 331–60.

THREE

The German Social Democrats' Anti-Imperialist Rhetorics and the Promotion of "Native" Rights during Reichstag Debates, 1904–1913

As I noted in chapter 2, the 1904–1908 conflict between indigenous tribes and the German *Schutztruppe* was a bloody affair, where warring parties accused each other of committing horrific atrocities. Each side also accused the other of starting the war, and the combatants viewed themselves as victims who suffered from the barbaric practices of their enemies. Ernst Graf Ludwig zu Reventlow, a conservative member of the Reichstag, warned his listeners during heated German parliamentary debates about German South West Africa that they should not "apply too much humanity to bloodthirsty beasts in the form of humans."[1]

Permutations of some of the same assimilationist and annihilationist rhetorics that circulated on the peripheries of empire in Southern parts of Africa (re)appeared in German metropoles as politicians and populations argued about the future of GSWA. During these debates, as well as during generational conversations about the historical significance of these Reichstag debates, there was evidence of what Manu Vimalassery, Juliana Hu Peugues, and Alyosha Golstein have called the "colonial unknowing," where some arguments tried to render "unintelligible the entanglements of racialization and colonization" in order to control what would "count as evidence, proof, or possibilities" in colonial or postcolonial settings.[2] Many participations in these parliamentary and public conversations in Germany about the war that was taking place in GSWA produced epistemic violence that complemented the physical violence that was taking place in this part of the Africa. In the process of naturalizing German colonial "rights" to quell Ovaherero and Nama "rebellions," defenders of the dispensation of massive military force also worked to make it impossible to return to the days when any African "prince" would be allowed to claim that "Hereroland" belonged to the Herero.

As is often the case in the Eurocentric narratives that were produced during these Reichstag debates, one's race, class, gender, and status influenced one's colonial subjectivity.

Ovaherero and Nama fighters might have been raised and educated in missionary schools, and they might have started wearing European clothes, and they may have purchased guns from nearby Walvis Bay, but in the eyes of many German colonizers, this did not mean that they could hide their inferior racial status. Sadly, the colonial archives that were co-produced by administrators, travelers, soldiers, and settlers contain rhetorical fragments that used the term "baboons" to describe the Africans who opposed them.[3] It would be the usage of this racist talk of subjugation of inferior races, and the geographical need for spaces for the mythic *Völk*, that would lead Jürgen Zimmerer to argue that there were structural parallels between what happened in GSWA and "the larger colonial war of conquest" that involved the Nazi invasion of Poland and Russia.[4]

Critical praxiological studies of genealogies of the assimilationist and annihilationist colonial rhetorics that were produced during and after the beginning of the 1904 German-Ovaherero "war" allow readers to see how both supporters and critics of aggressive German expansionist policies actually represented and treated indigenous communities. How one talked or wrote about the funding of more troops after hearing about the slaughter at places like Hamakari/Waterberg in 1904, for example, provided indicators of how average citizens may have felt about GSWA rights and duties. Professor Zimmerer went on to note that the "*situation colonial* penetrated all spheres of social action between colonizers and colonized," and that Africans were obligated to salute whites" and were forbidden to "use the sidewalk."[5] What Zimmerer called the idea of a "racially privileged society"—that allowed the poorest white to feel superior in the presence of the wealthiest African—would be a part of that colonial *dispositif* that helped maintain and police colonial boundaries.

I will be arguing in this chapter that Foucauldian analyses of many of the arguments that circulated during Reichstag debates and elections between 1904 and 1913 shows that many, if not most, Germans seemed to have shared Lieutenant General Lothar von Trotha's beliefs that uncivilized "races" were incapable of signing mutually enforceable treaties. Even those who articulated more moderate positions were still willing to argue that whatever rights the Nama and Ovaherero had before 1904 were lost when they "rebelled" against those who really "owned" GSWA.

Vocal minorities in both the metropole and on the peripheries of empire tried to argue that the Ovaherero and Nama should be viewed as fellow human beings who possessed legally enforceable rights that European imperialists had to protect, but all seemed hopelessly romantic or idealistic when thousands of settlers and soldiers boarded ships and embarked for German Southwest Africa so that they could defend the civilized.

As noted in chapter 1, German missionaries, settlers, administrators, and soldiers were well aware that their rifles and their machine guns and their artillery provided them with the power that they needed to defend "their" German colony. The lawyers who represented the Herero litigants in 2001, or the Ovaherero and Nama who file lawsuits in U.S. courts in 2017, could reference some of this power, but given formalistic judicial constraints they had to be careful as they contextualized some of this violence. If they cited too many colonial annihilationist arguments that might undermine some of the claimants' arguments regarding the status of "Native" property rights during the late nineteenth century. In order to make out part of their case in front of American judges, lawyers for the Namibians had to argue that most *informed* "European" or "German" legal opinion during the fin-de-siècle period treated the Ovaherero and other Africans as sovereigns who possessed land rights. In order to zealously advocate for their clients, twenty-first-century wordsmiths who wrote claimants' briefs had to create the impression that signed treaties were not mere pieces of unenforceable parchment "paper."

Third World Approaches to International Law (TWAIL) scholars have been arguing for years that we need to "decolonize" the rhetorics that have been produced by idealistic legal formalists who use ahistorical arguments to claim that Africans actually possessed rights that were respected by European legal experts. As Frédéric Mégret would argue, "there does seem to be something to the simultaneous proclamation of grand but abstract humanitarian principles and the sowing of devastation on the African continent."[6] He elaborated by noting that there was something "like the well-rehearsed hypocrisy of a European-centric universalism that co-existed happily with, and was oblivious to, profound exclusions in the international system."[7]

This obliviousness is "not simply a matter of collective amnesia or omission,"[8] but rather a type of agentic "willful ignorance"[9] that rendered invisible and incomprehensible the possibility that the German settlers or *Schutztruppe* had no business assuming that they could claim ownership of African lands.

Disputation about the status of imperialist gatherings like the 1884–1885 Berlin Conference or the legitimacy of the treaties that were signed by German civil servants or military decision makers impacted elite or public responses to requests that were made for more soldiers and more military supplies after 1903. Even a cursory review of most scholarly materials that have been produced on the topic of the 1904–1908 Ovaherero/Nama–German War shows that many writers were not always sure what to make of the notion that all of these signings of treaties with the Ovaherero or Nama were empty rituals that conferred few legitimate or enforceable rights. Professor Isabel Hull, for example, provided a masterful explanation of how some of these international agreements were more than just "scraps of paper,"[10] but much of her own research seems to support the positions of those who counter that colonial actions spoke louder than words, given the fact that so many Ovaherero and Nama "lost" "their" lands. Not everyone would agree with the *realpolitik* writers who noted that settler colonialism in places like GSWA was an inherently exploitive, brutal, and deceptive exercise in subjugation. Settler colonizers oftentimes appropriated talk of "humanity" when it suited their expansionist, assimilationist, or annihilationist purposes, but the "humanitarians" would be ridiculed when these same principles might constrain those same behaviors.

More than a hundred years ago German politicians in Reichstag debates argued with each other about the legal status of the rights of the "Natives" who signed treaties with the signatories who wanted to map out the borders of colonies like German South West Africa and German East Africa.

In this chapter I want to continue my study of some of the genealogical origins of the archival fragments that have been picked up by twenty-first-century Ovaherero and Nama activists by providing readers with critiques of the anti-imperialist rhetorics and the pro-expansionist discourses that were deployed during Reichstag debates and parliamentary elections. Between 1904 and 1913, German Social Democrats, Socialists, and some Central Party members waged a discursive battle with representatives of von Bülow's government as well as the Kaiser's militarists. Eventually this disputation became so heated, and so polarizing, that it led to what contemporaries called the 1907 "Hottentot" Election.

For a short period of time, it would be the violence in German South West Africa—more than talk about welfare or electoral rights for various classes—that would dominate metropole headlines. It would be the arguments that were used by the German Social Democrats and their allies during these few years that would also provide the rhetorical claims, the evidence, and the warrants that would be reassembled by future generations of legal and public arguers who wrote and talked about the need to protect the legal and moral "rights" of the Ovaherero and the Nama. The Social Democrats and their temporary allies tried to render visible what would be disavowed by the German pro-expansionists.

Critical scholars who track the evolving nature of these ideologies will quickly find that Ernst Graf Ludwig zu Reventlow was not the only person who believed in being vocal about the need to protect German settlers and soldiers. As long as the nomadic or pastoral Africans admitted their inferiority, showed their gratitude toward their betters, disarmed, provided needed labor, and were willing to accept segregationist or "reservation" policies in GSWA, then they would be allowed to live.

The Social Democrats in the Reichstag were oftentimes the recipients of dissident information about abusive practices in German colonies. Politicians interested in German imperial expansionism hated to hear talk of "atrocities" or the annihilation of Africans, and between 1904 and 1913 they fought endless discursive battles with supporters of more even-handed colonial policies.

THE SPD AND DEFENSES OF "NATIVE" RIGHTS IN THE REICHSTAG

Members of Germany's Social Democratic Party (SPD) and their allies were some of social agents in the Reichstag who made it impossible to forget about the carnage that was taking place on the peripheries of empire. Their supporters send them letters from soldiers in the field that provided details about what happened after Hamakari/Waterberg, and these Social Democrats occasional read newspaper clippings from the British Cape Colony. Some of the materials that were read out loud in the Reichstag also indicated that German politicians were familiar with some of arguments that appeared in the books that were written by German soldiers who gloated about the power of their Krupp guns and the triumphal nature of their victories during the suppression of the 1904 Herero "rebellion."

SPD leaders used some of these private and public materials when they produced a type of "subjugated knowledge" (Foucault) that drifted alongside more hegemonic ways of viewing GSWA affairs.[11] As noted below, the Social Democrats worked hard to overcome public perceptions that they were abandoning the colonial settlers and the soldiers who fought the indigenous "rebels" in GSWA.

The Social Democrats who were arguing for "native" rights in the Reichstag were some of the first vocal defenders of African rights, and they would bequeath to future generations archival arguments, speeches, and other archival parchments that were recorded in the *Stenographische Berichte über die Verhandlungen des Deutschen Reichstages*. These, in turn, became rhetorical shards of history and memory for other generations' future production of counterhistories and countermemories when these speeches were turned into scholars' "primary" evidence.

These Reichstag arguments were often recirculated in broader rhetorical cultures as conservative or moderate contributors to mainstream presses carried news of *Schutztruppe* victories or defeats. The authors of Social Democratic newspapers produced articles on the struggles of fellow African laborers overseas who were suffering under the whips of imperialist capitalists. It would be class and labor issues that would help Social Democrats identify with African oppression in German colonies.

Pro-imperialists challenged SPD contextualizations of colonial affairs. In the Reichstag it would be representatives of the Colonial Ministry, and the spokespersons for von Bülow, who would defend *Kaiserreich* policies. For Bernhard Dernburg, the German Colonial Minister, the losses that the Ovaherero and Nama suffered during the 1904–1908 war involved a case of *á la guerre comme á la guerre*—do what you have to during wartime with limited resources—that carried no unique legal or moral obligations.[12]

These who represented Kaiser Wilhelm II, when forced to mention "Native" land rights, usually talked about the ignorance of inferior Africans who signed treaties and simply made some bad deals. At other times, when the Kaiser's representatives could not openly deny that some treaties contained provisions that looked as though they protected "Native" sovereignty, the arguments would shift so that pro-expansions could mention the derogation of rights that had taken place when these Ovaherero "rebels" rose up and killed German settlers (see chapter 2).

Savvy defenders of empire in the Reichstag realized that patriotic listeners only wanted to hear about the heroism of the *Schutztruppe*, who were valiantly fighting uncivilized barbarians. This allowed citizens who supported the von Bülow administration to feel as though they were doing their part by voting for those who would fund the military campaigns on the African continent.

Did the German people think that the Kaiser, and his spokespersons, were going to abandon the volunteers, the German nurses, the health experts, and others who boarded ships and headed to GSWA shores?

The Social Democrats tried to cope with these waves of patriotism by arguing that they too cared about the troops, but they wanted to argue that the spilling of so much German blood would be avoided if parliamentary funds for colonial warfighting was cut off so that German diplomats would have to negotiate with the indigenous warriors. The Social Democrats tried to counter Bernhard Dernburg's wartime rhetoric by shifting the discursive terrain so that listeners or readers focused on the perpetration of alleged "atrocities" and the abuse of Africans.

Some SPD advocates were very conscious of the fact that they never actually traveled to German South Africa or East Africa and had little first-hand knowledge of conditions in the African colonies. They tried to compensate for this by quoting from the textual or visual materials that were supplied by the eyewitnesses who were "on the spot," but as Andrew Bonnell would note, oftentimes the German Social Democrats argued in "vicarious" and "theoretical" ways.[13]

The Social Democrats were vocal dissenters whose arguments about "Native" labor rights resonated with millions of German workers who toiled away and complained about the unjust enrichment of lazy capitalists. However, many of these arguments—especially the ones that focused on the protection of Ovaherero or Nama sovereign rights—were treated by the majority of Germans as cheap theatrics, unscientific sentimentalism that would be as problematic as the "old African" rhetorics that Lothar von Trotha had critiqued. Upper- and middle-class German communities could belittle the work of the SPD, and their spokespersons could argue that Social Democrats' claims were based on misrepresentations of capitalism, lack of colonial knowledge, or myopic assessments of civilian and military necessities.

Social Democrats who argued in the Reichstag created the impression that they grudgingly admired the stiff resistance that would be put up by the Ovaherero and the Nama after 1904, and they opined that this resistance provided positive proof that these were legitimate warriors fighting "defensively" to preserve their rights.

That said, few SPD advocates who argued in the Reichstag about indigenous rights were willing to go so far as to countenance the idea that the Africans were Europeans' equals, or that they were members of a cultured nation. SPD arguers expected that superior Europeans had the moral and imperial duty to protect their inferior African wards.

During the first weeks and months of 1904, Bernhard Dernburg and his supporters tried to justify the use of brutal coercive force in GSWA by circulating dehumanizing rhetorics that were purveyed by those who wanted to argue that any display of mercy on the part of the *Schutztruppe* would be interpreted by the Ovaherero as an overt sign of German weakness. The Social Democrats tried to rebut some of this by humanizing the Ovaherero, and they used some of the materials that they received from missionaries and others who wrote about how the Herero spared Britons, Boers, and German women.

SPD advocates were able to show that some settlers who were supposedly massacred by Africans were actually taken to safety by Ovaherero who seemed to be acting in civilized ways. Take, for example, how Social Democrats reframed matters when Herero warriors were castigated for their alleged cruelty to German settlers on farms. Two sisters, Mrs. Pickert and Miss Domski, were reportedly killed by the rebellious Ovahereros. Those pro-imperialists who recorded these events went on to claim that the African rebels mutilated their bodies by cutting each of these two sisters into four pieces and hanging them in some bushes. August Bebel, on March 19, 1904, tried to puncture holes in some of this mythmaking when he noting that both Mrs. Pickert and Miss Domski eventually arrived unharmed at the Okahandja Station. The two sisters, and a missionary by the name of Beckmann, had been prisoners of the Ovaherero for three weeks.[14]

Social Democrats wrote about wartime conditions and what happened to the Ovaherero and Nama after the 1904 war ended. SPD arguers in the Reichstag could rely on materials that were collected from informants who sent materials to socialist and social Democratic presses. Arguments, evidence, and warrants that appeared in those publications could then be used during parliamentary debates.

SPD arguers in the Reichstag also provided some of the first graphic and detailed pictures of what life was like for the Ovaherero and the Nama who were hunted down by the *Schutztruppe* during desert raids and then placed in von Bülow's concentration camps. An anonymous newspaper writer, who self-identified as a "concerned citizen in Lüderitz," sent in an article that was published in the socialist newspaper *Königsberger Volkszeitung*.[15] The author of this article reported that around "2,000" Nama "are presently under German imprisonment" and this person chronicled how the Nama had surrendered because they had been guaranteed their lives. Now, it was reported, in spite of these promises, the Nama were transported against their will to Shark Island in Lüderitz, where a doctor had assured the writer that they would "all die within two years due to the climate."[16]

Decades later interwar audiences in Europe would forget about many of the horrors of Hamakari/Waterberg or Shark Island, but for a time members of the Reichstag were constantly having to hear about everything from the alleged theft of Ovaherero and Nama cattle to the abuse of "Natives" in the concentration camps. Georg Ledebour, a deputy of the Social Democratic party, used some of the articles that appeared in media outlets like *Königsberger Volkszeitung* to embarrass those in the Reichstag who talked about the colonial regeneration of indigenous communities in GSWA. In 1906, as thousands were dying in the labor camps, Ledebour called on Chancellor von Bülow, and Minister Dernburg, to explain to the members of the Reichstag the causes of the "extent of mortality rates on Shark Island and in other camps."[17] David Olusoga and Casper W. Erichsen, writing in 2010, would later argue that thanks to Ledebour it was impossible for German parliamentarians "to claim ignorance on the matter after December of 1906."[18]

These commentaries on colonial military violence and camp abuses were used by the SPD to try to undermine support for the continued funding for the Ovaherero/Nama–German war. Many pro-imperialists sensed that some members of the working classes might be joining forces with middle-class skeptics who were unsure about the wisdom of continuing to fight indigenous forces in GSWA. A contributor to the *Militär-Literatur-Zeitung* in December of 1906 remarked, "Unfortunately our war in South West Africa is not "popular" in the usual sense."[19] Some of this may have had something to do with the fact that Colonel Deimling, on March 19, 1906, could report to members of the Reichstag that there were some fourteen thousand troops who were serving in South West Africa.[20]

Although interest in these colonial discourses would spike just before and after the so-called "Hottentot Election" of 1907, a host of synchronic and diachronic debates were waged for more than a decade as von Bülow's—and Kaiser Wilhelm's—supporters quarreled with the Social

Democrats and their allies. All sorts of contentious historical frames were used to either defend or to attack Second Reich plans for imperial expansionism in GSWA.

Many of the SPD topics that were discussed in the Reichstag would sound familiar to today's postcolonial scholars or critical genocide researchers. Von Bülow and his patriotic supporters had to listen to incessant talk of the abuse of "natives" in GSWA. Some of the topics that were covered in these Reichstag debates included the corporal punishment of indigenous communities, the theft of land, administrative corruption, the abuse of African women, and the problematic nature of militaristic responses to what the SPD viewed as civilian matters.

Some of the most infuriating commentaries on these topics came from some members of the left wing of the Center Party, that occasionally sided with the SPD. Members of the Center Party usually sided with von Bülow's political factions, but there was something about the violent treatment of the Ovaherero and Nama that perturbed some of the German centrists in the Reichstag. In a speech that underscored how all types of proprietary arguments could be melded together with ethnographic materials, August Erzberger had this to say in March of 1906:

> When the Germans came into Hereroland in 1885, land did not even belong to the tribe; it belonged to the entire nation as a whole. In this respect the Hereros were like other Negro [*sic*] races in Africa. The Germans, who later became acquainted with the laws and customs of the Hereros, were convinced of the inalienable community ownership of land.[21]

If this was true, then it meant that Samuel Maherero and others who signed treaties had no right to alienate land in the first place, and some SPD members and their supporters were willing to argue that this violated either German property laws or international laws.

If the land never belonged to the Ovaherero "tribe," then it could not be alienated, and this meant that those who sought to purchase the land were not following the strictures that were put in place by the Berlin Act or Hague provisions or the bilateral treaties that were signed by Africans. If Erzberg was right, then in theory, all German settlers were interlopers who violated the customary and formalistic legal rights of the African indigenous communities.

Erzberger was trying to take advantage of the grammatological "protection" claims that appeared in all sorts of international agreements of bilateral treaties with leaders of Herero and Nama tribes. He was raising the type of arguments that would reappear in the court filings of the Herero and Nama as they cobbled together the paperwork that would be filed in U.S. courtrooms in 2001 and 2017. These plaintiffs' lawyers would also note that the land in "Hereroland" or "Damaraland" belonged to the entire Herero nation, and they too argued that a few tribal leaders could not alienate communal Africa lands.

Those SPD parliamentarians or Central party members who wanted to critique von Bülow's colonial policies found inventive ways of bringing up the topic of indigenous rights. For example, in January of 1905, when the pro-imperialists waxed eloquently about the benefits that flowed to settlers from the building of the railroad from Swakopmund to Otavi, August Bebel berated both the Ovaherero "captains" and the Germans who failed to see that railroad owners possessed no rights whatsoever to cede lands that collectively belonged to tribes.[22]

Writers like August Bebel had been heavily influenced by Social Democratic versions of Marxist types of materialist ideas, and they were purveyors of the idea that African lands belong to "natives" who had an inherent right to defend their territories from imperialist invaders. Although Bebel also deployed arguments about social Darwinism, degeneration, regeneration, and "social efficiency," his particular brand of liberal humanism viewed ownership of land as a precondition for the advancement of purportedly inferior "races. Without land, and without the chance to develop that land, tribal growth was stunted and the "natives" could not move up the mythic Social Darwinian ladders.

All sorts of different villains and heroes served as the antagonists and protagonists in these competitive Reichstag social dramas. Georg Ledebour, for example, in his exchanges with Chancellor von Bülow and Minister Dernburg, claimed that the settlers in GSWA were some of the social agents who were stirring up trouble in the colonies. With their hunger for land they were joining the unscrupulous land speculators who tried to control as much land as possible. Ledebour opined that the settlers were unduly influencing civil administrators, and he averred that settlers had an inordinate say in how to carry out the suppression of the Ovaherero and Nama rebellions. Ledebour accused the German settlers, and their supporters in Berlin, of using the Ovaherero-German war of 1904 as an excuse for seizing indigenous lands and increasing colonial expenditures. "The farmer lobby," Ledebour argued, was wishing, hoping, and working toward the "continuation of the war in the hope that the land of the natives will ultimately be confiscated."[23]

This would be remarkably prescient, and Ledebour elaborated by explaining how all of this had little to do with Germany's avowed civilizing missions:

> It is tantamount to recklessness that the Government allows such people to drag it around by the nose and that it complies with these incomprehensible policies that will, inevitably, lead to the annihilation of some of the natives and the total slavery of others.[24]

This enslavement, in theory, was a type of "modern slavery" that violated the letter and spirit of the texts that were produced during the Berlin

Conference of 1884–1885 and The Hague Conference of 1899. These types of arguments would be presented by Georg Ledebour, Karl Kautsky, and Rosa Luxembourg.[25]

The radicalness of some SPD positions in the Reichstag would be noted by many empowered communities in Germany. German police kept on an eye on the working classes, and they were aware of how these classes talked about the unnecessary deaths of African "natives" in local saloons, trains, clubs, and other venues. This was characterized by some Germans as "short stories and bar tittle-tattle."[26]

A dynamic, recursive process was created whereby August Bebel would give speeches in the Reichstag that were then recycled in pamphlet form for workers who debated about these topics in German bars or libraries. Whether they realized it or not, these social agents were co-producing genealogical fragments that would reappear over and over again in many transgenerational legal and public texts about GSWA.[27] As one scholar would note in 2018,

> The SPD, despite embracing certain integrative and moderate tendencies during the years leading up to World War I, was the only political force in imperial Germany that not only rejected Germany's partially autocratic political system, but also the country's elites' extreme nationalism, its militarism, and its participation in Western imperialism and colonialism. When it came to the war in German South West Africa and Trotha's murderous tactics, SPD representatives did not mince words and repeatedly pointed out that the military's actions had resulted in mass murder.[28]

During this period Social Democrats and their allies consistently argued that the true humanitarians were the ones who respected the rights of indigenous communities in Africa, and SPD representatives used both tragic and comedic rhetorical frames as they ridiculed the idea that German soldiers and colonial settlers were the innocents who deserved the continued financial support from the Reichstag.

Although some radical Social Democrats seemed to be using arguments that implied that they were opposed to all types of overseas German colonial settlements, more moderate positions were often articulated that highlighted the differences that existed between inhumane and "prudent" colonization. On December 1, 1906, August Bebel informed his Reichstag colleagues that

> it is no crime to pursue a colonial policy. To pursue a colonial policy can under proper conditions be an act of culture; it only depends on what kind of colonial policy is pursued. There is a great difference between what colonial policy ought to be and what it is. If the representatives of cultural and civilized nations, as, for instance, the European and North American nations are, come to foreign peoples as deliverers, friends and organizers of culture, as helpers in need . . . then we Social Democrats are the first ones prepared to support such great missions of

> civilization. . . . But this is surely not the objective of your colonial policy. You come not as deliverers and educators, but as conquerors, suppressors, and exploiters. You come as conquerors in order to rob the Natives with brutal force of their possessions. You make them helots, compel them into drudgery to strangers for ulterior motives. You take the property of all, in order to give it to the few.[29]

Analogies were being made in the Reichstag between the historical Roman occupation of ancient Germania and *Kaiserreich* policies in GSWA.

In order to prevent this type of robbery and Spartan "helot" slavery the Social Democrats and their allies did their best to preserve the rights of Africans—or at least find ways of humanely segregated them from those who wished to annihilate them. On May 28, 1906, all seventy-eight Social Democrats in the Reichstag presented a resolution that petitioned the chancellor to allocate sufficient land for the natives so that they might again become self-supporting pastoralists.[30]

These SPD calls for native land reformation fell on deaf ears. In theory, if German colonizers didn't treat the suppression of the 1904 rebellion as a race war, then they allowed the Ovaherero to rebuild their cattle herds, and this meant that cattle could be sold to the British or other Europeans so that disgruntled Africans could buy guns and bullets. Besides, if the Ovaherero or the Nama returned to their pastoral ways, they would not be able to provide the needed labor for the building of wharfs, railroads, or German homes in and around places like Lüderitz.

In a host of ways, it could be argued that the November and December Reichstag debates of 1906 over these issues not only led to an impasse over the continued funding of the *Schutztruppe*, but helped with the education of German publics. German citizens knew that they would most likely be asked to go to the polls and break the impasse. They would either throw their support behind von Bülow's expansionist plans for the continued funding of the *Schutztruppe* or they could support those centrists and SPD speakers who wanted to recall the troops and bring them back home.

Would Germans put aside some of their imperialist ambitions as their rivals in Britain or France were colonizing many other parts of the globe?

For a few months in 1906 and 1907, a deeply divided German nation seemed to have populations that were unsure about what to do about the continued funding of military campaigns that many socialists and Social Democrats felt were being waged by Prussians and capitalists who followed the lead of Kaiser Wilhelm II. Under German law the Kaiser had incredible discretion in the way that he used his armies to fight the Boxers in China or in rebels in German East Africa, but he and his supporters still needed funding from the Reichstag. This meant that the "Hottentot" Election of 1907 was going to serve as a referendum on Second Reich colonial planning.

When Chancellor von Bülow decided to try and manage this impasse by seeking reelection, this triggered a bitter public struggle. As Olusoga and Erichsen would note, despite the "influence of the colonial lobby and their potent propaganda campaign, support for the settlers and von Bülow's government was far from universal."[31]

Germany's taxation system placed heavy burdens on the workers in that country, and many supporters of the Social Democrats realized that the Prussians who allegedly started the war against the Herero and Nama were not the only ones who were going to have pay for this costly adventurism. One worker, writing in December of 1905, noted, "How many thousands of people have been slaughtered there [German South West Africa] and all really pointless. The colonies have already cost us millions and people's lives as well."[32]

Years after von Bülow's conservative politicians prevailed in the Hottentot election of 1907, there would be Social Democrats and their supporters who refused to forget about the Herero war or the concentration camps. In 1912 a Social Democrat pointed out to his Reichstag colleagues that "because of Trotha's extermination strategy the Herero had been reduced from eighty thousand to twenty thousand. . . . Today, there is no doubt that nothing could be more condemnable than Trotha's tactics."[33] This exact same statistic—of some sixty thousand lost Ovaherero lives—continues to recirculate on the World Wide Web.[34]

In recent years many of the leading interdisciplinary researchers who study the symbolic impact of the "Hottentot" election of 1907 have argued that von Bülow's victories came when pro-imperialists—armed with racist, militarist, and imperialist rhetorics—defeated disheartened Social Democrats. The Reichstag leaders of the conservative German middle classes were able to convince just enough workers that they could control the "terms of a discourse or rule, shared across the political spectrum," that was a "part of larger, seamless orientalism that insisted on the silence of colonized peoples, denying them, literally, and figuratively, their humanity."[35]

Many discouraged Social Democrats were said to have become revisionists, willing to abandon their anti-imperialist rhetorics as they joined other patriots before the advent of the Great War. That said, it would be a mistake to dwell solely on the moral and legalistic arguments that were presented by the SPD in the Reichstag. Some of the most persuasive textual and visual arguments about "native" rights appeared in the materials that were produced by those who cared about what the ordinary German worker had to say about these issues.

In sum, a review of some of the Reichstag materials shows how the SPD advocates were kept busy responding to all types of annihilationist rhetorics, and in some cases it seems as though they heard some fascinating ways of configuring colonial contract obligations or wartime losses.

As I noted earlier in this book, when some settlers, soldiers, or administrators wrote or talked to Reichstag members about reparations, they were not talking about African losses, but alleged harms to settlers. It was their farmlands that were burned when the Herero or Nama raided their farms. Talk of colonial redress took the form of conversations about the money *that was owed German colonizers* who lost their farms during Herero and Nama raids. In May of 1906, for example, the von Bülow administration tried to present the German Reichstag with a proposal that went way beyond the mere compensation of settlers' losses during the rebellion years. Had it been approved, noted John Lowry, the aggrieved settlers would have received "forty-five percent restitution" that would have been more than "adequate compensation."[36] If this legislation had passed in 1906 it would have meant that the settlers would have been reimbursed some 7.5 million marks for direct Herero and Nama damage as well as an additional three million German marks in "unrealized cattle profits."[37]

Both the members of the German Center Party and the Social Democrats objected to what they viewed as unaccountable and unjustified compensation. One German jurist considered this to be one of the most foolish of the 1906 Second Reich's proposals.[38] Yet many of these same decision makers would have found it absurd to believe that African "savages" deserved the same type of compensation for their wartime losses.

The SPD advocates who argued in the Reichstag held their own in their discursive battles with the annihilationists or pro-expansionists, but these parliamentary arguments were not the only rhetorical weapons in the arsenals of those who continued to fight for "native" rights.

THE SOCIAL DEMOCRATIC RANK AND FILE, DER WAHRE JACOB, AND THE CRITIQUE OF THE COLONIAL WARS OF THE "PRUSSIANS"

Der Wahre Jacob was a satirical paper, published by J.H.W. Dietz of Stuttgart, that would be read by rank-and-file German workers in places like Hamburg pubs. Some of the same readers who were used to seeing caricatures of reactionary Junkers or intolerant priests or Prussian lieutenants were now being presented by contributors to this magazine with materials on the abuse of "slave" labor in GSWA.

The pictorial representations that appeared in outlets like *Der Wahre Jacob* provided visualized arguments about GSWA conflicts that were viewed by workers who may or may not read the specific arguments that were used during the Reichstag debates. Those who wrote essays, or those drew illustrations for these outlets, "did not shy away from accusing the German army of atrocities," and the depictions of Africans in their papers "ran the gamut from sympathetic portrayals that resisted stereotypical" caricatures to "more crass" representations.[39]

These vernacular spaces provided safe havens for those, when they were not drinking or playing dice, could read to each other passages that critiqued the decisions that were made by von Bülow or the Prussian officers who led their unsuspecting conscripts into colonial battles.

By 1907 hundreds of thousands of subscribers to *Der Wahre Jacob* received their copies in the mail, and oftentimes contributors acted as if implied audiences of Africans in German South West Africa were also seeing these same messages. One image, published on the cover of the January 9, 1907, issue of *Der Wahre Jacob*, was titled "People of Africa, Protect Your Most Sacred Possessions!" It shows a diaphanously drabbed woman, holding a sword and shield as Herero and Nama warriors and civilians cower behind her. "This allegorical figure," explains Andrew Bonnell, was "representing Social Democracy," as evidenced by "her Phrygian cap [the emblem of revolution]," as she stood "guard over a group of African women and children."[40]

This personification of Social Democracy is facing a cloud that is some distance way, where Chancellor Bernhard von Bülow is portrayed as a yellow Buddha, riding alongside Colonial Secretary Bernhard von Dernburg. This is a socialist critique of the allegory of the "Yellow Peril" that was produced by Hermann Knackfuss for Kaiser Wilhelm.[41] Professor Bonnell argues that this particular "illustration made a dramatic claim for solidarity between German Social Democracy and the African peoples in South-West Africa, and it stressed that the Herero had been fighting a legitimate war to defend their own lands against German imperialism."[42] The feminist SPD figure that appeared on that 1907 cover of *Der Wahre Jacob* represented the radicals who upheld socialists' codes of morality and egalitarianism, who refused to forget the international laws that protected workers. This image conjured up images of an SPD organization that had members who were unwilling to budget in the face of Prussian militarism.

For years *Der wahre Jakob* contained articles, poems, and pictorials that reflected and refracted the views of those who identified with indigenous workers who also suffered at the hands of elites who were obsessed with the pursuit of profit. In late 1906 Matthias Erzberger of the Centre party had famously talked about some procurement scandals that involved the firm of Tippelskirch, a supplier of goods for the German military, and Social Democrats now used outlets like *Der wahre Jakob* to ridicule the excessive profits that were lining the pockets of the shareholders of the Adolph Woermann shipping company.[43] This is the same Woermann shipping company that would be targeted by Herero claimants in a case that was filed in U.S. courts in 2001 (see chapter 7).

An assortment of texts and visualities in *Der wahre Jakob* were used to create the impression that the Prussian officers who usually led the

Schutztruppe overestimated their own abilities and underestimated the prowess of their African foes. One cartoon that appeared in an October 1904 issue of *Der Wahre Jakob*, titled "After the Victory," showed Lothar von Trotha on top of the Waterberg plateau, where he and five of his officers were using binoculars to try and find Ovaherero survivors.[44] As von Trotha looks down after the battle he says, "I have won the battle of Waterberg, but the gods only know where the Herero I defeated are hiding." An African wearing a German army uniform is shown stealing champagne from the general's picnic basket, symbolizing the wily indigenous fighters who eluded their German pursuers.

Another issue of *Der Wahre Jakob* contained an essay titled "Insolence!" that told the story of how Völkchen der Herero ("the little people of the Herero") were viewed as "model patriots." The Herero who were unwilling to do hard labor for settlers or soldiers were characterized as a "depraved rabble," who for inexplicable reasons continued to try to hold on to their land and cattle. The Social Democrat who authored this essay noted how impertinent Ovaherero had the temerity to shoot back at the "splendid lieutenants" who were leading those who murdered and hanged Africans.[45]

Democratic socialist workers who read these *Der Wahre Jakob* pages could fairly conclude that it was the Ovaherero or the Nama who were fighting a defensive war and not the settlers who were protected by thousands of troops, rapid-fire machine guns, and Krupp armaments.

The rank-and-file who were targeted by *Der Wahre Jakob* were no angels, and they often shared the racist beliefs of those they ridiculed, but they argued and acted as if the Ovaherero and Nama were fellow human beings who deserved fair court hearings in colonial courtrooms.

CONCLUSION: THE MEMORIES OF THE REICHSTAG BATTLES AND THE STRATEGIC TWENTY-FIRST-CENTURY USAGES OF THESE PARLIAMENTARY DEBATESF

As noted above, in spite of the best efforts of the SPD, in 1907 they barely lost the famous "Hottentot" election, which was considered a referendum that gauged German patriotism and continue funding an expensive war in GSWA.

Members of future Herero and Nama reparations movements would often cite the work of the Social Democrats who battled pro-imperialists in the Reichstag, but as usual, the victors oftentimes get to control what is placed in conventional colonial or canonical imperial archives. Those who supported von Bülow produced or read the adventure tales that appeared in the memoirs that were written by patriotic German officers who felt no need to apologize for either Hamakari/Waterberg or the concentration camps.

I agree with Andrew Bonnell's assessment that there are times when postcolonial scholars, in their rush to evidence the hegemony of the pro-expansionists, sometimes forget that there were anti-imperial agents who also once worked away in the metropole to try and reform imperialist missions as they defended the sovereign rights of Africans. No doubt the Social Democrats who circulated these anti-imperial messages were also caught in "webs of colonialist and racialized discourse,"[46] but I take the position that these admittedly flawed humanist critiques were better than the annihilationist rhetorics that were produced by those who welcomed the "extirpation" of the Africans. Anticipating the stances that would later be taken by members of Indigenous studies communities, settler colonial groups or postcolonial critics the SPD speakers in the Reichstag or the contributors to the pages of *Der Wahre Jakob* labored at producing dissent histories and countermemories of GSWA. They seemed to be trying to accomplish what Jodi Byrd once characterized as reconceptualizations of space and history to "render visible what imperialism and its resultant settler colonialisms and diasporas have sought to obscure."[47]

German Social Democrats who formed alliances with the Center Party parliamentarians during the Reichstag debates over colonial expansionism in GSWA were key social agents who helped produce some of the antecedent, anti-colonial rhetorics that for a time, gathered dust in musty, forgotten archives (see chapters 5 and 6).

The egalitarian rhetorics or solidarity discourses that were crafted by some of these Social Democrats were some of the first European commentaries that characterized some forms of aggressive settler colonialism in GSWA as a threat that interfered with the maturation and educational processes of these African "natives." It could be argued that the Social Democrats took some of the older missionary arguments and radicalized them for their own purposes.

In the Reichstag archives, and in the pages of outlets like *Der wahre Jakob,* scholars would later find the fragmentary arguments of the Social Democrats that would be handed down to later generations who were interested in recovering subjugated knowledges or producing new constellations of meanings. The members of the SPD were the losers of the "Hottentot" elections, and for a time their texts and visualities were rendered invisible by the mounds of materials that were left in the archives by the German pro-expansionists. It would only be later that these SPD rhetorics would be recovered, refurbished, and redeployed in (post)colonial debates about acknowledgments, expressions of regret, apologies, reparations, and other forms of equitable redress for the Ovaherero and Nama.

The German patriots who continued to pay for the *Schutztruppe* would control the conventional elite archives, but as Michel Foucault and others have pointed out, there are always fissures, ruptures, and cracks in any dominant *dispositif* that can help with the production of counterhistories and countermemories.

Would today's Social Democrats rise to the occasion and help the members of Ovaherero and Nama reparations movements? Professor Jens-Uwe Guettel, writing in 2018, argued that the hesitancy of the German Federal Republic to provide financial compensation to the Ovahere-ro and the Nama provided the perfect opportunity for the Germany's Social Democrats to "make amends" for the Second Reich's genocidal policies in Africa. By doing so, Guettel explained, the SPD would be returning to the party's anti-imperialist roots.[48]

Perhaps, just perhaps, some future generations of German and Namibian citizens may witness how those old SPD arguments will be deployed to secure some type of restorative justice for the descendants of those who once captured the imagination of Reichstag debaters.

NOTES

1. Graf Ludwig zu Reventlow, March 17, 1904, *Stenographiesche Berichte über die Verhandlungen des Deutschen Reichstages, 1903–1905* (Berlin: Verlag, 1905), I: 1900, quoted by Helmut Walser Smith, "The Talk of Genocide, the Rhetoric of Miscegenation: Notes on Debates in the German Reichstag Concerning Southwest Africa, 1904–1914," in *The Imperialist Imagination: German Colonialism and Its Legacy,* edited by Sara Friedrichsmeyer, Sara Lennox, and Susanne Zantop (Ann Arbor: University of Michigan Press, 1998), 107–24, 107.
2. Manu Vimalassery, Juliana Hu Pegues, and Alyosha Goldstein, "Introduction: On Colonial Unknowing," *Theory & Event* 19, no. 4 (2016), https://muse.jhu.edu/article/633283.
3. Amy R. Rivera, *Did the German Actions in the Herero Rebellion of 1904–1908 Constitution Genocide?* (Fort Leavenworth, Kansas: U.S. Army Command and General Staff College, 2012), 58.
4. Jürgen Zimmerer, "Colonialism and the Holocaust—Towards an Archaeology of Genocide," *Development Dialogue* (2008): 95–123, 95.
5. Ibid., 103.
6. Frédéric Mégret, "From 'Savages' to 'Unlawful Combatants,' A Postcolonial Look at International Law's 'Other,'" in *International Law and Its Others,* edited by Anne Orford (Cambridge: Cambridge University Press, 2006), 265–318, 4–5.
7. Ibid.
8. Vimalassery, Pegues, and Goldstein, "Introduction: On Colonial Unknowing," paragraph 1.
9. Ibid., paragraph 2.
10. Isabel V. Hull, *A Scrap of Paper: Breaking and Making International Law during the Great War* (Ithaca: Cornell University Press, 2014).
11. For a short, but interesting take on Foucauldian views of Ovaherero subjugated knowledges see Baligh Ben Taleb, "Misinformed Research Perpetuates Colonial Subjugation," *The Daily Nebraskan,* last modified January 14, 2013, http://www.dailynebraskan.com/opinion/ben-taleb-misinformed-research-perpetrates-colonial-subjugation/article_467416f0-5dfc-11e2-aa00-001a4bcf6878.html.
12. Bernhard Dernburg, quoted in Smith, "The Talk of Genocide," 109.
13. Andrew G. Bonnell, "Social Democrats and Germany's War in South West Africa, 1904–7: The View of the Socialist Press," in *Savage Worlds: German Encounters*

Abroad, 1798–1914, edited by Matthew P. Fitzpatrick and Peter Monteath (Manchester: Manchester University Press, 2018), 224.

14. Speech by August Bebel, March 19, 1904, cited in Arnold Valentin Wallenkampf, *The Herero Rebellion in South West Africa, 1904–1906. A Study in German Colonialism* (PhD diss., University of California, Los Angeles, 1969)

15. David Olusoga and Casper W. Erichsen, *The Kaiser's Holocaust: Germany's Forgotten Genocide* (London: Farber & Farber, 2010), 221.

16. Ibid.

17. Ibid.

18. Ibid., 221–22.

19. Wallenkampf, *The Herero Rebell i on*.

20. Deimling, quoted in Wallenkampf, *The Herero Rebell i on*.

21. August Erzberger. speech on March 24, 1906, quoted in Wallenkampf, *The Herero Rebell i on*.

22. Speech by August Bebel, January 30, 1905, quoted in Wallenkampf, *The Herero Rebellion*.

23. Georg Ledebour, quoted in Casper and Erichsen, *T he Kaiser's Holocaust*, 222.

24. Ibid., 222.

25. See Nicholas Stargardt, *The German Idea of Militarism: Radical and Socialist Critics, 1886–1914* (Cambridge: Cambridge University Press, 1994); Rosa Luxemburg, *Socialism or Barbarism*, edited by Paul Le Blanc and Helen C. Scott (New York: Pluto Books, 2010; Karl Kautsky, "Socialism and Colonial Policy," Marxists.org, n.d., https://www.marxists.org/archive/kautsky/1907/colonial/2-positive.htm. For a recent discussion of how socialists and Social Democrats tried to identify with the Ovaherero and Nama who fought colonial wars, see Adam J. Sacks, "All Humans Are Born Equal," *Jacobin*, last modified March 12, 2018, https://www.jacobinmag.com/2018/03/spd-kautsky-luxemburg-imperialism-africa-armenia.

26. John Phillip Short, *Magic Lantern Empire: Colonization and Society in Germany* (Ithaca: Cornell University Press, 2012), 133.

27. Here I am commenting on how some of the members of the German Central Party formed alliances with socialists and Social Democrats. See John S. Lowry, "African Resistance and Central Party Recalcitrance in the Reichstag Colonial Debates of 1905/06," *Central European History* 39 (2006): 244–69.

28. Jens-Ewe Guettel, "The SPD Should Return to Its Anti-Colonial Roots," *Jacobin Magazine*, August 2018, paragraph 18, http://www.jacobinmag.com/2018/08/spd-namibia-herero-nama-genocide-colonialism.

29. Speech by August Bebel, December 1, 1906, quoted in Wallenkampf, *The Herero Rebellion*.

30. This resolution is Document 516, cited in Wallenkampf, *The Herero Rebellion*.

31. Ibid., 222.

32. Bonnell, "Social Democrats," 226, endnote 9.

33. Guettel, "The SPD Should Return," paragraph 18.

34. See, for example, The Combat Genocide Association, "Herero and Nama Genocide," *Combat Genocide*, n.d., http://combatgenocide.org/?page_id=153.

35. Smith, "The Talk of Genocide," 108.

36. Lowry, "African Resistance," 260.

37. Ibid.

38. Ibid.

39. Bonnell, "Social Democrats," 209.

40. Ibid., 209.

41. "*Völker Europas wahrt eure heiligsten Güter,*' nicknamed "The Yellow Peril," was a, 1895 pen lithograph by Hermann Knackfuss. Knackfuss was one of Kaiser Wilhelm's favorite artists, and the allegorical image in this lithograph was intended to show how the leaders of Europe and United States needed to band together in order to stand tall against Asiatics who were threatening to storm Europe. The American version, titled "Peoples of Europe, Defend Your Holiest Possessions," appeared in *Harp-*

er's Weekly. See Kat Chow, "If We Called Ourselves Yellow," *National Public Radio*, last modified September 27, 2018, https://www.npr.org/sections/codeswitch/2018/09/27/647989652/if-we-called-ourselves-yellow.

42. Bonnell, "Social Democrats," 209.

43. Ibid., 215. For more on these alleged procurement and shipping scandals, see Klaus Epstein, *Matthias Erzberg and the Dilemmas of German Democracy* (New York: Howard Fertig, 1971); Klaus Epstein, "Erzberger and the German Colonial Scandals, 1905–1910," *English Historical Review* 74 (1959): 637–63.

44. H. G. J., "After the Victory," *Der Wahre Jacob* 476 (October 18, 1904): 4492, cited in Bonnell, "Social Democrats," 214.

45. Bonnell, "Social Democrats," 211.

46. Ibid., 207.

47. Jodi Byrd, quoted in Vimalassery, Pegues, and Goldstein, "Introduction: On Colonial Unknowing," paragraph 25.

48. Guettel, "The SPD Should Return."

FOUR

"Little Heaps of Sand," and the Transcontinental Debates about the Evidentiary Nature of the 1918 British Blue Book

In 1915, British troops and their Union of South Africa allies invaded GSWA, and this was the beginning of the end of German colonial rule in this part of the world. In interesting ways, those who invaded GSWA carried with them their assimilationist views regarding "native" rights and imperial duties, and this invasion would bring in social agents who questioned the ways that the settlers and administrators dispensed legal justice in German colonies.

After the Reichstag debates on the funding of the *Schutztruppe* in Africa few Europeans heard that much about what was happening in GSWA, but all of this changed when the leader of South African Union Army, General Louis Botha, returned to Cape Town to deal with a rebellion of Boer soldiers. While Botha was gone, the Defence troops who invaded GSWA found that they did not have to worry about any massive German army that might confront them in battle in this part of Africa. The only resistance that the invading South African soldiers encountered came from a few dozen German snipers who fired a few volleys, detonated some mines, and then fled.[1]

Tens of thousands of members of the South African expeditionary forces who traveled to places like Swakopmund and Lüderitz found that the absence of a large German colonial army meant that they now had plenty of time on their hands.[2] These bored members of British expeditionary forces would become some of the first chroniclers of what would later be called the Namibian genocide.

As noted in chapter 2, the British had always kept an eye on what was happening in GSWA, and the Nama leader, Henrik Witbooi, had sent many messages to British administrators hoping that they would intervene and stop the German takeover of indigenous African lands. Now, after 1915, with the presence of massive British armies, some Ovaherero and Nama dared hope that they, like the slaves liberated by the abolitionists, might receive help from a younger generation of British emancipators.

However, when help did come, it came from unexpected quarters. One medical doctor who traveled north with Botha's forces, Dr. Henry Walker, would record what he saw when he stumbled across a half-buried desert graveyard:

> Beyond the European cemetery is what is said to be the native burial-place. Rows and rows of little heaps of sand occupy about a thousand yards of desert. Some of these heaps have crude little crosses of sticks placed on them. It was puzzling to explain why so many natives were buried near Swakopmund, in a place that was not even enclosed.[3]

Dr. Walker had stumbled upon the buried remains of some of the tens of thousands of Ovaherero and Nama who lost their lives in the German detention and work camps that had been built following the 1904–1908 War.

The type of help that Dr. Henry Walker would provide the Ovaherero and the Nama had to do with imperial witnessing and the preservation of counterhistories, that at times were buried by German-speaking settlers who produced more dominant histories that would rather valorize the heroism of the *Schutztruppe*. Colonial violence would be followed by what Gayatri Spivak and other postcolonial scholars called "epistemic violence."[4]

Discoveries like these by members of the invading British and South African forces would eventually create situations where a few British imperialists would write journal articles, pamphlets, books, medical surveys, and military reports that critiqued the annihilationist rhetorics of their German rivals. While some of these authors sympathized with the plight of the Germans during times of rebellion, others did not hesitate to argue that British colonizers would never have treated the "natives" as slaves.

The phrase "little heaps of sand" would enter the academic lexicons of Africanists and other scholars who traced the thanatopolitics and the biopolitics of the 1904–1908 conflicts in Namibia, and many of the South African and British writers who joined General Botha helped revive interest in reviewing the past actions of German settlers and soldiers. Their critiques of indigenous life and death in the German colonies added more layers to the multilayered colonial archives, and the British and South African invaders' perceptual framings of the German "treatment" of the "natives" would later serve as "primary" sources for some of those who wanted to evidence the perpetration of German atrocities.

Genocide scholars, Namibian archivists, German history researchers and other investigators would later look back on some of these 1915 discoveries and write about colonial parallels, structures, continuities, or discontinuities that could be found in comparative analyses of "British" and "German" types of colonialism. In the process of critiquing the German practices in GSWA, these same British writers provided future generations with shards of competitive memories that provided the rhetorical arguments that were used by those who recontextualized the Second Reich's imperial decisions.

For my purposes here, it should be noted that some of the materials that were gathered after the South African invasion of GSWA would form what critical legal scholars call "ideological drifts,"[5] and captured German legal documents would be used by imperial rivals who produced what is now called 1918 British "Blue Book."

That Blue Book (*Report on the Natives of South-West Africa and Their Treatment by Germany* [1918]), is not always considered to be an "objective" source of "primary" information by some German scholars, but some of the texts and photographs that appear in that Blue Book are now being recycled and redeployed as legal experts, journalists, and others pay attention to what is happening in U.S. courtrooms where judges are presented with Ovaherero and Nama reparations claims. In 2018, for example, Matthias Goldmann, a legal expert on sovereign debt restructuring and other economic issues, was asked to produce a declaration for the claimants in *Vekuii Rukoro et al v. Federal Republic of Germany*. Goldmann cited the Blue Book's commentaries on the illegal confiscation of indigenous cattle that crossed German "borders," and he used other historical materials that came from the rhetorics that were produced by the Social Democrats in the Reichstag (chapter 3). Goldmann linked these materials with research from Horst Drechsler so that he could argue that during the early 1900s indigenous losses could be calculated.[6]

As I explain in more detail below, the commentaries of Dr. Walker, and the crafting of the 1918 Blue Book, aided members of future generations who wanted to debate another legal issue—the presence or absence of culpable "genocidal intent" in cases where tens of thousands of indigenous Africans lost their lives.

While Germany's imperial critics would use the British (some say Union of South Africa) 1918 Blue Book as a rhetorical weapon in the arsenal of those who felt that they were fighting against the lingering effects of Prussian militarism, others were equally convinced that this was a libelous text that did not paint an accurate picture of GSWA colonial development. Fragments from the Blue Book could be used in the crafting of either multidirectional or competitive memories.

During the first quarter of the twentieth century, German schoolchildren would be told about how German South West Africa was one of the "model" African colonies, where hardworking settlers could take in the aesthetic beauty of these African plains as they developed this part of Africa.

In this chapter I continue my critical genealogical study of twenty-first-century Namibian restorative justice rhetorics by asking several overarching questions. Can a military report on alleged German "atrocities" that was circulated by a rival imperial power ever be treated as an accurate "primary" source of historical information? Could the textual or visual evidence that appeared in that controversial Blue Book help future Ovaherero or Nama claimants who were looking for the "preponderance of the evidence" that "proved" that officials in German South West Africa knowingly perpetrated a genocide? Should observers really consider this to be an authoritative British Blue Book that gave "voice" to aggrieved African "natives" who survived colonial battlefields or the "*sjamboks*" (whips) that were used for floggings?[7]

Even those interdisciplinary scholars who openly worry about using tainted, politicized sources can nevertheless understand the perceptual value of the Blue Book. Reinhart Kössler, for instance, observed that the 1918 British Blue Book was "the first extensive treatment, from a critical perspective at any rate, of German colonial practice in Namibia."[8] Kössler elaborated by noting this was a text that was "based on a fairly broad range of materials, including oral sources, collected in the form of affidavits and similar testimonies" that were used to "convey the story, not only of colonial warfare, but also of everyday oppression in Namibia during the closing decades of German rule, in particular on the farms."[9] In 2003 editors not only republished the Blue Book, but they annotated it, and these scholars characterized it as a canonical text for German colonial studies.[10] Jeremy Sylvester and Jan-Bart Gewald opined that the Blue Book was a "key text in the production of colonial discourse,"[11] and others could note that materials from this text had also appeared in the work of writers like Horst Drechsler.

The British, armed with the textual and visual evidence from their Blue Book, were not simply trying to make a case for Lieutenant General Lothar von Trotha's individual failings at Hamakari/Waterberg. They were being more ambitious, and they were using materials from traders, missionaries, and survivors of concentration camps to argue in more functional or structural ways that German colonialism was totally different from other types of European imperialism and was inherently problematic. These types of claims would become the antecedent generic elements that would later be used by those participating in *Sonderweg* (special path) debates.

Readers can guess that academics are divided on the question of whether anyone should even be citing the Blue Book. In 1941 members of the British Foreign Office sent along a copy of the Blue Book to the Far East Bureau of the Ministry of Information in Singapore, but Foreign Office civil servants warned the recipients that the Blue Book should not be used for "publicity purposes" because it had been "composed in the heat of the last war" and is "historically somewhat suspect."[12] Years later, Andreas Eckl argued that since there was no way to get a copy of the "interviewees'" transcripts that appeared in the Blue Book, questions had to be asked about this text's "plausibility, consistency, and cohesion."[13] Had some of these captured German materials been altered to suit the needs of the British Foreign Office?

I will be arguing in this chapter that the Blue Book needs to be viewed as a major rhetorical text that was more than just "propaganda" or "prose." This work was a condensation symbol that needs to be viewed as a key archival parchment that reflected and refracted key ideological positions that were adopted by imperial critics who demanded a return to accommodationist positions. The Blue Book gained much of its rhetorical power because it became an iconic symbol of human liberation for those who despised annihilationist ways of thinking about colonial relationships.

In many ways the 1918 Blue Book that allegedly focused on the "desires" of African natives living in South West Africa was just one epistemic fragment in a much larger archival collection of imperialist investigative reports that were used to try to modify the behavior of those who had once been given "protectorates" and now would be given "mandates." The way that word and image came together in this particular 1918 Blue Book resembled Roger Casement's 1904 Report, that would be passed along to British diplomats who saw photographs of mutilated "Red Rubber" African workers in the Congo who were punished for not meeting quotas for rubber production. Casement's Report, along with the photographs that were taken by a missionary by the name of Alice Harris, was credited with helping put an end to Belgian King Léopold II's reign of terror in the "Congo Free State."[14] British and South African investigators hoped that similar benefits would come from Allied investigative reports that looked into ghastly German colonial abuses.

Yet if this was the case, then why didn't the British who lived in nearby places like Walvis Bay or the "Cape Colony" speak out about alleged abuses taking place in GSWA between 1904 and the time of the 1915 British invasion? When Mads Bomholt Nielsen tried to explain the absence of British public alarms, he argued that it would be a mistake to think that all British imperialists disagreed with German colonial policies. He contends that oftentimes Anglo-German colonial relationships were "ambiguous and contradictory," and at times it seemed that the British diplomats who kept an eye on German troop movements were interested *in helping the Germans* stop the spread of African rebellions that threatened to spill over into "British" territories.[15]

Those who assembled this particular 1918 Blue Book did not show any interest in helping the German expansionists cause, and they seemed to be producing a type of imperial counterhistory that might be read by responsible British lawyers, magistrates, and members of the public. These British investigators would provide revelatory information that was supposedly left out of more orthodox German tales of colonial benevolence.

The Blue Book would be co-produced by those who hastily cobbling together select materials that came from surviving German colonial court records of legal cases, interviews from African survivors, and translated transcripts that were based on conversations with workers who came up from the British Cape Colony. All these efforts produced an example of what Michel Foucault and others have called "effective histories," which seemed plausible to those who wanted to believe that the "Huns" should never have put in charge of any African colony.[16]

A hermeneutics of suspicion has haunted this Blue Book. Christina Twomey provided just one example of this hauntology when she raised the interesting point that some interviewees who acted as witnesses for the British had once fought *alongside the German Schutztruppe,* and they often admitted having participating in the killing of Ovaherero or Nama civilians. Were these culpable parties who served as witnesses for the British trying to deflect attention away from their own complicity?

The inclusion of materials taken from former German colonizers led Professor Twomey to conclude that anyone who treats Blue Book materials as legal or moral evidence has to "consider the possibility that these eyewitnesses were eager to distance themselves from a now discredited and defeated ruling power."[17] She also made the point that the coherence of the Blue Book came at the cost of producing a text that seemed to have been heavily edited, to the point where this "certainly" did not "read as verbatim transcripts of an oral interview."[18] It is very possible that some of those who were quoted or interviewed, if they understood the context behind the crafting of this Blue Book, might have objected to some of these usages of their contributions.

Like other imperial texts the Blue Book was partial, incomplete, political, and selective. Nevertheless, for many future audiences, this was an official text that proved to be a damning indictment of German colonial administrators. It confirmed what many already suspected, that the German militarists should never have been given control of places like GSWA, German East Africa, Togo, and so on.[19]

With this in mind, the rest of this chapter is organized in the following manner. First of all, I provide readers with some examples of the synchronic ways that those in the metropoles and peripheries of empire talked and wrote about the significance of the 1918 Blue Book. Second, I supply readers with some critical rhetorical analyses of the arguments that appeared in this inflammatory text. Third, I supply a relatively short critique of what this Blue Book *did not cover*. Finally, in the concluding segment I note how the 1918 Blue Book has also served the diverse needs of twenty-first century litigants and members of Ovaherero and Nama reparations movements.

THE CONTENTIOUS POLITICS THAT SET THE RHETORICAL STAGE FOR THE PRODUCTION OF THE 1918 BLUE BOOK

Those global audiences who had fought in the Great War were so horrified of the carnage that came from gas attacks, planes, machine guns, and trench warfare that they did what they could to prevent the spread of excessive faith in "–isms"—imperialism, militarism, capitalism, and Bolshevism—that they believed contributed to the beginning of World War I. Troops who fought alongside the British in the Great War had been brought from all parts of the British Empire—from Australia and British India and Canada and South Africa—and there were few regions of the world that were not touched by the traumas of World War I.

As I noted in previous chapters the theoretical work of Michael Rothberg on multidirectional memories reminds us of the promise and the perils that comes from comparing large-scale traumatic events,[20] and the victors in the Great War could not keep politicizing the conflict and placing blame for the war on the losers. For many generations both the victors, and the vanquished, tried to leave behind their contentious epistemic framings of the causes of the Great War, and there was no shortage of those who wanted to write about how to prevent its recurrence.

The range of suggestions that were offered—from talk of pacificism and an end to all wars to *realpolitik* suggestions that all nations would be deterred by disarmament or rearmament[21] —produced a surfeit of post-conflict remembrances of the Great War. It also led to many massive upheavals in colonial and imperial strategizing.

During the negotiations at Versailles the Russian and American delegates made it known that they would not be interested in hearing some of the same militaristic and imperialist talk that trumpeted the supposed benefits that came from older "protectorate" schemes. Americans like Woodrow Wilson were convinced that "Prussianism" and other forms of aggressive militarism had contributed to the underdevelopment of colonies.[22] Those who supported the Russian and American positions called for "mandate" systems that would help preserve "native" lands and rights of those living in the colonies. The involvement of the League of Nations in policing these affairs was supposed to help ensure compliance with customary international laws that preserve humanitarian principles.

This meant that the French and the British delegates at Versailles, who were trying to disempower German or Ottoman rivals, had to be circumspect in the ways that they used the term "annexation." The use of that term was viewed by many interwar audiences as signaling a complete disregard for the views of the indigenous populations living in colonized territories, who, before the Great War, had to watch as settler communities used legal terms like annexation to rationalize the dispossession of indigenous lands.

After the Great War, many diplomats and interwar communities preferred to talk about "mandates" and "trustees." Under Article 22 of the new League of Nations Charter, "South West Africa" replaced GSWA. This particular type of mandate was tailored to helping places that were said to be "inhabited by peoples not yet able to stand by themselves under the strenuous conditions of the modern world."[23]

In spite of the egalitarian sounding aspirations of the Americans and the Russians—who were dealing with their own segregationist policies at home—the very debates about these competing mandate classificatory systems illustrated how racism, eugenics, and talk of regeneration was still influencing diplomatic thinking, even after all the horrors of World War I. Few treated the Ovaherero or the Nama or Ovambo or the San or any other ethnic populations in these regions as autonomous groups who did not need the guiding hand of European powers.

The use of Article 22 of the League of Nations Charter signaled that the victors in the Great War were going to establish a type of nationalistic hierarchy that measured fitness to rule and levels of regional maturation. These hierarchies assumed that modern European notions of liberal imperialism should provide the measuring sticks that could be used to gauge fitness for self-rule. The announcement that the South African region would be classified as a "C" mandate colony—that would be governed by the laws of the Union of South Africa—implied that this was still a "wild" or semi-barbaric geopolitical space that would be controlled by the right sort of imperialists. Configuring the new "South West Africa" as a part of a larger "C Mandate" implied "indefinite control and a virtually free hand" for the new rulers.[24]

The Treaty of Versailles did not contain provisions that indicated that the British and South African troops were going to leave after being kicked out by the German imperialists. Instead, this became one more area controlled by British interests, yet another example of what Gilles Deleuze called "reterritorialization."[25] In the new South West Africa, these changes impacted everything from the name of spaces and places to the languages that had to be used in official or daily correspondence.

These African lands were not going to be given back to the Ovambo or the Ovaherero or any other indigenous community, but would be handed over to some of the victors in the Great War who were supposed to do a better job of developing this region while preserving the rights of the "natives."

In order to make this reterritorialization of former German colonial lands more palatable to interwar sensibilities this mandate system was not treated as vengeful victors' reoccupation of German lands but as apolitical "trusteeship." Civil servants, including Afrikaners, who traveled from the Union of South Africa to "South West Africa" were supposed to migrate to that region so that they could protect their African "wards." The presence of British allies was supposed to ensure that indigenous communities were not abused in the same ways that they had suffered under the older German "protectorate" arrangements.

Frustrated German communities—who once believed that they were on the cusp of winning the Great War after they controlled "the East" following the 1917 Russian Revolution—had to suffer through the humiliation of seeing Versailles delegates blame them for the militarism, the nationalism, and the other "–isms" that allegedly contributed to the outbreak of World War I. An editorial in the *London Times* in 1918 provided an example of some of the sentiments that animated those who sat around those Versailles tables:

> It had been widely supposed that in the oppression of Belgium the German capacity for wickedness had reached its limit. That was a foolish delusion. The inhuman outrages committed in Europe are insignificant compared to the savage abominations which were the foundation of German rule in Africa. Here we see the "blond beast" untrammeled. Here he [*sic*] gluts his appetite for blood, for plunder and for his bestial lusts.[26]

If the British had many any mistakes before and during the Great War, some of those mistakes supposedly came when they looked the other way and did not notice what was happening in places like East Africa or German South West Africa.

The losses in the Great War only added to the traumas of those who once believed themselves to be the dispensers of "*Kultur*" in Africa. Both during and after the Great War the allies mulled over how best to reign in these "blonde beasts," and the inclusion of Article 119 in the Treaty of Versailles called upon Germany, as a defeated power, to hand over its overseas colonies. The same German colonizers who once vilified Ovaherero and Nama fighters during the 1904–1908 rebellion, and lionized the heroism of the *Schutztruppe*, were now having to read European newspapers that will filled with stories about brutalizing colonial practices. Noel Buxton, the great grandson of the abolitionist Sir Thomas Buxton, opined that the argument about how "it would be cruel to the natives to restore them to their German masters" was a "stalking horse" that was being used "to advance other claims."[27]

In order to help the victors justify this taking away of German colonies they needed historical and legal texts that would document the extent of German "atrocities" in places like South West Africa. Major Thomas Leslie O'Reilly, a British colonial magistrate, was invited to be one of the authors of the 1918 Blue Book, and his portion of this report provided detailed critiques of how thirty years of German rule had destroyed indigenous lives and African cultures.

Detractors of the Blue Book would later belittle this text as just another example of the "atrocity" reports that were produced by victors in conflicts, but those who viewed this as an authentic representation of real colonial tragedies refused to dismiss the eyewitness accounts that were collected by Major O'Reilly.

As soon as the 1918 Blue Book's contents were publicized it catalyzed the efforts of both supporters and detractors. European travelers, administrators, soldiers, traders, and others weighed in and commented on this text's authorship, the motives for its production, and the reliability of its witness statements. German settlers who were allowed to stay in South West Africa joined those in Germany who argued that the 1918 Blue Book was just one of many libelous texts that were produced by propagandists who did not recognize the real "rights" and "duties" of imperialists. When the Blue Book was used to back up Georges Clémenceau's claims that Article 119 of the Versailles Treaty had to be added because "Germany's dereliction in the sphere of colonial civilization had been revealed too completely," German apologists responded by arguing that this was nothing more than a "colonial guilt lie."[28]

DECODING KEY ARGUMENTS AND PASSAGES IN THE 1918 BLUE BOOK

England's—or the Union of South Africa's—1918 Blue Book contained several key sections, that provided readers with a brief preface, part I on "Natives and German Administration," part II on "Natives and the Criminal Law," and an appendix that displayed photographs of chained Africans, hangings, and the disfigured bodies of those who suffered from German corporal punishment. E. H. M. Gorges wrote the preface, Major O'Reilly wrote part I, and A. J. Waters, a Crown Prosecutor, wrote part II.

In many ways the Blue Book was an intriguing and complex text that helped produce, as well as represent, British imperial identities as well as caricatures of German subject positions. The various parts of the Blue Book were used to create an imaginary binary world, where non-violent British imperialism could be contrasted with excessively violent German imperialism.

The authors of the Blue Book implied that African indigenous communities not only accepted, but desired, British tutelage. After all, wasn't it true that during the GSWA years many Ovaherero or Nama wrote letters to the British in the Cape Colony or Walvis Bay, asking for their intervention and help?

Portions of the Blue book were said to have been written by those who tried to provide a "voice" for those who risked much by coming forward and telling the British about German colonial atrocities. In his preface, the British administrator, E. H. M. Gorges, argued that he would not be surprised if some of those who provided "Native opinion" had to suffer again when "a smelling campaign" was carried out by reactionary South West Africa police who sympathized with the Germans and acted as "witch doctors" who might terrorize the witnesses.[29] This seemed to be an attempt to show that interviewees ought to be treated as truthful witnesses involved in what Michel Foucault would have called parrhesiastic practices.[30]

In his preface Gorges argued that readers of the Blue Book would be provided with "incontrovertible evidence of proved historical facts" that would allow them to see exactly why "Hereros and other native races in this area desired British Protection in preference to that of Germany."[31] From a Foucauldian vantage point, these are self-serving "elements" of British colonial *epistemes* that are produced by those who are trying to persuade others of the legitimacy of this South African takeover of what Germans viewed as one of their overseas colonies.

Postcolonial scholars or colonial settler researchers might note that these stark, binary ways of viewing the mandate system left little room for Ovaherero emancipation or the return of indigenous property, but the British viewed the publication of the Blue Book as a humanitarian venture. Gorges, for example, told his readers that publishing all of the materials that were collected for the writing of this report would have made this volume "too bulky," so the Blue Book contained only the "essential features" that were needed to show "the terrible courses pursued by the German colonial administration, the "Berlin Government," and "individual Germans" who were "settled or stationed in the country."[32]

This type of rhetorical framing—that was directed *at all* of those who "systematically subjected" the "natives" to "brutalities and robberies"[33] —served as a structural or as a functional way of viewing reprehensible colonial behavior. Instead of just singling out one particular German governor or one military officer for censure, the Blue Book was organized in ways that indicted an entire colonial apparatus. This type of framing—that made it difficult to find any redemptive German colonial scheme—produced the textured, accusatory materials that would reappear in many other texts that were produced in the future by those who quoted from the Blue Book.

Although Gorges did not reference some of the most sensational findings that were gathered by those who produced the Blue Book he wanted his readers to note that he thought that the worst might have passed. "One can" fairly "believe," he argued, that the German "colonists, or a portion of them, became "so satiated with the sight of the human blood that was shed" in the Herero war that German colonizers' worries about "their future labour supply and the loss of cattle forced them to call a halt to "the extermination of the Hereros."[34] In theory, the belated adoption of prudential assimilationist German practices put an end to more problematic exterminationist campaigns.

Gorges, unlike Major O' Reilly, seemed to be focusing on GSWA decisions that were made *before* the building of concentration camps in places like Lüderitz. Perhaps Gorges, like some in the British Foreign office, realized that trying to spend too much time on camp horrors might remind readers of the tens of thousands of Boer and African deaths that resulted from British camp internments during some of the Boer conflicts.[35] Instead of making that type of camp comparison, Gorges implied that some of the camp images and witness testimonies were so sensational that they would not be believed by many outside of South Africa, and so those images needed to be quarantined and placed in some other archival text.

The almost 150 pages of materials that Major Thomas Leslie O'Reilly provided in his section of the Blue Book were sufficiently damning, and he used a combination of textual and visual evidence to document the physical, cultural, and psychological destruction of the Ovaherero and Nama who lived under German tutelage. "At the time of the annexation by Germany," O'Reilly argued, "the Hereros occupied the heart of South-West Africa," and their "sphere of influence extended from Swakopmund in the west to the Kaihari border in the east," from "the mountains of Outjo in the north to Windhuk and Gobabis in the south."[36]

Long before academics like Horst Drechsler or Helmut Bley or Jürgen Zimmerer or Effa Okupa[37] wrote their GSWA histories (see chapters 6, 8, and 9) it would be Major O'Reilly who would write about the treaty signings of German Commissioner Heinrich Ernst Gŏring and the 1893 "massacre at Hornkranz" that was carried out by Kurt von François's forces. In order to help illustrate how the Ovaherero and Nama claimed ownership of their lands, O'Reilly highlighted how these indigenous communities had adamantly refused to give in to German pressures and openly contested European claims to ownership.

O'Reilly helped preserve some of the German colonial legal documents that went into the elite and public archives that I referenced in chapter 1. For example, he cited the correspondence between von François and Chief Hendrik Witbooi that was catalogued in captured German colonial files. As David Olusoga and Casper Erichsen would later note, Major O'Reilly's report came from the "mountain of translated German documents that had been assembled in Windhoek."[38]

This British Major tried to include materials that came from indigenous sources. O'Reilly quoted from some of the missives that Henrik Witbooi sent to the British in the Cape Colony, and in that correspondence Witbooi argued that "Namaqualand" had been "purchased by us in blood, twice over, from out grandfather's days to mine."[39] Showing some familiarity with the legalistic language that would be used by European militarists or legalists Witbooi went on to argue that he was "an independent chief" who had "not submitted" himself, his land, or is people "to German protection." Witbooi seemed to have viewed these performative acts as demonstrative jurisprudential evidence that he was complying with "all well-known laws of war."[40]

These textual fragments from the Witbooi correspondence would be cited over and over again by countless chronicles of the Ovaherero/Nama–German war and GSWA histories.[41] They also appeared in the multidirectional and competitive memories that were produced by journalists, academics, lawyers, lay persons, and others who argue about the presence or absence of "atrocities."

Major O'Reilly tried to show that after the killing of dozens of Nama by von François's troops the proud Chief Witbooi, surrounded by German troops and running out of ammunition, would be forced to sign one of those problematic protective agreements. Over the course of the next decade Hendrik Witbooi would have to send Nama warriors to fight alongside the *Schutztruppe* who fought the Ovaherero and other indigenous tribes. After some of these Nama fighters returned home from these German skirmishes, they told Chief Witbooi about what happened at places like Ohamakari/Waterberg, and Witbooi's Nama forces eventually joined the Ovaherero.

Some of the most graphic textual materials that Major O'Reilly included in the Blue Book came from captured letters and reports that were written by social agents like Governor Theodore Leutwein and Captain Kurt Schwabe. In one key passage Schwabe had this to say about his memories of the battle of "Hornkranz":

> Under an overhanging rock lay the corpses of seven Witboos, who in their death agony, had crawled into the hollow, and their bodies lay pressed tightly together. In another place the body of a Berg-Dramara woman obstructed the footpath, while two three-to-four year old children sat quietly playing beside their mother's corpse. . . . I estimate the losses of the enemy at about 150 persons, of which 60 were soldiers. . . . Unfortunately, there must be included women and children who had been in the *pontoks* during the fight.[42]

Long before the World War II victors at Nuremberg decided to rely on German documents to indict and convict Nazis, the British used captured German papers to put on public display the horrors of German colonial occupation, and reportage on the 1893 massacre at Hornkranz was a part of that inter-imperial rivalry framing of problematic colonial atrocities.

Major O'Reilly's Part I of the Blue Book was written in a chronological style that allowed him to link together incriminating statements from famous German pioneers with materials that the major had obtained from those who had witnessed the battle of Ohamakari/Waterberg. The British were worried about the historical gaps that were created when most German concentration camp records were destroyed, but O'Reilly filled in those gaps by gathering together sworn statements that came from hundreds of Ovaherero and Nama who had fled to places like Ovambo kingdoms, Angola and Bechuanaland.[43]

O'Reilly used these materials to assert that some ninety thousand Africans lost their lives during these turbulent times, and in in chapter 22 of his section of the Blue Book, he advanced this huge claim:

> [A]s early as 1905, a general peace would have been possible but for the obstinate adherence of von Trotha to his extermination policy. It was then that Marengo [a Nama leader] signified his willingness to surrender on terms. . . . [V]on Trotha lost all chances of an early peace by replying that the surrender had to be unconditional. . . . Little wonder, then, that Marengo decided to fight to the bitter end.[44]

Major Reilly conveniently left out the fact that it had been members of British border patrols who had actually tracked down Jakob Marengo and killed him when he crossed over into neighboring South Africa.[45]

In the British major's telling of the tale it would be German social agency that would take center stage and the German colonizers would be the antagonists in his morality play. After von Trotha was recalled, noted O'Reilly, the Germans decided to use indigenous men and women prisoners as laborers "on the harbor works at Lüderitzbucht and Swakopmund, and also on railway construction."[46] Just before he started to bombard his readers with quotation after quotation from witnesses who saw concentration camp horrors, he previewed what was to come in the Blue Book by mentioning that "probably 60 percent" of the "Natives" who surrendered to von Trotha's troops may have "died at the hands of the labour overseer and by the lash."[47] These "naked remnants of starving humanity" were put on the barren islets of Lüderitz and the "moisture-oozing shores of Swakopmund."[48] He was sure that the Germans who did this had to "take the fullest blame and submit to the condemnation of all persons with even an elementary feeling of humanity towards the native races."[49]

The Blue Book thus became a phantasmagoric imperial text that included some of the first detailed discussions of the *konzentrationslager*, or German concentrations camps in GSWA. This British and South African referencing of German labor camps served as a rhetorical weapon that was intended to put on graphic display the German dehumanization of the Ovaherero and other African tribes. It would be filled with raw numbers and other social science statistics that would appeal to those who wanted to see quantitative proof that this constituted a large-scale atrocity. As Professor Reinhart Kössler explained, the "Blue Book was not written as a pioneering feat in history" but rather as an "extensive South African government paper, hastily assembled to bolster South Africa's claims for permanent control" over the former areas called German South West Africa.[50] This Blue Book was also a British work that provided the generic template that would be picked up by others who wanted to read or write about what happened after von Bülow rescinded von Trotha's proclamation near the end of 1904.

The materials that came from the captured German archives were damning enough, but it was oftentimes the testimonial materials that came from the indigenous survivors or South African travelers that provided some of the most emotive portions of the Blue Book. In one section of this text Traugott Tjienda, a leader of the Hereros at Tsumeb, was quoting as stating this under oath:

> As our people came in from the bush they were made to work at once, they were merely skin and bones, and they were so thin that . . . they looked like broomsticks. . . . . Bad as they were, they were made to work. . . . The soldiers guarded us at night in big compounds made of thorn bushes. . . . The Herero women were compounded with the men. . . . When our women were prisoners on the railway work they were compelled to cohabitate with soldiers and white railway labourers. . . . Young girls were raped and very badly used.[51]

Commentaries from missionaries and other witnesses were used to discuss the cold ocean breezes, the typhus, the malnutrition, and the military indifference that was said to have contributed to the deaths of thousands. This helped create the impression that the "atrocities" did not begin and end with what happened at the battle of Ohamakari/Waterberg.

The Blue Book also provided some of the horrific statistics that would be recirculated over the course of the next century. Fritz Issac, for example, stated under oath that of the "3,500 Hottentots [Nama] and Kaffirs" who were sent to the Shark Island camp only "193" returned.[52] These statistics were even worse than the official German calculations that appear in the military or colonial archives that estimated that almost half of those detained in the concentrations camps lost their lives.

The authors of the Blue Book used thirteen photographs to help put on display the horrors of German rule in GSWA, and between page 100 and page 101 one finds an iconic image that would be captioned with this label: "Hereros Returning Starved from the Desert, Into Which They Had Been Driven by the Germans."

In 2014 the Namibian government would build the Independence Memorial Museum, and outside of that structure there appears what is called the "Genocide Statue." On one side of this statue, the side facing away from the street, one finds a "relief image" that transformed this iconic photograph into a commemorative artefact. In 2018 Ronald Niezen, in an excellent essay on competing Namibian memories and histories, argued that this particular image depicted a "group of starving Ovaherero, including an elderly woman, with ribs protruding."[53] Niezen went on to note that this image was "based on well-known archival photos."[54]

This very same iconic image of those survivors who trekked across the Kalahari continues to appear on countless web pages that discuss the importance of combating "African Holocaust" denialism or the need for Herero and Nama reparations.

Most scholars, law review authors, and others who peruse the Blue Book focus on O'Reilly's section of the Blue Book, but it seems as though early twentieth-century British audiences—perhaps aware of the symbolism of abolitionism—were equally concerned with the second half that covered German criminal cases of corporal punishment.

Some of the most controversial sections of the Blue Book were written by the British or South Africans who studied the German criminal cases that were brought by those who objected to German colonial floggings, known as *Väterliche Züneigung,* or "paternal chastisement."[55] Readers of this text learned that during the GSWA years police and other legal authorities in the colonies did little to intervene when corporal punishment was meted out to African laborers or servants who, in theory, needed to be educated like children.

I would argue that few of the writers who have commented on these paternal chastisements have recognized that colonial allowances for these types of floggings had their origins in neo-Lamarckian ways of thinking about education, genetic transmission of ideas, and colonial regulation of empires. Lamarckian approaches, unlike more Mendelian ways of viewing genetic determination, considered the "germplasm" of human beings to be alterable substances that were passed down from generation to generation.[56] In theory, if the German farmer, or the colonial administrator, or the soldier dispensed the right amount of "paternal chastisement," this meant that the children of those who were flogged would inherit these lessons. The idea here was that the future descendants of those who flogged would be less likely to commit crimes or rebel or disrespect their betters.

Sadly, this legitimation of paternal chastisement had everything to do with the popularity of the assimilationist or accommodationist rhetorics that I commented on in previous chapters, and these commentaries of Neo-Lamarckian ways of viewing corporal punishment resurfaced when German captors justified the use of harsh methods during the internment of Ovaherero and Nama laborers in the concentration camps.

The British and South Africans who produced the Blue Book had no trouble finding examples of German court cases that displayed excessive corporal punishment, and these writers' collective commentaries put on display for European audiences the sadism, the voyeurism, and the self-serving nature of German contractual relationships that hid what other Europeans called "modern slavery." As one Ovaherero witness would tell some white South African interviewers after the invasion by the British forces in 1915, "flogging" came "to our people more regularly than their meals."[57]

The use of the whip was a way of making sure that the Ovaherero, the Nama, and other indigenous communities in Africa were imprinted with figurate marks of their alleged inferiority. Moreover, the differential judicial treatment of settlers and Africans in German South West Africa was intended to send a message to humanitarians and other imperialists who believed in silly, egalitarian treatments of people of color that supposedly made them more insolent and ungrateful. Imperial Commissioner Theodor Leutwein, who was often viewed by twentieth century scholars as someone who used an "imperial" gaze instead of a "genocidal gaze" (Elizabeth Baer) when he viewed the African labourers,[58] could not help writing about the ways that barbaric communities in Germany colony knew little about the intricacies of European colonial legal regulations. "Beating to death was not regarded as murder" by civil administrators in German South West Africa noted Leutwein, but "the natives were unable to understand such subtleties."[59] Africans who killed whites were shot or hanged, often without trials.

The British who captured the files of German administrators in 1915 were horrified when they came across meticulous records of German colonial cases involving this differential treatment of settlers and police who flogged, and sometimes killed, Ovaherero and Nama laborers or prisoners. Some of the most horrific passages that appear in the Blue Book are the ones that have to do with descriptions of the actions of Ludwig Cramer and his daughter Hildegard, who ended up in court after several indigenous women who worked on the Cramer farm were brought to the hospital on the verge of death. Cramer, a farmer who worked with a large numbers of African field workers, was rumored to have purposely selected women as the targets of his "paternal chastisement." He would be accused in court of assault and battery of eight Africans, and seven of his victims were women.[60]

British reviews of captured German court records revealed that in 1912 two pregnant African women were flogged by Cramer with impunity, and both of them miscarried. Ludwig Cramer accused one of these women, Maria, of trying to hide poison for laborers on Cramer's farm, and with the assistance of Hildegard, Marie was beaten until she fell unconscious. Elizabeth Baer records that Marie's wounds festered, and that "a photograph of her back" appeared in the 1918 Blue Book.[61] Marie would eventually die of her wounds. To add to this chronicling of what the British called "beastly" horrors, a woman by the name of Auma, who was sent to the Cramer farm as a replacement for Marie, was also flogged to the point where she died two weeks later.

Readers might imagine how these floggings would have been handled by courts of law if all of this had taken place in European settings, but in German South West Africa these types of trials were "an anomaly."[62] For decades German farmers and other settlers in this colony could punish the "natives" without having to worry about any legal repercussions.

Ludwig Cramer's case received a great deal of publicity in Europe at this time because this was one of those rare instances when a colonizer would actually have to stand trial, and A. J. Waters noted that Cramer was initially sentenced to about nineteen months of imprisonment. This punishment, upon review by appellate German authorities, was downgraded to four months of imprisonment and a fine of 2,700 marks. When Professor Baer reviewed these Cramer cases in 2017, she was forced to conclude that the German colonial judicial system helped perpetuate the notion that Africans were "subhuman" creatures who "could be treated as ignorant children, or worse, as animals."[63]

From a critical Foucauldian perspective, the German floggings represented the type of daily, quotidian ways of maintaining racial supremacy that contributed to the creation of rhetorical situations where the dispensation of violence became an inextricably part of everyday colonial settler governance.

Not surprisingly, given the politicized nature of this particular Blue Book, for a time this text was read and reread by those who were convinced that the Kaiser's "Huns" had once again abused their imperial powers. In the same ways that European neighbors had read about the cruelties perpetrated by German soldiers traveling to China and East Africa, now they were having to read about the abuse of corporal punishment in GSWA.

The Blue Book would be credited with helping legitimate the taking away of German colonies, but few were willing to forget all the lawfare that swirled around this haunted text.

CRITICAL GENEALOGICAL READINGS OF BLUE BOOK RECEPTIONS BETWEEN 1918 AND 2018

Critical genealogical readings of the Blue Book, that trace the strategic use and abuse of fragments from this 1918 discursive assemblage, need to be read in the ways that I discussed back in chapter 1—along the grain and against the grain. Critics reading along the grain would note how Europeans who agreed Major O'Reilly would have read these "parchment" elements (Foucault), while those interested in reading against the grain would pay attention to the lamentations of those who were skeptical of British usage of the Blue Book.

Even before O'Reilly and Waters finished writing their respective parts of the Blue Book there would be those in the British Foreign Office and colonial departments who were not sure what to make of British colonial propagandizing efforts. This ambivalence, in turn, in many ways reflected the dominant British ways of viewing liberal imperialism and English colonial beneficence. It took a great deal to convince bystanders that British authorities needed to intervene in the affairs of German colonizers. Some wanted Major O'Reilly to produce a text that contrasted the evils of German colonialism with the enlightened "informal" approach of the British imperialists, while skeptics could not help viewing this as an atrocity tale that shouldn't be taken seriously by qualified scholars.

The polysemic and polyvalent features of this particular British episteme meant that it would become a part of many different sedimented knowledge formations. Depending on one's particular perspectives, the Blue Book could be viewed as a truthful, transparent container of "native" African viewpoints on colonial rule, a libelous imperial "lie," or a work that needed to be preserved or banned from the colonial archives. No wonder that Mads Nielsen, writing in 2017, could note that the "legacy" of the Blue Book had become entangled in a host of debates about Anglo-German rivalries, "the idea of colonial exceptionalism," and the "associated colonial *Sonderweg*."[64]

Was the Blue Book an attempted monumentalization of British greatness, or a testimony to the purported successes that came from avoiding German excesses? Was this text being used to show that the same Prussian militarism that had helped defeat the French and help unite the German nation in the early 1870s had also taken Germans on a "special path" that led *inexorably to the perpetration of two genocides?*

For many generations of Ovaherero and Nama, the 1918 Blue Book—that preserved half-forgotten sephia images—should be viewed as an authentic manuscript that put on display the agonies of those who were nearly exterminated after the battle of Ohamakari/Waterberg. The use of O'Reilly's work over the years helped descendants of those who were placed in Karibib, Okahandja, Otjihanena, Windhoek, and other concentration camps evidence what life was like before these places were covered up with buildings, gardens, forts, and other erasures of spaces and places. The Blue Book not only contained transcriptions of oral testimonies—it also helped provide some "primary" sources for interdisciplinary scholars in Namibia or Germany who needed to find this type of evidence before they were willing to treat the 1904–1908 events as genocidal in nature.

Those communities who were accused of having carried out these atrocities did not sit back and silently accept the British verdicts on GSWA practices. Disappointed Ovaherero and Nama survivors, who knew about O'Reilly's interviewing, had to watch as racist German governmentalities were replaced with British forms of mandate rule that helped the cause of those who sought to create alliances between empowered white minorities living in South Africa. "By 1924," argued Andrea Rosengarten, "the leaders of the Union government had completely changed their tune on the Blue Book findings and its survivor testimonies."[65]

What Ann Stoler has called the "debris" of colonial archives[66] set in as one form of monumentalism was destroyed to make room for a different type of monumentalism—apartheid. Major Reilly—who would become one many victims of the infamous "Spanish" influenza that killed more than 50 million souls—would not live to see the attempted dismantling of his Blue Book by those who wished to remember to forget as they forged a newly minted "South West Africa."

In 1925 the first all-white election for a legislative assembly took place, and the local Germany settler party, the *Deutscher Bund für Südwestafrika*, took the opportunity to demand that the colony's administrator, A. J. Werth, help with the abolition of the Blue Book.[67] The next year, Mr. August Stauch, a member of that legislative assembly, had this to say about what he characterized as a "war instrument": [T]he time has come to put this instrument out of operation and impound and destroy all copies of this Blue Book, which may be found in the official records and the in the public libraries of this territory.[68] The German settlers living in British-controlled South West Africa requested that the Union Government and the British government "expunge" the Blue Book so that it would not be regarded as an official document by anyone living in any part of the British empire.

The physical destruction of the Blue Book, or its sequestering, created difficulties for those members of future generations who wanted to write about the Namibian genocide or the need for reparations. Writing in 2003, Jeremy Sylvester and Jan-Bart Gewald were clearly bothered by the cultural amnesia that seemed to have gripped not only the German-speaking communities in Namibia but the European visitors who traveled to these regions during and after the apartheid years. Sylvester and Gewald argued that twenty-first-century Namibia had become a tourist destination where the "majority of tourists will be impressed by the legacy of German imperialism."[69] "In the coastal resort of Swakopmund," Sylvester and Gewald explained, "tourists gamble money in a converted railway station built by slave labor, drink coffee overlooking the site of a concentration camp, and ride dune buggies over the mass graves of Herero POWs."[70]

Tourists who traveled to Namibia during the twentieth or twenty-first centuries seemed to be more interested in taking pictures and participating in colonial nostalgia than acknowledging the lingering influence of colonial decisions that contributed to the impoverishment of many Namibians.

As the next few chapters will demonstrate, the Ovaherero and the Nama did not forget about these horrors, and they had their own ways of recording Namibian affairs,[71] and the renascent interest in evidencing genocidal claims goes hand-in-hand with recent efforts to dust off, and revisit, the texts and visualities of that old 1918 Blue Book.

CONCLUSION

Although some scholars would be bothered by the politicized nature of the 1918 British Bluebook, it would serve as a godsend to activists and lawyers. Both its contents and its rhetorical functions helped those who were trying to put together legal cases that showed the genocidal nature of the battle of Hamakari, the driving of women and children into deserts, the camps, and any other GSWA events that might qualify as culpable actions. The very partiality of the Blue Book, and the selective nature of the "German" evidence that would bother so many over the next century, did not bother all of the brief writers who had to assemble complaints for Herero and Nama claimants in 2001 and 2017 (see chapters 7 and 9).

Major O'Reilly would not be the last lawyer who might find fault with the treatment of the Ovaherero and Nama during the German colonial years. One of the lead attorneys for the plaintiffs in *Rukoro et al. v. Germany e. al.* (2017) case noted in a *Harvard International Law Journal* essay that what happened in the GSWA concentration camps had everything to do with twenty-first-century pursuits of restorative justice as more called for recognition of "Germany's responsibility." Kenneth McCallion, one of the lead attorneys in the *Rukoro* case, noted in a co-authored essay that after Lothar von Trotha issued the extermination order on October 2, 1904, the German "imperial authorities subsequently set up a system of concentration camps, which exploited captured Ovaherero and Nama during the war and survivors thereafter for forced labor until the year 1908."[72] These types of argumentative claims were permutations of claims that had been circulating for almost a hundred years after O'Reilly and other British officials produced that infamous Blue Book.

The lawyers for the Herero claimants, unlike some of the scholars who wanted to use a wider lens and view more than just the German camps, could concentrate on writing briefs that showed American judges the exceptional or unique nature of the Second Reich's genocidal acts.

With each and every passing day, as new generations on several continents hear about various colonial apologies, the return of Ovaherero and Nama skulls (see chapter 10), or the filing of lawsuits by Rukoro and others, more and more readers become familiar with the fragments that were cobbled together so quickly by Major O'Reilly and the other British imperialists. Now visitors to many parts of the World Wide Web can learn about von Trotha's "annihilation" orders and the responses of the German General Staff. Internet views can become autodidactic as they study how Alfred von Schlieffen, the chief of the Imperial German General Staff, once approved orders that led to the building of the "first" concentration camps in GSWA near the end of 1904.

Those who surf the net can also assess the importance of von Schlieffen's orders for lawyers working for Herero and Nama claims who are trying to construct their *prima facie* reparations cases.[73] Those "little heaps of sand" have not been forgotten.

NOTES

1. David Olusoga and Casper W. Erichsen, *The Kaiser's Holocaust: Germany's Forgotten Genocide and the Colonial Roots of Nazism* (London: Farber & Farber, 2010), 253.
2. Ibid., 254–55.
3. Henry F. B. Walker, *A Doctor's Diary in Damaraland* (London: Edward Arnold, 1917), 53.
4. An overview of some of the difficulties that confront those who try to track this type of "epistemic violence" appears in Kristie Dotson, "Tracking Epistemic Violence, Tracing Practices of Silencing," *Hypatia* 26, no. 2 (Spring 2011): 236–57.
5. For a helpful theoretical discussion of the importance of "ideological drift" in legal contexts see Jack M. Balkin, "Ideological Drift and the Struggle Over Meaning," *Connecticut Law Review* 25 (1993): 869–91.
6. Matthias Goldmann, Declaration of Matthias Goldman before the Southern District of New York Court, *Vekuii Rukoro et al. v. Federal Republic of Germany*, Civ. No. 17-0062, April 24, 2018. https://papers.ssrn.com/sol3/papers.cfm?abstract_id=3169852.
7. Reinhart Kössler, "Sjambok or Cane? Reading the Blue Book," *Journal of Southern African Studies* 30 (September 2004): 703–8.
8. Ibid., 703.
9. Ibid.
10. Jeremy Silvester and Jan-Bart Gewald, editors, *Words Cannot Be Found: German Colonial Rule in Namibia: An Annotated Reprint of the 1918 Blue Book* (Brill: Leiden, 2003).
11. Ibid., xxxiii.
12. Christina Twomey, "Atrocity Narratives and Imperial Rivalry: Britain, Germany and the Treatment of 'Native Races', 1904–1939" in *Evil, Barbarism and Empire: Britain and Abroad, c. 1830–2000*, edited by T. Crook and B. Taithe (London: Palgrave Macmillan, 2011), 201–25, 201.
13. Andreas Eckl, "The Herero Genocide of 1904: Source-Critical and Methodological Considerations," *Journal of Namibian Studies* 3 (2008): 31–61, 38.
14. For a discussion of the role that Roger Casement's reports played in trying to remove King Leopold II from rule over the Congo Free State, see Adam Hochschild, *King Leopold's Ghost: A Story of Greed, Terror, and Heroism in Colonial Africa* (Boston: Houghton Mifflin, 1998).
15. Mads Bomholt Nielsen, "Selective Memory: British Perceptions of the Herero-Nama Genocide, 1904–1908 and 1918," *Journal of Southern African Studies* 43, no. 2 (February 2017): 315–30, 326.
16. For a helpful overview of some of Foucault's critical genealogical approaches see Mitchell Dean, *Critical and Effective Histories: Foucault's Method and Historical Sociology* (New York: Routledge, 2003).
17. Twomey, "Atrocity Narratives," 203.
18. Ibid.
19. For just one of many examples of how these types of debates become topics for vernacular discussions as well, see Charles Brunsdon Fletcher, *Stevenson's Germany: The Case against Germany in the Pacific* (New York: Charles Scribner's Sons, 1920).
20. Michael Rothberg, *Multidirectional Memory: Remembering the Holocaust in the Age of Decolonization* (Sanford: Stanford University Press, 2009).

21. For some of these key deliberations regarding armament and deterrence in the interwar years, see Jeffrey L. Hughes, "The Origins of World War II in Europe: British Deterrence Failure and German Expansionism," *The Journal of Interdisciplinary Study* 18, no. 4 (Spring, 1988): 851–91.

22. Woodrow Wilson opined that the Great War was fought "to slay the beast of Prussian militarism." Geoffrey Wawro, "The Challenges America Faced at Versailles in 1919 are the Same the U.S. Faces Today," *Time*, January 18, 2019, paragraph 6, http://time.com/5506810/america-versailles-treaty-today/.

23. Jan-Bart Gewald, "Imperial Germany and the Herero of South West Africa: Genocide and the Quest for Recompense," in *Genocide, War Crimes and the West: History and Complicity*, edited by Andrew Jones (London: Zed Books, 2004), 59–77, 64.

24. Kössler, "Sjambok or Cane?" 703.

25. For examples of reterritorializations, see Gilles Deleuze and Félix Guattari, *A Thousand Plateaus*, translated by Brian Massumi (New York: Continuum, 2004).

26. Olusoga and Casper, *The Kaiser's Holocaust*, 274.

27. Noel Buxton, quoted in Twomley, "Atrocity Narratives," 211.

28. Commentaries on the "colonial guilt lie" appeared in British books as well. See, for example, George Lowther Steer, *Judgment on German Africa* (London: Hodder & Stoughton, 1939).

29. Union of South Africa, *Report on the Natives of South-West Africa and Their Treatment by Germany* (Windhuk: Administrator's Office, 2018), 11.

30. "Parrhesia" is a term that is used by Foucault and others to explain how some are willing to risk much by standing up and speaking truth to power. Michel Foucault, *Fearless Speech*, edited by Joseph Pearson (New York: Semiotext(e), 2001).

31. Gorges, in Union of South Africa, *Report*, 4.

32. Ibid.

33. Ibid.

34. Ibid., 5.

35. For some of the context behind the British camps during the Second Boer War, see S. B. Spies, *Methods of Barbarism: Roberts and Kitchener and Civilians in the Boer Republics, January 1900–May 1902* (Cape Town: Human & Rousseau, 1977).

36. Union of South Africa, *Report*, 36.

37. Effa Okupa would highlight how pre-colonial Namibian communities had their own African customary laws that were applied in disputes over land ownership. See Effa Okupa, *Carrying the Sun on Our Backs: Unfolding German Colonialism in Namibia from Caprivi to Kasikili* (Berlin: Lit Verlag, 2006).

38. Olusoga and Casper, *The Kaiser's Holocaust*, 262.

39. Ibid., 25.

40. Ibid., 25–26.

41. See, for example, *New Era* Reporter, "Hendrik Witbooi Papers: Reflections of Identity," *New Era Live*, last modified February 15, 2008, https://neweralive.na/posts/hendrik-witbooi-papers-reflection-of-identity; *Deutsche Welle* Staff, "Hendrik Witbooi, A Strategic Political Fighter," *Deutsche Welle*, last modified May 15, 2018, https://www.dw.com/en/hendrik-witbooi-a-strategic-political-fighter/a-43457319.

42. Olusoga and Casper, *The Kaiser's Holocaust*, 27.

43. Ibid., 263.

44. Union of South Africa, *Report*, 97.

45. For more about Jakob Marengo see J. R. Masson, "A Fragment of Colonial History: The Killing of Jakob Marengo," *Journal of Southern African Studies* 21 (1995): 247–56. Marengo would be remembered as one of the last of leaders of the indigenous communities who held out against German control of "German" South West Africa.

46. Union of South Africa, *Report*, 98.

47. Ibid.

48. Ibid.

49. Ibid.

50. Ibid.

51. Traugott Tjienda, quoted in Union of South Africa, *Report*, 101–2.
52. Union of South Africa, *Report*, 99.
53. Ronald Niezen, "Speaking for the Dead: The Memorial Politics of Genocide in Namibia and Germany," *International Journal of Heritage Studies* 24, no. 5 (2018): 547–67, 556.
54. Ibid.
55. Silvester and Gewald, *Words Cannot Be Found*, 204; Elizabeth Baer, *The Genocidal Gaze* (Detroit: Wayne State University Press, 2017), 2.
56. For an example of the influence of Lamarckian ways of viewing eugenics in German race science studies, see Fritz Lenz, "Eugenics in Germany," *Journal of Heredity* 15, no. 5 (May 1924): 223–31.
57. Silvester and Gewald, *Words Cannot Be Found*, 135.
58. On the theoretical differences that existed between the "imperial" and "genocidal" gazes, see Baer, *The Genocidal Gaze*.
59. Silvester and Gewald, *Words Cannot Be Found*, 204; Baer, *The Genocidal Gaze*, 2.
60. Baer, *The Genocidal Gaze*, 2.
61. Ibid.
62. Ibid.
63. Ibid.
64. Mads Nielsen, "Selective Memory," 329.
65. Andrea Rosengarten, "'A Most Gruesome Sight': Colonial Warfare, Racial Thought, and the Question of 'Radicalization' during the First World War in German South West Africa," *History: The Journal of the Historical Association* (2016): 437.
66. Ann Stoler, *Duress: Imperial Durabilities for Our Times* (Durham: Duke University Press, 2016).
67. Jan-Bart Gewald, *Herero Genocide in the Twentieth Century: Politics and Memory* (New York: Brill, 2003), 288.
68. Ibid.
69. Silvester and Gewald, *Words Cannot Be Found*, xxxv.
70. Ibid.
71. See, for example, Kirsten Alnaes, "Oral Tradition and Identity: The Herero in Botswana," *Collected Seminar Papers. Institute of Commonwealth Studies* 11 (1981): 15–23.
72. Kenneth F. McCallion and Robert Murtfeld, "Germany's Responsibility under International Law to Compensate the Ovaherero and Nama Peoples of Namibia for the 1904–1908 Genocide," *Harvard International Law Journal* (2018): 1–4, 2.
73. Felicia Stephan, "The First Genocide of the 20th Century before a Domestic Court," *Võlkerrechtsblog*, May 28, 2018, paragraph 18, https://voelkerrechtsblog.org/the-first-genocide-of-the-20th-century-before-a-domestic-court/.

FIVE

Apartheid, Colonial Aphasia, and Decolonizing Remembrances, 1919–1969

Oftentimes, when litigants interested in bringing colonial reparations lawsuits attempt to file twenty-first-century torts, human rights, or other cases, they are rebuffed by those who contend that too much time has passed, that a statute of limitations stands in the way, or that the deaths of potential witnesses makes it difficult to try these types of cases. Courts have been more sympathetic when the claimants are still alive to testify about their losses—when South Korean women can tell courts about their treatment by imperial Japanese soldiers or elderly Mau Mau survivors of the 1950s British Kenyan detention centers can testify about torture—but it is not easy for twenty-first-century jurists to find jurisdiction when cases are filed a hundred years after the perpetration of alleged atrocities. Today's Namibian claimants face incredible judicial hurdles when they seem to have a difficult time answering this question: Why didn't you file these genocidal cases decades ago? After all, the Ethiopians immediately appealed to the League of Nations when they were gassed by the Italians during the 1930s, and Holocaust survivors sought restitution for World War II abuses during the Cold War years.

This chapter helps readers understand some of the historical, political, and other situational factors that made it extremely difficult to even think about filing of lawsuits in colonial courts or international forums in the decades following the closing of the last concentration camps in 1908. In some cases scholars have written about the dual legal systems that meted out justice in drastically different ways to the colonized and the colonizer, but that is only one of the factors that inhibited the filing of these types of lawsuits. As I point out in this chapter, some Ovaherero and Nama lived in refugees in the diaspora, some in South West Africa feared reprisals, and others lacked access to the traditional archival resources that were prized by Western litigants interested in formal lawfare. Moreover, a confusing array of pro-settler histories and memories—that often treated privileged whites as victims in South Africa—made it difficult to produce reparations counterhistories and countermemories.

I will also be arguing in this chapter that there were indeed episodic times when the Ovaherero did indeed try to ask for reparations for what happened at places like Ohamakari/Waterberg—especially after the passage of the UN's Convention against Genocide—but few domestic or international social agents viewed these in the same ways that they viewed the Armenian genocide or the Holocaust.

It will be my contention that the lack of public will made it nearly impossible for some indigenous African communities living in South West Africa to gain access to courts of public opinion or courts of law before the last quarter of the twentieth century. Between 1919 and the 1960s, relatively few Western scholars, diplomats, administrators, or journalists expressed any public interest in providing social redress for Ovaherero and Nama victims. Portions of this chapter will also show that oftentimes indigenous communities who were almost exterminated during colonial wars or genocidal campaigns had to live as vagrants and squatters during apartheid regimes.

In place of any open, public debates on reparations for aggrieved Ovaherero or Nama communities, empowered white communities circulated different versions of accommodationist or assimilationist rhetorics during mandate and apartheid years that were used to rationalize the use of segregationist "reserve" systems that supposedly helped maintain law and order. In theory, the provision of modern medicine, roads, buildings, and so forth was supposed to help with innumerable "native problems." These white supremacist efforts were also used to stave off interference from the League of Nations and later, by members of the United Nations who cared about decolonization or the need to end discriminatory practices. For a time, there was little talk in South West Africa of remembering the near annihilation of rebellious Africans, and the focus was on the need to provide restitution to aggrieved whites in controversies over land dispossession.

Some members of German-speaking communities who were adjusting to life in South West Africa wanted to reminisce and monumentalize the sacrifices of the *Schutztruppe* at the same time that these particular social agents found that some of their histories and colonial *epistemes* would be questioned by others.[1]

Between 1900 and 1914, German farmers in GSWA—oftentimes retired soldiers—seemed to show little interest in debating their critics as they worked away at turning a protectorate into a productive colony. During this period railroads were built that connected coastal areas to interior mining regions, and by 1903 some 334 German farmers had settled in the Windhoek-Okahandja-Karibib region.[2] After the declared end to the Ovaherero war in 1907, German colonial administrators "set the stage for apartheid policies" when they "placed severe restrictions on nonwhites" by subjecting them to a "system of labor registration and contracts and pass laws."[3] Indigenous Africans in GSWA were removed from "areas selected for white settlement," and by 1913 "approximately 80 percent of the white population was German."[4]

Everything from surveys to topographic mapping was used to ensure that "large areas of native territory" would be treated as German "crown lands."[5]

Within a short time after South African Defence forces arrived in places like Lüderitz or Windhoek, the winds of change were in the air as Afrikaners from South Africa were encouraged to migrate to South West Africa by the Union of South Africa government. As late as 1985 some academics were stilling using the rhetoric of *terra nullius* as they noted that from "1920 to 1930 1,519 farmers, most of them Afrikaners, settled on previously unoccupied land."[6]

Reterritorialization of these various communities in South West Africa meant that both Afrikaner migrants and African survivors would eventually be presenting regional and international audiences with competing ways of remembering fraught and tangled pasts.

In some ways the focus on the horrors of what would be called "international wars"—World War I and World War II—temporarily overshadowed remembrances of what Rudyard Kipling once called "savage wars of peace."[7] As Richard Dale would note in 2001, researchers seemed to have forgotten about the 1923 South African-German agreements, the World War II internment of German-speakers in South West Africa, and the contentious nature of the 1950 Namibian elections.[8]

Sadly, instead of bringing more equitable land redistributions, decisions made during mandate and apartheid periods created even more challenges for the Ovaherero and other indigenous communities. As noted in previous chapters, the Ovaherero and Nama communities, after waging war against the Germans between 1904 and 1908, had to watch as the Kaiser's military governors and civil servants took away what little land and cattle they possessed because of their "rebellion," and the segregationists who backed South African apartheid regimes showed an interest in backing white supremacist agendas.

During the interwar years, colonizers in Africa, influenced by eugenical talk of "race suicide," regeneration, or degeneration, asked public health officials, doctors, and others to keep a social scientific eye on the health of South West African populations and demographic changes.[9] There would be those who wrote about the "dying" Damara, Nama, or Ovaherero races, in much the same way other Africanists or public health officials or colonial administrators wrote about the "last" of the Tasmanians[10] or depopulation in the "Belgian Congo."[11] Yet, as George Steinmetz would note, German settler commentary on "Native policy" or the extermination of the rebels did not always reflect material realities. It was "unambiguously clear," argued Steinmetz, "that the Ovaherero were neither exterminated physically nor decimated culturally, even if their suffering was enormous and the changes in their cultural extensive."[12]

Critical indigenous studies scholars might quibble with Steinmetz's framing of these Ovaherero losses, but the point that he was trying to make was that the "dying race" colonial rhetorics were used in self-serving ways to legitimate the continued, and incremental, alienization of indigenous lands in West Africa. The Nama and the Ovaherero did not disappear, and they remembered the loss of their leaders and their loved ones in places like Ohamakari/Waterberg or Shark Island or the deserts in the West. On August 26, 1923, remnants of the once proud Ovaherero nation were granted permission by the Union of South Africa authorities to reassemble in Okahandja so that they could rebury chief Samuel Maherero. This ceremony, that was attended by some three thousand Ovaherero survivors and a hundred whites, would be remembered by many indigenous African communities as the beginning of the commemoration of "Herero Day" or "Red Flag Day," and these acts would come to symbolize anti-colonial heroism.

Perhaps realizing that the new South African rulers in Pretoria were not going to give their land back, indigenous groups like the Ovaherero or Nama ended up "squatting" on the edges of large white farms as they tried to survive and rebuilt their traditional herds of cattle. They were considered by the ruling white communities to be outcasts who were trying to survive on the peripheries of empire, and it would have been unthinkable to believe that they would have any say in South African governmental decision making.

No doubt the Ovaherero were not the only indigenous communities who suffered during these interwar years, but this did provide an example of what Judith Butler has called "precarious" living. As she noted in 2011, there are times when, because of "forced emigration or the redrawing of the boundaries of a nation-state" there were populations that were "living in conditions of unwilling adjacency" and were suffering.[13] Fences and barbed wire and police were used to enforce segregationist laws and boundaries in South West Africa, and reserves were used by the South African government in order to help maintain segregationist policies.

After the end of the 1904 war, some Ovaherero and Nama were deported, others worked in the mines of South Africa, and some became a part of a diaspora where those who traveled abroad to places like the British protectorate of Bechuanaland.

German-speaking communities living in South West Africa would express ambivalent feelings about the sudden influx of Britons and Afrikaners during the war years, because they could see that these new residents were now coming to compete for land rights, cattle, and other scarce resources. In theory, compromises had to be made among whites who still lived among black majorities. White hegemonic rule depended on the maintenance of racial and ethnic hierarchies.

These aphasiastic problems would grow over the years, and as I explain in more detail below, some of those who lived in South West Africa later heard calls for the internment of the German "enemy" during World War II, and heated disputes over the morality and legality of apartheid regimes led to South Africa's later refusal to turn over its mandate to the United Nations.[14] Some postcolonial critics or Third World Approaches to International Law researchers (TWAIL), convinced of the longitudinal nature of structuralist colonial or imperial legacies, might go so far as to argue that German colonial abusive behavior and apartheid misrule had something to do with the difficulties that Namibians felt when they had to watch as other Africans experienced "decolonization" decades before Namibian independence in 1990.

Many of those who crafted these generational mnemoscapes did not totally forget about what happened during the 1904 to 1908 years, and those who suffered from bouts of colonial aphasia had a difficult time deciding how to frame those remembrances.

With this in mind, the first major subsection of this book reviews what was happening in Germany after the colonies were "taken" from the Germans at Versailles. In the second portion of the chapter, I provide readers with a critical genealogical analysis of how Nazi rhetorics became entangled with some of the imperial and mandate rhetorics that were produced after the Union of South Africa took over GSWA. There I explain how white communities in South West Africa who mentioned "reparations" talked about their own rights and the duties of "natives" who were still living in South West Africa. This portion of the chapter also explains how the "South westers" contributed to all of this aphasia by crafting their own "revisionist" histories and public memories. They used word and deed to underscore the point that the German-speaking communities who "owned" large tracts of land in South West Africa were not leaving.

The third portion of the chapter provides a synchronic look at how audiences in Europe and in South West Africa reacted to the reparations efforts of Reverend Michael Scott. Ovaherero activists who joined Scott were some of the social agents who used the work of Reverend Michael Scott after World War II to critique repressive apartheid laws.

The fourth subsection of this chapter explains why some of these African activists, during the apartheid years, started to pay attention to the rhetorical strategies that were used by those who demanded that West Germany pay reparations to Israelis and to Jewish survivors of the Holocaust. This part of the chapter helps readers see how Cold War politics and South West African realities influenced the constitutive formation of discursive and ideological constructs that linked atrocious colonial behavior to the Holocaust.

The fifth, and concluding subsection explains how those who suffered from colonial aphasias dealt with calls for twenty-first-century reparations, a topic that will discussed in greater detail in later chapters.

THE INTERWAR YEARS, NAZI REMEMBRANCES OF "LOST" OVERSEAS COLONIES AND IMPERIAL FANTASIES ABOUT "THE EAST"

Many readers may already be familiar with some the racial rhetorics that were produced by the Nazis that contributed to acceptance of euthanasia programs, but interdisciplinary scholars are still working at unpacking some of the other rhetorical dimensions of Nazi military operations like Barbarossa, the pervasive anti-Semitism that led to the Holocaust, and the nexus that existed between colonial desires and German policies. As George Steinmetz would point out, oftentimes those who wrote and talked about German expansionism or the annihilation of troublesome indigenous foes oftentimes produced statements that reflected the "wishful fantasies" (*Wunschfantasien*) of some colonizers.[15] These fantasies could be used to symbolically link the expansionist efforts of those who wanted to "restore" Germany's overseas colonial empire as well as those who thought it would be more prudent to focus on expansionism in Eastern Europe or Russia or other regions that served as homes for ethnic Germans.

During the interwar years, a key ideograph in these multifaceted transcontinental debates would be the evocative term "*Kolonialschuldluge*" or "colonial guilt lie" that I mentioned in chapter 4.[16] This ideograph would be one of the discursive fragments—what Michel Foucault called "elements"—that would help make up what Sara Friedrichsmeyer, Sara Lennox, and Suzanne Zantop called the German "imperialist imagination."[17]

When those at Versailles were encouraged to read that infamous 1918 British Blue Book, written in part by Major O'Reilly, the German Colonial Office did more than just complain about the "lies" found in this text. In 1919 those who worked in that office collected legal, ethical, and political evidence of their own about the colonial transgressions of rival imperial activities, and they published what would be called the German "White Book." One portion of this German manuscript set the tone for readers of the White Book by asking this key question: "Is England of all nations called upon to sit in judgment upon questions affecting the treatment of native populations?"[18]

Germans working in the Colonial Office must have realized that the 1918 Blue Book had been written in a legalistic style that was meant to make the "case" against continued German control of their overseas colonies, and the White Book was published in order to rebut these claims and explain the German Colonial Office's positions on these subjects.

It was no coincidence that the horrors of the British concentration camps during the Boer War were a major topic that would be covered in the German White Book. The authors of this text noted that between June of 1901 and May of 1902, some 115,000 Boer children, women, and men may have died in the camps and some estimated that twenty thousand Africans also died in this camps. This death toll, if accurate, would have represented about 10 percent of the total Boer population that was living during that period.[19] Using their own argumentative variant of the atrocity genres, the German authors of the White Book outlined, in graphic detail, the horrors that were experienced by the Boers and Africans who died in British concentration camps.

At the same time that the German colonial office circulated information about British concentration camps during the Boer War, there would be those writers during the interwar years who complained about the misrepresentations of the "good" Germany colonies. For more than a dozen years before Hitler took power, German lawyers, diplomats, scholars, film makers, book authors, and others worked to counter the suasory power of that "colonial guilt lie." For example, in a 1924 article in the *Süddeutsche Monatschefte*, Heinrich Schnee, the former governor of German East Africa, tried to write about why so many in Europe were smearing the good name of Germany.[20] As Willeke Sander notes,

> [The notion of the] "colonial guilt lie" . . . encapsulated [German] colonialists' antagonism to the Blue book and the larger context of opposition in which they operated. The term "lie" in particular indicates the sense of betrayal colonists felt and their resentment of what they saw as the conniving deceit (rather than humanitarian motivation) behind the Allies' actions. Similarly the concept of guilt suggested a burden of responsibility that colonialists refused to accept.[21]

This obstinate refusal to accept responsibility for colonial atrocities is a manifestation of that colonial aphasia that I referenced above.

In the same way that German-speaking farmers in South West Africa encouraged the burning of copies of the Blue Book, many Germans living in Europe used the grammatology of the "colonial guilt lie" to argue that Article 231 of the Treaty of Versailles was both ahistorical and unfair. In his 1926 Book, *German Colonization, Past and Future: The Truth about the German Colonies*, Heinrich Schnee argued that "there rests upon the German nation just the same necessity of refuting the ungenerous fiction of 'colonial guilt' as of repudiating the charge that it alone must bear responsibility for the late war."[22]

Many critical scholars often point out how material conditions impact the formation of colonial and imperial imaginaries, and in this particular case the Allied governments, after Versailles, sent troops to the Ruhr areas of Germany. These regions were some of the main centers of coal and iron output for a modern nation, and Allied occupation by French troops and others was intended to deter German rearmament. This type of occupation, however, also made it difficult, if not impossible, for the Germans living in the interwar years to pay all of the supposed "war reparations" that were owed to the Allies who suffered from "Prussian" aggression during the Great war. The February 10, 1923, issue of America's *The Literary Digest* contained an article titled "Germany's Triumph of Despair," that showed rows of French troops marching down German streets. The American author of this article explained that Germany's Weimar government had "failed to remit a portion of the 33 billion dollars it owed under its obligations agreed to at the Versailles Treaty."[23] All types of diplomatic, economic, and legal strategies were discussed for possible debt relief for those Germans who suffering from the ravages of hyperinflation.

Talk of "reparations" was thus in the air during the interwar years, but this was not viewed by most Europeans as having anything to do with Ovaherero or Nama suffering. This would not be the first, nor the last time, that German populations dealt with occupation, and few of those who produced these particular victimage tales publicly voiced any concern for Ovaherero, Nama, or other indigenous grievances.

Instead of producing the type of multidirectional memories that Professor Michael Rothberg was writing about—that would have allowed for comparative studies of the suffering of several communities, including those African "rebels" who died during the GSWA colonial wars[24] —what many Germans, or German speakers, produced during the interwar years were competitive memories that prioritized their own suffering.

The colonial-guilt-lie ideological formations resonated with German-speaking audiences on several continents who used these narrative frameworks to try and make sense of Weimar economic dislocation or treaty losses of colonial lands. This type of *dispositif* invited German readers to feel as though they had a responsibility to fight two related public lies—the lie that German settlers and soldiers had committed atrocities against the "natives" during the German South West Africa years, and the lie that German soldiers were solely responsible for the carnage of the Great War. They could treat some "atrocity" rhetorics in the same way that they treated the "propaganda" that Germans had abused Belgians during the Great War.

These would be some of the key rhetorical topics that would later reappear in countless Nazi texts that asked for the "return" of German lands that had been taken by those who did not care about racial preservation and the "vŏlk." Very different permutations of these argumentative clusters also resurfaced during disputes over German exceptionalism or comparative European colonial atrocities.

Countering the Allies' colonial guilt lie involved the rhetorical assemblage of many different pro-imperialist or pro-settler narratives. All sorts of fantastical revisionist memories about the productive farm life in the "taken" "German" colonies were produced by writers like Hans Grimm, whose novel *Völk ohne Raum* ("nation without space") (1926) was dedicated to the German colonial causes in Africa.[25] This would become a best-selling book that would become a "byword for expansion" into the European "East under the National Socialists."[26]

The anxieties that were produced by those who were obsessed with the mythic loss of African colonies were not the only interwar factors that contributed to the production of what Ann Stoler and others had called colonial "dissociation."[27] Millions of German militarists during World War I had had a chance to see a bountiful "East" when many of the Kaiser's divisions were sent to the Eastern Front to save Europe from the Russian "Asiatics." Just a few months before Major O'Reilly wrote his portion of the Blue Book the Russian Revolution led to the Bolsheviks' call for an armistice with Germany, as well as the signing of the Treaty of Brest-Litovsk. Under the terms of this treaty Russia handed over to Germany about a quarter of Russia's population, "almost 90 percent of her coal reserves and a third of her agricultural output."[28]

No wonder that when the Western Front collapsed so many Germans were in shock, and at a loss for words, when it was said the Kaiser's troops were the ones who were held responsible for starting World War I. Confident that they almost won the Great War the German armies on the Eastern Front looked for scapegoats for their misfortunes, and small libraries could be filled with the texts that they produced to counter a host of wartime and colonial "lies.'

When interwar generations in Europe argued about "reparations," they were thinking about the unfairness and shame that came *when Germans were not compensated* for their "lost" colonies. The loss of Eastern lands and overseas colonies was bad enough, but they also had to witness what was called the "Black Horror on the Rhine,"[29] where Senegalese and other African soldiers serving under French Army occupation forces were accused of perpetrated sexual war crimes against Germans between 1918 and 1930.

These competitive interwar German memories were produced by those who tethered together a variety of racialized, sexualized, and territorialized *epistemes*. The old British stories about the abuse of Africans in that politicized 1918 Blue Book were repudiated by those who refused to connect any of this to other rumors of "atrocities" committed in places like Louvain, Belgium.[30] No doubt the argumentative threads that were produced during these years became some of the rhetorical strands that woven into the tapestries of claims that would later be made by those advancing "*Sonderweg*" theses.

In the same way that the 1919 German White Book had been published to counter British Blue Book claims about "atrocities" committed against the Ovaherero and the Nama, now interwar German authors produced rows of books and countless articles on the dangers that Aryan populations faced under occupation by African "barbarians" serving the French. German writers—especially those who once served in places like German East Africa or German South West Africa—put pen to paper and wrote about how German women were being raped and were killed by the "mulatto." In one popular 1921 novel, *Die Schwarze Schmach: Der Roman des geschändefen Deutschlands* (The Black Shame: A Novel of Disgraced Germany) Guido Kruetzer portrayed Moroccan and Senegalese soldiers as rapists who violated thousands of innocent "Aryan" girls who had white skin, blue eyes, and blond hair. E. D. Morel, who once helped form the Congo Reform Association that revealed Léopold II's "red rubber" atrocities, now used all sorts of racist tropes to join those who complained about the "black horror on the Rhine."[31]

The discursive, structural template of the European colonial rescue metanarratives remained the same, but the content and the names of the victims and the perpetrators evolved to fit presentist circumstances. While some German lawyers and lay persons continued to demand compensation for lost German colonies after Versailles, other futuristic planners during the late 1920s and the early 1930s began arguing that German populations had already paid their dues and that they ought to be allowed to join the League of Nations. Some went to far as to argue that it was time for Germany to be provided with its fair share of "mandate" colonies.

A few popular German colonial organizations continued to recommend that German emigrants leave for South West Africa or Central Africa, but many Nazis viewed these as outdated ways of thinking about modern colonization. Instead of dwelling on overseas possessions many German race hygiene experts, eugenicists, ethnographers, and population planners during the late 1920s and 1930s joined the militarists who remembered the days when they had occupied Polish and Russian lands. These social agents came up with all sorts of imaginative German schemes that outlined how settlement communities that might serve as the future homes for aggrieved "ethnic Germans" and others in Prussia or Berlin who worried about the "polenization" with German emigrants who would travel East. Germanization efforts were supposed to counter Polish attempts at territorializing "German" lands.

After the Nazis came to power, the *Kolonialpolitisches Amt der NSDAP* (KPA) (Colonial Policy Office of the NSDAP) would be organized to help prepare legions of civil administrators, politicians, and social workers who would have to help with the supervision of new colonies in "the

East." Elaborate "colonial legal arguments about the right to colonial possessions"[32] were conjured up by German lawyers and jurists who wanted to join those who dreamed about regenerative, clean farms and urban communities that would be built hundreds or thousands of miles away from Berlin.

Some of the old "African hands" who had once fought with General Lothar von Trotha at Ohamakari/Waterberg were now expected to lend a guiding hand to the lawyers, geographers, population planners, race hygiene experts, German Red Cross workers, and others who might be traveling East to help with the new colonization. Professor Schmokel, would derisively write that it "may well be questioned whether at any time in history a non-existent empire had been so well administered!"[33]

As noted above, the Nazis and other Germans who lived during these interwar and World War II years didn't actually "forget" about the GSWA years as they dreamed of expansionism in the East. Instead, they reframed their remembrances of Eastern provinces in aphasiastic ways that allowed them to paint distorted pictures of some imaginary "blood and soil" activities that were used to produce a contiguous Third Reich that restored the glory of Germania.

Those who study Nazi racial science and this obsessive interest in the "East" often mention how the Nazi scientist, Eugen Fischer, would be one of the figures who appeared in the chronicles of both GSWA affairs as well as the rise of the Third Reich. Much has been made of the fact that Fischer once traveled to GSWA after the Ovaherero-Nama War so that he could study "mixed-race" African communities before he dug up indigenous human remains and brought them back to Germany. Other researchers focus on familial or organizational connections that can be made between individual families (the Görings) or the former *Schutztruppe* who later served with the Freikorps during the Weimar years. These relationships are then used by colonial genocide scholars or other researchers to advance arguments about a "continuity thesis" that exists between several different genocides (see chapters 8, 9, and 10).

Sadly, when the Nazis referenced the Ovaherero, Nama, or San communities in their interwar texts, they were usually bringing up these names of ethnic groups so that they could treat them as the foreign "others," the objects of study who helped evidence German or European or Aryan racial superiority. The ethnologists, anthropologists, eugenicists, and race hygiene scientists who worked with the Nazis to prove African inferiority were some of the last researchers who would use some of the skulls and human remains that were collected during and after the 1904–1908 Ovaherero/Nama–German War (see chapter 8).

These speculative racialized ideas were turned into praxiological studies of "applied eugenics," and legal restrictions were put in place to prohibit the "race-mixing" that allegedly polluted the purity of German blood. In 1933 the minister of justice for the Third Reich, Franz Gürtner, wondered how a law might be written that would effectively ban "mixed" marriages between Aryans and non-Aryans.[34] The passage of the infamous "Nuremberg laws" indicated that citizenship had everything to do with "German blood" and "German honor," and Jews who had different blood or "germplasm" were not supposed to have sexual relationships with "Aryans." Other studies focused on the race mixing that was taking place between German settlers overseas and indigenous communities.

Some of the language that appeared in the Nuremberg laws was copied directly from some of the older imperial laws that were once passed during colonial times when governors and other administrators banned intermarriage between Germans and Africans in German South West Africa in 1906. Similar regulations, with sanctions, had been introduced in "German" Togo and "German East Africa."[35]

The passage of formalistic legal restrictions that were supposed to help with the prevention of race mixing made sense to those who were reading colonial memoirs or travelogues that spread similar eugenical messages. Romance novels that were written about frontier life in German South West Africa before the loss of the overseas colonies were now read by Nazis and others who wanted to make sure that real Germans did not marry "coloured Germans" or "half castes" who might produce "woolly-haired grandchildren."[36] The heroes in many of these tales were the protagonists who managed to restrain themselves from cohabiting with allegedly inferior African women so that they could marry upstanding white women.

These horrific racist tales and other colonial figurations were recirculated and modified to suit the needs of Nazis who dreamed of modernizing and replacing lazy and inefficient Poles or Russians or Ukrainians with stalwart German farmers in the East. In place of "old" colonial models that prioritized the inclusion or assimilation of the Poles the Nazis came up with exclusionary plans that explained why hundreds of thousands of inferiors needed to be "resettled" in order to make room for superior Germans or "ethnic" Germans. Some Nazis made sure that the Reich Commission for Strengthening the Germandom (RKFDV) would have the power that was needed during World War II to effectively "resettle" Poles and others who did not belong to the *Völk*.[37]

Although wartime exigencies meant that Heinrich Himmler and other Nazi planners could not carry out all of their schemes, "the colonization of the eastern frontier" was supposed to involve the use of a process that was said to be similar to the colonization of the North American heartland by German immigrant farmers in the nineteenth century. Following the lead of Americans who ruthlessly put down indigenous Native American resistance was supposed to result in the "salvation of the German *Völk's* endangered peasantry."[38]

After the end of World War II, German populations who suffered from Stalinist invasions or Allied reoccupation remembered the bombings of Dresden or the abuse of German prisoners of war as they produced their own victimage tales. Those who had to listen to Allied talk of German rehabilitation or the benefits of the Nuremberg trials could produce their own counternarratives.

This leads into a discussion of the impact that the Cold War years or decolonization periods had on the production of German victimage tales. As Jürgen Zimmerer would note, the "early loss of its colonial empire spared Germany the post–World War II frictions that decolonization imposed on other countries such as Great Britain, France, the Netherlands or Portugal, and both the public and the scholarly community forgot about the very existence of a German colonial empire."[39]

I would of course prefer to call this another example of colonial aphasia, where many Germans didn't necessarily forget about their colonizing years, but had a difficult time trying to master several different fraught pasts. Their own personal losses and wartime traumas did indeed make it difficult for them to talk about these issues in the same ways that Allied audiences framed these rhetorical situations.

After the perpetration of the Holocaust, and after the recording of the loss of more than 55 million lives during World War II, it would have been extremely difficult for Ovaherero or Nama activists to petition German courts or international forums for compensation for what took place during and after the Battle of Ohamakari/Waterberg. Situational factors play a huge role in determining how individuals and societies cope with "colonial unknowing."

No doubt many scholars are right when they claim that the carrying out of the Great War and World War II oftentimes overshadowed the older "small wars" or savage wars of peace. David Olusoga and Casper W. Erichsen explained some of this in *The Kaiser's Holocaust* (2010), where they noted,

> During World War II, both German scholars and members of the Nazi elite came to recognize that the war in the East, and the regime's murderous treatment of its racial enemies, were redolent of the bloodier episodes in colonial history. Yet during the Nuremberg Trials in 1946 and 1947, the International Military Tribunal and the governments it represented avoided making similar connections. The memory of the German genocides committed in South-West Africa, so important at Versailles in 1919, were overlooked at Nuremberg a generation later. This is partly explained by colonial amnesia[;] . . . victorious and liberated powers of Europe had more immediate reasons for wanting to close their eyes to the darker aspects of colonial history.[40]

However, as noted above, this did not mean that German communities totally avoided the topics of victimage status or reparations. They simply redefined those terms so that they could focus on their own victimage.

In this next subsection I want to shift readers' attention so that they can see what was happening in South West Africa during these same years so that they can get a comparative, synchronic perspective on these issues.

THE FORMATION OF SOUTH WEST AFRICAN NATIONAL IDENTITIES AND THE MISRECOGNITION OF TRAUMATIZED OVAHERERO AND NAMA PASTS, 1915–1945

Throughout the interwar years, the focus of attention of many German-speaking locals in South West Africa was on maintaining positive relationships with the South African administrators and the new Afrikaner settlers who were sent from Pretoria. During one of his 1920s visits to South West Africa, Prime Minister Smuts assured German-speaking delegates that "there will be no further reference to the Blue Book on South West Africa."[41]

Those who traveled to this region from South Africa were asked to put up a united front and stop quarreling about land rights so that both the German-speaking farmers and the Afrikaners could help with the regeneration of a unified white South Africa. The Ovaherero and Nama "who died in the genocide were dismissed and forgotten in the interests of white settler cooperation."[42]

During the 1920s, 1930s, and early 1940s, both the descendants of the German settlers and those who emigrated from places like Cape Town worked together to build an apartheid state, and for years talk of establishing racial harmony depended on the establishment of a thick *dispositif* that could be used to rationalize the segregation of neighborhoods and entire populations. "For a number of years after 1926," argued Jan-Bart Gewald, "nothing was heard of the Herero genocide" in dominant European diplomatic circles.[43]

Elderly Ovaherero and Nama survivors had to find ways of coping with these dissociative discursive practices. They wanted to preserve the memories of the sacrifices of warriors like Samuel Maherero, but they did not want to make waves, and they stayed out of South West African governmental politics. They withdrew to assigned native "reserves," while frustrated members of younger generations of Ovaherero or Nama tried to use human rights talk at the time that they critiqued discriminatory Afrikaner practices. Oftentimes it would be members of younger generations who publicly complained about the monuments that had been put up to commemorate the sacrifices of the *Schutztruppe* and the German marines who died between 1904 and 1908.

During the 1920s and 1930s, demographic and migration reports became the topic of conversation as thousands of German speakers found themselves surrounded by tens of thousands of white immigrants who came into the country. Christo Botha argues that some German speakers who decided to stay in the GSWA after 1915 seemed to feel as if they were an "oppressed minority" who were suffering from a type of "internal colonization."[44] Yet those Germans who chose to stay prospered; and they, and their descendants, consolidated their farmlands, while impoverished Ovaherero and Nama survivors were often treated as "vagrants" by South African police.

Once again that pesky Blue Book became entangled in disputation over property, personal rights, and power relationships. As Botha explains,

> The political future of South West Africa was decisively shaped in the years between 1915 and 1920. Immigration of Afrikaner trekboers from the northern Cape region in South Africa were permitted, thereby laying the foundation of an eventually numerically dominant element in the white community. Apart from publication of the Blue Book, the South African military administration also launched a "hearts and minds" campaign to discredit Germans among the local African population and portray themselves as essentially benign overlords.[45]

German speakers in South West Africa—who were already familiar with talk about the Versailles "lies"—were now adding new layers of victimage commentaries that helped to explain what Brigette Lau meant by "internal colonization."[46] Those who once fought the Ovaherero, the Nama, and the British during World War I faced new psychological and social challenges when they were maligned by Afrikaner immigrants.

In order to try and placate some of these German speakers, those in Pretoria used a new "accommodationist approach," whereby the London Agreement of 1923 was passed to provide citizenship to those who wanted to continue living in South West Africa. Most Germans accepted this citizenship offer, but they were not pleased when the South African Unionists turned around and started to implement "a land resettlement program" that was supposed to help with the relocation of Anglo-Boers in 1928.[47]

All of this was used to help with the production of colonial victimage narratives where South Africans were "subjugating" German-speaking communities who were said to be treated as "second class" citizens in South West Africa.

Granted, compared with the Ovambo or the Ovaherero or the Nama living conditions, German speakers in South West Africa were fairly privileged, but perceptions mattered. By 1936 census records showed that some 9,634 Germans were living alongside 18,088 Afrikaners.[48]

Young German speakers, who sympathized with the rise of the National Socialists in Germany, now resented the support the Afrikaners in South West Africa were getting from Unionists in Pretoria. Afrikaners—in spite of their power at the ballot box—were still viewed as "trekboers," with "all of the negative connotations associated with the term, such as cultural backwardness, and Afrikaans was perceived as an inferior language (*kitchen-Dutch*)."[49] All sorts of class hierarchies and ethnic perceptions shaped the contours of South West Africa politics and grammars. Post-structuralists who viewed these affairs would invite us to see how many different ethnic communities could configure themselves as disempowered and aggrieved communities who needed legal or moral redress.

To complicate matters, the "growth of a rampant ethnic chauvinism in German ranks was paralleled by a similar movement among Afrikaners, which drew to some extent on German ideological resources."[50] When pressed, the Afrikaners could always claim that German's poor treatment of the "Natives" had everything to do with the League of Nations "C" mandate status of this region. Afrikaners could argue that German speakers had nothing to complain about, given that the League of Nations had been in charge of the mandate allocations. Those who carried about pointing out the contradictions of apartheid states could note that German speakers were provided with opportunities that were not afforded people of color.

By the time World War II arrived, the German speakers living in South West Africa seemed to be faced with some major choices—they could either accept dominance by the Afrikaners and embrace the notion that they were in living in the "Southwest" or they could continue to feel they were a part of the German "Heimat."[51] These choices would influence how some whites talked and wrote about the legality of land settlements, reparations, anti-British sentiments, Afrikaners, and indigenous populations.

APARTHEID, THE GLOBAL RECEPTION OF THE WORK OF REVEREND MICHAEL SCOTT, AND THE REVIVAL OF INTEREST IN CALLS FOR OVAHERERO REPARATIONS

After World War II, members of the South African government realized that the newly formed United Nations might have members who might try to dismantle and critique their apartheid regime, so they tried to preempt these moves by arguing for the incorporation of Namibia as the "fifth province" in the Union of South Africa. Before the formation of the United Nations (UN), it had been the responsibility of the League of Nations to supervise the mandate system that led to the empowerment of the Union of South Africa, and now those responsibilities were transferred over to the UN.

Occasionally one heard the dissenting voices of those who refused to accept the normality or the legitimacy of South Africa's apartheid state, and there would be those who kept alive the idea of Ovaherero and Nama restitution. For example, Reverend Michael Scott, between 1947 and 1952, was an enigmatic figure who would eventually become *persona non grata* in South Africa for his parrhesiastic advocacy.

As Michel Foucault once argued, the "parrhesiastes" is someone who takes risks, and is willing to speak truth-to-power in the name of some transcendent moral cause.[52] Reverend Michael Scott, who had witnessed Mahatma Gandhi's work, had already worked as an activist who called attention to the horrid living conditions in Bethel, one of Johannesburg's "native locations," and after moving to Ovaherero regions in South West Africa, he worked for the cause of Namibian independence.[53] Scott, along with African survivor informants, "used the atrocities perpetuated in the Herero genocide as a weapon at the United Nations against the incorporation of Namibia into South Africa."[54]

The vast majority of scholars who write about the Ovaherero and Nama reparations movement have forgotten about, or have inadvertently marginalized, the efforts of the supporters of activists like Reverend Michael Scott, who would become an iconic figure in Ovaherero folklore. For more than a year Scott camped out near Windhoek, and Ovaherero storytellers would chronicle how he met regularly with Ovaherero residents who told him tragic stories about the horrors of German rule. It was said that he listened attentively to what they had to say about the dispossession of their land, the various types of banishments, and the herding of more and more indigenous communities onto "reserves." As Scott talked to these informants, he learned about how the best grazing lands were now in the hands of empowered whites who patrolled their property. In an essay that was published in Britain's *The New Statesman and Society*, a journalist in 1949 tried to summarize Scott's interpretative framing of affairs:

> Then came the German colonists, hungry for land; and finally, von Trotha, a general whom Hitler would have delighted to honor. . . . In 1904 he issued the "Extermination Order." All Hereros [,] whether man, woman or child, were to be killed. An orgy of looting, torture, and massacre followed. To read the records is exactly like reading the accounts of the obliteration of Poland, except that the Germans had no gas chambers then, but killed babies with their own hands, or burned sick old women in their huts. The tribe broke and fled. . . . The majority, all but fifteen thousand out of ninety thousand, were hacked to pieces by the Germans or died of thirst.[55]

This type of multidirectional discourse, coming from Reverend Scott, infuriated many of the leaders in South Africa who prevented him from returning to South West Africa. He had dared compare the Ovaherero and Nama genocide with the World War II Holocaust.

This response from apartheid officials seemed to have everything to do with the way that Reverend Michael Scott was received in some European circles, and those who listened to him, and quoted him, were co-producing counterhistories that ruptured conventional Afrikaner ways of explaining land dispossession.

However, it would not only be the Afrikaners who would be blamed for misrepresenting colonial treatment of indigenous African communities. In Scott's rending of affairs, after the Great War the Ovaherero had been "lured by British promises" that "Native lands would be returned" if they came back.[56] When the Ovaherero returned, instead of having to deal with the British "mandatory power," they had to deal with the South Africans, who "never for a moment considered giving back their tribal lands. Some pastures were left to the German settlers who remained. More went to the Afrikaner settlers."[57]

From a critical genealogical vantage point, this 1949 journalistic fragment served several rhetorical functions. First of all, it provided an early example of what would later be called the "continuity thesis," where the horrors of von Trotha's "annihilationist order" would be treated as precursors for Nazi colonial settlement plans in "The East," that involved the destruction of the Polish nation-state. *The New Statesman and Society*'s summary of Michael Scott's claims, linking African and Polish struggles, also provides an excellent example of the "multidirectional" types of arguments that Professor Michael Rothberg alluded do. This outlet was using this analogy in a way that reminded us of both the horrors of the Nazi death camps as well as the GSWA concentration camps.

Second, the 1949 passage that was paraphrasing Michael Scott clearly inverts the traditional colonial stories that were told about the beginning of the 1904 "rebellion," and instead of blaming vengeful Ovaherero for the uprising, it is the German colonists who are said to have started the war.[58] This anticipated some of the "revisionist" arguments about the start of the Ovaherero rebellion that emerge during the 1990s when Jan-Bart Gewald and others wrote about the social agency of panicking German soldiers and settlers.

Third, the 1949 use of specific numbers of Ovaherero dead—the figure of fifteen thousand out of ninety thousand—echoed the claims that were once made by Social Democrats in the Reichstag (see chapter 3) as well as the claims made by Major O'Reilly in the 1918 British Blue Book (chapter 4). This provided yet another example of those parchment papers that Michel Foucault indicated were scrawled over time and time again.

Post–World War II representations of Michael Scott's parrhesiastic practices thus added new rhetorical layers to the dense "public" or "elite" archives that I mentioned in chapter 1. During some very difficult times for impoverished Ovaherero and Nama communities the episodic journalistic coverage of arguments like Scott's provided some hope, some evidence, that not everyone ignored indigenous framings of what happened after the battle of Ohamakari/Waterberg.

REMEMBERING THE 1952 REPARATIONS AGREEMENT BETWEEN ISRAEL AND THE FEDERAL REPUBLIC OF GERMANY

When the members of the Ovaherero and Nama reparations movement wrote and talked about their rights, their need for reparations, and the existence of legal precedents for restitution, it was no coincidence that they often referenced the payments that were made following World War II to Jewish victims of the Shoah.[59] In September of 1952, Israel and the Federal Republic of Germany signed the Reparations Agreement, and it entered into force the following March.

It would not be a foregone conclusion that this 1952 reparations agreement would be signed by all the parties, and a great deal of advocacy had to take place on several continents before this agreement would eventually be concluded. German Chancellor Konrad Adenauer of West Germany addressed the German parliament in 1951 and referenced the "unspeakable crimes" that "have been committed in the name of the German people, calling for moral and material indemnity." He went on to say that the "German Government" was prepared, "jointly with representatives of Jewry and the State of Israel," to "bring about a solution to the material indemnity problem, thus easing the way to the spiritual settlement of infinite suffering."[60]

After this Nahum Goldmann of the Jewish Agency for Israel, and president of the World Jewish Congress, assembled together almost two dozen Jewish national and international organizations whose representatives put together what would be called the Conference on Jewish Material Claims Against Germany.[61] Thus began the process of negotiation that would eventually lead to the signing of the Reparations Agreement in 1952.

The reparations agreement that was signed between Israel and West Germany would provide the archetypal materials that would be emulated by countless other communities seeking reparations over the next six decades. Ryan Michael Spitzer, writing in the *Vanderbilt Journal of Transnational Law* in 2002, noted how Germany "voluntarily agree to compensate the survivors of the Holocaust under the leadership of Chancellor Konrad Adenauer, who believed that the German people owed a moral duty to compensate the Jewish people for their material losses and suffering."[62] Six years later Jeremy Sarkin and Carly Fowler observed that no "legislation existed during the time of the Holocaust that would give genocide victims the right to reparations, yet Germany paid reparations anyway."[63]

Sarkin and Fowler used this argument as a not-so-veiled way of indicating that perhaps it was time to stop using lack of formalistic precedents as an excuse not to take seriously Ovaherero reparations claims. Why weren't colonial genocide grievances treated in the same ways that courts were treating Holocaust litigation?

This, however, is an important retrospective analysis that may not have been available to the Ovaherero and Nama communities who were living in an apartheid state during the 1940s, 1950s, and 1960s. The Namibians had their oral histories of what happened at Ohamakari/Waterberg, and they did form organizations like the South Western African National Union (SWANU)[64] so that they could keep alive talk of land rights.[65] However, where were those social movements or receptive audiences who were willing to push for African reparations for colonial wrongdoing during these years?

As the Ovaherero communities watched the negotiations that took place between West Germans, Israelis, and private parties over reparations they had to strategize about the best ways of presenting their own case during the turbulent apartheid years. In order to try and prevent the formation of any anti-colonial political campaigns the South African authorities clamped down on existing nationalistic political organizations in Namibia, and this in turn hindered the building up of reparations movements.

For many living in South West Africa, reparations talk was merely aspirational, because indigenous communities faced a situation where larger and larger populations were expected to live on less and less land that was set aside by the apartheid government. The complexities of the situation created yet another example of how the lingering effects of colonial aphasia could be felt by those who searched for a language that could explain their predicament.

It seems as though younger and older communities of Ovaherero disagreed about how to react to the passage of South African legislation like the Apartheid Group Areas Act. Jan-Bart Gewald notes that during this period some Ovaherero pursued a policy of "appeasement," where they "sought to play down the ideas of conflict and tension engendered through the remembrance and commemoration of the Herero genocide."[66] These leaders talked about these policies with members of the German-speaking communities in SWA as well.

Those Ovaherero leaders who pursued these appeasement policies crafted rhetorics that would look nothing like the discourses that circulated in Ovaherero and Nama legal complaints in 2001 and 2017. For example, in August of 1964 the *Windhoek Advertiser* contained this commentary from Herero chief Hosea Kutako:

> We do not want to cling to the past or to have old war grudges. Our aim is to forget the past and to look forward rather than backward and

> to have good relations with all sections of the populations, but good relations cannot exist if some people try to remind us of the bad past.[67]

Obviously not all Ovaherero spoke in monolithic ways, and this type of grammatology seemed to echo the arguments that were produced by the German-speaking victors after the Battle of Ohamakari. This way of talking and writing about forgetting "the past" also sounded very much like German diplomatic responses to calls for reparations that were circulating between 1998 and 2019.

Many elderly Ovaherero were thankful that some German speakers were willing to mention the loss of indigenous dead during commemorations of the Ovaherero/Nama–German War, but some of the younger speakers refused to forget the genocidal nature of some of this violence. Clemens Kapuuo, who would eventually succeed Chief Hosea Kutako, managed in one short fragment to produce arguments that look very familiar to those who are acquainted with the debates about the "continuity thesis" and a "*Sonderweg*":

> To our minds, there is little difference between the extermination order of General von Trotha and the extermination of Jews by Adolph Hitler. The members of the *Alte Kamaraden* [Old Comrades] are today a free people whereas the Hereros are not and are under a foreign Government which was elected partly by members of the *Alte Kameraden*. It is natural that the Hereros would be opposed to the celebration of a battle [Waterberg] which placed them under foreign domination up to this day.[68]

Clemens Kapuuo was advancing a permutation of a claim that would reappear in many future constellations of symbolic meanings.

CONCLUSION

It may be an open question whether colonial aphasia can be remedied by mastering of difficult pasts, but what this chapter has shown is that far from always "forgetting" about the 1904–1904 Ovaherero/Nama–German war some were trying to find the grammars that would allow them to articulate their positions in strategic ways. The German-speaking communities who had to cope with the arrival of the Afrikaners could form alliances with those who might try and ban that infamous Blue-Book, but in Germany those who worried about the "colonial guilt lie" had their own victimage tales to tell.[69]

The Nazis who studied the Ovaherero and the Nama did so in the name of "race hygiene," the prevention of "race-mixing," and the resettlement in the "East." Any overseas failures that were experienced by the "old Africans" could be disassociated from the more modern successes of expansionist planners like Heinrich Himmler.

That said, the type of analogies that Clemens Kapuuo made between the GSWA genocide and the Holocaust would reappear in scholarly garb as those interested in colonial genocide studies tried to extend the work of Holocaust scholars. Some researchers went so far as to argue that the decolonization of legal remembrances of some genocidal acts might improve international law practices. Felix Lange had to say this about how international and colonial laws were configured by those who looked back on those Nazi years:

> Despite this new interest in international law's colonial past, that link between colonialism and international legal argumentation has attracted little attention. . . . When international lawyers have engaged with Germany's colonial history, they have addressed the question of reparations for the Herero genocide in Germany. South-West Africa. . . . [Germany's colonial] discourse, an important discourse for understanding international legal argumentation . . . is . . . overlooked . . . Even though Hitler's government never successfully gained colonies overseas, it developed far reaching plans for a German-controlled Central African Empire. . . . Some historians today argue that Hitler's *Lebensraum* policy in Eastern Europe was nothing other than colonialism on the European continent.[70]

Lange was alluding to permutations of that "continuity thesis" that I critique in other chapters of this book. He was also suggesting that some researchers were convinced that perhaps the Holocaust could be configured as another colonial genocide.

If we broadened our lens to take into account other facets of German colonial discourse and international legal debates, then we would pay attention to how social agents like Reverend Scott were imploring the UN to acknowledge the Oveherero and Nama genocide. We would pay attention to the ideological nature of some of these cold war multidirectional and competitive memory formations.

The rise of what would be called "critical genocide studies" after 1990 meant that Holocaust scholars were now joined by Namibian experts and others who wanted to debate about the presence or absence of "evidence" that showed symbolic or material links between German colonialization in GSWA and East Africa and the rise of the Nazis. As I will explain in later chapters the academic phrase "Windhoek to Auschwitz" started to appear in academic books and law review articles on Herero reparations cases.[71]

These efforts would help the lawyers who searched for historical and legal materials that would show that the Ovaherero and Nama indigenous communities never relinquished their sovereign rights, but critical genealogists should not forget the colonial aphasia that afflicted many of the empowered Afrikaners and the German speakers during the interwar and apartheid years.

NOTES

1. See, for example, the work of Professor Tilman Dedering and Reinhart Kössler that I cite in many chapters of this book. For another example note the work of Henning Melber, "How to Come to Terms with the Past: Revisiting the German Colonial Genocide in Namibia," *Africa Spectrum* 40, no. 1 (2005): 139–48.

2. Guido G. Weigend, "German Settlement Patterns in Namibia," *Geographical Review* 75, no. 2 (1985): 156–69, 161.

3. Ibid., 163.

4. Ibid., 163, 168

5. Ibid., 161.

6. Ibid., 164.

7. Critiques of contemporary usages of "savage wars of peace" rhetorics can be found in Thomas Donnelly, "The Past as Prologue," *Foreign Affairs* 81, no. 4 (July/August 2002): 165–70.

8. Richard Dale, "Reconfiguring White Ethnic Power in Colonial Africa: The German Community in Namibia, 1923–50," *Nationalism & Ethnic Politics* 7, no. 2 (Summer, 2001): 75–94.

9. Marion Wallace, "'Making Tradition': Healing History and Ethnic Identity among Otjiherero-Speakers in Namibia, c. 1850–1950," *Journal of South African Studies* 29, no. 2 (June 2003): 355–72.

10. For a journalistic overview of debates about the "last" of the Tasmanians and the debates over Aboriginal identity see Richard Flanagan, "The Lost Tribe," *The Guardian*, last modified October 13, 2002, https://www.theguardian.com/world/2002/oct/14/australia.features11.

11. A. Wauters, "Belgian Policy in the Congo," *Journal of the Royal Institute of International Affairs* 9, no. 1 (January 1930): 51–62.

12. George Steinmetz, "From 'Native Policy' to Exterminationism: German Southwest Africa, 1904, in comparative Perspective," *University of Michigan's Theory and Research in Comparative Social Analysis*, 4–5, Los Angeles: University of California, 2005, https://escholarship.org/uc/item/11z1k021.

13. Judith Butler, "Precarious Life and the Obligations of Cohabitation," *Nobel Museum, Stockholm*, May 2011, 1, https://www.terada.ca/discourse/wp-content/uploads/2012/06/Butler_Sweden2011.pdf.

14. In 1940, after South Africa officially entered World War II, most ethnic German males living in this part of Africa were placed in internment camps near Kimberley, South Africa. Those between the ages of twenty and sixty had their property temporary placed under the authority of a Custodian for Enemy Property regulation. Weigend, "German Settlement Patterns," 164.

15. Steinmetz, "From 'Native Policy,'" 4.

16. For a helpful discussion of how the "colonial guilt lie" impacted German-Herero relationships, see Britta Schilling, *Postcolonial Germany: Memories of Empire in a Decolonized Nation* (New York: Oxford University Press, 2014).

17. Sara Friedrichsmeyer, Sara Lennox, and Suzanne Zantop, *The Imperialist Imagination: German Colonialism and Its Legacy* (Ann Arbor: University of Michigan Press, 1998).

18. Willeke Sandler, *Empire in the Heimat: Colonialism and Public Culture in the Third Reich* (New York: Oxford University Press, 2018), 26.

19. Paul Harris, "'Spin' On Boer Atrocities," *The Guardian*, last modified December 8, 2001, paragraph 6, https://www.theguardian.com/world/2001/dec/09/paulharris.theobserver. For more on the Boer camps see Elizabeth Van Heyningen, "The South African War as Humanitarian Crisis," *International Review of the Red Cross* 97 (2015): 999–1028.

20. Heinrich Schnee, *German Colonization, Past and Future: The Truth about the German Colonies* (New York: Knopf, 1926). For some overviews of the arguments of Heinrich Schnee see Daniel Steinbach, "Schnee, Heinrich," *1914–1918 Online: The Interna-*

tional Encyclopedia of the First World War, last modified April 13, 2016, https://encyclopedia.1914-1918-online.net/article/schnee_heinrich.

21. Sandler, *Empire in the Heimat*, 26.

22. Heinrich Schnee, quoted in Sandler, *Empire in the Heimat*, 26.

23. *The Literary Digest* Staff, "Germany's "Triumph of Despair," *The Literary Digest*, February 10, 1923, 1–4, http://www.oldmagazinearticles.com/Ruhr-Valley_French_Occupation-pdf. See also *Time* Staff, "Germany: Arithmetic," *Time* 1, no. 1 (March 3, 1923).

24. Michael Rothberg, *Multidirectional Memory: Remembering the Holocaust in the Age of Decolonization* (Stanford: Stanford University Press, 2009).

25. Hans Grimm, *Volk ohne Raum* (Munich: Albert Langen, 1926).

26. Felix Lange, "The Dream of a Völkish Colonial Empire: International Law and Colonial Law during the National Socialist Era," *London Review of International Law* 5, no. 3 (November 2017): 343–69, 348.

27. For more detailed accounts of Ann Stoler's position on colonial aphasia see Ann Stoler, *Duress: Imperial Durabilities in Our Times* (Durham: Duke University Press, 2016).

28. David Olusoga and Casper W. Erichsen, *The Kaiser's Holocaust* (London: Farber & Faber, 2010), 265.

29. See Letter to the Editor, "The Horror On the Rhine," *The Spectator*, October 2, 1920, 12; Keith L. Nelson, "The 'Black Horror on the Rhine': Race as a Factor in Post–World War I Diplomacy," *The Journal of Modern History* 42, no. 4 (December 1970): 606–27. For an excellent recent analysis of these affairs see Iris Wigger, *The "Black Horror on the Rhine": Intersections of Race, Nation, Gender and Class in the 1920* (London: Macmillan, 2017).

30. See Bruno Waterfield, "The City That Turned Germans into 'Huns" Marks 100 Years Since It Was Set Ablaze," *The Guardian*, last modified August 25, 2014, https://www.telegraph.co.uk/news/worldnews/europe/belgium/11053962/The-city-that-turned-Germans-into-Huns-marks-100-years-since-it-was-set-ablaze.html.

31. See Robert Reinders, "Racism on the Left: E. D. Morel and the "Black Horror on the Rhine," *International Review of Social History* 13 (1968): 1–28.

32. Lange, "The Dream of a Völkisch," 345.

33. Wolfe W. Schmokel, *Dream of Empire, German Colonialism, 1919–1945* (New Haven: Yale University Press, 1964), 160.

34. Olusoga and Erichsen, *The Kaiser's Holocaust*, 302.

35. Ibid.

36. Matthew P. Fitzpatrick, "The Threat of 'Woolly-Haired Grandchildren': Race, the Colonial Family and German Nationalism," *The History of the Family* 14, no. 4 (2009): 356–68.

37. See Robert L. Koehl, *RKFDV: German Resettlement and Population Policy, 1939–1945* (Cambridge: Harvard University Press, 1957).

38. Alan E. Steinweis, "East Europe and the Notion of the 'Frontier,' in Germany to 1945," *Yearbook of European Studies* 13 (1999): 56–69, 64.

39. Jürgen Zimmerer, "Colonial Genocide: The Herero and Nama War (1904–8) in German South West Africa and Its Significance," in *The Historiography of Genocide*, edited by Dan Stone (London: Palgrave Macmillan, 2008), 323–43, 329

40. Olusoga and Erichsen, *The Kaiser's Holocaust*, 344.

41. Dale, "Reconfiguring White Ethnic Power."

42. Gewald, "Herero Genocide in the Twentieth Century: Politics and Memory," in *Rethinking Resistance: Revolt and Violence in African History*, edited by Jon Abbink, Mirjam de Bruijn, and Klaas van Waraven (Boston: Brill, 2003), 279–304, 289.

43. Ibid.

44. Christo Botha, "Internal Colonization and an Oppressed Minority? The Dynamics of relations Between Germans and Afrikaners against the Background of Constructing a Colonial State in Namibia, 1884–1990," *Journal of Namibian Studies* 2 (2007): 7–50.

45. Ibid., 15.
46. Ibid., 15–17.
47. Ibid., 17.
48. Ibid., 19.
49. Ibid.
50. Ibid., 20.
51. Ibid., 20.
52. On Michel Foucault's discussion of *parrhesia* and risk taking, see Maria Tamboukou, "Truth Telling in Foucault and Arendt: *Parrhesia,* the Pariah and Academics in Dark Times," *Journal of Education Policy* 21, no. 6 (2012): 1–17.
53. For a well-known discussion of Michael Scott's advocacy, see Freda Troup, *In Face of Fear: Michael Scott's Challenge to South Africa* (London: Faber & Faber, 1950).
54. Gewald, "Herero Genocide," 290–91.
55. *The New Statesman and Nation* staff, "Michael Scott and the Hereros," *The New Statesman and Nation*, March 5, 1949, cited in Gewald, "Herero Genocide."
56. Gewald, "Herero Genocide," 292.
57. Ibid.
58. The notion that the Germans may have started the war is one of the key claims that would be advanced by Jan-Bart Gewald's revisionist essays. Before this Henning Melber made similar arguments about German hysterical overreactions to indigenous group movements.
59. See, for example, Andrew Connelly, "Africans Take Germany to Court in New York over 'Forgotten genocide,'" *USA Today*, last modified July 31, 2018, https://www.usatoday.com/story/news/world/2018/07/31/africans-take-germany-court-new-york-over-forgotten-genocide/877191002/.
60. See Susan Slyomovics, *How to Accept German Reparations* (Philadelphia: University of Pennsylvania Press, 2014), 22–23.
61. For an overview of key reparations issues in West Germany and Israel during these Cold War years, see Nicholas Balabkins, *West German Reparations to Israel* (New Brunswick, NJ: Rutgers University Press, 1971).
62. Ryan Michael Spitzer, "The African Holocaust: Should Europe Pay for Reparations to African for Colonialism and Slavery?" *Vanderbilt Journal of Transnational Law* 35 (October 2002): 1313–48.
63. Jeremy Sarkin and Carly Fowler, "Reparations for Historical Human Rights Violations: The International and Historical Dimensions of the Alien Torts Claims Act Genocide Case of the Herero of Namibia," *Human Rights Review* 9 (2008): 331–60, 355.
64. See Zedekia Ngavirue, *Political Parties and Interest Groups in South West Africa (Namibia): A Study of a Plural Society* (Basel: P. Schlettwein Publishing, 1997); Tony Emmkett, *Popular Resistance and the Roots of Nationalism in Namibia, 1915–1966* (Basel: Schlettwein Publishing,1999).
65. Gewald, "Herero Genocide," 292.
66. Ibid., 293.
67. Hosea Kutako, quoted in Gewald, "Herero Genocide," 293.
68. Clemens Kapuuo, quoted in "Hereros Oppose Waterberg Celebrations: *Alter Kamerad* Denies "Extermination," *Windhoek Advertiser*, last modified July 29, 1964, cited in Gewald, "Herero Genocide, 293. See also Larissa Förster, *Postkoloniale Erinnerungslandschaften: Wie Deutsche und Herero in Namibia des Kriegs von 1904 gedenken* (New York: Campus Verlag, 2010), 204.
69. See Monica Van der Haagen-Wulff, "Decloaking Invisibility: Remembering Colonial South-West Africa," in *Postcolonial Justice*, edited by Anke Bartels, Lars Eckstein, and Nicole Waller (Leiden: Koninklijke Brill, 2017), 277.
70. Lange, "The Dream of a Völkish," 345–46.
71. For a fine overview of some of these academic conversations see Henning Melber, "Genocide Matter-Negotiating a Namibian-German Past in the Present," *Stichproben: Wiener Zeitschrift für kritische Afrikastudien* 17, no. 33 (2017): 1–24.

SIX

Academic Scholarship, Cold War Politics, and the Revival of Scholarly Interest in Ovaherero and Nama Restitution

In this particular chapter, I will be showing how all sorts of researchers who had their own agendas—anti-colonialists, critics of rampant capitalism, political analysts who complained about totalitarian regimes, and so on—co-produced arguments between 1945 and 2000 that would be selectively picked up and reassembled by twenty-first-century lawyers and activists.

It is not always easy to discern some of the ideological motivations, or the representative nature, of some academics who produce the texts that become entangled in the German or Namibian memories of the GSWA years, but occasionally critical genocide scholars do get clues that help with critical analyses of these rhetorics. Some, like Henning Melber, were willing to admit that they belonged to organizations like the South West Africa's People's Organization (SWAPO) at the same time that they wrote their Namibian histories or critics of SWGA genocidal acts,[1] but there also times when educated guesses have to be made about the politics and cultural assumptions that swirl around the circulation of particular scholarly fragments.

As I noted in chapter 1, international presses in 2015 and 2016 noted how empowered German decision makers were finally willing to recharacterize the GSWA atrocities of 1904–1908 as a colonial "genocide," and academics were credited with helping with these consciousness-raising efforts. As Katharina von Hammerstein would note in 2016, for the "first time in 111 years, top government officials of the Federal Republic of Germany, legal successor not only to Nazi Germany but also to the German Empire that ended in 1918, had joined postcolonial historical scholars, literary authors and political activists in recognizing part of the 1904–1908 German-Herero Nama Colonial War for what it was: the first genocide of the twentieth century."[2]

Journalists wrote about how Germany was confronting its "other genocide,"[3] or was "mastering" its controversial colonial past. Jason Burke, for example, writing in the UK's *Guardian*, explained to readers that a series of events had contributed to the witnessing of a "policy U-turn in Berlin," helping to pave the way for negotiations "between the German and Namibian governments over possible reparations payments . . . and "an official apology."[4]

It was considered to be a major achievement of the German legislators that they were able to overcome some of the colonial nostalgia, historical fragmentation, and political wrangling that stood in the way of acknowledgments of Ovaherero and Name grievances.

This did not mean that purveyors of the "colonial guilt lie" or genocide revisionists or deniers or skeptics were going to go away—official German acknowledgment merely reflected the fact that more German politicians and their constituencies were willing to recognize at least some of the "social," and "historical"—if not "legal"—features the Ovaherero and Nama reparations claims.

I would argue that the achievement of that "U-turn" that was mentioned above was not simply a matter of having a few legislators in the German Bundestag change their minds. These legislative acknowledgments were also reflecting changes in elite and vernacular ways of conceptualizing colonial genocides in general, and the Ovaherero/Nama-German war in particular. Younger generations, for example, were willing to revisit postcolonial issues or reparations questions that were not seriously considered by some of the older generations.

In the same way that material conditions and ideological forces during the colonial years had gradually influenced the production of the assimilationist and annihilationist rhetorics that destroyed Ovaherero and Nama cultures (see chapters 2–4), incremental epistemic shifts during the twentieth and the early twenty-first centuries had contributed to the decolonizing of those same epistemic structures.

Public acknowledgments of the Ovaherero and Nama genocide by German leaders were matters that were influenced by the convergence of many post–world war trends, including renascent interest in studying German imperial history, the willingness to hear colonial apologies, the rise of postcolonial studies, and young scholars' willingness to study colonial genocides in the same detailed way that earlier generations of researchers had dedicated their lives to the study of the World War II Judeocide.

In this chapter, I want to focus on the role that academics played in all of this transgenerational disputation, and I want to outline for readers the scholarly fragments on these reparations topics that would be selectively appropriated by judges, jurists, and commentators who participated in the courtroom and public debates about the 2001 and 2017 Namibian reparations cases.

As I noted in earlier chapters, a host of social scientists and humanists appeared to be bothered by the instrumental usage of some research on the Holocaust or the Namibian genocide by those who might be affiliated with some of the participants in the U.S. federal reparations cases. In 2012 Reinhart Kössler, in a review of several books, complained about the ways that Professor Sarkin was trying to represent the Herero Reparations Corporation and how he was also writing a book that alleged distorted German and Namibian histories.[5] Kössler complained that Sarkin's book on the Namibian genocide was filled with assertions, confused ethnonyms of Nama groups, obscured "African agency," and focused too much on Ovaherero anti-colonial activities. Kössler was convinced that part of the reason that Sarkin was having difficulties had to do with shortcomings that came from having "an agenda" that was "different from writing history."[6] Professor Kössler averred that "Sarkin dons the role of the attorney out to persuade the jury," and in the process Sarkin was making exaggerated claims about the overriding importance of the GSWA to Germany or the role that Kaiser Wilhelm II played in perpetrating the Namibian genocide.[7] Kössler opined that Sarkin that was trying to find "circumstantial evidence" that the German emperor had directly ordered Lothar von Trotha to annihilate the Ovaherero in order to try to "establish responsibility or liability."[8]

This is an intriguing claim for Professor Kössler to make because his own work, and his coauthored work, has been used for many years by activists and investigative journals on several continents for consciousness-raising about the Namibian genocide. Was he arguing that Sarkin's work was legalistic but his own was not? Was he arguing that Sarkin was purveying partial or incomplete or erroneous information about the treatment of the Ovaherero and Nama, or was he objecting to the ways that Sarkin simultaneously adopted several subject positions, posing as an advisor to Ovaherero litigants while playing the role of academic chronicler of these affairs? Was Professor Kössler implying that his own work as a historian had little to do with the entangled German politics and Namibian histories that he wrote about elsewhere?

As I noted in chapter 1, those who assume that mythic dividing lines exist between the production of persuasive "legal" advocacy and the formulation of "histories" or "historiographies" are obfuscating the ways that all interventionists in these disputes over Namibian genocide are involved in this lawfare and representations of colonial warfare. From a Nietzschean or Foucauldian perspectival way of viewing discourse/power/knowledge formations there are no apolitical essentialist truths out there to find about these colonial or genocidal matters.

I join those theorists who treat rhetorical historical study or critical genealogical inquiry as a "field of eruptions, forces, emergencies and partial formations."[9] Here, in this portion of the book, readers can be apprised of the contested nature of the scholarship that would be produced by researchers like Horst Drechsler and Helmut Bley.[10] Their work is now cited in countless mainstream journals, alternative press outlets, and blog sites on the World Wide Web, but for a time the work of writers like Drechsler and Bley was marginalized by those who wanted to focus on the future, and not the past, of Namibian-German relationships.

Before I begin my critical genealogical critiques of some of the post–World War II academic work that influenced the trajectory of Herero and Nama claims, let me provide a brief interlude that helps readers contextualize some of my critiques.

UNDERSTANDING THE DEBATES ABOUT THE LEGAL AND PUBLIC "POLITICIZATION" OF COLONIAL OR IMPERIAL RESEARCH

Some researchers, trained to believe in the existence of bright lines between mundane "politics" and dispassionate "scholarship," are worried about the strategic usage of scholarly materials by members of Ovaherero and Nama reparations movements. The above quotations that I referenced in Reinhart Kössler's review of the work of Jeremy Sarkin only provide a typical example of how one person's empirical claim may be another's rhetorical assertion in colonial genocide disputation.

Given the varied methodological and epistemic assumptions that are made by social scientists who study the Holocaust, modern genocides or colonial atrocities—who are oftentimes trained to be objective, unbiased, and apolitical writers—it is not always easy to see *how archival research often creates, and not just reflects, available evidence, the narrative framing of that evidence, and the normative usage of those materials.* As Michel Foucault's followers are fond of arguing, the colonial archives are places of knowledge *production,* where decisions are made about what can be said, or not said, about fraught imperial pasts.

Not all of the post–World War II researchers who collected historical and cultural materials on German settler colonial pasts or the near annihilation of the Ovaherero or Nama viewed themselves as active, empowered social agents who were producing usable pasts. Even fewer self-identified as public intellectuals or activists who enjoyed intervening in public disputation when their work was selectively appropriated for lawfare causes.[11]

While some post–World War II experts did not hesitate to write and talk about the applicability of Hague Conventions or Geneva principles in their studies of colonial figures like Lieutenant General Lothar von Trotha, other academics interested in legal formalisms or objectivist histories objected to the ways that the work of Drechsler, Bley, or Jürgen Zimmerer was starting to appear in journalistic essays or court filings.

Between 1945 and 2018 there were those who seemed to sense that this blurring of mythic lines was turning academic research on GSWA into a form of atrocity discourse that some found problematic. There are those who strenuously objected to the ways that this supposed "politics of compensation" was influencing traditional studies of colonial Africa, Namibia, or South African post-apartheid rule. For example, David Bargueño, in an essay titled "Cash For Genocide?," outlined the reasons why he was bothered by the blurring of legalistic and historical reasoning in Namibian reparations cases. He opined that legal studies and historical studies served "different masters."[12] Writing in 2012, he lamented the ways that some of his colleagues were ignoring the differences that purportedly existed between legal ways of viewing adversarial evidence and historiographic ways of sifting through colonial or imperial evidence. Bargueño claimed that that "neat binaries" that were required by lawyers and judges—"of rights and wrongs, victims versus perpetrators, individual deviance from collective behavior"—ran "counter" to the supposed historiographic approaches that took into account "the complexities, ambiguities, and complicities found in historical records, archives and individual memories."[13] David Bargueño was worried that when colleagues or lawyers took advantage of the rhetorical power of law to confer legitimacy, this blurring of binary lines led to the acceptance of some preferred "history" that came at the cost of silencing dissident histories. More "muddled paths of causation" were set aside as lawyers were said to be validating victors' justice.[14]

Bargueño, like Professor Kössler, seemed to be assuming that trained historians, who were carrying out their craft, could, or should write in objective, apolitical ways that ideally took into account the dissident histories that were left behind in archival contests. Historians and other scholars were not supposed to be activists seeking reparations, and for Bargueño pure research had little to do with disputation over the "fraught terrain of colonial Africa."[15]

In the rest of his 2012 essay, Bargueño critiqued both the historical and the legal choices that were made by those involved in the Ovaherero and Nama reparations cases, and he tried to provide a praxiological type of analysis that showed his readers some of the interesting legal angles that were not pursued by Namibian claimants. Bargueño implicitly argued that lawyers involved in reparations cases were cherry-picking their histories, reducing the complexities found in orthodox historical scholarship in order to advance the political causes of their clients.

In theory, the best Namibian histories and other interdisciplinary studies of settler colonialism or Ovaherero and Nama cultures were the systematic or comprehensive ones that were coming from those who produced knowledge for knowledge's sake. These apolitical writers cared little about the potential usages of their work by lawyers, investigative journalists, and others.

I beg to differ, and I would argue that *there no arhetorical texts in the archives that have been written in apolitical ways that do not reflect and refract the ideological positions of some community.* Authors of articles on the Holocaust or the Armenian Genocide or what happened after Ohamakari/ Waterberg may hide their politics and their motivations, and they may try to cover over the traces of the origins of the arguments and the research that they use in their knowledge production, but the evidence, the narrative emplotments that they use, and the choices that they make about what not to cover in their studies speak volumes. Professor Kössler may complain about Professor Sarkin's use of "secondary" instead of "primary" sources, or the lack of proof that Sarkin visited this or that "archive," but Professor Kössler may not admit is that every single major claim that he makes about the Namibian genocide or German "history" is itself a tiny sliver of rhetorical archival materials that can always be turned into politicized weapons by dominant and dissident communities.

Is it any coincidence that those who profit from present Namibian-German bilateral relationships see little reason to engage in indigenous lawfare or the open politicization of scholarship?

I would argue that Professor Bargueňo's description of legal argumentation, the use of binaries, the referencing of normative assumptions about right and wrong, and the selective nature of judicial disputation may be *an apt description of all writings, including allegedly objective historical or historiographic writing*. From a critical genealogical perspective, there are no innocents here, and the Foucauldian parchments that are "grey," meticulous, and scribbled over and recirculated over time are always in those colonial or imperial archives for a reason.[16] Theodore Leutwein, for example, left us shards of memory that might let future generations see that during his lifetime he had objected to von Trotha's decisions. This allowed him—as a representative of the assimilationists or the accommodationists—to distance his supporters from the annihilationist rhetorics of his age. Since that time the "muddle" that Bargueňo describes has been an inherent part of all historical and legal treatments of Namibian and German pasts.

When any scholar puts pen to paper, or when that researcher hits those computer keys, she or he has to make motivated decisions about what will be viewed as a "primary" or "secondary" source, and what texts will be viewed as relevant or irrelevant sources for their rhetorical production. Lawyers and judges are not the only social agents who "rewrite history" (Bargueňo), and more than a few circulate all types of ignoble or noble lies. What Friedrich Nietzsche had to say about the use and abuse of history during the nineteenth century can be applied to all humanly produced arguments about colonial or imperial or postcolonial "histories" that are recirculated in all sorts of strategically produced academic and legal texts.[17]

A host of conscious and unconscious motivations influence how promoters and detractors of Ovaherero and Nama reparation efforts choose to defend their preferred methodological styles as they simultaneously critique applications of various theories and methods. This has impacted the ways that we view everything from the alleged perpetration of a "genocide" to the acceptance of this or that "continuity thesis."

Note the discursive origins, and the tenor, of the arguments that have been circulating from the time of German colonization in German South West Africa to the time when German decision makers finally acknowledged the Herero/Nama genocide in 2015–2016. Were these decisions based on apolitical, arhetorical framings of the 1904–1908 events as a "war" instead of an atrocity?

We are living in the "age of apology,"[18] where academics are some of the public intellectuals who get caught up in all sorts of of "U-turns" and lawfare. Note, for example, how Caroline Elkins, a Harvard historian working on the Mau Mau "Emergency years," was asked, in 2008, to become involved in lawsuits for compensation for alleged torture that had taken place in Kenya during the 1950s. Elkins had dared to critique the conventional historiographies that were often used to paint pictures of benevolent British imperial practices that were supposed to look very different from German or Belgian colonizing activities. One writer characterized Elkins's involvement as an "idea" that was "both legally improbable and professionally risky." Elkins's idea—that the detainment of hundreds of thousands of Kikuyu during the post–World War II emergency years bordered on "genocidal"—was considered "improbable," in that at one time it was unlikely that the UK's highest court was going to hold "Britain accountable for atrocities perpetrated 50 years later."[19] It was also risky because many experts in British imperial or commonwealth studies had attacked her for her supposed instrumentalist and revisionist interpretations of what happened in British "rehabilitation" camps and villages.[20]

Notice how all of this assumed that the orthodox military histories or legal accounts of the suppression of the Mau Mau that were produced by writers during the 1950s or 1960s were treated as more representative or more authoritative or more orthodox ways of conceptualizing British imperial or commonwealth histories.

Yet in spite of this legal improbability and all of this riskiness, the Mau Mau survivors eventually won a 2013 settlement, and UK diplomats were forced to acknowledge the problematic nature of some of the horrific colonial abuses that were carried out by the British and their "loyalist" African allies during the "suppression" of the Mau Mau "rebellion."

The legalistic cases in the Mau Mau settlement were partially built on Elkins's academic efforts, and even though these particular cases never reached the trial stage, Elkins was credited with helping provide equitable redress for thousands of elderly Kenyans. It was said that Elkins, when she signed on to join that Mau Mau compensation team, could not have realized that this "lawsuit would expose a secret: a vast colonial archive that had been hidden for half a century."[21]

These Mau Mau settlement cases, like the Holocaust reparations cases (see chapter 5), would become classical studies of how courtrooms could be viewed as forums that dispensed both justice and edifying social knowledge about historical wrongdoings.

The academic work of Caroline Elkins and others who produced similar critiques of colonial or imperial abuses would be cited over and over again, and on occasion, they would become a part of what Reinhart Kössler has called "postcolonial entanglement." This is where "a surprising array of actors" co-produce the "historical record" that may include materials from "divergent trajectories of remembrance that are related to the genocide, both in Namibia and in Germany."[22]

If we juxtapose the arguments of Bargueňo and Kössler we would note that both seemed to be arguing that we needed to take into account dominant and dissent histories—they simply had disagreements about whether some of this activism was helping or hurting the cause of those who wanted to see more historical pluralism, more complexity, and more nuance.

In spite of what Reinhart Kössler argued in his critique of Sarkin's work, he was not always shying away from involvement in the production of "postcolonial entanglement" or engagement with that "historical record," and he seemed to sense that all types of complementary and contradictory historical information could be reassembled in politicized ways.

If we pay particular attention to the rhetorical usage of these historical and other archival materials on the Namibian genocide or German colonial histories we would find that the production of that "U-turn" that was mentioned above oftentimes meant decolonizing the lingering influence of colonial pasts in (post)colonial presents. More than a few used academic sources to try and make it difficult for German parliamentarians or others to deny, or evade, the fact that German soldiers may have committed not one, but several genocides.

Politicians—regardless of what choice that they made—had to decide how best to deal with those hagiographic pictures of heroic *Schutztruppe* obeying military norms or international laws as they carried out a "defensive" "war" against the barbaric "rebels." Would twenty-first-century German politicians and diplomats follow the scholars who took this line or the revisionists who critiqued this sanitized version of GSWA affairs?

As noted earlier in this book, Professor Kössler also invites researchers to use the term "mnemoscape" when they look for an umbrella term that might describe the place where all of these contested Namibian rhetorical units of analysis might coalesce. In academic contexts, a "mnemoscape" might be formed when ideographs, characterizations, colonial myths, and imperial gazes came together to form a larger *dispositif*.

Here I need to let readers know that a cursory web search will show that Professor Kössler has now interjected himself into some of these debates about Ovaherero and Nama reparations and other forms of Namibian social justice, and this may provide some context for the ideologically loaded ways that he seems to be operationalizing this notion of "mnemoscapes." His own lines of intellectual inquiry involve the study of the contrasting memory practices and concerns of various indigenous communities or German-speaking communities living in places like Namibia. He argues, for example, that if we really want to understand the politics of memory in Namibian contexts, then we have to unpack the ways that both "governments and non-state actors" address national, transnational, and "post-colonial politics of apology and reconciliation."[23]

I would argue that it is also time that academics and readers pay attention to the ways that scholarly research and lawfare materials become a part of these mnemoscapes. Instead of thinking of "politics" as something that takes place apart from, or after, the writing of academic texts or legal writings we need to see how all academic and judicial work—regardless of intentionalities—has the potential to be picked up and entangled in all of this structural and functional politics of historicizing. Who, in 1789, when the Alien Torts Act was first passed, could have predicted that this would having anything to do with the 2001 and 2017 filings of Namibian cases in U.S. courtrooms?

I join those postcolonial, post-structural, and other critical scholars who take the stance that we cannot, and should not, treat some elite academic writings as arhetorical materials that are produced by unmotivated bystanders. Regardless of their alleged credentials and their acumen there are no Platonic guardians—Jacques Derrida called them *archons*—who should stand above the fray and arbitrate between conflicting "public" readings of social justice arguments.[24]

Given all of the aphasia, the disassociations, and the refusals to take seriously Ovaherero complaints during the mandate and apartheid years (chapter 5), how, and why, did a few scholars start to produce the histories and the historiographies that would be picked up and appropriated by members of the Ovaherero and Nama reparations movement?

In the next subsection of this chapter, I will be unpacking and critiquing some of strategic usage of the work of writers like Horst Drechsler or Helmut Bley, and I will note how the blogosphere now contains many websites that take for granted the realities of the "Kaiser's Holocaust" (Olusoga and Erichsen).[25] I will also try to explain why those interested in reparations continue to reference the work of writers like Hannah

Arendt, W. E. B. DuBois, Aimé Césaire, Frantz Fanon, and Peter Katjavivi.[26]

DECOLONIZING SPECTERS OF PARTIALLY FORGOTTEN GENOCIDAL PASTS, 1945–1970

The advent of the World War II Holocaust led to the questioning of many humanistic and Enlightenment principles, and for decades it would be argued by some that the Nazis' misdeeds that were "perpetrated upon white/Europeans" constituted the "same outrages" that were "routinely carried out against nonwhite/non-European colonial populations with relatively little outcry on the part of Europeans."[27] While the bulk of academic work on genocides, especially after the Adolf Eichmann trial, focused on the role that the perpetrators, bystanders, and victims played during the Shoah, there were some writers who did more than hint that there were historical precedents and material precursors for these Nazi practices. An entire library could be filled with critiques of the work of Raphael Lemkin, who had written about colonial genocides and the Ovaherero-German 1904 war.[28]

After the Rwandan genocide interdisciplinary scholars started to adopt all sorts of comparative approaches that raised the sorts issues that Michael Rothberg was interested in when he wrote about multidirectional and competitive memories.[29] While Holocaust scholars—oftentimes interested in preserving the "uniqueness" of the Judeocide—were not always pleased when they encountered some of these comparative approaches, others were convinced that parallels could be made between genocides without participating in that zero-sum game that concerned Rothberg.

The more that some scholars studied the violence that was waged during colonial times the more difficult it became not to make associational or causal claims about the parallels that could be found between different genocides. Michael A. McDonnell and A. Dirk Moses, for example, noted in 2005 that those who thought that the "genocide is a synonym for the Holocaust" were ignoring how studies of Raphael Lemkin's archival notes and research showed that he considered the Shoah to be a "consequence of Nazi imperialism and colonialism in Europe."[30]

In other words, if Raphael Lemkin himself had been willing to find parallels and precedents in his own archival work, then why shouldn't those who followed him make similar comparisons between genocides perpetrated during different colonial or postcolonial periods?

McDonnell and Moses argued that the "German imperium" between 1939 and 1945 involved a radical, bureaucratic mode of governance that had its roots in the earlier European colonial ages. McDonnell and Moses were convinced that, in all likelihood, after Lemkin coined the term genocide in 1944, his research during the 1940s and 1950 helped him become aware of the long-term impact of colonial genocides.[31]

For a host of law review writers, lawyers, and judges, it would be the UN General Assembly's adoption of permutations of Lemkin's work by the Convention on the Prevention and Punishment of the Crime of Genocide, on December 9, 1948, that would ensure that genocidal issues were often framed in legalistic frames of analysis.[32] Not surprisingly, some of the victorious Allies after World War II were willing to treat the Holocaust as a genocide, but they assiduously avoided including portions of Lemkin's work on "cultural" genocide that might lead to probing investigations of their own historical and contemporary colonial practices.

The British may not have wanted studies of their Boer camps, the French had no reason to have scholars looking into the scorched earth policies of 1830s French colonizers in North Africa,[33] the Russians may not have wanted studies of the treatment of Cossacks,[34] Poles, and so forth, and the Americans may not have wanted academic studies of their treatment of the rebellious "Moro" during military campaigns in the Southern Philippines.[35] The Allies had their own reasons for keeping the spotlight on German prewar aggressions and Nazi genocidal horrors.

Lemkin, however, used library materials that allowed him to study incidents like the early nineteenth-century "extirpation" of the Tasmanians and other colonial massacres. No wonder Dominik Schaller would note that a fair reading of Lemkin's entire corpus of work showed that this Polish lawyer was torn between "condemnation and admiration" for imperial ventures when he compared and contrasted German, British, and other forms of colonialization.[36]

Lemkin seemed to be one of those readers of colonial texts and acts who was genuinely torn when presented with competing assimilationist and annihilationist ways of explaining what happened in places like Tasmania or German South West Africa. His faith in the constraining power of international law made it difficult for him to accept positions that viewed imperialism in general as an inherently exploitative activity.

While writers like Lemkin joined those who wanted to make distinctions between "good" and "bad" forms of colonialism, there were some African Americans and African writers who had no qualms about discussing the problematics of settler colonialism or imperialism in general. W. E. B. Du Bois would have this to say in 1947:

> There was no Nazi atrocity-concentration camps, wholesale maiming and murder, defilement of women or ghastly blasphemy of childhood-which Christian civilization or Europe had not long been practiced against colored folks in all parts of the world in the name of and for the defense of a Superior Race born to rule the world.[37]

Rothberg would contend that Du Bois changed some of his opinions when he visited the Warsaw Ghetto,[38] and yet in 1947 Du Bois may simply have been articulating the positions of many people of color who did not have the same access that he did to Western media outlets.

Permutations of this type of anti-colonial language would later be used by advocates of African American and African reparations who believed that formal and informal means of redress ought to be provided to the descendants of those who suffered from transatlantic slavery and slave trades.

Other strands of related arguments in these commentaries about imperialism came from the responses to the political philosophical work of Hannah Arendt.[39] Some readers may remember the controversies that arose from her critiques of the ghetto *Jüdenrat* and her discussions of the "banality of evil" in her *Eichmann in Jerusalem,*[40] but after the 1990s it would be her work on the intersectionalities that existed between capitalism, imperialism, and totalitarianism that garnered the attention of critical genocide scholars.

Hannah Arendt would be credited with helping produce some of the texts that helped her theorize about what others would call the "continuity thesis" and the "boomerang effect."[41] One particular continuity thesis posited the idea that philosophical parallels could be found between the ideologies that circulated during the German South West Africa periods and the Nazi years. The boomerang effect had to do with the notion those living in the colonies witnessed horrors that would not have been tolerated in Europe, and that European colonizers were caught off-guard when these overseas cruelties that were visited upon the colonized migrated to European shores.

Arendt became a seminal figure for generations of writers who wanted to question the traditional canons that seemed to relegate genocide studies to only a few, well-known genocides—the Holocaust, the Armenian genocide, the Rwandan genocide, and perhaps what was happening in Darfur. "Hannah Arendt," argued Jan-Bart Gewald, "became the first academic to alert the world to the linkages that exist between Germany's colonial past and the later development of the national socialist state."[42]

In The *Origins of Totalitarianism,* Arendt claimed that overseas colonies were "breeding grounds of race thinking and . . . sites of ubiquitous massacre."[43] Robert Gerwarth averred that Arendt's "masterpiece" provided an insightful interpretation of the "morally corrupting effects of imperialism on Europe."[44] Gerwarth elaborated by noting that according to "Arendt, Europe's colonial realm served a laboratory for racial doctrines and practices that were subsequently imported back into Europe."[45]

Yet many close readers of Arendt's text claimed that her primary interest was in critiquing problematic "pan-national" influences on German or European cultures. Gerwarth cautioned those who used Arendt's work to not jump to hasty conclusions about her alleged promotion of mono-causal links between GSWA activities and the Nazis. Gerwarth joined the ranks of those scholars who worried about the instrumentalist usage of some academic work.

George Steinmetz has provided one of the best close readings of Arendt's philosophical work, and he explained that Arendt was complaining about general imperial abuses when she referenced what was happening in South Africa, before and after World War II. He was convinced that she was not that interested in investigating concrete or unique German colonial policies in German South West Africa.[46] Steinmetz explained how Arendt revealed some of her own biases when she described how descendants of the Dutch Boers in South Africa were stooping to "the allegedly precivilizational level of African natives" who were exhibited the "rootlessness, antistatism, racism, and hordelike behavior of the European 'pan' movements that spawned fascism.[47] In theory, the appearance of some pan movements was contributing to the spread of colonial pathologies.

Arendt, in order to quarantine European political philosophizing, was using primitivist epistemic arguments about some "precivilization" that betrayed the racialization of the "other." This was a variant of the old canards that appeared in so many colonial books about whites losing their moral compass when they were living in tropical regions that allowed them to "go native."

Those who were trying to treat Arendt as some egalitarian who would have been in favor of reparations or African land redistribution were reminded that in 1950 she once characterized some Africans as "vegetating" "savages" who lacked not only a "culture and history of their own," but even a "specifically human character."[48] In Arendt's theorizing on the origins of apartheid politics, the Boers' failings came when they escaped the political constraints that came with the imbrication of European culture and civilization. The Boers' isolation moved them in other directions, where they lived "outside the ambit of the colonial state."[49]

In other words, Arendt argued that the Boers who lived too far from European colonial influences resembled the uncivilized black Africans, and the Boers had failed to take advantage of their proximity to the best colonial practices that were based on sound Enlightenment political thought. In theory, the adoption of apartheid ideologies by Boer descendants meant a move away from the "cultural" influences of true European political philosophizing.

Steinmetz critiqued the work of some admirers of Arendt's work when he noted that Arendt was not some anti-imperialist who was interested in attacking all forms of colonization. "Colonialism for Arendt," argued Steinmetz, *contributed* to the civilizing process of changing "the country into a normal producing part of Western civilization."[50] Unlike other academics who used Arendt's arguments to make empirical linkages between colonialism and the Holocaust, Steinmetz noted how she appeared to be making comparative and not causal arguments when she juxtaposed Afrikaner and European totalitarianism.

From a postcolonial vantage point it might be argued that Arendt was interjecting herself into much larger cold war conversations that included responses to the work of W. E. B. Dubois, Frantz Fanon, and Aimé Césaire. Steinmetz explained how Hannah Arendt's commentaries on colonial abuses became the "breeding grounds for race thinking" that migrated across generations and influenced the arguments of young writers like Jürgen Zimmerer.[51]

Whether scholars who extended Arendt's work used or abused her writings may be an open question, but there is little doubt that many of those who followed in her footsteps produced the type of argumentative constellations that appealed to academics as well as lay persons who wanted to find historical links between many colonial practices and future modernist twentieth century behavior. Benjamin Madley, writing in 2005, argued that in 1952 Arendt had "postulated that European imperialism played a crucial role in the development of totalitarianism and associated genocides."[52] Madley would go on to study the Tasmanian genocide, the Ovaherero/Nama atrocities, the destruction of indigenous communities in California, and other colonial genocides.

It would only be a short step to take this even further and use some of those linkages for legalistic purposes. For example, Chief Riruako, who led efforts to file the Ovaherero reparations case in the United States in 2001, told reporters, "What Hitler did to the Jewish people was something that originated in German colonization in Namibia. The Holocaust started with us here."[53]

The instrumentalist use of these types of comparative colonial studies did not escape the attention of writers who wanted to maintain that bright line that I mentioned earlier in this chapter. Professor Bargueňo noted how "court papers" seemed to be using Arendtian connections when lawyers argued that the Federal Republic of Germany, in "brutal alliance with German multi-national corporations," "relentlessly pursued" the enslavement and genocidal destruction of the Herero Tribe" that foreshadowed, "with chilly precision," the "European Holocaust."[54] This, Bargueňo seemed to argue, went too far.

Readers can readily appreciate that there were both legal and historical reasons why these linkages were being made. The legal reasons had everything to do with the successes of lawyers who had helped provide reparations for Holocaust victims in U.S. and other courts, while Arendtian claims about historical ties to colonialism helped those who wanted to move away from "Auschwitz-centered" genocidal talk.[55] Why, some argued, should the term "genocide" only be used in those rare, Holocaust-type situations?

However, from post-structural and postcolonial vantage points, the Arendtian arguments about imperialism or pan-national movements were only some of the strands that went into those complex tapestries of arguments that were produced by researchers between 1945 and 2000. Readers who care about the production of influential mnemoscapes need to be presented with a short section that shows some of the ways that deniers and revisionists tried to counter the allegations that were presented by supporters of various continuity or boomerang theses.

CONTESTED MNEMOSCAPES, REVISIONISM, AND DENIALISM, 1971 TO 1990

Before the Namibians gained their independence in 1990, some fought for years with South African Defence forces, and when freedom came they wanted to remember the sacrifices that were made by the Ovambo and all of the other African communities who fought against apartheid. As far as they were concerned, some of the Ovaherero and Nama claims asking for redress for only a few Namibian ethnic communities sounded like divisive "tribalism" that hindered efforts to form nationalistic Namibian identities. Not everyone was appreciative of the efforts that were made to appropriate the work of Michael Scott and others who followed him.

For several decades before Namibian independence, the paucity of historical research on the GSWA atrocities complicated matters for the younger Ovaherero who were demanding that the world not forget about these histories. Some of these problems were alleviated when Africanists and others started to read the work that would be produced during the late 1960s and 1970s by authors like Horst Drechsler or Helmut Bley.

Before Drechsler and Bley came out with their books, many public reminisces of places like East Africa or Togo or Cameroon focused on the beneficence that came from how German missionaries, doctors, engineers, and others had helped improve the lives of "natives." For decades there would be little mention in Germany of the battle of Hamakari/Waterberg. Instead school children in Germany were reading textbooks filled with stories of colonial adventurers in search of treasure, the religious teachings of missionaries, the development that came from railroads, and the improved health of those who were inoculated with drugs that helped with sleeping sickness, malaria, smallpox, polio, and other diseases. In the same way that Belgian students were learning about the good "Belgian Congo," German students were invited to participate in the co-production of rhetorics that had to do with German exceptionalism or imperial nostalgia.[56]

The turbulent 1960s—which heralded the arrival of college activism on German campuses, critiques of French and American involvement in Indochina, and the liberation efforts of decolonizing national movements—also witnessed ruptures, contradictions, and interrogations of the conventional archives by those who tried to resurrect the suasory power of old texts like the 1918 Blue Book. As Professor Steinmetz noted in 2009,

> German colonialism in Southwest Africa has proven oddly difficult for historians to interpret, or even narrate. Only a few writers have taken up the challenge of providing an analytic account of the entire thirty-year course of German colonial rule in Namibia. The two most influential studies, by Horst Drechsler and Helmut Bley, where written more than three decades ago. Both are invaluable and pioneering studies, yet neither offers a convincing and coherent interpretation of colony's development. Much can be learned by focusing on the lacunae in these texts. [57]

Like all influential texts, the work of Drechsler and Bley might have been incomplete and had blind spots, and yet referencing of colonial horrors would force generations of readers to grapple with the possibility that GSWA had been the scene of some atrocities that had been conveniently forgotten since the time when Germany "lost" her overseas colonies.

Horst Drechsler's work would later be viewed as canonical by some Africanists, Namibian writers, critical genocide scholars, and legal brief writers, but his work during the late 1960s and early 1970s was considered shocking, unorthodox, controversial, and potentially libelous. Drechsler's 1966 book, *Südwestafrika unter deutscher Kolonialherrschaft* (Southwest Africa under German Colonial Rule), would be translated and published in 1980 under the title *Let Us Die Fighting, the Struggle of the Herero and Nama against German Imperialism*.[58] The title was taken from some of the missives that were sent from Henrik Witbooi when he warned Ovaherero warriors that the "Red tribes" needed to set aside their differences, stop signing "protection" agreements with German administrators, and realize that the Germans were duping the Africans (see chapter 2).

Drechsler's "East German" critique of GSWA's colonial affairs was a product of its time, and his book on German colonialism was filled with commentary on labor exploitation and the inherent evils of rampant capitalism. Although some might read it as a follow-up to the work of the Social Democrats in the Reichstag during the Second Reich, others could claim that Drechsler's book seemed to resonate with global audiences who were witnessing the rising power of anti-colonial movements during the cold war decolonization periods. Some could configure his work as a text that was simply trying to critique West German capitalism.

For those who were interested in Marxist or social critiques of capitalism, it made sense that many portions of Drechsler's work focused on issues of labor and capital exploitation before he turned to the portions of his manuscript that provided detailed discussions of von Trotha's annihilationist order and the 1904 war.

Drechsler used critiques of free market capitalism to explain how some forms of exploitive imperialism contributed to the destruction of Ovaherero and Nama cultures. Drechsler would be remembered as one of the first academics who openly used the word "genocide" to describe what happened to the indigenous communities living under German colonial rule in Africa.

Drechsler's 1966 book was filled with the types of historical materials that would appeal to those trying to put together a "case" that demonstrated the complicity of many in carrying out the German colonial enterprise. He wrote about German land ownership, mining societies, and the power of the German Colonial Society for South West Africa (*Kolonialgesellschaft*), and his thorough analysis covered many different economic dimensions of colonial life. For example, this was a book that described the entrepreneurial efforts of Adolf Lüderitz, the sale of his companies to German organizations when he went bankrupt, the formation of the Otavi Mine and Railway Company, and the copper mines at places like Tsumeb.[59]

In Drechsler's rendering of the 1904–1908 Herero-German War, the German soldiers, settlers, and civil administrators found ways to use the exigencies of war as a cover for the continued exploitation of indigenous labor and lands. The fact that the settlers and the GSWA government no longer had to negotiate with indigenous "*Kapteins*" meant that there was the potential for huge profits, and all of this attracted the attention of German companies and European shareholders who saw all of this creative destruction as an opportunity that could not be ignored. Drechsler noted how German companies profited by "plunging" into the "trading business."[60]

Drechsler's academic work stitched together several different genres and argumentative frames, and it was based on what he could find in East German archives. His evocative discussions of the shooting and the killing of African women and children were sometimes juxtaposed with the dry recital of statistical information. His book may not have appealed to interdisciplinary scholars who were not enamored with his neo-Marxist historical methods, and it was probably the case that many Germans preferred to read the conventional histories about the "good" German colonizers. Yet the materials that Drechsler collected allowed future genocide scholars to link the 1918 Blue Book to his work and other evidence of imperial wrongdoing during the GSWA years.

It soon reached the point when generations of Namibian and German scholars interested in genocidal claims about GSWA could not avoid discussing Drechsler's work. They could read it selectively; they could always leave out his Marxist theorizing as they concentrated on the factual information that he was providing readers on mining activities, the building of wharfs, the construction of railroads, and concentration camp activities. Yet they had to at least cite his work as they agreed or disagreed with his assumptions, his conclusions, and his historiographic methods.

Drechsler's influence bothered those who felt that he knew very little about GSWA affairs. Brigitte Lau, a Namibian archivist and historian, was no fan of his "genocide thesis." However, she admitted that Drechsler's account is "so well researched" that his factual materials could be used as evidence that supported her own, alternative framings of GSWA affairs.[61] Yet she disputed the claims that Drechsler made about what happened during and after the Battle of Ohamakari/Waterberg.

Postcolonial critics in the West may not have shared Drechsler's deterministic views regarding classical Marxism and labor abuse, but as George Steinmetz notes writers like Tilman Dedering could use some of Drechsler's work in their own guarded discussions of "modes of production."[62]

For my purposes here, I would like to note that Drechsler's meticulous chronicling of economic factors in GSWA was exactly what lawyers for Herero and Nama litigants needed when they filed cases in places like Washington, DC, or New York City (see chapters 7 and 9).

Helmut Bley's English-translation work *South-West Africa under German Rule, 1894–1914* is often treated by academics as a companion text that complemented Drechsler's earlier work.[63] George Steinmetz argued that this West German book was written during a period when the "exceptionalist approach to German history was extremely influential," and Bley's study used a scholarly frame for colonial analysis that contrasted the harsh brutalities of German colonialism with the "supposedly more normal British or Western" colonial versions.[64] This seemed to echo the strategy that had been used by Major Thomas O'Reilly.

I would argue that from a critical rhetorical vantage point, Bley's work was important for members of the Ovaherero and Nama reparations movement because it provided them with a persuasive textual example of a West German scholarly work that tried to show a generation's willingness to argue about the possible existence of a German *Sonderweg*.[65] Those who extended Bley's work could raise the issue of whether Prussianism, Kaiser Wilhelm's brand of militarism, or German colonialism in general, contributed to the formation of annihilation ideas or practices that supposedly were not found in other colonial contexts.

For more than forty-five years the work of Horst Drechsler and Helmut Bley would serve as seminal, canonical works for reparations activists, but their books could be read in polysemic ways by different interpretive communities. The more that Drechsler's and Bley's work was used to critique GSWA policies, the more that it attracted the attention of apologists, revisionists, or denialists who refused to conceptualize German colonial histories in these ways. Defenders of German culture, German military history, or the *Schutztruppe* in GSWA could always argue that writers like Drechsler and Bley were interlopers who did not truly understand Namibian landscapes or what happened before and after Ohamakari/Waterberg.

German-speaking Namibians, who had their own favorite authors and preferred archival manuscripts, argued that colonial wars had nothing to do with genocides, that the Herero and Nama had acted in barbaric ways and massacred settlers, and that reparations advocates were trying to retrospectively apply concepts that had no currency in nineteenth-century cultures. More than a few living in South West Africa or Germany denigrated the work of those they felt were promoting that "genocide thesis" that politicized German colonial history or Namibian history.[66]

Decades would pass before any large groups of scholars started to once again show more than a passing interest in the work of writers like Drechsler or Bley, but some of their more critical strands of argumentation were kept alive by writers like Jon Bridgman. Writing during the 1980s, Bridgman helped popularize the historical study of the Ovaherero/Nama–German War when his jacket cover explained how "for the Hereros the war was the greatest historical event they ever experienced. It was their Marathon, their Cannae, and their Hiroshima."[67]

While the work of writers like Drechsler, Bley, and Bridgman would be used by indigenous activists, it would later be argued that between the 1980s and the first decades of the twenty-first century that Africanists and genocide scholars *were not always citing the work of Namibians who were also chronicling some of these events.* Some felt that this problem was partially remedied when scholars and other writers started to cite Peter Katjavivi's 1988 book, *A History of Resistance in Namibia.*[68]

Katjavivi's way of framing what happened during the German South West Africa years was different from the chronicles that appeared in many Ovaherero and Nama oral histories or German textual framing of the 1904–1913 period in that the metanarrative tale that he had to tell was about the *nationalist struggles* of those Africans who fought to resist South African apartheid. In Katjavivi's telling of the tale the Ovaherero and Nama who fought German conquest set the stage for later attempts to prevent mandate and apartheid exploitation of land and labor, and it would be the South West Africa People's Organizations' (SWAPO) leaders who played the role of protagonists in his book.

This nationalistic type of chronicling of Namibian history would appeal to Ovambo and other majorities in Namibia who wanted to end tribalism and ethnic conflict, and those who shared these sentiments could relate to Katjavivi's critique of nationalist responses to South Africa's "Bantustan policy" before the 1990 independence.

Katjavivi would later become one of the empowered Namibian politicians who would become involved in efforts to repatriate human remains from Germany, and he was willing to participate in conversations about other forms of restorative justice possibilities.

Another figure who produced work that resonated with some Namibian communities was Brigitte Lau. She shared an interest with Katjavivi in trying to highlight the agency of indigenous communities, and yet her usage of that agency took her in other directions. Lau served as a Namibian archivist, and she was bothered by those who may have used a Eurocentric lens to critique Namibian affairs. She was convinced that only those who took the time to travel to Namibia, and only those who visited the Namibian archives, really knew that much about the presence or absence of alleged GSWA atrocities. Lau ridiculed some of Drechsler's theoretical assumptions and his methods, and she belittled the idea that the *Schutztruppe* were some "cool killers" involved in the intentional and systematic annihilation of the Ovaherero communities.

Lau's work—that appeared during the late 1980s—would appeal to German speakers in Namibia who felt that European writers like Drechsler were unfairly critiquing the activities of the German protection forces. Lau's writings—filled with commentary on the suffering of German troops, their decimation by disease and their disorganization—would resonate with those who would argue that there was no central imperial governmental plan for the genocide. Lau and her followers underscored the point that the German troops who went into the deserts after the battle of Ohamakari/Waterberg were in no shape to perpetuate any genocide against the Ovaherero or the Nama.[69]

Lau was writing during a period when some German-speaking amateur historians and other writers were recirculating familiar arguments about German interwar colonial guilt or the lack of concrete evidence for claims that were made about the perpetration of war crimes during a typical colonial "war." By 1993 there were so many amateur historians producing all types of denialist-type claims that Tilman Dedering felt that he had to write an essay titled "The German-Herero War of 1904: Revisionism of Genocide or Imaginary Historiography?"[70]

The declaration of Namibia's independence in 1990 seemed to have revived interest in traditional and revisionist studies of GSWA. For many years the vast majority of scholars—including those who read the work of Drechsler or Bley—followed the "conventional" story that had been told by the German General Staff in 1904, that the Ovaherero had started this "rebellion." A new wrinkle was added to these debates when Jan-Bart Gewald started to claim that it was an incompetent German lieutenant—Ralph Zürn—who had erroneously interpreted the arrival of a large gathering of Ovaherero as evidence that a "rebellion" had started.[71] Gewald—who reviewed the claims of Rhenish missionaries and a few Ovaherero—argued that it would be the Germans who were responsible for starting the 1904–1908 Ovaherero/Nama–German War.

Before Casper Erichsen came along, academics knew very little about the Shark Island camp in Lüderitz.[72] Those who wanted to make the argument that the German concentration camps were not the "end" of the annihilation colonial periods needed this type of work, which helped lawyers and public intellectuals as they argued about the need to compensate descendants for the coercive labor, pain, and suffering of the plaintiffs' ancestors. In some of his work Erichsen listed the names of the Shark Island prisoners, including Jacob Fredericks, Samuel Kariko, and Cornelius Fredericks. It is telling that even though most of those who died at places like Shark Island were women and children, we don't know their names, and Casper Erichsen dedicated some of his work to the "more than 4000 other names that history has since forgotten."[73]

By the end of the twentieth century, all sorts of multidirectional and competitive memories had been constitutively produced by growing numbers of interdisciplinary scholars who showed an interest in revisiting GSWA histories and historiographies.

So how would twenty-first-century investigative journalists, lawyers, politicians, or laypersons use or abuse the materials that were gathered by authors like Drechsler, Bley, Bridgman, Lau, Katjavivi, and others?

CONCLUSION

Given the nature of Namibian reparations claims—which are often based on Holocaust reparations analogies—I felt that readers needed to be provided with a chapter that illustrated the suasory power of the ideological formations that were produced by those who used the work of writers like W. E. B. DuBois, Raphael Lemkin, Hannah Arendt, Horst Drechsler, and Helmut Bley as they fought for acknowledgment of the Ovaherero/Nama genocide. These scholars' representative works contained the ideological fragments and the rhetorical reservoirs of symbolic meaning that could be used by future generations who would debate about whether the Ovaherero and Nama deserved moral or legal redress.

During these restorative justice debates it mattered a great deal how particular writers or speakers or others producing mnemoscape materials on GSWA, and how academic observers of Nama and Ovaherero reparations efforts framed contentious historical events. Strategic choices had to be made about what archival materials were going to be cited in textbooks, and what texts or pieces of parchment would be left alone to gather dust in the German or Namibia archives.

Readers by now may sense that I view academic work as politicized materials that are instrumentalized in ways that blur those mythic bright lines that some researchers believe are supposed to exist between "advocacy" and "scholarship." As long as critical genealogists keep an eye on the ruptures, the elisions, and the absences that are found in these clusters of reparations *epistemes*, I see no reason why scholars cannot admit the rhetorical nature of all GSWA historicizing. As Ann Stoler noted in her book *Duress*, one of the goals of critical genealogists is to interpret and to contextualize texts in ways that allow readers to see "occulded, genealogies of imperial effects."[74]

I am convinced that we can grant that all this research has been politicized without summarily dismissing any of this as tainted or unscholarly work. Are most observers willing to throw out or be dismissive about genocidal claims simply because activists and public intellectuals are using some of the work of researchers for ideological purposes?

Although the historiographic frames that were used by Horst Drechsler, Helmut Bley, and others who extended their work may not have satisfied Professor Steinmetz, they did provide some of the popular academic templates and the praxiological materials that would later be needed by future generations who cared deeply about reparations, repatriation of remains, and other forms of restorative justice.

Granted, the selective usage of this material should raise issues for those who are trying to read along and against the colonial archival grains. Even when we support particular causes we should be able to see how all lawfare conceals as it reveals.

When twenty-first-century lawyers for Ovaherero and Nama claimants are trying to outline the legal elements of their cases, their choice of preferred histories matters, especially in situations where they are trying to overcome the jurisdictional hurdles and reach the "merits" portions of these cases. It makes complete sense that the authors of the 2001 and 2017 amended complaints in the Ovaherero and Nama cases would cite the scholarly work of Drechsler, Bley, Bridgman, and others as they tried to advocate for reparations payments from Germany or German companies.

Critical genealogists ought to be able to find constructive ways of helping readers see the argumentative elements that are revealed and concealed in the academic claims, evidence, and warrants that migrated into twentieth-century and twenty-first-century mnemoscapes about GSWA.

Now that readers have been presented with a wealth of materials on various diachronic and synchronic work on representations of GSWA pasts, it is time to actually trace how lawyers for the Herero and the Nama argued about these topics when they prepared for the reparations cases that would be filed in U.S. courtrooms.

The next chapter takes up the question of how American and global audiences responded when the Ovaherero, in 2001, tried to argue that they, like the Holocaust victims before them, deserved legal redress from the Americans.

NOTES

1. Henning Melber, "Namibia: The German Roots of Apartheid," *Race & Class* 27, no. 1 (1985); 63–77.

2. Katharina von Hammerstein, "The Herero: Witnessing Germany's 'Other Genocide,'" *Contemporary French and Francophone Studies* 20, no. 2 (2016): 267–86, 264.

3. See, for example, Gabriele Steinhauser, "Germany Confronts the Forgotten Story of Its Other Genocide," *The Wall Street Journal*, July 28, 2017, https://www.wsj.com/articles/germany-confronts-the-forgotten-story-of-its-other-genocide-1501255028.

4. Jason Burke and Phillip Oltermann, "Germany Moves to Atone for 'Forgotten Genocide' in Namibia," *The Guardian*, last modified December 25, 2016, paragraph 2, https://www.theguardian.com/world/2016/dec/25/germany-moves-to-atone-for-forgotten-genocide-in-namibia.

5. Reinhart Kössler, "Review Article: Genocide in Namibia, the Holocaust, and the Issue of Colonialism," *Journal of Southern African Studies* 38, no. 1 (March 2012): 233–38.

6. Ibid., "Review Article," 234.

7. Ibid.

8. Ibid.

9. Wendy Brown, *Politics Out of History* (Princeton: Princeton University Press, 2001), 117; Ann Laura Stoler, *Duress: Imperial Durabilities in Our Times* (Durham: Duke University Press, 2016), 23.

10. Given my post-colonial, post-structural, and post-modern leanings, I am not interested in evaluating each of these individual's contributions to any genocidal "canon," but instead, I want to show how their collective work provided layers of arguments that could be used, and abused, by those who argue about various forms of restorative justice. For example, it could be argued that although Horst Drechsler would be remembered as one of the first "modern" scholars to call the Ovaherero/Nama–German war a "genocide," he was also accused of relying too heavily on the work of Major O'Reilly and the British who produced that infamous 1918 Blue Book.

11. Where. for example, does one place the work of Peter Kajavivi, who served SWAPO in London, wrote as a scholar about the history of Namibia, and then served as a politician in the National Assembly of Namibia. Not to mention that he became a chancellor of the Namibian University of Science and Technology. As early as the 1960s Kajavivi had joined SWAPO. For commentaries on Kajavivi's academic contributions see Reinhart Kössler, "Entangled History and Politics: Negotiating the Past between Namibia and Germany," *Journal of Contemporary African Studies* 26, no. 3 (2008): 313–39.

12. David Bargueño, "Cash for Genocide?: The Politics of Memory in the Herero Case for Reparations," *Holocaust and Genocide Studies* 26, no. 3 (Winter 2012): 394–424, 394.

13. Ibid.

14. Ibid.

15. Ibid.

16. For Foucault's extension of the work of Nietzsche and his discussions of gray, meticulous, and scribbled-over parchments in archives, see Michel Foucault, *Language, Counter-Memory, Practice* (Ithaca: Cornell University Press, 1984). In many future chapters of this book, I will be referring back to this particular Foucauldian missive.

17. For Nietzsche's discussion of the use and abuse of history, see *Friedrich Nietzsche, Unfashionable Observations,* translated by Richard T. Grey (Stanford: Stanford University Press, 1995). For some intriguing overviews of how some have used Nietzsche's insights on critical histories in critiques of colonial violence, see Nancy Rose Hunt, *A Nervous State: Violence, Remedies, and Reverie in Colonial Congo* (Durham: Duke University Press, 2016).

18. Mark Gibney, Rhoda E. Howard-Hassmann, Jean-Marc Colcaud, and Niklaus Steiner, *The Age of Apology: Facing Up to the Past* (University of Pennsylvania Press, 2008).

19. Marc Parry, "Uncovering the Brutal Truth about the British Empire," *The Guardian*, last modified August 18, 2016, paragraph 1, https://www.theguardian.com/news/2016/aug/18/uncovering-truth-british-empire-caroline-elkins-mau-mau. Professor David Anderson would also be asked to get involved in some of this litigation.

20. For an overview of some of these disagreements, see Pascal James Imperato, "Review: Differing Perspectives on Mau Mau," *African Studies Review* 48, no. 3 (December 2005): 147–54.

21. Parry, "Uncovering the Brutal Truth," paragraph 7.

22. Reinhart Kössler, "Facing Postcolonial Entanglement and the Challenge of Responsibility," in *Reconciliation, Civil Society, and the Politics of Memory*, edited by Birgit Schwelling (Berlin: Transcript Verlag, 2012), 277–312, 277–78.

23. Ibid., 278.

24. For an intriguing extension of Derrida's work on this topic, see Leswin Laubscher, "Facing the Apartheid Archive, or the Archons and Researchers," *South African Journal of Psychology* 40, no. 4 (2010): 370–81.

25. David Olusoga and Casper Erichsen, *The Kaiser's Holocaust: Germany's Forgotten* Genocide (London: Faber & Faber, 2010).

26. Peter H. Katjavivi, *A History of Resistance in Namibia* (London: Zed Books, 1988). Katjavivi has served Namibia in several capacities, including working as Namibia's ambassador to Germany. See, for example, *New Era* Reporter, "President Briefed on German Reparations Visit," *New Era*, last modified July 12, 2007, https://neweralive.na/posts/president-briefed-on-german-reparations-visit.

27. John Torpey, "'Making Whole What Has Been Smashed,': Reflections on Reparations," *The Journal of Modern History* 73, no. 2 (June 2001): 333–58, 344.

28. See, for example Michael A. McDonnell and A. Dirk Moses, "Raphael Lemkin, A Historian of Genocide in the Americas," *Journal of Genocide Studies* 7, no. 4 (2005): 501–29.

29. Michael Rothberg, *Multidirectional Memory: Remembering the Holocaust in the Age of Decolonization* (Stanford: Stanford University Press, 2009),

30. McDonnell and Moses, "Raphael Lemkin," 502.

31. Ibid.

32. See Josef L. Kunz, "The United Nations Convention on Genocide," *The American Journal of International Law* 43, no. 4 (October 1949): 738–46; William A. Schabas, *Genocide in International Law* (Cambridge: Cambridge University Press, 2000); UN Office of Genocide Prevention and the Responsibility to Protect Staff, "Definitions: Genocide: Background, n.d.,

33. Some consider the strategic use by the French colonial forces of the "*razzia*" as a type of population-centric counterterrorist strategy. See, for example, Thomas Rid, "Razzia: A Turning Point in Modern Strategy," *Terrorism and Political Violence* 21 (2009): 617–55.

34. See, University of York staff, "Soviet Order to Exterminate Cossacks Is Unearthed," *University of York*, last modified January 21, 2003, https://www.york.ac.uk/news-and-events/news/2003/cossacks/.

35. See Mark Derewicz, "A Long-Buried War with the Moros," *Endeavors*, last modified January 1, 2006, http://endeavors.unc.edu/win2006/feature_04.php.

36. Dominik J. Schaller, "Raphael Lemkin's View of European Colonial Rule in Africa: between Condemnation and Admiration," *Journal of Genocide Research* 7, no. 4 (December 2005): 531–38.

37. W. E. B. DuBois, *The World and Africa* (New York: Viking Press, 1947), quoted in Robin Kelly, "Poetics of Anticolonialism," *Monthly Review* 51 (1999): 6.

38. Michael Rothberg, "W. E. B. DuBois in Warsaw: Holocaust Memory and the Color Line, 1949–1952," *The Yale Journal of Criticism* 14, no. 1 (Spring 2001): 169–89.

39. See Hannah Arendt, *The Origins of Totalitarianism* (1951; London: Allen & Unwin, 1967).

40. See Christopher J. Lee, "Locating Hannah Arendt with Postcolonial Thought: A Prospectus," *College Literature* 38, no. 1 (Winter 2011): 95–114.

41. Patricia Owens, *Between War and Politics: International Relations and the Thought of Hannah Arendt* (Oxford: Oxford University Press, 2007).

42. Jan-Bart Gewald, "Herero Genocide in the Twentieth Century: Politics and Memory," 291n35.

43. Arendt, *The Origins* . Arendt's work has influenced the thinking of many interdisciplinary scholars. See, for example, Robert Gerwarth and Stephan Malinowski, "Hannah Arendt's Ghosts: Reflections on the Disputable Path from Windhoek to Auschwitz," *Central European History* 42, no. 2 (2009): 279–300; George Steinmetz, *The Devil's Handwriting: Postcoloniality and the German Colonial State in Qingdao, Samoa, and Southwest Africa* (Chicago: University of Chicago Press, 2009), 10–11; Richard H. King and Dane Stone, *Hannah Arendt and the Uses of History: Imperialism, Nation, Race and Genocide* (New York: Berghahn Books, 2007).

44. Robert Gerwarth, "Drawing a Line from Africa to Auschwitz," The *Irish Times*, July 31, 2010, paragraph 7, https://www.irishtimes.com/culture/books/drawing-a-line-from-africa-to-auschwitz-1.630972.

45. Ibid.

46. Steinmetz, *The Devil's Handwriting*, 10n31.

47. Ibid., 11n31.

48. Ibid. See also Arendt, *The Origins of Totalitarianism*, 194, 190, 186, 192.

49. Ibid.

50. Steinmetz, *The Devil's Handwriting*, 11n31 (his emphasis). See Arendt, *The Origins*, 205.

51. Steinmetz, *The Devil's Handwriting*, 10–11.

52. Benjamin Madley, "From Africa to Auschwitz: How German South West Africa Incubated Ideas and Methods Adopted and Developed by the Nazis in Eastern Europe," *European Historical Quarterly* 35, no. 3 (2005): 429–64, 429.

53. Chief Riruako, quoted in John C. Torpey, *Making Whole What Has Been Smashed: On Reparations Politics* (Cambridge: Harvard University Press, 2006), 135.

54. *Herero People's Reparations Corporation v. Deutsche Bank*, 370 F. 3d 1192, 361, U.S. App. D.C. 468, 21, quoted in Bargueño, "Cash," 402–3.

55. For a related critique of this "Auschwitz-centered" discourse see Timothy Snyder, "In Defense of Bloodlands," *Tablet*, last modified August 3, 2012, https://www.tabletmag.com/jewish-arts-and-culture/books/108229/in-defense-of-bloodlands.

56. See Susanne Grindel , "Educating the Nation. German History Textbooks since 1900: Representations of Colonialism," Mélanges de l'École française de Rome - Italie et Méditerranée modernes et contemporaines (2015):127–2 | 2015, http://journals.openedition.org/mefrim/2250; DOI: 10.4000/mefrim.2250; Lars Müller, "'We Need to Get Away from a Culture of Denial?' The German Herero in Politics and Textbooks," *Postcolonial Memory Politics in Educational Media* 5, no. 1 (March 2013): 50–71.

57. Steinmetz, *The Devil's Handwriting*, 135.

58. Horst Drechsler, *Let Us Die Fighting: The Struggle of the Herero and Nama against German Imperialism (1884–1915)*, (London: Zed Press, 1980).

59. Steinmetz, *The Devil's Handwriting*, 136.

60. Drechsler, quoted in Steinmetz, *The Devil's Handwriting*, 136.

61. Brigitte Lau, quoted in Steinmetz, *The Devil's Handwriting*, 136–40.

62. Steinmetz, *The Devil's Handwriting*, 139–41.

63. Helmut Bley, *South-West Africa under German Rule, 1894–1914* translated by Hugh Ridley (London, Heinemann, 1971).

64. Steinmetz, *The Devil's Handwriting*, 140.

65. For a helpful overview of how some of these GSWA *Sonderweg* arguments resembled some of the 1980s debates on German Holocaust histories, see Matthew P. Fitzpatrick, "The Pre-history of the Holocaust? The *Sonderweg* and *Historikersteit* Debates and the Abject Colonial Past," *Central European History* 41 (2008): 477–503.

66. For a very different take on this alleged genocide denialism or cultural forgetting, see Lars Müller, "'We Need to Get Away from a Culture of Denial'?: The German

Herero War in Politics and Textbooks," *Journal of Educational Media, Memory, and Society* 5, no. 1 (2013): 50–71.

67. Jon Bridgman, *The Revolt of the Hereros* (Berkeley: University of California Press, 1981)

68. Peter H. Katjavivi, *A History of Resistance in Namibia* (London: Zed Books, 1988).

69. Brigitte Lau, "Uncertain Certainties: The Herero-German War of 1904," *Mibagus* 2 (April 1989): 4–5, 8.

70. Tilman Dedering, "The German-Herero War of 1904: Revisionism of Genocide or Imaginary Historiography?" *Journal of South African Studies* 19, no. 1 (1993): 80–88.

71. Jan-Bart Gewald, *Herero Heroes: A Socio-political History of the Herero of Namibia, 1890–1923* (Athens: Ohio University Press, 1999).

72. Casper W. Erichsen, "Shark Island, 1904–1907: A Historical Overview," Namibia Digital Repository , accessed September 26, 2018, http://namibia.leadr.msu.edu/items/show/154.

73. Erichsen, "Shark Island, 1904–1907," 7.

74. Stoler, *Duress*, 9.

SEVEN

The 2001 Herero People's Reparations Case Filed in U.S. Courts

Earlier in this book I underscored the point that talk of "indemnities," the return of stolen lands, and other types of moral or legal redress for colonial wrongs had been circulating for at least a century before Paramount Chief Kuaima Riruako and his supporters filed the first of the Herero reparations cases in a Washington, DC, federal courtroom in 2001. This would be a type of legal action that focused exclusive attention on Ovaherero grievances.

Many supporters of the Ovaherero reparations movement talked and wrote as if 2001 American courts had to follow the legal precedents that were set by the 1952 German-Israeli reparations agreement, but the judges who heard these cases had other plans. Legal interpretations change, and so do situational factors and the rhetorical climates that set the stage for the passage of particular legislative measures.[1] I share Sidney Harring's opinion that by 2001 there really wasn't any "consistent" rationale that was being used for any modern "reparations regimes."[2] It was not always easy to predict how groups of American judges were going to interpret and apply provisions of the Alien Tort Statute (ATS) in reparations cases. As Anthony Bellia Jr. and Bradford Clarke would note in a 2011 essay in *The University of Chicago Law Review*, the ATS was rarely "invoked for almost two centuries," but in "the 1980s lower federal district courts in the U.S. began reading this statute "expansively to allow foreign citizens to sue other foreign citizens for all violations of modern customary international law that occurred outside the United States."[3] However, since that time American judges had oftentimes read the ATS in much more restrictive ways.[4]

Although law review authors tried to make sense of the mixed bag of successes and failures of reparations lawsuits that were filed in both domestic and international forums after the 1952 West German-Israeli agreement, it seemed as though the best that observers could come up with were some insights regarding the situational factors that seemed to influence post-1952 reparations decisions. Having living witnesses who suffered through genocides helped those who filed these reparations cases, and it mattered whether scholars and diplomats viewed particular violent activities as warranting the label of "genocide."

In this particular chapter I want to show readers how lawyers, judges, activists, governmental officials, and other commentators reacted when they were confronted with the Ovaherero's 2001 lawfare, and I want to explain some of reasons why these claimants may have decided to file these reparations claims in U.S. courts.

In theory, the Ovaherero could have sued in German courts, Namibian courts, or sought out hearings in international tribunals. Talk of the growth of international criminal law and the influence of international humanitarian law (IHL) was in the air. Although Michael Scott had failed to convince UN officials to intercede on behalf of the Africans in South West Africa during the apartheid years, perhaps the passage of time might help new reparations Namibian advocates.

By the end of the twentieth century it was astonishing to note just how many reparations cases were being filed across the globe. Jeremy Sarkin pointed out that legal cases involving "former colonial communities" have been filed in many national and international forums. For example, courts in the United Kingdom heard cases on damages for Maasai farmers in Kenya who have been killed or maimed over the last fifty years by British Army explosives that have been left behind during counterinsurgency efforts, and the British Ministry of Defence (MoD) has been sued for failing to prevent the rape of some 650 women by soldiers.[5] Other cases have been filed by Ugandans complaining about human rights abuses. Tanzanians wanted legal redress for the killing of two hundred and fifty thousand Makonde, Makua, Matumbi, Ngoni, Waluguru, and Yao.[6] In Asia there were cases involving complaints about Japanese imperial misbehavior during the occupation of Korea and China.[7]

Those who watched the filing of these types of lawsuits may have felt this was a good time for the Ovaherero to pursue their reparations claims in American courtrooms. First of all, the more than two-hundred-year-old Alien Tort Claims Act of 1789 seemed to allow for these types of civil law suits.[8] Philip Musolino, the lawyer who was chosen to head up the legal team working for the Ovaherero plaintiffs, had already made a name for himself suing to help South African litigants and other aggrieved parties. A second reason for traveling to U.S. courts had everything to do with Namibian governmental reluctance to back these types of cases. Minister Hifikepunye Pohamba and former president Sam Nujoma valued the signing of bilateral agreements with Germany, because these agreements helped with the infrastructural development in Namibia.

The Ovaherero activists interested in pursuing reparations claims were aware of this hesitancy, but they were convinced that their impoverished communities in Namibia would receive little of that German developmental money. The activists were also aware that many of the Ovambo who held the power in Namibia were suspicious of alleged Ovaherero opportunism and "tribalism."

The Ovaherero activists who initiated this 2001 U.S. suit thus had the unenviable task of trying to take German corporations and other defendants to court without the public support of the Namibian government because Namibian officials did not believe that any single ethnic "tribe" in Namibia needed to be singled out as recipients of German reparations payments.[9] Ovaherero favoritism was viewed as a potential threat to Namibian unity, given the fact that most Namibians believed that they had all suffered during the colonial and apartheid years.

Critical genealogical scholars who review some of the texts produced by Kuaima Riruako and the other litigants during the mass-mediated coverage of this first reparations case will get the textured sense that there was a great deal of improvisation taking place as these litigants tried to deal with the intricacies of U.S. lawfare. Those who track the multiple trajectories of the *Riruako* case will find that the presses seemed to be reporting on all sorts of trial and error tactics, and more than a few journalists and interviewees wondered if impoverished Namibians would ever receive any help from American jurists.

I will be arguing that the lawyers for Kuaima Riruako and the Herero People's Corporation decided to assemble together historical arguments and legal texts that were drawn from the materials that documented those annihilationist colonial rhetorics that were circulating between 1893 and 1908. A close reading of the plaintiff's complaint that was filed in Washington, DC in September of 2001 shows the selective nature of the sources that would be used to put together the "merits" portions of this case.

Interestingly enough, the three sources that were primarily used to rhetorically craft this 2001 complaint depended on materials from that infamous "Blue Book," the academic writings of Jon Bridgman,[10] and the 1999 "revisionist" work of Jan-Bart Gewald (see chapter 6).[11] Readers will recall that Professor Gewald was the one who tried to claim that it had been anxious and misguided German officers who started the 1904 Ovaherero-German war and not the indigenous Africans.

Synchronic readings of national and transcontinental responses to these 2001 filings that circulated before, during, and after the filing of the *Riruako* case show that opinions differed regarding the wisdom, the feasibility, and the impact that these efforts might have on Namibian-German relationships. Gesine Krüger averred that the Herero restitution claims might help open up a multifaceted debate on Namibian history's "violations of human rights."[12] Manfried Hinz reminded readers that at the beginning of the 1990s, an American citizen, Hugo Princz, had tried to sue Germany for compensation for forced labor during his stay in a German concentration camp, and that the *Princz* case had been filed in the same court, the District Court of Columbia, which received the first Herero reparations filings.[13]

Manfried Hinz's critique underscored the point that America's appellate courts were not necessarily helping litigants win their reparations cases. He was writing these comments while the Ovaherero lawsuit was pending, and he explained to readers that a U.S. Court of Appeals had quashed a lower court judgment in the *Princz* case. The appellate court in the *Princz* case accepted Germany's argument that bilateral agreements on sovereign immunity meant that Germany could not be judged by a U.S. court.[14]

Hinz would be prescient when he argued in 2004 that future litigants, who were trying to emulate the successes of those who filed the earlier Holocaust reparations cases, should not assume that courts in America were going to automatically accept jurisdiction over claims for damages against nation-states for alleged atrocities that were committed in foreign countries.[15]

While some reviewers of these cases might want to use formalistic or positivist analyses of these decisions, my interest in extending the work of Third World Approaches to International Law (TWAIL) and post-structural writers influences the ways that I note the ruptures, the contradictions, the indeterminacies, and the contingencies of these particular reparations efforts. I view these reparations cases as types of lawfare that blurred the purported lines that existed between politics and law, and rhetoric and the "rule of law." Moreover, I agree with Catherine Lu's assessment that addressing and redressing colonial injustices often means that those interested in pursuing reparations claims need to focus on structural, and not individuated features of large-scale atrocities:

> [R]eparation in the forms of official acknowledgment, apology, and financial compensation to individual victims is one important component of interactional justice and reconciliation. . . . [S]eeing colonialism as structural injustice illuminates objectionable social structures—often based on race, class, and gender categories that transcend nationalistic and statist divides.[16]

It matters how reparations litigants frame their legal and public commentaries as they discuss the long-term impact of colonial rule.

As I noted in earlier chapters, many Ovaherero litigants and their supporters seemed to have been convinced that their case was just good as the Holocaust reparations precedents. What the Ovaherero may not have known is that they were walking into a prefigurative world where

American configurations of the ideograph "human rights" influenced how participants in all this lawfare viewed allegations of colonial genocide. All the politics that swirled around old colonial claims, U.S. jurisdictional requirements, the predispositions of judges, and narrow interpretations of the Alien Torts Claims Act complicated all of this and made it extremely difficult for the Ovaherero litigants to win this 2001 reparations case.

Take, for example, the issue of whether or not the Ovaherero had exhausted all of their other remedies and were filing a justiciable legal claim that warranted U.S. federal court intervention. The more that the Ovaherero and their lawyers showed the horrific "genocidal" nature of the South West African militarism that affected many indigenous communities after the Ohamakari/Waterberg 1904 battle, the more difficult it became to show that the Ovaherero had suffered in disproportionate ways. After all, the thousands of *Schutztruppe* who arrived in 1904 killed many Nama, San,[17] and other indigenous groups during the fighting who were not Herero.

As Jan-Bart Gewald would note, when the "Herero camps were finally abolished in 1908," they found themselves "confined within a tangled web of legislation that sought to control the lives, in their entirety, or all black people living in German South West Africa."[18]

The more that the lawyers for the Ovaherero commented on the reprehensible actions of the Germany protection forces, the banks who bankrolled the war, and the ships that carried the troops and weapons, the more this *involved non-Herero victims.*

I will also be arguing in this chapter that the Ovaherero litigants may have committed some political and legal blunders when they did not include the Nama in their early reparations efforts. The initial recruiting of members of the Herero People's Reparations Corporation involved the inclusion of Ovaherero from Namibia, but it should be pointed out that they had left out some U.S. citizens who were of Ovaherero descent.

Moreover, the temporal and spatial distances involved with documenting the harms that were suffered nearly a hundred years earlier created legal headaches for Philip Musolino and the other attorneys who were trying to establish the "connections" that were needed for jurisdiction under the Alien Tort Claims Act.[19]

With this in mind, my critical genealogical critiques in this chapter will begin with a subsection that helps readers to get a contextual sense of the catalytic events that led to the filing of the 2001 Herero lawsuit. During the 1990s, when German officials continually refused to even consider talking with Herero leaders about reparations, this forced Paramount Chief Kuaima Riruako's supporters to consider taking the unusual step of trying to seek restorative justice in foreign venues.

In the second portion of the chapter, I highlight presences and absences that can be found in the initial complaint that Philip Musolino and the other lawyers would file for the Herero People's Reparations Corporation in the fall of 2001. This was a class action suit that involved more than two hundred claimants who argued that they spoke for one hundred twenty-five thousand Ovaherero in Namibia.

The third part of the chapter focuses on how public and legal communities in the United States, Namibia, Germany, and elsewhere reacted to these efforts, and in that portion of the chapter, I note how many of these commentators seemed to be recirculating arguments about colonial wars and Ovaherero aggression that echoed some of the lamentations of the German colonial farmers and soldiers who rationalized their treatment of the Ovaherero "rebels."

Finally, in the concluding portion of this chapter, I explain what all this Ovaherero lawfare has to do with twenty-first-century restorative justice practices.

THE 1990S MARGINALIZATION OF OVAHERERO AND NAMA REPARATIONS CLAIMS

As noted in previous chapters, the Ovaherero's oral traditions, and their sense of "tribe" or "nation," helped them survive the colonial and apartheid years, and since 1923 their annual performative rituals commemorating the efforts of Samuel Maherero and those who followed him. Even when Ovahereros who confronted the power of German-speaking farmers and Afrikaners disagreed about the wisdom of pursuing reparations claims, they nevertheless shared the belief that their pastoral communities were almost wiped out by German soldiers and settlers.

During some of the last apartheid years in South West Africa, advocates who wanted to see belated acknowledgment of these German colonial atrocities seemed to take heart when a United Nation's organization, the Economic and Social Council on Human Rights, decided to include what happened in German South West Africa in their list of historical "genocides." In an influential July 1985 report, Benjamin Whitaker indicated that although there was some dispute about the exact numbers of Ovaherero lives that were lost during the GSWA years, there was evidence of an "intent to destroy" an entire ethnic community, and on that basis this colonial warfare against the Herero and Nama constituted the first genocide of the twentieth century.[20]

There were several reasons why this Whitaker Report stood out. First of all, it could be used as a rhetorical weapon in the arsenal of those who debated with genocide denialists or revisionists. The Namibian historian, Brigitte Lau would write in her "Uncertain Certainties" that Lothar von Trotha's troops did not have any intent to wipe out the Herero after Ohamakari/Waterberg, that scholars misinterpreted his proclamations, that the Herero warriors held their own during battles, and that there was no central colonial plan to get rid of the German colony's labor pool.[21] Those who rhetorically crafted the Whitaker Report countered this type of revisionism.

The Whitaker Report also stood out because, as I noted earlier, most genocide anthologies or monographs that were produced during this period did not include what happened in German South West Africa as one of the century's genocides. UN officials and foreign diplomats knew about the legacy of the Armenian genocide, or the World War II Holocaust, but few included large-scale colonial atrocities in their lists of "historical" genocides. The Whitaker Report seemed to provide the UN's ratification of the claims that appeared in the 1918 Blue Book and the work of Horst Drechsler (1966) and Helmut Bley (1971).

The stance that the authors of the Whitaker Report took needs to be recognized, however, as a minority position, a type of counterhistory or multidirectional memory that was adopted by those who did see how recognizing this particular genocide might threaten conceptualizations of other genocides.

During the 1980s it would be the "*Historikerstreit* debates" in Germany and elsewhere that grabbed the headlines, as conservative German historians started to write about the suffering of German soldiers who were captured by Russians, the treatment of ethnic Germans living in "the East," and the horrors of Allied bombings of places like Dresden.[22]

There were some scholars during this period who tried to revive interest in reconsidering the place of the Ovaherero/Nama genocide in the scholarly canons of Holocaust and genocide studies, but few public communities were receptive to this idea when they first heard these messages. As Henning Melber would argue in 2017, "during 1984, a century after the infamous Berlin Conference, several initiatives" about the Herero genocide "failed to translate into wider public awareness."[23] These disputes stayed within academic circles, and those circles often included Africanists but not necessarily leading Holocaust or modern genocide scholars.

The stories that were told about the Ovaherero rebellion that appeared in the Whitaker Report had to compete with other victimage tales that circulated synchronically during this same period. For example, during the 1980s many global communities were arguing about what to do about South Africa's apartheid practices. Namibians, led by the South West Africa People's Organisation (SWAPO) party, were fighting for independence, while those in public spheres who talked about reparations were usually commenting on compensation for Holocaust victims.

In ironic ways some of the Ovaherero arguments during these turbulent times were kept alive by more empowered rhetors who *ridiculed* the idea of Ovaherero reparations! Wealthy and middle-class German speakers in South West Africa seemed to be suffering from imperial nostalgia or colonial aphasia as they gave speeches about the heroism of the *Schutz-*

truppe. The white "South Westers" maintained their own traditions, they tended their own German graveyards, and they gave speeches attacking Ovaherero versions of Hamakari/Waterberg and the concentration camps. Professor Melber recalled how, during the late apartheid years, "colonial-apologetic reasoning remained more effective than the critical reminders provided by emerging anti-colonial civic actors demanding a decolonization of the mindset."[24]

In the same way that German settlers during the 1920s had demanded the destruction of copies of Blue Books (chapter 4), now groups that included some academically trained historians were demanding that the 1904–1908 violence be viewed as regrettable colonial "wars" and not "genocides." Personal identities, and power politics in Namibia or Germany, became entangled in historiographic disputation and public memory contestation.

After the 1990 announcement of Namibian independence most Namibians—who were led by Northern Ovambo communities and the SWAPO party—wished to unify the nation and celebrate the "special" relationship that they had with Germany.[25] Like many in nearby South Africa Namibians wanted to talk about "reconciliation" and mutual forgetting. The Ovaherero—who comprised somewhere between 7 to 10 percent of the population in Namibia—fought uphill political and cultural battles when they tried to convince their Namibian compatriots that reparations for the Ovaherero were warranted.

During the 1990s, whenever any leading German dignitary came to visit Namibia, a battle of wills took place as various individuals and factions fought over the trajectory of Namibia's future. Those who took part in these diplomatic and social maneuverings were "in the shadow of the genocide," as various social agents on several continents were asked to admit that nations after decolonization were still traumatized by fraught colonial legacies.[26] When German Chancellor Helmut Kohl visited Namibia on September 14, 1995, he stunned many Namibian administrators when he hosted a reception for the German-speaking minority living in Namibia, and he greeted these guests with the words, "my dear fellow-countrymen." Spontaneous applause broke out as the German-speaking minority—who had been asked to become "Namibians"—realized that they did not have to forget their German colonial heritage.[27]

While Chancellor Kohl was visiting that Germany community in Namibia, he ran into three hundred members of "the Herero tribe led by Paramount Chief Kuaima Riruako," who marched toward the German delegation and "handed a petition for Kohl" that contained their requests for acknowledgments of colonial massacres.[28] Riruako was accompanied by an "army" of "*truppenspeiler*" (troop players), who were wearing old, but mended, colonial German uniforms as they carried on a tradition that dated back to colonial days.[29] The petition demanded that Kohl and Germany seriously consider paying reparations, and a meeting with Herero leaders was requested. Instead the German chancellor visited the coastal town of Swakopmund.[30]

Chancellor Kohl's visit was not the only time when the Ovaherero activists gained notoriety for their efforts. Several years later, when Federal President Roman Herzog visited Namibia, instead of talking about reparations or other forms of social redress, he made a show of complaining about how post-Independence Namibian language policies were having a negative effect on the lives of the German-speaking minority in that country.[31]

Visiting German leaders on official state visits did their best to sidestep some of the lingering questions that still hovered over those "special" German-Namibian relationships. They occasionally expressed remorse that horrid things that had happened in some abstract colonial past, but these politicized comments were not linked in any way to any specific acknowledgment of German moral guilt or legal culpability

Yet within that proverbial "court of public" opinion the Ovaherero activists were having better luck as sympathetic media outlets carried stories of Chancellor Kohl's visits and the need for reparations. The British Broadcasting Service (BBC), for example, carried stories about the "Herero tribal members'" attempts to gain Kohl's attention.[32] Several years later South Africa's *Mail and Guardian* carried a story about the "Hitler's Forgotten Namibian Victims,"[33] an obvious example of a vernacular rendering of that academic "continuity" thesis. That same news outlet contained a story in 1998 about how the Ovaherero were the "tribe Germany wants to forget."[34] John Grobler explained that unlike the "politically dominant Ovambo people—who were represented by the South West African Peoples Organization (SWAPO)—the Hereros during and after colonial wars had lost most of the lands that their cattle needed for grazing."[35] Donald McNeil, Jr., writing for the *New York Times*, assured readers that the Ovaherero were the type of tribe that wore "its past on its sleeve" as it sought apologies from the Bonn government.[36] This, of course, implied that most of those who followed German or Namibian colonial or postcolonial affairs did not wear their past on their sleeves.

Law review writers during this same period also helped spread awareness about the Ovaherero reparations cause. Oftentimes the authors of the law reviews published in the 1990s speculated about the strength of potential cases that could be filed by all types of litigants. Lynn Berat, in the *Pace International Law Review*, floated the idea that the Namibian government itself might have had its own reparations case against Germany if Namibians wanted to pursue that route.[37] However, given SWAPO's power, and Namibia's "special" relationship with Germany, this was highly unlikely.

During this period Namibian governmental officials tried to stay out of the Ovaherero reparations debates. Instead, it would be Kuaima Riruako who would receive the lion's share of media attention as he started to talk to the press about the potential filing of reparations suits. Riruako talked about how the Herero Traditional Authority was still waiting on Bonn to act on their requests for meetings and reparations, and he did more than hint that if those efforts failed then the Ovaherero might have to ask for UN interventionism.

One of the arguments that Riruako's supporters would hear time and time again was that the *Schutztruppe*, between 1904 and 1908, had indiscriminately killed any African who possessed a dark skin. If this was the case, then why should the Herero be the only plaintiffs? This was a time of moral equivalence argument that could deployed to try and discourage the Ovaherero from seeking lawfare redress in legal venues.

Many listeners who heard these 1990s arguments seemed to sense the contradictions and the politics that swirled around these Ovaherero reparations claims. More than one hundred twenty thousand Ovaherero were being pulled in different directions—by those who wanted them to be "Namibians" and set aside their "tribalism," and by those who were equally adamant that the Herero had been the special ethnic targets of German colonial annihilationists.

Riruako, however, did not seem to worry about these tensions, and he tried to cope with German governmental indifference. In 2001 he helped assemble the Herero People's Reparation Corporation, and this led to the filing of a lawsuit in the Superior Court of the District of Columbia in the United States.

Those who wrote about Riruako's efforts often emphasized the communal nature of this lawsuit. One newspaper in Namibia later reported that some two hundred prominent Ovaherero agreed to become a part of Riruako's lawsuit. Journalists explained to readers of their newspapers that these litigants were asking the U.S. federal courts to hear their demands that billions of dollars be paid by German corporations, and later a related filing would accuse the German government of carrying out atrocities that killed many Ovaherero who were living under colonial "occupation."[38] Media sources averred that Herero People's Reparation Corporation (HPRC) was asking for $2 billion from the German government, and the same sum from the German corporations.[39]

In 2003 the reparations case that was filed in the Superior Court in Washington, DC, was transferred to New York.[40] Some observers regarded this as a frivolous suit that had no chance of winning, but others believed that the Herero People's Reparation Corporation was using lawfare in productive ways to advance the cause of tens of thousands of Ovaherero.

How would the lawyers representing the Ovaherero cope with the archival materials that contained both accommodationist and annilationist clusters of colonial arguments? Would they purposely avoid using that infamous British Blue Book, and what types of materials from the German Kaiser's General Staff would make their way into the legal texts in these cases? Given the importance of the Alien Tort Statute (ATS), what type of "connections" would the plaintiffs' lawyers try to make between what happened between 1904 and 1908 and U.S. shores in 2001?

In this next section I provide readers with a critical reading of the Ovaherero's reparations complaint that was assembled by the legal team working for Musolino and Dessel, because I view this text as a condensation symbol for the collective views of many Namibian indigenous communities.

A CRITICAL TEXTUAL READING OF THE 2001 OVAHERERO REPARATIONS COMPLAINT

The 2001 complaint that was filed for the Herero People's Corporation was a forty-five-page text that was arranged chronologically, and it was arranged this way so that it might help American judges conceptualize the gradual dispossession, and the inhumanity, of what would took place in German South West Africa between the early 1880s and August of 1907. The defendants in the case included Disconto-Gesellschaft (acquired by Deutsche Bank in 1929), and Terex, the successor in interest to, or merger partner of, Orenstein-Koppel. Another defendant was Deutsche-Afrika-Linien, a German corporation that had acquired the older Woermann Shipping Line of Hamburg, Germany. Deutsche Bank had played a leading role in financing most of the banking and financing projects in GSWA from 1890 to 1915, Orenstein-Koppel had been in charge of most of the railway construction during that period, and this was an organization that would be accused by the plaintiffs' lawyers of prospering for 125 years by taking advantage of a "slave labor system" without ever showing any "degree of remorse" for the suffering of the women and children who were treated as slaves before they died.[41]

Adopting language that seemed to have been taken from that old 1918 British Blue Book, the authors of the Ovaherero complaint argued that the three German corporations were part of a "German colonial enterprise" that contributed to the genocide of the Herero.[42] Woermann was also accused of employing slave labor and of running its own concentration camps.

These characterizations of German colonial banking, railway, and shipping enterprises was very much a product of their time, given the fact that during the late 1990s American courts and other judicial forms were hearing cases about the involvement of Swiss banks in the formation of Holocaust enterprises.[43] This type of GSWA corporatized contextualization also resembled the legal cases that had been filed against corporations involved in South African apartheid cases.[44]

Many of these civil cases tried to maintain a focus on matters of international law as well as domestic law, and the plaintiffs who bring these civil suits usually try to argue that some "*jus cogens* norm"—or a major principle of international law that is widely accepted by the larger communities or states as a norm—cannot be derogated and needs to be heard by a competent court. The lawyers who file these cases in American courts then argue that this involves matters of "universal jurisdiction," and then they go on to claim that U.S. courtrooms have been, and should be, used to punish violations of those international law norms. In a key precedent, *Princz v. Federal Republic of Germany* (1994), a U.S. federal district court in the District of Columbia had made the observation that a court was in the presence of violations *jus cogens* norms if a state

> practices, encourages, or condones (a) genocide, (b) slavery or slave trade, (c) murder or causing the disappearance of individuals, (d) torture or other cruel, inhuman, or degrading punishment, (e) prolonged arbitrary detention, (f) systematic racial discrimination, or (g) a consistent pattern of gross violations of internationally recognized human rights.[45]

In this particular case the Ovaherero plaintiffs tried to argue that their claims were based exclusively on a federal common law claim.

The lawyers who prepared the complaint for the Herero Peoples' Reparations Corporation, the Herero Tribe of Namibia,[46] and individual members of the Herero Tribe, took the position that German banks, railway construction companies, and shipping lines had not only profited, but had employees who participated in, some of the genocidal acts that almost wiped out the Ovaherero. The authors of the complaint could show their American readers that the Ovaherero nation had been reduced from a population of eighty thousand to fifteen thousand. U.S. jurists were informed that those Ovaherero who survived—including some 10,632 women and children—were then placed in horrid German concentration camps.[47]

The implicit, enthymematic argument was clear—how did these women or children pose any threat to this German "colony," and for what possible reason were they placed in camps to die away if there was no genocidal intent on the part of the traders, settlers, bankers, miners, shippers, and so on, who were a part of this "colonial enterprise"?

As readers might imagine, those who authored this 2001 complaint did not cite the work of the German-speaking "hobby historians" (Professor Kössler's phrase), or the German or Namibian writers who questioned the genocide thesis or the continuity thesis or the *Sonderweg* thesis. Instead, they used the academic work of Horst Dreschler, Jon Bridgman, and Jan Bart Gewald[48] to craft a metanarrative of how a once proud "indigenous people" who were engaged in "pastoralism, horticulture, and hunter-gathering" were reduced to a state of colonial subservience and slavery.[49]

The Ovaherero complaint was well written, and the historical trajectory of the claimants' position was relatively easy to follow. In one key portion of the 2001 complaint, the authors of this class action tort suit noted how in today's Namibia, some "25,000 German farmers" "now owned the millions of hectares that comprised Herero land before the tribe's genocidal destruction by Imperial Germany and the defendants at the turn of the century."[50] This was a transparent way of implying that today's Ovaherero were still suffering from the lingering effects of colonialism, and that claimants' lawyers could document the collective traumas that were experienced by the descendants of those who suffered at Ohamakari/Waterberg or died in the camps.

After mentioning contemporary Namibian inequities, the authors of the Ovaherero complaint showed how, from the early 1880s to the beginning of the 1904 Herero-German war, descendants of the plaintiffs had to watch as their lands, their herds of cattle, their economies, their "cosmology," and their "spatio-political" organization were lost as German settlers violated protection agreements and ignored international law provisions that were in place at the time.[51]

In the historical sections of this complaint, Jon Bridgman's work was cited to explain what life was like for the Ovaherero before the arrival of the German colonizers. The Ovaherero were described as Bantu-speaking groups from the North who were, and should be, labeled as "tribes" or "nations."[52]

The use of this grammatology was important because it allowed the lawyers for the Ovaherero to argue that the Herero tribes possessed sovereign rights that should have been respected by the defendants and others involved in the "German colonial enterprise."

The authors of this claimant brief wisely chose to avoid using the old German colonial assimilationist arguments that assumed that most of these lands were "*terra nullius*," unoccupied and unused in the colonial mythologies that configured these indigenous communities as wandering, nomadic African tribes. Instead of viewing the pre-colonial Ovaherero as scattered groups of pastoralists who were disunited and fighting amongst themselves, the Ovaherero were configured as members of a premodern or modern society that was already in the process of becoming centralized and federated at the very time the German occupiers arrived in this part of Africa. The Ovaherero complaint contained sections that indicated that the Ovaherero had "chieftances centered upon specific geographic areas."[53] These chieftances were ignored when Europeans who attended the Berlin Conference of 1884–1885 ratified "German's intrusion into Southwest Africa."[54]

One of the defendants in this legal action, Deutsche Bank, was characterized as a "principle investor" in the new German ventures in this part of the world when that bank helped Adolf Lüderitz and the *Deutsche Sudwestafrika Gesellschaft* corporation gain illicit control of areas in and around Lüderitz. The Ovaherero lawyers showed how in April 2, 1885, in Berlin, the defendant Deutsche Bank obtained a corporate commitment to "take over the exercise of state sovereignty, as far as that can be transferred to the company on behalf of its territories."[55]

In the social dramas that were produced for U.S. judges in this complaint, Otto von Bismarck is depicted as someone who had deal with emboldened corporate investors who leveraged their power to have a say in the running of German South West Africa. In the complaint's chronicling of events, these German corporations' exercise of sovereignty was done in destructive ways that had little to do with constructive settlement policies.

Some of the most important parts of this lawfare reframing of select academic works came when the authors of this complaint tried to explain to readers some of the pivotal decisions that were made that showed the disdain and the racial animus of the defendants and the soldiers and administrators who were sent to German South West Africa. From a critical indigenous vantage point, this was another example of what Manu Vimalassery, Juliana Hu Pegues, and Alyosha Goldstein characterized as the "colonial unknowing."[56]

Instead of respecting the Ovaherero communities and preserving their sovereignty, the Germans were said to have acted as occupiers who worked away at grabbing up land and herds of cattle. A pivotal moment in time came when Otto von Bismarck, in June of 1889, sent twenty-one German soldiers under the command of Captain Curt von François to GSWA. This decision, argued the authors of this Herero complaint, meant that the Kaiser's Second Reich was changing its level of commitment, so that now GSWA became a "German colony" that would be governed by the "German colonial enterprise."

Von François's arrival also signaled that this colonial enterprise was now moving from civilian to military oversight. "Military force," and not reliance on "treaties" signed with indigenous Herero tribes," would guide colonial decision making.[57] The Ovaherero lawyers averred that by 1890 the "overriding objectives and demands of the German commercial enterprise were tragically and inalterably fixed."[58] From a *realpolitik* standpoint, there would be fewer pretentions that this was Ovaherero land that was protected through treaties.

Although some portions of the complaint mentioned the wording of bilateral treaties and early twentieth-century interpretations of international humanitarian law or international criminal law, there was little citation of German legal sources on the relevance of treaties and the need to protect indigenous rights. This would be one of the major differences between this 2001 complaint and the one that would later be filed in 2017 for Ovaherero and Nama litigants (see chapter 9).

In the 2001 complaint readers were invited to see how the defendants' actions violated post–World War II anti-genocide norms. The defendants were accused of "willfully violating fundamental principles of international law, and willfully" engaging in "crimes against humanity."[59]

In many ways it seemed as though the Ovaherero plaintiffs were trying to use expansive definitions of genocide that came from writers like Raphael Lemkin, who reasoned that genocidal acts involved more than just the systematic, "physical," or "biological" destruction of ethnic communities. Here it was assumed that the destruction of Ovaherero "cultures" by colonial corporations also constituted genocidal acts. As noted in early chapters, critical genocide scholars or settler-colonial scholars call this "cultural genocide."

Note the wide range of practices that were mentioned by the plaintiffs' lawyers as they tried to outline which specific acts carried out by the "German colonial enterprise" warranted judicial redress: (a) initiation of and implementation of a race war against the Herero; (b) initiation of and implementation of an implicit and explicit campaign of genocide, extermination ,and extirpation of the Hereros; (c) the brutalization and enslavement of the Hereros, and the systematic use of forced labor; (d) the systematic forced degradation of Herero women held as captives; and (e) the systematic destruction of the Herero culture.[60]

Many critics of Ovaherero reparations lawsuits don't like to see legal commentaries on reparation claims that are based on *retrospective* applications of post–World War II IHL norms, so the writers of the claimant's brief included some historical material on late nineteenth-century and early twentieth-century international criminal laws and international humanitarian laws. For example, mention was made of the German pledges that were made when, in July of 1890, German diplomats attended the Anti-Slavery Conference in Brussels. During these conference proceedings the German delegates had promised that they would protect "native" races in African from slavery and oppression. "In German Southwest Africa," argued these legal authors, "that pledge evaporated in the face of brutal demands of the German commercial enterprise."[61] Now the surviving Herero were treated as "helots" and slaves who died after being placed in labor camps.

Note how this echoes some of the socialist or Marxist claims that appeared in some of the work of Horst Drechsler and others who wanted to include class critiques in their analysis of the Namibian genocide.

Ovaherero attorneys also cited diverse materials that came from all types of colonizers who supported the efforts of those who accepted, or demanded, the brutal treatment of the Herero. Paul Rohrbach. a famous colonial apologist, was quoted extensively, and one portion of the Herero complaint highlighted the ways that Rorhbach was writing as if colonization itself was deemed to be an acceptable and violent activity:

> The decision to colonize . . . means nothing less than the Native tribes must withdraw from the lands on which they have pastured their cattle

> and let the white man pasture his cattle on the self-same lands. If the moral rights of this standpoint is questioned, the answer is that for people of the cultural standard of South Africa natives, the loss of their free national barbarism and the development of a class of worker in the service of and dependent on the whites is primarily a law of existence in the highest degree.[62]

It would be difficult to find a better example of how European ideological theories about Social Darwinian were being operationalized in self-serving ways to naturalize white settler dispossession of indigenous lands. Note also the similarities that existed between Rohrbach's views and the views of Governor Theodor Leutwein that I referenced in chapter 2.

In intriguing ways, those who crafted this particular rhetorical text were able to find arguments from early twentieth-century German decision makers that sounded much like the claims that were advanced by twenty-first-century critics of Ovaherero reparations payments! One portion of the complaint critiqued some of the remarks that were made by German Chancellor Count von Caprivi before the Reichstag on March 1, 1893. There he had said, "We have South West Africa. . . . I shall avoid retrospective consideration as to how we got it. . . . Now it is a German land and must remain a German land."[63] Compare this with how German diplomats talk about the need to avoid applying UN standards for genocide, as well as other investigative journalist commentaries on "retrospective" postcolonial analyses.[64] The lawyers for the Ovaherero, writing in 2001, were trying to do exactly what German Chancellor Count von Caprivi claimed should not be done.

By the early 1890s it seemed as though fewer German settlers or soldiers or bankers or railway engineers or shippers wanted to even pretend that they were occupying, or "renting," indigenous lands. Now the Kaiser's government, working with banks and corporations, were selling concessions to land companies, and this in turn aided settlers who thought it was safe to travel to places like "Hereroland" or "Damaraland." Colonial governmental authorities, especially those working in and around Windhoek, granted lands to the *Deutschen Kolonialgesellschaft*.[65] It was argued that by this time "each of the defendants, or their predecessors, had assumed significant, influential and profitable roles in the German commercial enterprise."[66]

After making these claims the authors of this class action complaint could then spend more time outlining the specific activities of that "German commercial enterprise" that were problematic. For instance, before turning to the beginning of the 1904 war with the Herero, these legal writers could mention Chief Henrik Witbooi's reactions to the massacre of some 150 Nama men, women, and children at Hoornkrans. The Ovaherero fared no better when von François was replaced by the more moderate Major Theodor Leutwein.[67] The complaint implied that only the pace of dispossession changed. Major Leutwein—who had a legal background—would later become a governor, and he may have been chosen for all these important positions because he had a classical education. He could use a different type of wordsmithing to preserve what the plaintiffs' lawyers called the "power of the German colonial enterprise."[68]

The authors of the 2001 complaint alleged that Major Theodor Leutwein used divide-and-conquer strategies that pitted the Ovaherero against other tribes like the Nama, and this German governor worked to help with the building of railroads and harbors that would allow for the mobilizing of troops who could police these German lands. Jan-Bart Gewald was quoted as arguing that Leutwein was hoping that the those in "Hereroland" who moved northward to avoid German settlement would soon be pressured into selling their huge herds of cattle to the European settlers.[69] The Ovaherero's political and economic power would disappear, and they would be forced to work for the German rulers.

This 2001 complaint was a prime example of how select materials from academic secondary sources can be marshalled together in powerful ideological and legalistic ways. Like all lawfare texts, the Ovaherero complaint would be filled with contingencies, contradictions, and partial argumentative claims, but it took advantage of Jan-Bart Gewald's 1990s academic arguments that placed the blame for the start of the 1904 war on the shoulders of the Germans. The plaintiffs' lawyers, following the lead of Gewald, argued that it had been panicking German soldiers, and not the Ovaherero, who started the Herero-German war.

Unlike many previous attempts at documenting colonial genocidal acts—that focused primarily on the social agency of single individuals like General von Trotha—this particular complaint highlighted *the many structural of functional features* of German capitalist ventures in GSWA.

Foucauldians or postcolonial scholars would be able to recognize both the biopolitical and thanatopolitical arguments that were used by some of these plaintiff's lawyers. "The German colonial enterprise," they argued, "imposed new borders on the indigenous people of South West Africa by force of arms, by threat of arms, and by exorbitant commercial pressure, including fraud, unconscionable debt collection practices and withholding [of] medicines and vaccines."[70] This referencing of vaccines was meant to underscore the point that Germans could use their modern medical knowledge to inoculate their herds to protect their herds from the Rinderpest diseases that would wipe out Ovaherero herds in 1897 that were not vaccinated.

Clearly the physical massacres that were carried out at places like Ohamakari/Waterberg were not the only thanatopolitical ways of bringing the creative destruction that was supposed to be a precondition for the biopolitical emergence of what I would call a "Herero free" GSWA.

These types of plaintiff arguments anticipated, and countered, the arguments that might be made by defense attorneys who could try and argue that the land owned by twenty-five thousand German-speaking Namibians was legally purchased from Ovahereros and other indigenous communities. As the authors of the 2001 Herero complaint would note, Herero lands were considered to be communal lands. Those who wrote this complaint wisely avoided discussing the social agency of Samuel Maherero and others who grew rich profiting from the sale of land to the Germans. By 1895, according to these writers, it seemed as though the German banks and commercial organizations that were influencing GSWA policies had awarded concessionary companies land rights, and mining rights to "virtually all" of GSWA.[71]

Many neoliberal writers often view Theodore Leutwein as a more moderate German colonizer who expressed some cultural sensitivity in his dealings with indigenous African tribes, but there others, like Gewald, who are very critical of Leutwein's brand of liberal racial colonialism, Writers like Jon Bridgman and Gewald have noted that under Leutwein's leadership soldiers and settlers continued to talk about the need for reservations for the "natives," and the German administrators prioritized the completion of railroad projects that helped ensure that by the end of 1903, the Ovaherero had lost "three-and-one half million acres out of a total of thirteen million hectares" of land.[72]

This 2001 complaint was written by those who did a fine job of explaining how Leutwein's colonizing efforts were criticized by settlers as being too respect of Herero rights, and those who knew about his meetings and letter exchanges with individuals like "Kaptein" Henrik Witbooi were convinced that Leutwein, and some sentimental missionaries, were standing in the way of even more German settlement expansionism. The lawyers who prepared this complaint mentioned how Carl Weiss, a settler representative, sent petitions to those in Berlin complaining that Leutwein's milder form of "*Eingeborenen politik*"—the politics with foreign non-Europeans—was threatening the security of GSWA.[73] In spite of the fact that from 1896 to 1903 the Herero "saw much of their best lands and a good portion of their cattle pass" into the hands of the colonizers,[74] settlers were viewing these matters through other lens as they demanded that the Kaiser's advisers sent over military officers who knew how to treat inferiors.

In the second part of their 2001 complaint the authors could now use this historical contextualization to make more pointed case-brief type of arguments about genocide and jurisdiction. Quoting the work of Jon Bridgman, these lawyers alleged that the defendants, "as part of the German colonial enterprise, fomented racial hatred, which led to genocide." It was added that the newer arrivals who immigrated from Germany with many of the *Schutztruppe* seemed to be less charitable than those who arrived earlier, and now some of these new settlers and soldiers wondered whether the colony might not be better off "if the black population were completely eliminated."[75] This was a clear adoption of legalistic arguments based on evidencing of annihilationist reasoning. This complemented, and at times, contradicted, the positions that appeared earlier in the complaint that highlighted indigenous ownership of land.

The authors of this 2001 complaint could now write about the raping of Herero women, the flogging of Ovaherero workers and prisoners, the desecration of the graves of the great chiefs Tjamuaha and Kamaherero, cattle confiscation, and forced labor. Banks and shipping lines were characterized as major contributors to that "enterprise" that seemed to adopt as its mantra, "leniency towards the native is cruelty to the whites."[76]

Deutsche Bank, the Otavi Mines and Railway Company (OMEG), and the Woermann Shipping Land corporation were characterized in this 2001 complaint as entities that controlled travel by land or water. All of this building of needed colonial infrastructures required even more lands, more "slave" labor, and the "elimination of the Herero as a racial, political, ethnic and tribal entity."[77]

To make matters worse it seemed as though the defendants were complicit in the ushering in of a "phoney war" that served to cover the actions of those who how helped fund the building of concentration camps for the Herero and other indigenous detainees. After all, those who "envisaged" a "dream of living as a colonial landed gentry"[78] had to segregate those threatened the colony.

At this point readers might guess that the complaint authors' commentary about the "German colonial enterprise" had to include material on Lothar von Trotha, and it did. It would be the 1918 British Blue Book that provided most of the quotations and citations for this part of the complaint. When it came to the formation of the concentration camps, it was argued that the Woermann Line, OMEG, and other companies, "with the financial support of Deutschebank," had "brutally used the concentration camp system for their economic benefit."[79]

After reading all of this, and after seeing materials on the racial studies of Eugen Fischer, the death rates in the labor and concentration camps, and the use of Ovaherero as "guinea pigs,"[80] readers of this complaint could fairly conclude that the defendants' predecessors had played major roles in carrying out of genocidal, or near-genocidal, acts.

The conclusions of most complaints contain a summary wrapping up of inductively produced arguments, and in this particular case judges were presented with the claim that defendant Deutsche Bank had "individually and jointly with its co-defendants and with Imperial Germany" had been "an active and responsible participant in the German colonial enterprise."[81] This particular defendant was accused of initiating a "race war," of implementing a campaign for the "extirpation" of the Ovaherero, of brutalizing and enslaving the Hereros, of systematically degrading Herero women, and destroying Herero culture.[82]

Would this strong stance that appeared in the 2001 Ovaherero complaint, be accepted by members of the "court of public opinion" or "court of law"? Soon after the filing of the lawsuit against the three German corporations the lawyers for the Herero filed a second lawsuit that was aimed at the German government itself.

LEGAL AND PUBLIC REACTIONS TO 2001 OVAHERERO LAWFARE ACTIVITIES

Between 2001 and 2007, as federal judges at various U.S. judicial levels of review responded to the cases that were filed by Kuaima Rikuako and the Herero People's Reparation Corporation, a host of observers from many different fields discussed the wisdom of filing these lawsuits. John Torpey argued that it was logical to expect that lawsuits like this might be filed in order to make "whole what has been smashed."[83]

While some who commented on the 2001 Ovaherero reparations cases tried to focus on the more formalistic jurisdictional dimensions of these cases, others were paying close attention to the extra-judicial arguments, the politics, the histories, the historiographies, and the memories that became entangled in these judicial controversies. Professor Gesine Krüger explained in 2005 how Paramount Chief Kuaima Rikuako seemed to be inviting listeners to dwell on both the land question in Namibia and on remembrances of the Holocaust.[84] Using rhetorical frames that appeared to be disciplinary in nature, Professor Krüger treated all of this as "symbolic" rather than substantive, because she was convinced that any distribution of land—"even if possible"—would "never" solve Namibia's social and economic problems. She came to this conclusion because experts "unsuspicious of rubbing shoulders with the group of white commercial farmers that is still dominating the agricultural sector" had analyzed all this before.[85]

Using permutations of the social scientific arguments that were often made about the mythic divide that was supposed to exist between "scholarship" and "advocacy" (see chapters 1, 6), Professor Krüger opined that the Herero lawsuits were really built on different theoretical and historical frames. One frame located claims for restitution in an "African colonial context," while the other frame—that depended on linkages to the World War II Holocaust—placed these equitable claims at the center of more global debates about justice, histories of human rights, and memory.[86]

Depending on one's politics, one could either reconcile or separate these two strands that Professor Krüger mentioned. Those who did not share Professor Krüger's pessimist view might argue that the Herero People's Reparation Corporation's lawfare was encouraging the crafting of multidirectional, and not competitive memories. Those who adopted these idealistic stances could even argue that this Ovaherero litigation was helping legal and public audiences see the connections that existed between GSWA colonial abuses, the Holocaust, and the South African apartheid years. As Barbara Kurowska would note, it appeared as if the Ovaherero lawsuits were used to help put pressure on the Namibian government while "shaming Germany into reparations."[87]

Yet detractors who did not support the filing of the Ovaherero lawsuits in American courts could counter by arguing that all of this was divisive, and that the analogies that were being made between some Namibian genocide and the World War II Holocaust were not warranted. Critics could aver that U.S. lawyers should not be added to the ranks of those who were already finding too many similarities, parallels, and continuities between colonial transgressions and other Nazi activities.

Many of the American judges who reviewed the Herero People's Reparation Corporation case between 2001 and 2006 seemed to be on the same page when these interpretative legal communities looked over the arguments that were presented by the plaintiffs' lawyers. A typical formalistic analysis of the issues in *Herero People's Reparation's Corporation et al. v. Deutsche Bank AG, et al.* would be presented in July of 2003 by U.S. federal district Judge Colleen Kollar-Kotelly of the United States District Court, District of Columbia. She would explain that according to the amended complaint of the Ovaherero litigants, this American court was being asked to "examine the absolute depths of human existence, from the evils of imperialism to institutional slavery and genocide."[88] She reminded her readers that the claims against another defendant, Woermann Line, had been previously dismissed for lack of personal jurisdiction, so the focus now was on the role that Deutsche Bank and other German banks may have played in what the plaintiffs called the "German colonial enterprise that was said to have led to the systematic murder of thousands of Herero men, women and children." [89] The amended complaint covered alleged atrocities that were committed by the defendant banks spanning a twenty-five year period between 1890 and 1915.

As Judge Kollar-Kotelly pointed out, initially the plaintiffs tried to sue Deutsche Bank AG, Terex Corporation, and the Woermann Line—because all three were German entities that were supposed to have cooperated with the government of Imperial Germany. The filing of some motions to dismiss on the part of several defendants led to a situation where Deutsche Bank and other banking institutions became the sole defendants in this particular legal action. The German banks were said to have engaged in "explicitly sanctioned extermination, the destruction of tribal culture and social organization, concentration camps, forced labor, medical experimentation, and the exploitation of women and children in order to advance their common financial interests."[90]

Most of the U.S. judges who first heard some of the Ovaherero arguments in the District of Columbia, and later in New York courts after the case against Deutsche Bank was refiled, were apparently convinced that the plaintiffs were not stating a defensible cause of action. A District of

Columbia Court of Appeals affirmed one dismissal in June of 2004, and when the appellants appealed that decision to the U.S. Supreme Court, the nation's highest court denied *certiorari* to hear the case.[91] One New York court determined that they could dismiss the case against Deutsche Bank because the arguments of the appellants' lawyers were basically the same ones that had been heard in District of Columbia courts.

By the time that the Third Circuit Court of Appeals heard the *Hereros v. Deutsche Afrika-Linien GMBLT & Co.* case in 2007 it seemed as though at least some American judges could be persuaded that the Ovaherero during the GSWA years may indeed have been abused by some German corporate entities who used slave labor and ran their own concentration camps. However, that did not mean that they had to take the next logical step and accept the plaintiffs' argument that private Namibian citizens should be allowed to sue the German government or German corporations in U.S. federal courts.

When the members of the Third Circuit were asked to review the decision that was made by the lower district court to dismiss the case—for failure to state an actionable claim in their complaint—this dismissal was affirmed by the Third Court of Appeals.

The members of the Third Circuit court of appeals provided three strong legalistic reasons why the Ovaherero, the appellants, were not going to get help from this court under the provisions of the U.S. Alien Tort Statute. While the members of the Third Circuit Court of Appeals admitted that they were inclined to believe that the defendant German bank may have engaged in conduct that might have violated the international norms that governed imperial behavior during the early twentieth century, they also noted that this "inclination does not support a cause of action."[92]

The circulation of that type of legal reasoning was enough to do in the Ovaherero case, but the members of the Third Circuit Court of Appeals went on to argue that courts in general, who heard these types of cases, should not be using their discretion in order to review conduct that occurred about a century before this case was filed.[93] This echoed many of the arguments that had been made by German government officials and international lawyers since at least 1990. It was also the type of argument that went beyond jurisdictional commentary.

One of arguments that most law students would expect to hear being made in a case like this was that private parties like the Ovaherero should not be bringing politicized critiques of foreign policy decisions into courts of equity. This seemed to be a permutation of the "political question" doctrine that assumes that bright lines existed between legislative "political" decisions and "judicial" interpretations of those legislative enactments. The Third Circuit was thus willing to stand by their decision that there were "no judicially discoverable or manageable standards" for deciding on a case involving about one hundred twenty-five thousand plaintiffs.[94]

Third World Approaches to International Law (TWAIL) scholars who might read this case would ask that critics pay attention to the ideological features of decisions like this, and there were some pundits who did just that. Some, like Felix Würkert, would try to explain in 2015 why the Ovaherero had not gained a hearing in international forums and why they might have sued in U.S. courts:

> The source of colonial injustice lies in this non-recognition of organized indigenous societies as equal subjects under public international law. So, of course, the staunch application of a state-centered public international law cannot help to redress this injustice. The fact that the Herero People's Reparation Corporation initially intended to sue Germany in the ICJ [International Court of Justice] can either be seen as an implied critique of a concept of statehood that did not accommodate the Herero nation, or as a critique of a public international law that only accommodates states. But regardless of the interpretation, barring the way for reparation claims by referring to the lack of subjectivity of Herero and Nama, leaves no room to acknowledge the illegal nature of colonialism in general. The argument continues the colonial legacy.[95]

The American jurists were often willing to admit that a Ovaherero nation once existed, and that they may have suffered during German colonial periods, but they, like members of the ICJ, were not always willing to overlook the jurisdictional hurdles that prevented them from hearing the merits of these types of colonial reparations cases. This "colonial unknowing" also meant that they were not going to discuss the inherent problematics of colonialism in general, or the exclusionary nature of early twentieth-century international laws that discriminated between "civilized" and "uncivilized" "races."

As many TWAIL scholars have noted, there are times when even legal formalists or legal positivists end up writing opinions that provide hints of how jurists actually feel about the substance of some claims, and in this particular case it is intriguing that members of the Third Circuit used a variant of the "Pandora's Box" argument that I discuss elsewhere in this book. When the judges on the Third Circuit studied the "intentions" of the drafters of the U.S. Alien Tort Statute these appellate judges concluded that those legislators could not possibly have wanted to open of doors that would have led to filing of "countless aggrieved groups for human rights violations."[96]

These appellate judges on the Third Circuit must have conjured up all sorts of visions of (post)colonial cases being filed by critics of French, British, German, Spanish, Ottoman, and other imperial empires. These appellate judges claimed that they understood the "gravity of the crimes," but they were convinced that by itself did not mean that the ATS had to be interpreted in liberal ways to provide redress for Herero appellants in U.S. courtrooms.

Other federal judges and law review writers placed more hurdles in the paths of Overaherero reparations litigants when those judges and writers mentioned the bilateral agreements that were signed by U.S. and German diplomats that protected Germany's "sovereign immunity."

Some critics of these Ovaherero cases, after reviewing these types of jurisdictional hurdles, were convinced that this showed that lawfare reparations efforts went nowhere. Norman Paech, for example, argued that the failure of the Ovaherero lawsuits provided empirical proof that "politics" and "law" did not mix, and that there were other ways of coming to terms with complex Namibian or German pasts.[97] Manfred Hinz speculated that cases that involved the criminal prosecution of transgressions committed by former governments were complicated enough, but that the Ovaherero lawsuits showed that "nearly insurmountable" political and legal challenges came when one was dealing with "cross-border dimensions and transgressions," such as the legal cases involved with apartheid reparations.[98] Given other issues, including "socio-political anthropological ones," and "imperfect international legal orders," Hinz wondered if Herero pride would be restored by the international development of a "culture of public apologies" that he thought began with Willy Brandt's kneeling in front of the memorial for the victims of the Warsaw Ghetto in 1970.[99]

Jeremy Sarkin was more optimistic when he claimed, in 2014, that collective reparations were warranted for the Ovaherero and that "reconciliation in some form" was still sorely needed.[100] He seemed to be inviting his readers to believe that with the passage of time, U.S. federal judges would eventually relent and provide redress for the Herero.

During the middle of this lengthy American appellate process, many were shocked when it appeared that at long last some German official was willing to come visit Namibia and express some contrition over what happened in GSWA between 1904 and 1908. The year 2004, the centennial anniversary of the battle of Ohamakari/Waterberg, would be one of those key pivot times for assessing German-Namibian relationships. In August of that year German Economic Co-Operation Minister Heidemarie Wieczorek-Zeul appeared at one of the traditional Herero commemorative gatherings. At that gathering Wieczorek-Zeul presented a speech in front of audiences who expressed their ambivalence when she asked for "forgiveness for our sins." She deftly argued that what happened at Hamakari would be regarded as a "genocide" by today's standards, and she referenced the horrific nature of the carnage that devastated Ovaherero and Nama communities. Yet when this economic minister failed to use the word "apology," Ovahereros who were there that day shouted, "*Zahlen, Zahlen*" (pay, pay) and "*mariva*" (money)."[101] Her response to this adamant call for concrete restitution was to publicly argue that her entire speech was an apology, and that she would later spend part of her ministerial budget on minor developmental projects in Namibia.

Minister Heidemarie Wieczorek-Zeul's 2004 address would often be cited by researchers who critiqued that 2001 Ovaherero lawsuit in American courtrooms. A year after her public presentation it was noted that she had been a part of negotiations with President Hifikepunye Pohamba, where, during a visit to Berlin, it was said that Germany was offering to pay "reparations" that amounted to some 20 million Euros that would be paid over a ten-year period.[102] Others refused to call that 20 million Euros "reparations," and they noted that the federal German government did not publicly back Wieczorek-Zeul's acts of contrition, and they pointed out that other German officials openly argued that they were not going to talk about Namibian reparations.

When many Ovaherero finally learned about some of the specific details regarding the amounts of development aid that would be coming from Minister Heidemarie Wieczorek-Zeul's agency, they viewed this as a paltry and insulting sum that looked nothing like Holocaust settlement payments. This particular 2004 German offer of development aid from a German minister became entangled in discussions of Namibian development policies and the expropriation of some white-owned farms in Namibia.

CONCLUSION

Those critical scholars who review this 2001 Ovaherero reparations case will find that this is a situation filled with many ironies, contingencies, and incommensurable ways of viewing GSWA histories and memories. In order to have a chance at winning the case, select decisions had to be made about who would be considered to be the primary victims of the 1904–1908 conflict. For lawfare purposes, and for political reasons, the Nama and the other indigenous communities were left out of the indigenous narratives that circulated in these particular Ovaherero complaints.

In spite of the African communal ways of viewing ownership of land—the people belonged to the land—the lawyers for the Ovaherero plaintiffs wrote as if the "paramount chief" might indeed be the legal representative of a Herero "tribe" or "nation" that was said to have lost sovereign rights. It seemed as though U.S. jurisprudential expectations were forcing claimants' lawyers to make hard decisions about how to write and talk about European property laws, the sale of indigenous lands, and national "sovereignty." This uneasy melding of Ovaherero and European views on land created contradictions that were not easy to paper over when filing complaints that had to address both American jurisdictional statutes and merit types of concerns.

These sorts of essentialist, legalistic ways of viewing individual indigenous subjectivity were reifying, rather than decolonizing, many German colonial knowledge formations. In order to look as though they were "buying" land or signing enforceable "protection" treaties, German administrators like Heinrich Ernst Göring and Theodor Leutwein played the role of antagonists in legal social dramas that made it appear as though they violated the treaty agreements that they signed with leaders like Henrik Witbooi or Samuel Maherero. Yet doing this also meant focusing *on individual decision making* by Nama or Ovaherero leaders who supposedly "sold" many acres of indigenous lands to the German colonizers.

Even those who agreed with the need to acknowledge historical genocidal acts were unsure if the Ovaherero reparations efforts in American courtrooms were the best routes to take for purposes of consciousness-raising. As Brigitte Weidlich would note in 2009, if the "Hereros won this case, other ethnic groups who suffered during colonization of western countries would have followed" and they would have inundated the "Columbia Federal Court with claims."[103]

Ovaherero litigants respond by asking, Where were these worries about opening Pandora's box of reparations claims when Holocaust litigants were filing suits in American courtrooms? Why didn't these same jurisdictional issues, or discussions of "political" question doctrines, or talk of "sovereign immunity," hinder the efforts of those who used U.S. courtrooms to go after other defendants who were accused of perpetrating the Holocaust or the Armenian genocide?

Some, however, seemed to deflect attention away from studies of the impact of losing in U.S. courts as they focused on the idealistic, didactic features of these Ovaherero court filings. Howard Rechavia Taylor, writing for Al Jazeera, recalled how the 2001 case filed by the Herero People's Reparation Corporation had been "unsuccessful in court," but had sparked "a debate that continued to affect German and Namibian civil society."[104] Perivi John Katjavivi, writing in 2017, noted how the Chief Hosea Kutako Foundation, headed by Riruako, had demanded in September of 2001 that $2 billion be paid out by the German government, and how the lawsuit had named several companies, including *Deutsche Bank*, for having helped with the perpetration of the Namibian genocide.[105] He was convinced that the publicity that followed in the wake of the filing of the case helped convince the Namibian government that reparations for GSWA wrongdoing was not just an Overherero issue but a "national cause" as well.[106]

Was the ushering in of that "debate" really that important if it did not result in any German policy or societal change, if it did not lead to any legal court victories or settlements that might provide the monies that were needed by impoverished Ovaherero to buy back lands owned by the German-speaking Namibians?

By 2007, the Ovaherero had learned a valuable lesson—if they were going to talk about the importance of consciousness-raising, or if they were going to ask for more public debates or more acknowledgements of the Namibian genocide, then they needed to work with the Nama and they needed to put up a united front in their reparation efforts. That year, Herero Chief Kuaima Riruako, standing beside Nama Chief David Frederick, appeared before reporters as they presented a joint position paper on reparations. In that joint paper these representative of their respective ethnic groups demanded that they be included in dialogues that touched on their concerns. In one portion of the joint position one finds these contentious claims: "What happened to our ancestors was genocide as defined in international law, and in view thereof we demand just reparation for damages and losses to our ancestors in terms of their own lives, their land, their livestock and other forms of their property."[107]

In chapter 9, I will have more to say about these "lessons" that were learned as the Ovaherero and the Nama tried to present a united front when they approached the U.S. courts once again in 2017.

NOTES

1. For a helpful overview of some of the political factors that influence the trajectory of reparations cases see John Torpley, *Making Whole What Has Been Smashed: On Reparations Politics* (Cambridge: Harvard University Press, 2006).

2. Sidney Harring, "German Reparations to the Herero Nation: An Assertion of Herero Nationhood in the Path of Namibian Development?" *West Virginia Law Review* 104, no. 2 (2002): 393–417.

3. Anthony J. Bellia, Jr., and Bradford R. Clark, "The Alien Tort Statute and the Law of Nations," *The University of Chicago Law Review* 78, no. 2 (Spring 2011): 445–51, 445.

4. See Stephen P. Mulligan, "The Rise and Decline of the Alien Tort Statute," *Congressional Research Service* (Washington: Congressional Research Service, June 6, 2018), https://fas.org/sgp/crs/misc/LSB10147.pdf.

5. Jeremy Sarkin, "Should Reparations for Massive Human Rights Abuses Perpetrated on African Victims during Colonial Times Be Given?" in *Justice for Victims: Perspectives on Rights, Transitions and Reconciliation,* edited by Inge Vanfraechem, Antony Pemberton, and Felix Mukwiza Ndahinda (New York: Routledge, 2014), 89–104. 94.

6. Sarkin, "Should Reparations," 94.

7. See, for example, Jonathan Watts, "Japan Guilty of Germ Warfare against Thousands of Chinese," *The Guardian,* last modified August 28, 2002, https://www.theguardian.com/world/2002/aug/28/artsandhumanities.japan.

8. See the *Alien Tort Claims Act of 1789*, Title 28 U.S. Code, Chapter 85, Section 1350.

9. See Dinah Shelton, "The World of Atonement: Reparations for Historical Injustices," *Miskolc Journal of International Law* 1, no. 2 (2004): 259–89.

10. Jon M. Bridgman, *The Revolt of the Herero* (Berkeley: University of California Press, 1981).

11. Jan-Bart Gewald, *Herero Heroes: A Socio-political History of the Herero in Namibia* (Athens, Ohio: Ohio University Press, 1999).

12. Gesine Krüger, "Coming to Terms with the Past," *German Historical Institution Bulletin* 37 (Fall 2005): 45–49, 49.

13. Mamfred O. Hinz, "One Hundred Years Later: Germany On Trial in the USA: The Herero Reparations Claim for Genocide," in *Bürgerliche Gesellschaft: Idee und Wirklichkeit,* edited by Manfred Hahn (Berlin: Trafo-Verlag, 2004): 375–90, 381.

14. Ibid., 381.

15. Ibid., 382.

16. Catherine Lu, "Redress and Addressing Colonial Injustice," *Ethics & Global Politics* 11 (2018): 76–80, 77–78.

17. For background on the difficulties that San communities had in many parts of South Africa, see Mohamed Adhikari, *The Anatomy of a South African Genocide: The Extermination of the Cape San Peoples* (Cape Town: University of Cape Town Press, 2010); José Manuel De Prada-Samper, "The Forgotten Killing Fields: "San" Genocide and Louis Anthing's Mission to Bushmanland, 1862–1862," *Historia* 57, no. 1 (2012): 172–87.

18. Jan-Bar Gewald, "Herero Genocide in the Twentieth Century: Politics and Memory," in *Rethinking Resistance: Revolt and Violence in African History,* edited by Jon Abbink, Mirjam de Bruijn, and Klass Van Walraven, (Leiden: Brill, 2003), 279–304, 285.

19. For some helpful overviews of the scope of the U.S. Alien Tort Claims Act of 1789, sovereign immunity, and colonial or postcolonial cases, see Jason Allen and Barbara Ann Hocking, "Unlocking the Alienation: A Comparative Role for Alien Torts Legislation in Post-Colonial Reparations Claims?" *Human Rights Review* 11, no. 2 (June 2010): 247–76. See also Jeremy Sarkin, "Reparations for Historical Human Rights Violation: The International and Historical Dimensions of the Alien Torts Claim Act Genocide Case of the Herero of Namibia," *Human Rights Review* 9, no. 3 (2008): 331–60; Jeremy Sarkin, *Colonial Genocide and Reparations Claims in the 21st Century: The Socio-Legal Context of Claims under International Law by the Herero against Germany for Genocide in Namibia, 1904–1908* (Westport, CT: Praeger Security International, 2009).

20. Benjamin Whitaker, *Revised and Updated Report on the Question of the Prevention and Punishment of the Crime of Genocide,* United Nationals Economic and Social Council Commission on Human Rights, July 1985, 8, http://dag.un.org/handle/11176/351399?show=full.

21. See Brigitte Lau, "Uncertain Certainties: The Herero-German War of 1904," *Mibagus* 2 (1989): 4–5, 8.

22. See Matthew P. Fitzpatrick, "The Pre-History of the Holocaust? The *Sonderweg* and *Historikstreit* Debates and the Abject Colonial Past," *Central European History* 41, no. 3 (September 2008): 477–503.

23. Henning Melber, "Genocide Matters—Negotiating a Namibian-German Past in the Present," *Stichproben: Wiener Zeitschrift für kritische Afrikastudien* 17, no. 33 (2017): 1–24, 10.

24. Ibid., 10.

25. For an excellent overview of someone who played several roles in these disputes—fighter for independence, educator, and ambassador to the European Union and Germany, see Peter H. Katjavivi, "Namibia's Bilateral Relations with Germany: A Critical Relationship," in *Namibia's Foreign Relations: Historical Contexts, Current Dimensions, and Perspectives for the 21st Century,* edited by Anton Bösl, André du Pisani, and Dennis U. Zaire (Windhoek: Konrad Adenauer Stiftung, 2014), 135–68.

26. Henning Melber, "In The Shadow of Genocide: German-Namibian Reconciliation a Century Later," *Freiburg-Postkolonial.de,* September 2006, paragraph 1, http://www.freiburg-postkolonial.de/Seiten/melber-reconciliation2006.htm. See also Reinhart Kössler, "Two Modes of Amnesia: Complexity in Postcolonial Namibia," *Acta Academica* 47, no. 1 (2015): 138–60.

27. Melber, "In the Shadow," paragraph 3.

28. Harring, "German Reparations," 393–94. For more on the rhetorical significance of Kohl's visit, see Tom Bentley, *Empires of Remorse: Narrative, Postcolonialism and Apologies for Colonial Atrocity* (New York: Routledge, 2016), 86.

29. For commentary on the performative roles of the "*truppenspeiler*," see Wolfgang Werner, "Playing Soldiers: The Truppenspieler Movement among the Herero of Namibia, 1915–1945," *Journal of South African Studies* 16 (1990): 485–502.

30. Harring, "German Reparations," 393–94.

31. Melber, "In the Shadow," paragraph 3.

32. Harring, "German Reparations," 393–94.

33. Delroy Constantine-Simms, "Hitler's Forgotten Namibian Victims," *Electronic Mail and Guardian*, last modified September 26, 1997, https://allafrica.com/stories/199709260086.html.

34. John Grobler, "The Tribe Germany Wants to Forget," *Electronic Mail and Guardian*, last modified March 13, 1998, http://www.raceandhistory.com/Science/germany-namibia.htm.

35. Ibid.

36. Donald G. McNeil, Jr., "Its Past on Its Sleeve, Tribe Seeks Bonn's Apology," *The New York Times*, last modified May 31, 1998, https://www.nytimes.com/1998/05/31/world/its-past-on-its-sleeve-tribe-seeks-bonn-s-apology.html.

37. Lynn Berat, "Genocide: The Namibian Case against Germany," *Pace International Law Review* 5 (1993): 165–210, 207–11.

38. Brigitte Weidlich, "Time Now to Heal the Wounds," *The Namibian*, last modified October 5, 2007, paragraph 9, https://www.namibian.com.na/index.php?id=38540&page=archive-read.

39. Eddie Bruce-Jones, *Race in the Shadow of Law: State Violence in Contemporary Europe* (New York: Taylor and Francis, 2017), 147.

40. For an overview of this particular Ovaherero court case, see Sidney Harring, "German Reparations," 393–417.

41. The Herero People's Reparation Corporation, *The Herero People's Reparation Corporation et al. v. Deutsche Bank AG et al.*, First Amended Complaint (District of Columbia: Superior Court of the District of Columbia, 2001), 28.

42. For other critiques of this "German colonial enterprise" see Mohamed Adhikari, "'Streams of Blood and Streams of Money': New Perspectives on the Annihilation of the Herero and Nama Peoples of Namibia 1904–1908," *Kronos*, 34 (2008): 303–20.

43. See Charissa Jones, "In Lawsuit against Swiss Banks, A Hope to Do Justice to a Father's Memory," *The New York Times*, last modified November 12, 1996, https://www.nytimes.com/1996/11/12/nyregion/in-lawsuit-against-swiss-banks-a-hope-to-do-justice-to-a-father-s-memory.html.

44. Patrick Bond and Khadja Sharife, "Apartheid Reparations and the Contestation of Corporate Power in Africa," *Review of African Political Economy* 36, no. 119 (March 2009): 115–25.

45. *Princz v. Federal Republic of Germany*, 26 F. 3d 1166, 1173 (D.C. Cir 1994).

46. The authors of the 2001 Ovaherero complaint explained to their readers that they were going to use the term "Herero" to reference all of the Otijeherero-speaking people who suffered from the near-annihilation carried out by the German colonizers.

47. Colleen Kollar-Kotelly, *The Herero People's Reparations Corporation et al. v. Deutsche Bank Ag et al.* Civ. No. 01-01868 (CKK), July 31, 2003. 2003 WL 26119014.

48. For example, the authors of the Overaherero complaint cited the work of Jan-Bart Gewald, *Herero Heroes: A Socio-political History of the Herero in Namibia* (Athens, Ohio: Ohio University Press, 1999).

49. The Herero People's Reparation Corporation, *The Herero People's Reparation*, 30.

50. Ibid., Another text that would be cited in the Oveherero complaint was Mary Evelyn Townsend, *The Rise and Fall of Germany's Colonial Empire, 1884–1918* (New York, Macmillan Company, 1930).

51. The Herero People's Reparation Corporation, *The Herero People's Reparation*, 31.

52. Jon M. Bridgman, *The Revolt of the Herero* (Berkeley: University of California Press, 1981), 14.

53. The Herero People's Reparation Corporation, *The Herero People's Reparation*, 32, quoting Gewald, *Herero Heroes*, 28.

54. The Herero People's Reparation Corporation, *The Herero People's Reparation*, 35.
55. Ibid., 36–37.
56. Manu Vimalassery, Juliana Hu Pegues, and Alyosha Goldstein, "Introduction: On Colonial Unknowing," *Theory and Event* 19, no. 4 (2016): https://muse.jhu.edu/article/633283.
57. The Herero People's Reparation Corporation, *The Herero People's Reparation*, 37.
58. Ibid.
59. Ibid., 60.
60. The Herero People's Reparation Corporation, *The Herero People's Reparation*, cited in Kollar-Kotelly, *The Herero People's*, 1.
61. The Herero People's Reparation Corporation, *The Herero People's Reparation*, 38.
62. Bridgman, *The Revolt*, 51.
63. Ibid., 43.
64. See, for example, Andrew Connelly, "Africans Take Germany to Court in New York over 'Forgotten Genocide,'" *Global Post*, last modified July 31, 2018, https://www.pri.org/stories/2018-07-31/africans-take-germany-court-new-york-over-forgotten-genocide.
65. Gewald, *Herero Heroes*, 48.
66. The Herero People's Reparation Corporation, *The Herero People's Reparation*, 39.
67. Ibid., 41.
68. Ibid.
69. Ibid., quoting Gewald, *Herero Heroes*, 101.
70. Ibid., 42.
71. Ibid., 42–43.
72. Ibid., 43.
73. Ibid.
74. Bridgman, *The Revolt*, 50.
75. Ibid., 60.
76. The Herero People's Reparation Corporation, *The Herero People's Reparation*, 45, quoting Great Britain, *Report on the Natives of south West Africa and Their Treatment by Germany* (London: HMSO, 1918), 53.
77. The Herero People's Reparation Corporation, *The Herero People's Reparation*, 46.
78. Ibid., 46, quoting Gewald, *Herero Heroes*, 144.
79. The Herero People's Reparation Corporation, *The Herero People's Reparation*, 54.
80. Ibid., 57.
81. Ibid., 59.
82. Ibid., 60.
83. Torpey, *Making Whole*, 50, quoted in Barbara Kusowska, *Reparations Politics-A Case Study of the Reparations Demands of the Herero Towards the Federal Republic of Germany* (Foundations for European Study, 2008): 1–29, 22.
84. Gesine Kruger, "Coming to Terms with the Past," *German Historical Institute Bulletin* 17 (Fall 2005): 45–49, 45.
85. Ibid., 45.
86. Ibid.
87. Kurowska, *Reparations Politics*, 29.
88. District Judge Kollar-Kotelly, *The Herero People's Reparation Corp.*
89. Ibid., 1.
90. Ibid.
91. *Herero People's Reparation Corp. v. Deutsche Bank, A.G.*, 543 U.S. 987, 125 S. Ct. 508, 160 L. Ed. 2d 371 (2004).
92. *Hereros v. Deutsche Afrika-Linien GMBLT & Co.* (3rd Cir. 2007): 9.
93. Ibid., 9–10.
94. Ibid.
95. Felix Würkert, "Yes, Redressing Past Wrongs in the Present!" *Võlkerrechtsblog*, last modified October 28, 2015, https://voelkerrechtsblog.org/yes-redressing-past-wrongs-in-the-present/.

96. *Hereros v. Deutsche Afrika-Linien GMBLT & Co.* (3rd Cir. 2007): 9–11.
97. Norman Pach, quoted in Kurowska, *Reparations Politics*, 21.
98. Hinz, "One Hundred Years later," 383.
99. Ibid., 383–84.
100. Sarkin, "Should Reparations for Massive Human Rights Abuses," 100.
101. Weidlich, "Time Now to Heal the Wounds," paragraph 17.
102. Al Jazeera staff, "Namibia Spurns German Reparations," Al Jazeera, last modified November 30, 2005, https://www.aljazeera.com/archive/2005/11/20084913272340595.html.
103. Brigitte Weidlich, "105 Years Ago: Herero Uprising against Colonialism," *The Namibian*, last modified January 12, 2009, paragraph 16, https://www.namibian.com.na/print.php?id=1981&type=2.
104. Howard Rechavia Taylor, "U.S. Court Hears Case Against Germany Over Namibia Genocide," Al Jazeera, last modified July 31, 2018, paragraph 17, https://www.aljazeera.com/news/2018/07/court-hears-case-germany-namibia-genocide-180731201918543.html.
105. Perivi John Katjavivi, "The German Namibian Genocide—What Is to Be Done?" *Africa Is a Country*, last modified February 15, 2017, paragraph 7, https://africasacountry.com/2017/02/the-german-namibian-genocide-what-is-to-be-done.
106. Ibid.
107. Weidlich, "105 Years Ago," paragraph 27.

EIGHT

Realpolitik Entanglements of Namibian-German Relationships and the *Dingpolitik* of Ovaherero Herero and Nama Human Remains

In 2017 American judges must have been intrigued by some of the topics that were covered in plaintiffs' briefs and other documents that referenced the Ovaherero and Nama genocide. Along with the usual discussion of the need for expansive or liberal readings of the Alien Tort Claims Act (ATCA) was the strange mention of how skulls and human remains were some of the artefacts that were stolen by German colonizers and needed to be returned to indigenous communities. Some of these abject objects of thanatopolitical commentary were the remains of those who either died during the 1904–1908 Ovaherero/Nama–German War or were victims of the Kaiserreich's concentration camps. After a German television program reported that thousands of skulls were still housed in German medical institutions, museums, or private collections, the Ovaherero activists continued to talk with reporters about how these skulls provided "proof" of genocide. Iconic images of German *Schutztruppe* placing skulls in crates that were sent off to the homeland for German racial experimentation soon graced the pages of newspapers, journals, books, and blog sites. By 2019 American jurists were so used to seeing mention of these Namibian skulls and other human remains in reparations claimant briefs that one judge, Laura Taylor Swain, called this "Germany's bone activities."[1]

During the first quarter of the twenty-first century the inferential leaps, talk of restorative justice, and stories about all sorts of Namibian racializations, race hygiene, eugenics, and German genocidal intents and other colonial entanglements seemed to be omnipresent, but this was not the case in the half century before this. The disavowals and the studied ignorance of the many facets of colonial wrongdoing—characterized by Manu Vimalassery, Juliana Hu Pegues, and Alyosha Goldstein as a form of "colonial unknowing"[2] —contributed to the fragmentation of both discursive and physical evidence. Those who spent generations writing about the Schutztruppe who once put down rebellions—or who wrote about the social agency of the German speakers who commemorated those efforts—aggressively and effectively co-produced archives that made it difficult for future generations to see how the transportation of indigenous skulls had anything to do with colonial atrocities or any acts of collective amnesia.

Twenty-first-century decolonizers, drawing from the work of critical indigenous studies, settler-colonial studies, postcolonial criticism, critical genocide studies, and related disciplines thus had to find ways of explaining the links that existed between the physical or biological extermination of ethnic communities like the Ovaherero and the Nama and the epistemic violence that would become a part of so many "ignorance contracts." As more and more indigenous scholars are noting, this did not simply involve acts of passive forgetting but rather active use of cultural, political, diplomatic, and legalistic frames that consciously or unconsciously hid the parallels and continuities and symbolic links that could be made between physical traces of colonial atrocities and the occluding of painful and dissonant imperial heritages.

That said, a vocal few critics are intent on demonstrating that not everyone is willing to accept the willful ignorance that can be used to exonerate colonial or imperial agents who may have helped perpetrate colonial atrocities or war crimes. Variants of arguments about what Reinhart Kössler would call "imperial skullduggery"[3] had now resurfaced, and the stories that once appeared in indigenous oral histories about the lost ancestors are now recirculated in twenty-first-century accounts of scurvy experiments in concentration camps or physical anthropological bone collections that were used by Wilhelmine anatomists or physical anthropologists. Some who revisit—and reinvent—the elite and public archives are even willing to recount the time when Colonel Governor Heinrich Ernst Göring made the foolish mistake of trying to build over indigenous remains.

As we shall see in the rest of this chapter, objects and topics that earlier generations might not have seen as having anything to do with objective historicizing about the Namibian genocide were appearing in new constellations of meaning that helped twenty-first-century lawyers, jurists, and other audiences decide what would be regarded as "evidence, proof, or possibility."[4] At the same time, talk of the repatriation of Ovaherero, Nama, San, and other indigenous remains would become parts of larger conversations about the need for acknowledgments, heartfelt apologies, monetary reparations, and even revolutionary land redistribution in Namibia.

In this particular chapter, my critical genealogical critiques will also be extending the work of Bruno Latour and others who have written about the importance of both *"dingpolitik,"* the politics of things, and *realpolitik*, the traditional way we think about deliberative argumentation in places like parliaments.[5] I will be arguing that all of these twenty-first-century conversations about the repatriation of Ovaherero or Nama ancestors reminded global audiences of the symbolic and material links that could be established between skulls, illegal taking of indigenous property, and the old German annihilationist ideologies.

Sadly, even death may not have ended the abuse of the colonized, and generations of descendants of indigenous victims of colonial wars or labor camps were still traumatized by the ways that human remains were treated by those who had little respect for indigenous burial practices or Ovaherero or Nama rituals. As Professor Katharina von Hammerstein would tell reporters in March of 2019, the murder of Ovaherero and Nama during the colonial wars was terrible, "not only because so many people died, but also "because on top of that" survivors "could not bury the dead" and they could not "give them the honor of being buried."[6]

While some decolonizers may have hoped that most Namibians and European postcolonial activists would unite and work together to put pressure on German or Namibian governments to support the repatriation of many more human remains that could be used in evidentiary hearings or courtrooms, this did not happen. The existence of varied cultural perceptions regarding religious rituals, proper commemorative practices, respect for the dead, and conflict ways of approaching colonial legacies meant that oftentimes those interested in these human remains worked at cross-purposes. For example, schisms in the ranks of the Namibian communities were created when Ovaherero and Nama recipients of repatriated skulls argued about whether these ancestors should be buried, or whether these few repatriated human remains should be put on display in national museums or should be used as evidence in legal reparations cases.

Many of the investigative journalists who commented on the activist efforts of the members of the Ovaherero and Nama reparations movement also wrote about how the tracing of the historical origins of these human remains invariable led to emotional discussions of how thousands of Africans had died in colonial wars or in camps. A host of multidirectional and competitive memories surfaced as twenty-first-century commentators wrote or talked about why German soldiers, traders, or other colonizers collected, or dug up, these African remains and used them for trophies or profitable materials that could be sold to physical anthropologists and other European scientists. Researching the "provenance"—or the geographic or temporal origins of these human remains—

allowed transcontinental scientists and public intellectuals to join the contemporary discussions that were taking place about how best to "re-humanize" some of these remains.

At times it seemed as though readers of articles on Namibian skulls or internet bloggers who learned about experimentation in places like Shark Island were participating in a form of "dark tourist" activities when they learned about the skullduggery associated with GSWA colonial practices. At the same time that twenty-first-century audiences were learning about the Ovaherero and Nama requests for repatriation of these human remains, they were also being bombarded with fragmentary vignettes about everything from the passage of colonial "race-mixing" laws to some of the sales of human remains that ended up in American or European museums.

All of these consciousness-raising efforts soon morphed into discussions of colonial knowing and unknowing, and arguments about why this type of information had been kept out of German textbooks or traditional accounts of German colonization practices. Oftentimes iconic images that were taken from Holocaust contexts were juxtaposed with the vignettes about skulls taken from Shark Island so that both experts and ordinary citizens could visualize the continuities and the claims that were being made about real and imagined parallels that existed between Nazi behavior and Schutztruppe attacks on women and children after Ohamakari/Waterberg.

Critical genealogists who extend Latour's work on the nexus that exists between realpolitik and dingpolitik could argue that at the same time that readers and viewers learned about the pernicious racist colonial ideologies that drifted along from generation to generation they also found out that Namibian remains could be treated as trophies, "specimens," physical data, and so on. Colonial knowing and unknowing in these Namibian and German colonial contexts thus depending on how audiences felt about imperialist circumstances, settler activities, indigenous rights, presentist needs, and the subject positions of those who possessed these remains. What were twenty-first-century audiences and their elected decision makers supposed to do when they learned that thousands of African ancestors were kept in many European private and public collections?

In many ways the aphasia that I described in earlier chapters once again manifested itself when some German spokespersons who represented some of the institutions that housed Namibian skulls had a difficult time explaining to Namibians who came to bring back their ancestors why German anatomical communities or museums or private collectors still kept those old ethnographic, eugenic, and physical anthropological collections. Why, indigenous activists asked, didn't places like the University of Freiburg simply *hand over all of the "tainted" human skulls* that they found in archives like the Alexander Ecker Collection to the Ovaherero or the Nama or to the Namibian government? If the German government was not going to pay reparations, then why couldn't knowledgeable German scientists or other academics admit that these Namibian "ancestors" needed to return home so that they could receive a proper burial?

As readers might imagine issues of provenance and restitution were soon inextricably tied to a plethora of other volatile topics, ranging from the acknowledgment of the Ovaherero and Nama genocide to the institutional ownership of human remains that may, or may not, have archival records or markings that connect them to alleged colonial atrocities. After all, couldn't a German medical institute argue that most "untainted" human remains needed to be used for the dissemination of medical knowledge that should be made available to all doctors and students? Could European museums who were reluctant to participate in repatriation ceremonies argue that in the past, when they did turn over some skulls and other objects to indigenous communities, those very same objects appeared on black markets or were lost?

Just as colonial genocide debates followed in the wake of Holocaust disputation, the twenty-first-century public, journalistic, and academic debates about the repatriation of Ovaherero and Nama remains were taking place after German scholars and scientists had spent decades mulling over what to do with the human remains of those who may have been linked to Nazi experimentation in the Holocaust death camps.[7]

Oftentimes well-intentioned representatives of German institutions, who voluntarily arranged for the private handing over of some of these Namibian ancestors, were puzzled when they were bombarded with political or historical questions by members of Ovaherero and Nama communities who traveled abroad to receive their ancestors. Activists who wanted more than just the return of a few dozen skulls were frustrated when they learned about the extent of some of these collections, and they realized that the handover of some human remains might serve as purification rituals that allowed German institutions to maintain control of the vast majority of the "untainted" remains.

All sorts of presences and absences, spoken and unspoken assumptions about the past and the present, tales of blame and innocence, swirled around these particular "bones of contention."[8] Ovaherero and Nama activists—who were already having to deal with poverty back home and the costs of reparations lawsuits—were now learning that the handover of remains by a few private German institutions did not automatically lead to participation of indigenous activists in meaningful dialogues with official German governmental representatives who purposely stayed away from these repatriation ceremonies.

Did the repatriation ceremonies that were carried out by private institutions help display Germany's "special relationship" with Namibia, or did they represent not-so-veiled attempts to bring to an end talk of reparations or Namibian land redistribution? Were these efficacious acts of decolonization, or were these more examples of what Vimalassery, Pegues, and Goldstein called mutable historicizing and "colonial unknowing"?[9] Given the fact that no one seems to use lawfare in Germany to try and stop the handover of these remains isn't this positive proof that repatriation is a necessary, and perhaps sufficient, form of redress for colonial matters that happened long ago?

In order to help answer those types of questions in this chapter, I use my own variant of what some call "praxiological" studies to help readers understand the role that these Namibian-German repatriation ceremonies play in contentious debates about moral and legal responsibilities for GSWA wrongdoing.[10] Although I will be focusing most of my attention on the first of these handover ceremonies in Germany in 2011, I will also critique elite and public responses to several other repatriation ceremonies that were held in 2014 and 2018.[11]

Let me begin my critiques in this chapter by providing readers with a brief contextual overview of some of these twentieth-first century Ovaherero and Nama repatriation debates.

CONTEXTUALIZING THE TWENTY-FIRST-CENTURY OVAHERERO AND NAMA REPATRIATION DEBATES

For various reasons German institutions and museums or private parties hesitate to turn over all of "their" African skulls, skeletons, and other human remains to indigenous communities like the Ovaherero and Nama, and each and every time that global presses have announced that more human remains were found, and were going to be returned, the topics of colonial reparations, apologies, acknowledgments, and "denials" resurfaces.

At the time of this writing there are have been three different major German-Namibian repatriation ceremonies that have taken place—in 2011, 2014, and 2018—and the press coverage of these repatriation activities usually includes commentary on the American legal cases or the best way to acknowledge the "first" genocide of the twentieth century.[12]

The polysemic and polyvalent nature of these repatriation ceremonies created situations where some Germans and other Europeans regarded the handover of human remains as performative acts that would end or settle colonial matters, while Namibian activists and their supporters viewed these same performances as the opening of talks or the beginning of restitutional efforts. Not everyone was pleased when they read that true reconciliation was going to have to take the form of "continuous reclamation processes" that would be "interrogating the systematic legacies of genocide."[13]

The ready availability of social media materials, as well as ample mainstream coverage of these repatriation rituals, allowed countless numbers of the world's denizens to become vicariously involved in conversations about some very old topics. Many of the issues that I discussed in previous chapters—about whether Lieutenant Zürn started the Herero-German war of 1904[14] or whether German settlers legitimately purchased and owned colonial lands—became inextricably linked to twenty-first-century conversations about provenances, the limits of restitution, and the postcolonial rehumanization of those who were once dehumanized. The more that local, regional, national, and international presses presented the arguments of the Ovaherero and Nama activists, the more that defenders of German institutions realized that they could not stay silent if they wished to keep their museum "relics" or their scientific "specimens."

As twenty-first-century arguers debated about what to do with the Ovaherero, Nama, and other indigenous human remains, they invariably added new parchment layers to the already-crowded colonial and postcolonial archives. All sorts of humanist and anti-humanist arguments, accommodationist and annihilationist rhetorics, and stories of guilt and innocence were rhetorically crafted as diverse groups of stakeholders joined in these conversations.

Few academics who wrote about related topics, and then found out about these reparations debates, could sit on the sidelines. Vilho Amukwaya Shigwedha, who watched the burial of other human remains that came from Angola, was bothered by the instrumentalist treatment of some of these remains in "post genocide Namibia."[15] His own "genealogy" led him to conclude that the parties involved should have followed traditional indigenous burial practices. He opined that they should have respected the wishes of the "majority of affected communities," and buried the "ancestors" instead of trying to preserve the remains for political purposes. He was convinced that these repatriated remains could be buried in ways that ensured that the "deceased's wandering spirit" was "put to rest."[16]

Shigwedha disagreed with the Ovaherero and Nama activists who wanted these ancestral remains to be preserved in Namibia's Independence Memorial Museum so that they could be used for pedagogical or evidentiary purposes. For Shigwedha, the failure to carry out proper burial underscored the point that "treating the bones respectfully" had become entangled in the politics of memory and restorative justice, where the issue of reparations "for the affected communities" was considered to be of "paramount importance."[17] Were Eurocentric ways of viewing legal genocidal evidence interfering with Namibian cultural practices?

As pressure mounted for another German "mastering" of colonial pasts, some of the same organizations that once dealt with the fallout from the discovery of Nazi remains now had to cope with journalistic commentary on how the Namibian human remains were tied to German "scurvy" experiments in Shark Island. The horrors of the Nazi concentration camps or death camps were bad enough, but now retrospective reviewers of post-Ohamakari camps were treating the existence of thousands of skulls as conclusive proof of the "Windhoek to Auschwitz" continuity thesis.

In order to respond to these mounting public, academic, and journalistic pressures, private German institutions that housed these human remains did not follow the lead of South African or Australian scientific communities that often included indigenous communities in repatriation decision making. Instead, German medical institutions in Berlin or Hamburg or Freiberg put together *ad hoc* German committees that painstakingly reviewed natural science and social science archival records in order to determine, which, if any, skulls or other human remains were "tainted" and needed to be returned to Namibians.

Many German researchers and curators were embarrassed by what they learned about the work of Eugen Fischer or the hauntology that shadowed these remains. Academics, curators, and others involved in tracking down the provenance of these alleged Namibian remains were not even sure how many skulls and other human remains could still be found in German medical institutions, museums, or private attics, but fascinated journalists, activists, and critical researchers estimated that there were tens of thousands of human remains housed in Europe.[18] At one time, Andrew Zimmerman notes, German physical anthropologists needed these skulls for not only their racial "science" but their "ideology," and they "both created and presupposed certain relationships between colonizing and colonized bodies, constituted by asymmetric practices of measuring, representing, and collecting."[19]

THE ARCHIVAL REDISCOVERY, AND REPATRIATION, OF THE "SHARK ISLAND" SKULLS AND OTHER HUMAN REMAINS

In many ways the indiscriminate killing and the studied neglect of the "other" in colonial and imperial contexts has made it extremely difficult to "positively" identify the historical origins of some of the indigenous skulls, skeletons, and other human remains that can be traced back to the early twentieth century. Some of these abject objects were taken away after German hangings of indigenous prisoners, and sometimes soldiers or scientists dug up remains that had been buried in Swakopmund or Lüderitz gravesites. They were then used by race scientists and their students for a few decades, and then placed in storage boxes.

Sometimes these remains were taken from shallow grave sites where many Ovaherero and Nama died of unnatural or natural causes, and eugenicists like Eugen Fischer traveled to German South West Africa so that they could collect the remains of supposedly inferior Africans before they boarded ships that took them back to their European laboratories.

In rare cases eugenicists or physical anthropologists, in the name of objective racial science, left us helpful archival labels that aided the tracking down of the provenances of these human remains, and occasionally European numbers were etched on skulls that helped render visible the invisible. Andrew Zimmerman is surely right when he notes that these skulls were once a part of some Foucauldian "biopower" colonial apparatus that helped with the production of racialized imperial knowledge formation.[20] "The empiricism that led anthropologists to desire a complete collection, to constantly want more," noted Zimmerman, "meant that the discipline found its ideal and practical realization in genocide."[21]

Physical anthropologists and Second Reich soldiers or German scientists were not the only social agents who were involved in the digging up, the collecting, the transporting, the cataloguing, and the display of these abject "specimens." We will never know how many of these human remains were used during European academic lectures on anatomy, anthropology, ethnology, eugenics, geography, and so on. Skulls could be treated as trophies by returning *Schutztruppe*, cabinet curiosities for those who never left Europe, or empirical evidence of the superiority of German "*Kultur*."

Before 2008 one found few commentaries on these human remains outside of scientific circles, but all of this changed when Markus Frenzel, a German television reporter, produced a documentary film that "proved the existence of human remains of Namibian origin in Germany in 2008."[22] After this announcement the Namibian government formally requested that some human remains be returned that were thought to be stored at the facilities of the Pathological Institute (now called the Center for Anatomy) at the prestigious Charité University in Berlin.

The administrators of the Charité University were gracious enough to assemble an interdisciplinary team—called the Charité Remains Project—that was tasked for several years with the responsibility of coming up with the guidelines that would help with the determination of which, if any human remains, ought to be transferred over to some Namibian communities.

For several years Dr. Andreas Winklemann (anatomist), Dr. Karin Koel-Abt (anthropologist), Professor Thomas Schnalke (director of the Charité's medical history museum), Nils Seethaler (ethnologist), and Dr. Holger Stoecker (historian) worked together as a team as they sifted through their archives and determined that twenty skulls may have been collected during a "context of injustice." These tainted objects/ancestors could be then prepared for repatriation.[23]

Larissa Förster noted that some of the difficulties that this team encountered had to do with the fact that "colonial medicine considered the remains" to be "mere specimens for racial variety," and this meant stripping them of their individual identities so that they could be "inventorised as typological objects."[24] Those who sought to universalize and generalize in the name of science needed to bracket out human individuality. Förster, an expert on the cultural dimensions of both historical and contemporary treatment of human remains from Namibia, would be one of many researchers who were influenced by renascent interest in the study of postcolonialism, indigenous rights, and mastering of German or Namibian pasts.

For many Namibians, the twenty skulls found in Charité archives were ancestors who had waged anti-colonial wars before the Ovambo and other Namibians fought for Namibian independence before 1990. Planners in both Germany and in Namibia in 2011 prepared elaborate ceremonies for the handover of these Namibian remains, and this allowed many of the parties involved to properly grieve and commemorate the return of their Namibian ancestors. German and international presses provided mediated coverage of the press conference that was held at the Charité, the question and answer session that was witnessed by more than seventy visitors from Namibia, the memorial service at St. Matthew's Church, the actual handover, and the arrival of these human remains at Windhoek's Hosea Kuako Airport in Namibia. During each of these events journalists wondered when, and if, official German representatives would show up at these repatriation ceremonies.

Officials in the German government—perhaps sensing the symbolic importance of these exchanges for the Namibians—treated this as a private affair that had little to do legal restitution or land reformation in Namibia.

German postcolonial scholars at major universities who mentioned this repatriation kept pushing for more restorative justice efforts, but German government representatives constantly argued that twenty-first-century citizens in both Germany and Namibia needed to look forward and not backward. Anke Bartels, Lars Eckstein, Nicole Waller and Dirk Wiemann—who reviewed this 2011 handover and watched similar ceremonies for the repatriation of humans to Australian "traditional owners"—argued in 2017 that there "was little political interest in proactive research into German's colonial past," which meant that any help for the Ovaherero or other indigenous communities was "reactive, responding to diplomatic pressure from nations and interest groups powerful enough to make such claims."[25]

Some global communities were willing to consider the possibility that the presence of human remains was an ominous sign that if investigative journalists or scholars did more digging then they would discover even more buried colonial or imperial secrets. After the 2011 news coverage of the Charité handover, international viewers learned that several other places, like the Alexander Ecker Collection, had come across more human remains that might be linked to German colonial periods. It was said that the Ecker Collection, that was based at the Albert-Ludwigs-Universität Freiburg, might have over two hundred human "skulls of African origin."[26] Was this evidence of more skullduggery?

Observers started to follow these events as if they were putting together a historical puzzle or reading a novel, where interested parties could track the misdeeds of collectors like Eugen Fischer—one of the "fathers" of Nazi eugenical policies. Even before the discovery of human remains in the Ecker Collection, Fischer's work on the "Rehoboth Basters" of German South West Africa had been discussed by many interdisciplinary scholars who extended the work of Horst Drechsler, Helmut Bley, or Jan-Bart Gewald.

Those who followed the media coverage of Namibian reparations efforts discovered that Eugen Fischer had once served as the curator of the Ecker Collection. Conjectures were made that Fischer's desire to provide empirical support for his theories about the racial positionality of the "Rehoboth Basters" has something to do with his massive collection of human remains. These Basters—who also had to cope with German colonial administrators during the GSWA years— became the object of Fischer's attention because they were regarded as communities who were neither "white" nor "black" because of their alleged breeding practices.[27] Physical anthropologists often argued that the Rehoboth Basters were descendants of Dutch colonizers who once lived in South Africa's northern Cape, and in the 1860s it was said that they trekked up from South African into the Namibian "wilderness." Fischer, in an attempt to add more detail to studies of racial hierarchies was one of many European researchers who sought to study isolated groups of "mixed race" descendants whose blood allegedly mixed together Dutch and African blood.

In theory, if German settlers learned about the dangers of this type of race mixing from authors like Fischer, then they would alter their bad habits and quit mating with inferior Africans—especially the Rehoboth Basters. This would stop the dilution of pure German blood, prevent degeneration, and preserve the Germany "germplasm" in the German South West Africa.

Based on his published studies of the Rehoboth Basters, Fischer gained the international reputation of being one of the world's foremost experts on the perils of "race mixing," and his work was used to justify colonial prohibitions of legal marriages of Africans and Europeans, segregation in the colonies, the need for "native reserves," and eventually, Nazi "race hygiene" policies. Prejudiced colonizers or Nazis didn't always need Fischer's work to make their points, but it often did not hurt to cite his work.[28]

Like many scientists who sought to make large claims about populations Fischer was a collector, who realized that the scientists of his age only respected findings that were based on information that could be gathered from the micro-study of large aggregates of human remains.

Those of us who view some of Fischer's praxiological work through post-colonial or critical genocidal lens are horrified, but critics need to remember Ann Stoler's admonition that scholars need to read "along the grain" so that they can understand certain collective mentalities.[29] Although the studies of skulls appealed to anthropologists, anatomists, enthnologists, or eugenicists, many also dreamed of actually measuring living "specimens." This explained some of the reasons why scientists visited "human zoos" or museum exhibits[30] on many continents, and why we have been bequeathed photographic collections that were used for that imperial gaze. The same Fischer who took back those remains to Freiburg was also the person who wrote a letter in 1913 to the German colonial government in GSWA asking for permission to procure body parts from male "Bushmen." In that same correspondence he referred to these Bushmen as criminals and suggested that it might be best if live African Bushmen be sent to Freiburg, where they would probably die off because they were not acclimated to Germany's climate![31]

Other colonizers collected butterflies, ivory, and many other "cabinet curiosities," but perhaps scientists like Fischer felt that they were helping the cause of humanity and social efficiency by fetching good from evil, by treating specimens from "dying" races or dead criminals as materials that might help with the progress of racial science. Those sciences, in turn, were supposed to help Social Darwinians preserve the *Völk.*

Here I need to mention that many of today's professors and students in places like Freiburg are some of the harshest critics of these colonial practices, and many go out of their way to help Ovaherero and Nama communities. Those in Freiburg, for example, often joined those in Berlin or Hamburg who were willing to help provide the historical contexts that were missing from some reviews of these repatriation ceremonies.

The documentary work of Markus Frenzel catalyzed the efforts of Ovaherero and Nama activists who asked the German government and scientific institutions to hand back the descendants who were killed during GSWA period. Chief Kuaima Riruako—who had been one of the plaintiffs filing those first Ovaherero reparations lawsuits in America (see chapter 7)—now asked that the Namibian government start diplomatic negotiations with the German government for the return of Namibian skulls. The Namibian ambassador to Germany, Neville Melvin Gertze, met with some of the administrators and researchers at the Albert-Ludwigs-Universität Freiburg to discuss whether there was evidence that these tainted remains were on the premises. All of this was taking place at the same time that Australian Aboriginal communities were also asking for the repatriation of other human remains.[32]

Yet in spite of all of the recent press coverage of these activities in Freiburg, it would be the Charité, a university hospital in Berlin, that would be remembered as the first institution in Germany that actually handed over ancestors to Namibians during 2011 ceremonies. The Centre for Anatomy at Charité took center stage as international journalists reported on how that organization's planners anticipated the arrival of more than fifty Namibian delegates. The World Wide Web started filling up with countless stories about Ohamakari/Waterberg, von Trotha, conditions in "death camps," prior legal proceedings, and the demands of the Ovaherero and Nama activists.

Later in this chapter, I will have more to say about the Charité ceremonies, but before I go there, I want to briefly explain how *dingpolitik* German "provenance" research can impact the *realpolitik* trajectory of some of these repatriation conversations.

SCIENTIFIC "PROVENANCE" RESEARCH AND GERMAN FRAMINGS OF "A CONTEXT OF INJUSTICE"

While many journalists, trained to pursue objectivity and impartiality, sympathized with the plight of German researchers who wanted to do a thorough job of carrying our provenance research, impatient Ovaherero and Nama activists were demanding the immediate handover of their ancestors. According to one summary report that came from the Embassy of the Republic in Berlin, investigations had revealed that the skulls that would be handed over during repatriation ceremonies had been identified as human remains that definitely came from German South West Africa.[33]

Not many details were provided about the specific historical or cultural research that was used to draw these conclusions, and not much was written about the thousands of other human remains that were stored all across Germany. A review of specific provenance reports shows that a few of these researchers who carried out provenance studies of human remains were citing the work of Casper Erichsen, but few mentioned the annihiliationist rhetorics that were sometimes used by soldiers or collectors who collected, shipped, or analyzed these skulls.

Some of the skulls that would be handed over during that fall 2011 Charité repatriation ceremony were believed to have come from Shark Island, and this fueled the (perhaps unfounded) World Wide Web speculation that the German researchers had discovered the skull of Cornelius Fredericks, a beloved Nama leader who died in the camps.[34]

Throughout 2011 mainstream and alternative press outlets used the word and the image to educate global viewers about the anthropological collection of African human remains, the transportation of crates of indigenous skulls, camp experimentation, Nazi scientific research, race-mixing laws, and the Holocaust. Unlike some of the restrained missives that were coming from German spokespersons for medical facilities who hesitated to mention the word "genocide,"[35] the blogosphere started filling up with commentaries that treated the repatriated skulls as irrefutable evidence of colonial wrongdoing. More than a few mainstream writers or bloggers mentioned how the perpetration of the "Kaiser's Holocaust" should have led to criminal trials at places like The Hague or Nuremberg.[36] Edwin Black, for example, writing in *The Times of Israel* in 2016, opined that "Germany's extermination program for black Africans" had set the "template for the Holocaust."[37] Again, note the viral spread of various continuity theses.

Many mainstream journalists and alternative press writers did mention how contrite German leaders of medical hospitals or museums had expressed their personal regrets at the handover of dozens of skulls, but this invariable led to more questions about why German governmental officials in places like Hamburg or Berlin were not speaking out about these findings. This led inexorably to questions about the contents of history textbooks about German colonialism[38] or the "decolonization" of German museums.[39]

More skeptical critical indigenous scholars, or postcolonial critics, might ask, Were these well-publicized repatriation ceremonies serving as performative ways *of avoiding grappling with complex issues like reparations or Namibian land redistribution*? How, one might ask, was all of this talk of "confronting" dark pasts through the return of skulls helping impoverished Ovaherero and Nama communities? As critical colonial settler scholar, Lorenzo Veracini, would note—citing the work of Eve Tuck and Wayne Yang—if real "decolonization" was going to be more than a "metaphor," then critical consciousness-raising was going to have to "translate into the action that disrupts settler colonialism."[40]

Some German spokespersons refused to tackle those broader colonial settler issues, and they argued that the repatriation decisions that had to be made by German decision makers or institutional employees should be governed by some of the formal and informal codes that had been vetted by committees that had reviewed similar postcolonial calls for repatriation of human remains. For instance, representatives of German medical schools could point to some museum guidelines that were recently promulgated by the *Deutscher Museumsbund* (DMB).[41] The authors of these guidelines indicated that those requesting repatriation of these remains had the burden of proving that skulls and similar objects were actually sent to German shores in a "context of injustice."

As far as I can tell, before 2013, indigenous communities did not participate in any meaningful dialogues that led to the promulgations of these first museological rules on colonial human remains, and the German natural scientists, social scientists, and other members of the committee who produced these rules assumed that they could study and outline what did, and did not, constitute adequate proof to overcome these types of burdens.

Instead of treating entire collections of materials from the German colonies as "tainted," spokespersons for German institutions, using provenance grammars, had talked as if only a few skulls or descendants needed to be turned over to the Namibians. The indigenous Ovaherero or Nama activists who made repatriation requests would have to follow German museological guidelines that required positive identification of each and every human remain that had anything to do with grave robbing, the illicit sale of body parts, or German South West African camp experimentation. As Lars Eckstein explained in 2017, it seems as though there was a "wide consensus among legal scholars, museum practitioners and curators of scientific collections in particular that colonial regimes were in principle legitimate concerns of imperial acquisition."[42]

Micro-aggressions practiced during repatriation ceremonies thus spoke volumes about national reluctance to view many German colonial acts as problematic in nature. Twenty-first-century social agents in Germany could apologize for the few documented acts of a small group that theoretically contributed to that "context of injustice," but from a poststructural or postcolonial vantage point, this all assumed this could be contrasted with much more normative, and just, German settler contexts.

This type of rhetorical framing of both the skulls and the "context" for their procurement individuated the taint, prevented decolonization, and disaggregated the human remains that were found in public or private German collections.

I would go even further and ask this question: Is it possible that part of the reason that German governmental officials were refusing to become involved in any German—Namibian activist talk of reparations or repatriation is that all of this was leading to questions about some German colonial "*Sonderweg*"? Were they worried that after being asked to "master" Nazi pasts they might have to go through similar processes as they had to answer for the Second Reich's colonial genocides?

For decades many Germans had taken pride in the fact that they had made amends by paying reparations to Holocaust victims, and thousands of monuments, museums, and other spaces and places were now used to teach younger generations about the Judeocide. Would the acknowledgment of other German genocides erase some of the psychic and social distance that had been created between the Nazis and today's generations? Would all of this be another example of Vimalassery's, Pegues's, and Goldstein's "colonial unknowing"?

Few members of nation-states want outside parties rummaging through their colonial or military archives, and readers can readily imagine the anxieties of German leaders or European citizens who find academics or investigative journalists are now mentioning how buildings, medical anatomical collections, or research facilities are linked to colonial genocidal acts or Nazi race hygiene practices.

All of this praxiological focus on the provenance of skulls was doing more than just raising questions about the origins of some human remains—it was also leading some to question the orthodox histories, traditional historiographies, and dominant public memories that were crafted by those who wanted to think positively about German colonial legacies. Articles on Namibian human remains started to contain paragraphs on Germany's particular brand of imperialism and the annihilations sentiments of some colonizers in places like German South West Africa or German East Africa.[43] Scientists carrying out provenance studies could argue that far too many were making inferential *realpolitik* leaps based on just a little bit of *dingpolitik* research.

Fairly or unfairly, the German museological rules for the repatriation of remains, that focus on demonstrating a "context of injustice," raised myriad philosophical, social, political, and legal questions about settler colonialism or Namibian indigenous rights that cannot be adequately answered by a few experts who join a well-intentioned museological committee.

The more restrictive German rules for the return of museological human remains can be contrasted with other ways of viewing burdens of proof or inclusive decision making. Michael Pickering, for example, has acknowledged that while Australian archaeologists and anthropologists may have different ways of dealing with skulls and other human remains, Australian government officials still try to be inclusive in the ways that they handle repatriation requests from Australian Aboriginals and Torres Strait Islanders. Pickering would commend some of the German writers who crafted key 2013 recommendations for working on these guidelines, but he noted that "respect and sympathy for the dead" did not always translate into "automatically conceding to the requests of the affiliates."[44] Ciraj Rassool, who compared the German guidelines to those used by South Africa's Iziko Museums, explained that South Africa's national policy seemed to be that "any remains stolen or acquired for racial research should be regarded as having been unethically collected."[45]

In fascinating ways this twenty-first-century postcolonial German reluctance to hand over all remains from indigenous lands seemed to provide one more example of the lingering influence of colonial collecting obsessions. "Colonialism refers to more than just the formal political experience of colonialism," explains Rassool, and "there needs to be a deeper appreciation of how categories, institutions, and disciplinary formations may be marked by coloniality, even long after colonialism's end."[46] Those who crafted the museological repatriation guidelines for the *Deutscher Museumsbund* may have been inadvertently or unconsciously perpetuating what critical indigenous scholars have called the "colonial insistence on epistemic mastery."[47]

By putting in place restrictive guidelines those who crafted the rules that were supposed to help with the orderly transfer of human remains were assuming that in cases of doubt and uncertainty materials collected from places like German South West Africa must have been a part of a legal trading regime. The writers of these guidelines acted as if their own categorizations, and their own "provenance" studies were totally innocent and had little to do with work of individuals like Eugen Fischer. Yet note the ways that they assumed that "races" existed, and so forth.

The hauntology surrounding these human remains from places like Shark Island warrants more than just the brief mention of historical "context" that may be used to supplement longer, more technical, portions of German provenance investigatory reports. Some of the very same ontological and epistemic assumptions that helped produce colonial arguments and accommodationist or annihilationist ideologies drifted along in these European archives. Like the skulls that were transported, the racist ideologies appeared, disappeared, and resurfaced, and now those who were carrying out provenance research were convinced that their twenty-first-century efforts had little to do with nineteenth-century eugenical prejudices. Those who studied the old racist photographs of Ovaherero, Nama, San, and other indigenous communities, or those who studied old physical anthropological reports that referenced these human remains, tried to distance their own provenance research from the packing of skulls or the measurement of supposedly "inferior" races.

This type of disaggregation and disassociation allowed more than few to assume that their "objective" provenance work had little to do with activist talk of genocide.

It is no coincidence that so many of those who were involved in the provenance research before the 2011 handovers wrote and talked about how their own scientific research differed from more humanist, textual types of historical studies. They could treat their own provenance findings as "primary" materials, and the work of someone like Horst Drechsler or Helmut Bley or Casper Erichsen as a producer of "secondary" materials.

Those who produced these disciplinary hierarchies or formulated these museological guidelines were having trouble seeing the instrumentalist nature of their own work. What did DNA investigations, in theory, have to do with more humanistic, holistic work that involved studies of rhetorical cultures, colonial apparatus, colonial settler mindsets and even Wilhelmine assumptions regarding the collection of human remains?

It was unthinkable to contemplate a situation where thousands of human remains were characterized as "tainted" and quickly turned over to the Namibians or other indigenous communities. That would have obviated the need for the provenance research that protected untainted scientific collections. Emptying museological cupboards and witnessing the total decolonization of anatomical institutions were not a part of the mission statements of these German provenance teams.

By not taking seriously the harsher critiques on Fischer, Shark Island, or related topics that appeared in the 1918 British Blue Book, or the work of Casper Erichsen, today's committee members who write these provenance reports produce very narrow guidelines that reify some (post)colonial assemblages. Consciously or unconsciously, those natural scientists or social scientists who wrote German guidelines for the museological return of human remains were acting as pseudo-lawyers or autodidactic investigators who could discover—without having lawyers or indigenous representatives on their committees—what was just or unjust. This privileging of physical anthropological ways of defining, describing, and explaining the origins of human remains helped instantiate the idea that all of humanity profited from keeping most human remains in the hands of German museum curators or anatomy professors and out of the hands of Ovaherero or Nama activists.

I realize that many Westerners might respond to these critical genealogical critiques by asking, Shouldn't dispassionate researchers, instead of emotional activists, be the decision makers who can operationalize that ideographic "context for injustice"? Shouldn't these human remains stay in the hands of elite researchers who could continue to use them to train generations of doctors?

Remember, I am writing not just about individual intents or motivations but about the ideological formations that can be found in large scale rhetorical structures. Note the politicized nature of the grammars that were used to explain how that "context for injustice" guided German decision making. Those who conversed about physical certainties and uncertainties wrote about the "ambiguous provenance," and the need to clarify issues regarding regional origins or time periods by using triangulating "scientific methods" such as "historical research," studies of "methods of acquisition of human remains," "morphological sex and age-of-death verification," "morphological estimation of ancestry," and even "molecular" biological approaches (mtDNA).[48] This was a part of the rhetorical arsenal of those who oftentimes co-produced, or accepted, the findings that were then used to rationalize the normalization of more restrictive repatriation policies.

European investigatory groups like the Charité committee were the twenty-first century gatekeepers, some of the custodians who get to decide what did, and did not, constitute a "context for injustice." Their expert guidance could then be used by empowered decision makers to justify particular framings of German colonial practices.

No wonder that some of those who reviewed these types of guidelines averred that these twenty-first-century skeletal investigations "have discomforting continuities" with "19th century raciology," where data bases that depend on "cranial measurements" seem to be a product of racial science techniques.[49] After all, didn't one have to believe in the ontological existence of "races," or human differences, before one could produce epistemic conclusions about skeletal origins?

I realize that these are contentious claims, and that not all readers are going to agree that these issues about provenances have everything to do with moral or legal culpability, so let me provide a more detailed critique of some of these same human remains so that readers can see how critical genealogical work helps with critiques of that "colonial unknowing."

DECOLONIZING "PROVENANCE" RESEARCH AND A CRITICAL GENEALOGICAL REVIEW OF THOSE "TAINTED" "SPECIMENS"

Earlier I briefly alluded to Bruno Latour's work on *dingpolitik* and *realpolitik,* and here I need to show how those theoretical insights help decolonizers understand some of the complexities that swirl around those Namibian human remains. If we applied Latour's notion of *realpolitik* in these repatriation or reparations situations, we would be highlighting the Namibian parliamentary commentaries of someone like Kuaima Riruako, or the Bundestag conversations or U.S. Congressional Record statements on the need to recognize the "Namibian genocide."

Bruno Latour, however, was convinced that there were other, more open and inclusive ways of thinking about public participation in efficacious deliberative processes, and he was bothered by the inordinate attention that was lavished on *realpolitik* ways of conceptualizing public participation in deliberation. He argued that cosmopolitan readers and others needed to also take into account the potential rhetoricity of something he called *dingpolitik,* a neologism that explains the agentic nature of material objects. He was convinced that for "every one of those objects, you are spewing out of them a different set of passions, indignations, opinions, as well as different ways of carrying out their partial resolution."[50] In order to provide his readers with a concrete example of the persuasive power of objects Latour, writing in the middle of the Iraqi phase of the global war on terrorism (GWOT), mentioned the "latest beheading by fanatics in Falluja,"[51] that led to the leveling of that entire town by U.S. Marines. This all took place after the circulation of graphic images of cheering Iraqi crowds that were shown celebrating the deaths of some Blackwater security guards. The beheadings, in other words, involved agentic objects that brought together *realpolitik* and *dingpolitik* agency as ideologies were produced that impacted societal and military decision making in Iraq and elsewhere.

If we applied some of these Latourian insights to the Ovaherero and Nama reparations situations we might better understand not only the ways that indigenous communities felt about the return of their ancestors but the operative assumptions that guided some of the decisionism that swirled around the Charité repatriation performances. We would no longer view these human remains as "specimens" as physical, unchanging laboratory items that can be studied, classified, measured, identified, and then hastily put them on planes to get the "taint" out of Germany. Instead, we would trace the ways that skulls/ancestors speak, or interact, with those who viewed them at various times as war trophies, collectible items for sale, data for Wilhelmine racial science, or evidence that can be used in New York courtrooms.

Critical genealogists, who would keep in mind the praxiological interest in these human remains, would try to track the "anatomy" of these skulls as they were photographed for a 1907 German soldier's memoir or were taken "out of context" by savvy youngsters who could put up web pages using these same images to tell visitors to this part of the World Wide Web about the Namibian genocide. We could bring together Michel Foucault's and Ann Stoler's work on the archives, and regimes of truth, with Latour's concerns about *dingpolitik*. This merger would help with the study of the symbolic and the material links that can be made between the provenances that were written up before the Charité repatriation performances and the ways that those living during the German South West Africa years treated these very same human remains.

The skulls that were handed over during twenty-first-century repatriation ceremonies in Germany or Namibia may have at various times been treated as the remains of prisoners of war, specimens used for scurvy experiments at Shark Island, or the relatives of indigenous claimants from Australia[52] and Namibia.

If we go back to the work done on those provenances we can readily appreciate the arguments of Larissa Förster and Sarah Fründt, who noted that the "German museum community has been somewhat slow with entering the debate, but has recently started to catch up with international standards."[53] I am of course arguing that all of this goes way beyond simply assessing the fairness of the museological standards articulated by a few elite natural or social scientists that might govern the orderly return of a few human remains.

From a critical genealogical standpoint, the sedimentations and layering of the texts and visualities of those Shark Island skulls and other Namibian human remains, have, over the course of a century, become entangled in acts of selective colonial or imperial remembrance. Indigenous scholars might argue that they have everything to do with agnosia, or the study of disavowals, or willful ignorance.[54]

As noted above, there seems to be a palpable desire to dissociate objectionable studies of "race mixing" and eugenics from population studies or provenance research, or the perceived need to produce "balanced" rules that take into account present or future scientific needs. Osteologists, for example, could argue that the very rarity of some of "tainting" of these indigenous remains, as well as the massive rise in repatriation requests, has contributed to the rising demand of training and practice in this area of "skeletal biology."[55] The past becomes prologue as more expertise is needed to decide what metaphoric "cupboards" filled with curiosities have to be emptied.

In order to provide readers with just one example of this way of contextualizing matters, note how Ursula Wittwer-Backofen and her coauthors wrote about the experiences with provenance analysis of human remains from Namibia that could be found in the Ecker Collection of Freiburg University in Germany. This was a particularly sensitive topic, given the fact that many humanists have written about how the Ecker Collection was tied to the work of Eugen Fischer. In their essay, Wittwer-Backoften and her coauthors explain how they began to "pre-select" which skulls might be problematic by using UV light that could be "applied to decipher faint signatures" that would "help reveal those that are invisible in daylight." They explained that all skulls and their "signatures" were then "thoroughly photographed."[56] Using this procedure, these researchers concluded that some nineteen skulls might be "determined to be relevant" for repatriation purposes.[57]

Few of the journalists who covered the Charité University Hospital repatriations ceremonies in 2011 seemed to realize that presence also signified absence, and that the handing over of a few dozen skulls was signifying that many other, "untainted" remains were going to stay in Germany. These Charité and Freiburg processes for provenance determination meant that many thousands of other skull or human remains that might have been collected during German colonial or imperial periods—that may or may not have come from the old "German South West Africa"—would not be considered "relevant" and would no longer be the object of Charité investigations. Now, the members of these investigative teams explained, they had already carried out detailed, and costly, studies of skull labels, imaging techniques, morphometrics, and other scientifically applied methods. The use of these varied techniques led them to avert their gaze away from thousands of human remains to focus on nineteen skulls—eight that had a "direct reference to the Herero," five that were labeled "*Hottentotte*" (a derogatory name for Nama), and several others that had labels that suggested that they came from "Southwest or South Africa."[58] Later on in their study they noted that in all "19 cases, acquisition is not documented," and these researchers treated historical sources are materials that provided little "information on acquisition," which in turn led to "specific skulls out of this subsample."[59]

Again, in theory, these researchers could do little about the gaps that supposedly existed in provenance timelines. Reading the rest of the article helps contextualize what Wittwer-Backofen and her researchers considered to be "historical research"—the texts that were produced by scientists who actually used the skulls in their research or mentioned Eugen Fischer's name or provided clues that would help establish the provenance of each skull. Given the lack of specificity and inadequate historical research, Wittwer-Backofen's team made these decisions:

> Of the 19 examined skulls, six most likely are not relevant to the project as they are probably not Herero or Nama remains from Namibia (744, 745, 749, 756, 769, and 794). . . . Six other skulls are also labeled or referenced to be Herero. Of those, 748 is said to have been found near Rehoboth. 750, 751 and 752 are said to be have been excavated near Swakopmund, possibly by Eugene Fischer himself. 754 and 755 are said to have been presented by medical officer Jacobs, whose identity could not be verified. Both might have come from concentration camps, 754 from Swakopmund, 755 from Shark Island, where an extermination camp existed, and thus might be related to the colonial war from 1904 to 1908.[60]

These authors concluded their 2014 essay by arguing that the "preponderance of the evidence" for "an origin from the region of today's Namibia" could be claimed for fourteen out of the nineteen skulls, and these they suggested should be candidates for repatriation.[61] Wittwer-Backofen and her coauthors also recommended that in order to help with this type of work, those involved with skeletal remains and "practical" repatriation efforts needed to get in "contact with the country of origin and the population concerned at an early state of research" so that mutual agreements could be set up regarding provenance analysis that might or might not include invasive testing methods.

Here I need to pause and make several observations about these investigative rhetorics. First of all, notice the ways that these researchers talked about the "preponderance" of the evidence, a standard that finds parallels with legal usages of that term in civil cases. Second, even though the end of the Wittwer-Backofen et al. essay mentions the need for future inclusion of input from indigenous communities, there is little evidence that they were actually involved in this particular labeling process. Moreover, instead of talking about stolen materials, or the racial politics behind these collections, we get a sanitized, neutral-sounding discussion of "acquisition."

Third, the report produced by Wittwer-Backofen and her coauthors commendably calls Shark Island an "extermination" camp, but there is precious little attempt to go on and explain, in any detail, the complicity of so many German soldiers, doctors, and others in these colonial collection regimes. The framing of this provenance analysis allows for the clinical discussion of Shark Island without having to mention that this was part of a massive colonial governmental apparatus that may have been genocidal in nature.

That said, there is a great deal of laudable commentary in this type of provenance analysis. Some of these investigators did review the work of Paul Bartels (1911) and C. Fetzer (1914), so these provenance researchers and other workers were showing that they were familiar with the applied race science work of those who used some of the skulls found in the Ecker Collection.

The Freiburg researchers seemed to be genuinely interested in being precise and transparent about their methods, but they, or those who used their findings, could carry out investigations in ways that hindered repatriation efforts. The fleeting mention, in passing, of the rights of indigenous communities who view these remains as ancestors, seems to be an afterthought, presented at the end of an essay that focuses on the social agency, and the acumen, of those who seem to know more about what the skulls have to say. Here the Wittwer-Backofen et al. essay makes no mention of the grave robbing, the exportation of skulls by German soldiers like Ralph Zürn,[62] the photographs of skulls placed in crates and sent to Berlin, the scurvy experiments at Shark Island that were conducted by Dr. Blofinger, or the Nazis who produced anti-black and anti-Semitic tracts based on the work of Fischer's studies of the GSWA "Rehoboth Basters."

These researchers may have believed that they were generous in suggesting that eleven skulls be handed over for repatriation, but this could also be viewed as a public relations damage control measure, that helped purify their own disciplines. As Lars Eckstein explains, these are examples of tactics that can be used by those who "reject the notion of a systematic context of injustice for colonial collections," that protect collections from indigenous repatriation requests by treating the "acquisition and trafficking of subaltern bodies in the name of racial science" in ways that are "*a priori*" defined as "ethical and legitimate."[63]

Are these provenance scientists emulating the actions of German diplomats who also avoiding using the dreaded "g" word? In the case of the Freiburg investigators it seems as though they were unwilling to defend the position that the very collecting of skulls during three decades of German overseas colonization might constitute evidence of genocidal behavior or what Raphael Lemkin called "cultural genocide." By narrowing gazes that only looked for "relevant" objects for repatriation provenance researchers could avoid commenting on the systematic nature of colonial violence in GSWA.

These researchers may not have viewed themselves as participants in the "cultural wars" or the "memory wars" or "history wars" of the twenty-first century, but this type of provenance research produced *realpolitik epistemes* and *dingpolitik* fragments. Their involvement in disciplinary or institutional micro-politics need to be linked to more macro ways of viewing the praxis associated with this type of research.

Removing the "taint" from human remains collected during colonial years is inextricably related to removal of historical, archival, historiographical, or even *nationalistic* "stains."[64] Krüger, who was trying to explain how the human remains themselves may be agentic, had this to say about the connections that could be made between provenance research and the formation of thanatopolitical or biopolitical archives:

> The skeletons and skulls which travelled like an army of the dead into European and American archives and collections can themselves be regarded as archives. They contain a whole range of scientifically reconstructable information on the personal life of an individual and about given or assumed population groups. From anatomical comparison to modern DNA analysis, research methods changed over time, and in tandem, so did the question and theories of osteology, physical anthropology, archaeology, palaeoanthropology, bioarchaeology, and other disciplines. . . . Mortal remains are biological and biographical archives.[65]

Are these "mortal remains" telling us anything about collective colonial agency?

Instead of openly discussing how most imperial collections of indigenous human remains might have anything to do with genocidal behaviors, many German spokespersons and researchers who discuss repatriation invite members of the press to record the solemn nature of ceremonies that chronicle the return of indigenous ancestors. In 2014 the University of Freiburg circulated a press release on the topic of the "Repatriation of Skulls from Namibia." Readers who read this press release would find that the University of Freiburg planned on holding a ceremony that involved the work of an "extensive research project," and that the University would work with the Namibian Embassy. The rector of the University of Freiburg, Professor Dr. Hans-Jochen Schiewer, supervised the handover of the fourteen skulls to a Namibian delegation led by the Minister of Youth, National Service, Sport, and Culture Hon. Jerry Ekandjo, deputy chairman of the Council of Traditional Leaders Chief Immanuel /Gaseb (the slash represents a clicking sound), and head of the National Museum of Namibia and chairperson of the National Heritage Council Esther Mwoombola-/Goagoses.[66]

Note the absence of any commentary on any evidencing of a genocide, or any discussion of other, future repatriation efforts that might involve the transportation of hundreds or thousands of human remains. Was this a door-opening or a door-closing performance for those in charge of Freiburg skeletal archives? Was this postcolonial knowing or "colonial unknowing"?

The 2014 Freiburg handover took place with relatively little fanfare, but that would not be the case with reparations requests that involved other German institutions.

CONTEMPORARY REPATRIATION MOVEMENTS AND "REHUMANIZATION" EFFORTS

At the University of Hamburg, academics like Professor Jürgen Zimmerer have become public intellectuals who are using postcolonial societies and conferences to help educate publics about the importance of performances like the ritualistic handover of Namibian human remains in 2011, 2014, and 2018. German postcolonial scholars are now forming solidarity movements with the activist Namibians, and many are not afraid to talk about colonial genocides or the need to have radical land reformation in Namibia.

Many members of these transcontinental alliances do not mind using the "g" word, and they have worked at encouraging some of UNESCO's world heritage organizers to consider preserving some of the spaces and places that once served as concentration camps or burial grounds for those who died in German South West African wars.

From a praxiological standpoint, theory turns into praxis as stories about the return of human remains are tethered to narratives about the eugenical studies of Eugen Fischer, and the larger cultural need to acknowledge what happened at places like Shark Island. Stories of "bone" collecting are linked to those academic studies of Horst Drechsler or Helmut Bley that were some of the first academic investigations that referenced GSWA genocidal acts.

All sorts of inversions and strategic appropriations of the past are used to rehumanize those who were once dehumanized by colonial settlers, soldiers, civil administrators, or scientists. Throughout 2018, as more writers commented on these repatriation efforts, journalists across the globe who wrote about the skulls of the Nama or the Overaherero were also discussing the need for more indigenous involvement in bilateral restorative justice negotiations, the need to change some of the names of streets in German metropoles, the taking down of some statues, and the payment of postcolonial reparations.

Those iconic skulls/ancestors were not soon forgotten. For many these skulls were speaking to us from the grave about past transgressions. Vilho Amukwaya Shigwedha has explained how Fausy Kambombo, an employee of the Namibian Independence Memorial Museum, once commented on the relational dynamics of encounters with these descendants:

> It is emotionally charged when one comes into contact with the skulls and skeletons in their current environment and situation. When I escorted the Brazilian team [working on a documentary] to the room where the skulls are kept, I opened some of the boxes that contain the skulls. Mind you that apart from the skulls, four human skeletons are also inside that room. . . . It's painful that these people continue to be treated this way. . . . You cannot just walk into that room and come out clean.[67]

Again, the taint discussed in those provenance reports involves more than just locating the place where a "specimen" was first picked up and shipped off to Europe.

The rehumanization efforts that are being performed in Namibian-German contexts need to be contextualized by viewing all of this as a part global efforts at decolonizing all types of difficult imperial pasts, and I would argue that German institutions should not be singled out as some unique or atypical repositories of inexplicable colonial evil. Researchers are finding that many other European collectors brought back to England or France or Belgium similar artefacts or ancestors.

Rehumanization efforts need to involve many international parties, because some researchers estimate that by the beginning of World War I, tens of thousands of skulls, tissue, brains, skeletons, and other human remains were placed in tins and crates as they were taken from the peripheries of empire and taken to Europe. The British, French, Dutch, Belgians, and other colonizers either bought, found, or stole countless artefacts from Asia, Australia, and Africa and then placed them in the universities, museums, hospitals, military barracks, or private homes of many Europeans.

A critical review of these "bones of contention" shows the diverse nature of some of the transcontinental responses of those who come across large collections of contested remains.

Decision makers in the Netherlands, instead of waiting on claims from private parties in Indonesia, simply destroyed some of these remains that were no longer considered to be of any scientific value.[68] Alternatively, one might follow the advice of writers like Ciraj Rassool who has called for the return, reburial, and "rehumanization" of many of the remains that were taken during colonial times. Instead of having so many European or other museums find ways of rationalizing why they need not return that many "specimens." Rassool argues South African, European, and Namibian institutions that house these remains need to participate in a complex, but needed, relational process of "undoing Empire."[69]

Instead of stalling in the face of indigenous requests, or circulating universalist, Euro-centric rhetorics that comment on the continued need for the "scientific" specimens, some are willing to part with these human remains. Rassool contends that members of twenty-first-century institutions who warehouse or display these human remains need to admit that indigenous communities regard these skulls and other materials as human ancestors, who in some cases deserve proper burial. Instead of trying to distance themselves from the "pseudo-sciences" of the past, physical anthropologists, curators, and others need to see how their own disciplines, institutional histories, or national legacies were, and are, entangled in "hierarchical and stratified relations of knowledge," that were used to found the very colonial or imperial racial sciences that are being critiqued.[70]

Those interested in the rehumanization of remains have to involve many indigenous communities in the decision making that is needed to decide what to do with the skulls, corpses, skeletal remains, casts, and other artefacts that were a part of massive markets for these objects during imperial pasts.[71]

Accepting some forms of rehumanization may mean decolonizing and dismantling imperial buildings, colonial ideologies, and other assemblages. Having been a part of the discovery of some remains in an Austrian facility that led to the return and reburial of Klaas and Trooi Pienaar—a couple who had been buried on a frontier South African farm—Rassool argued that even after the passage of some one hundred years researchers could help with needed consciousness-raising. Using archival sources investigators could still find the Pienaar name, their status as a married couple, and other information that helped "provide a research-based provenance that made their continued presence" in that Austrian museum collection "untenable."[72]

However, what does one do in situations where hermeneutics of suspicion can be used by scientists, diplomats, and researchers in a city or country that has to worry about countless indigenous requests, or interminable calls for apologies, reparations, or land redistribution? Can these skeptics question whether an organization really is "indigenous," and who has the right to speak for the dead? Are some activists actually naïve interlopers who confuse the eugenical pseudo-science of Eugen Fischer's age with today's twenty-first-century DNA or genetic provenance techniques?

Gesine Krüger has argued that disputes over human remains were at the center of post-1990s demands for repatriation, restitution, and reburial.[73] Claudia Prinz similarly remarked that tens "of thousands of human remains—from bones to mummies, from modified pieces of hair to bodily organs—are part of museum and scientific collections at German institutions, and Germany is no exception in that respect."[74]

Yet recognizing the problematic nature of some of these collections often places workers in European universities, medical hospitals, and museums in difficult positions. As Wittwer-Backofen and her colleagues explain, up "until very recently there has been very little discussion of the context in which acquisitions of human remains for historical research collections" that were accumulated during "the period of colonialism."[75]

This, I argue, has everything to do with the lingering effects of the asphasia that I discussed in earlier chapters. During portions of what A. Dirk Moses has called the "racial century" (1850–1950), it was not unusual for many European colonizers to bring back their "trophies" or "specimens." African human remains ended up in places like the Blumenbach collection in Göttingen, the Anatomical Collection at the Charité Berlin, or the Alexander Ecker collection in Freiburg.

Providing reporters or Namibian activists with documents that show the exhaustive work of the authors of these provenances will not end matters. Some of those who are asked to study these human remains may be working in buildings that are named after some of those who did the collecting during imperial years. Imagine how a German scientist, trained in the natural sciences to believe in the importance of DNA and "race," reads and interprets the work of someone like Ciraj Rassool, who writes about how places like South Africa, Namibia, and Germany are parts of an "understanding of empire" that was "premised upon extractive, hierarchical and stratified relations of knowledge" that was also "founded on disciplinary rituals of expeditions, fieldwork and collecting, as well as the appropriation of corpses, body parts, skeletal remains and artefacts between continents and across borders."[76]

Rassool argues that those who try to use narrow interpretations of the rules and procedures for repatriation guidelines in places like Europe are making the mistake of demanding that indigenous communities prove, on a case-by-case basis, the empirical links that causally connect skulls to reprehensible acts like grave digging or the transportation of materials from concentration camps. This, Rassool argues, ignores the ways that expeditions to Oceania, Asia and Africa were a part of the "trade in such materials, in addition to theft and grave robbery."[77]

If Rassool is right, then this means that those who work at German institutions that warehouse thousands of skulls, skeletons, and other human remains need to accept the fact that in addition to "theft and grave robbery," some of these human materials were transported "amid histories of bartering, gifting, and purchasing." Rassool worried that well-intentioned members of the German Museums Association were producing repatriation guidelines that did not take into account the concomitant "epistemic violence" that had everything to do with the "entry of human remains and artefacts into a classificatory order of collections, museums, and knowledge."[78]

Rassool's stance may anger those who realize that their DNA measures, their "invasive" or "non-invasive" instruments, their X-rays, MRIs, CT scans, or 3D scanning plans[79] were now being symbolically and materially linked to the colonial activities of those who collected the objects they were studying. At the same time that some scientists in charge of crafting repatriation protocols were trying to disassociate themselves from the "political" side of postcolonial restorative justice demands, many academic advocates of more liberal repatriation practices were critiquing apparently clinical approaches to provenance preparation.

What Ann Kakaliouras has called "osteological subjects" now gained social agency as social historians, colonial scholars, cultural anthropologists, and others who alleged that decisions regarding the repatriation of human remains needed to include both the active involvements of members of indigenous communities as well as acknowledgment of the lingering effects of that massive historical trade in skulls and skeletons. Krüger, approaching this topic from a different angle, wrote about how the mortal remains that were at the center of African and other requests for repatriation were "collected systematically during colonial times all over the world in order to study the racial evolution and differences of mankind."[80] This collecting, in turn, was used to convince the "colonized world" that so called "native peoples" who confronted the "encroachment of modernity would soon be vanishing." This was part of the reason why so many European, American, and Australian scientists "rushed with a certain urgency to collect as many bones as possible."[81]

So why not explain all of this to Ovaherero and Nama supporters who are aware that their communities—in spite of the efforts of some—did not vanish? While many interdisciplinary scholars and activists are convinced that the work of writers like Hannah Arendt, Horst Drechsler, Helmut Bley, Jan-Bart Gewald, Andrew Zimmerman, and David Olusoga and Casper Erichsen[82] has helped make us aware of the origins of some of what Westerners call "relics" or "specimens," many other German researchers are still convinced that in "Germany research into the history of anthropological collections is yet scarce."[83] Those interested in rehumanization will find that there are massive disconnects within disciplines, across disciplines, and across national boundaries.

CONCLUSION

During each of the ritualistic exchanges of Namibian human remains that were discussed above, it became very obvious that the parties involved had very different ways of contextualizing what they were witnessing. How one felt about the universalist claims of anatomists, indigenous claims, tribal religious practices, Namibian ethnic customs, physical anthropology or metaphysics seemed to influence how one felt about rights and duties in these complex rhetorical situations. Depending on one's historical or contemporary subject position, at various junctures in time these human remains could be configured as Namibian ancestors, abject reminders of brutal wars and "death camp" conditions, profitable materials that were collected and packed off by soldiers to German research institutions, "race hygiene" data for aspiring graduate students, or "evidence" to be used in courts of law.

I want to argue here that rehumanization efforts also had the potential to impact legal framings of Namibian pursuit of repatriation and reparations. American lawyers who prepared the 2018 amended class action complaint for Veukuii Rukoro, Johannes Isaack, Barnabas Veraa Kutuuo, and the Association of the Ovaherero Genocide in the USA Corporation seemed to be aware of the symbolic importance of these ancestral remains. Note how the claimants' attorneys contextualized the collecting of these remains as they formulated arguments about proprietary "takings" and jurisdiction:

> Defendant's unlawful takings in connection with genocide, as well as its refusal to negotiate with Ovaherero and Nama representatives in

> violation of the U.N. Declaration, has had a direct and proximate effect on class members residing in the United States. . . . In September 2017, the American Museum of Natural History ("AMNH") in New York City confirmed to Plaintiffs that it was in possession of Namibian remains, which related to the 1904–1908 German genocide of the Ovahero and Nama peoples. The human remains were originally collected by Professor Felix von Luschan, a German anthropologist and ethnologist at the Museum of Ethnology in Berlin from 1885-1910. . . . Luschan built up two large collections containing thousands of specimens: one for the Berlin museum and one in his private possession.[84]

Writing to American judges about those Namibian human remains at the American Museum of Natural History helped claimants' lawyers establish jurisdiction under the U.S. Alien Tort Act, but it also hinted that all this collecting involved transatlantic human rights issues and judicial critiques of colonial practices. The attorneys for the Federal Republic of Germany argued that the human remains found in the American Museum of Natural History were from von Luschan's private collection, and that von Luschan's work, in turn, could be linked to many European and American racial studies. The defense attorneys argued that these private sales had little to do with American public or governmental interests, and that meant that the American courts did not have the jurisdiction to hear these cases.

While some scientists, diplomats, administrators, and laypersons are puzzled by the money and time that is spent on these repatriation or reparations disputes, others realize that much more is at stake than the simple provenance identification of a few dozen skulls. How one contextualizes the treatment Namibian ancestors speaks volumes about how one feels about colonial genocide claims, indigenous rights, and the attempted rehumanization of these *dingpolitik* artefacts. Professor Krüger has noted that human remains, "like archives, not only document and contain data but construct its subject," and for that reason those human remains "do not provide stable, fixed and unequivocal information."[85] Joan Schwartz and Terry Cook similarly argue that some archives are not "passive storehouses of old stuff, but active sites where social power is negotiated, contested, confirmed."[86]

Whether we like it or not the normative talk of the right of indigenous communities to receive repatriated human remains becomes entangled in epistemic and ontological debates about the realities of "race," anthropological typologizing, or the "pseudo" or real scientific knowledge that was accumulated by generations of European anatomists, physical anthropologists, ethnologists, eugenicists, and others. These conversations ideological drift in discussions of colonial genocidal acts.

The collection of human remains from the peripheries of empire was not something that a few European soldiers or doctors or traders dabbled in; it was an entrepreneurial activity that pre-occupied many on several continents who aspired to be social scientists or natural scientists during the nineteenth and twentieth centuries. Oftentimes massive collections of bones and other human remains were collected by amateur hunters, elite members of royal families who went on hunting trips, missionaries, or ordinary soldiers who fought during colonial wars. When they got bored with their trophies, or when they wanted to leave behind something to posterity, they frequently handed over these human remains to European scientific institutions in Brussels or London or Paris or Berlin.

During the late nineteenth or early twentieth century, proving one's "Aryan" or "Anglo-Saxon" or "Germanic" superiority oftentimes meant using bones or other human remains to prove racial difference or the inferiority of indigenous "others." Katharina Schramm, writing in 2016, could argue that these "substances of indigeneity" had everything to do with former settler colonies, notions of indigeneity, "historical fault lines, collective memories, and "contemporary affiliations."[87]

After reading the above, I hope that readers can readily understand why one writer could claim that the "treatment of human skulls" discloses "issues of humanitarian, cultural and ethical concerns."[88] I would extend this analysis and argue that the histories and the memories of those "little heaps of sand" (see chapter 4) should also influence the ways that we contextualize those 2001 and 2017 cases that were filed in American courtrooms.

NOTES

1. *Vekuii Rukoro et al. v. Federal Republic of Germany*, U.S. District Court for the Southern District of New York, No. 17 CV 62-LTS, March 6, 2019, 8.

2. Manu Vimalassery, Juliana Hu Pegues, and Alyosha Goldstein, "Introduction: On Colonial Unknowing," *Theory and Event* 19, no. 4 (2016): https://muse.jhu.edu/article/633283.

3. Reinhart Kössler, "Imperial Skullduggery, Science and the Issue of Provenance and Restitution: The Fact of Namibian Skulls in the Alexander Ecker Collection in Freiburg," *Human Remains and Violence* 4, no. 2 (2018): 27–44.

4. Vimalassery, Pegues, and Goldstein, "Introduction," paragraph 1.

5. Bruno Latour, "From Realpolitik to Dingpolitik, or How to Make Things Public," in *Making Things Public: Atmospheres of Democracy*, edited by Bruno Latour and Peter Weibel (Cambridge: MIT Press, 2005): 14–44.

6. Katharina von Hammerstein, quoted in Amanda Ottaway, "For Victims of a Little-Known Genocide, a Long Journey to Justice," *Courthouse News*, last modified March 20, 2019, paragraph 21, https://www.courthousenews.com/for-victims-of-a-little-known-genocide-a-long-journey-to-justice/.

7. On some of the thorny issues that were raised by those who wanted to use medical knowledge that came from Nazi experimentation, see Sabine Hildebrandt, *The Anatomy of Murder: Ethical Transgressions and Anatomical Science during the Third Reich* (New York: Berghahn Books, 2016).

8. See Dunia Zongwe and Bernhardt Tjatjara, "Namibia: The Bones of Contention in the Ovaherero-Nama Genocide Case," *All Africa*, last modified March 15, 2019, https://allafrica.com/stories/201903150452.html.

9. Vimalassery, Pegues, and Goldstein, "Introduction," paragraphs 1–5.

10. Praxiological studies involve investigations of the ways that practitioners and others put into practice certain ideological theories. For a praxiological study that shows how graduate students and researchers used some of those Ovaherero or Namibian remains in their racialized studies, see Leonor Jonker, *"More than Just an Object": A Material Analysis of the Return and Retention of Namibian Skulls from Germany* (master's thesis; Utrecht: Universiteit Utrecht, 2015). I am indebted to Leonor Jonker for her excellent discussion of the heuristic value of praxiological studies.

11. Kirsten Grieshaber, "Germany Returns 27 Sets of Colonial-Era Remains to Namibians," AP News, last modified August 29, 2018, https://www.apnews.com/4d0d65b1f0f3427cad384180ded754d6.

12. See, for example, BBC staff, "Germany Returns Skulls of Namibian Genocide Victims," BBC, last modified August 29, 2018, https://www.bbc.com/news/world-africa-45342586.

13. Memory Biwa, "Afterlives of Genocide: Return of Human Bodies from Berlin to Windhoek 2011," in *Memory and Genocide: On the What Remains and the Possibility of Representation*, edited by Fazil Maradi, Ralph Buchenhorst and Maria Six-Hohenbalken (New York: Routledge, 2017), 91–106, 102.

14. See Chief Alfons Kaihepovazandu Maharero, "On the Occasion of the Official Handing-Over Ceremony of the Namibian Skeletal Remains That Were Expatriated to Germany Following/During the 1904 Genocide in Namibia," Genocide.Namibia.net, September 30, 2011, http://genocide-namibia.net/wp-content/uploads/2015/03/ocd_1904_chief_maharero.pdf.

15. Viho Amukway Shigwedha, "The Return of Herero and Nama Bones from Germany: The Victims' Struggle for Recognition and Recurring Genocide Memories in Namibia," in *Human Remains in Society: Curation and Exhibition in the Aftermath of Genocide and Mass-Violence*, edited by Jean-Marc Dreyfus and Elisabeth Anstett (Manchester: Manchester University Press, 2016). 197–219.

16. Ibid., 212.

17. Ibid., 213.

18. Javier Pes, "It's Not Just Art That Indigenous People Are Fight to Reclaim from Museums," *Artnet News*, last modified November 29, 2018, https://www.apnews.com/4d0d65b1f0f3427cad384180ded754d6.

19. Andrew Zimmerman, "Adventures in the Skin Trade: German Anthropology and Colonial Corporeality," in *Worldly Provincialism: German Anthropology in the Age of Empire*, edited by Matti Bunzl and H. Glenn Penny (Ann Arbor: University of Michigan Press, 2003), 156–78, 156.

20. Ibid., 160.

21. Ibid., 178.

22. Shigwedha, "The Return of Herero and Nama Bones," 199.

23. Jonker, *"More than Just an Object,"* 94.

24. Larissa Förster, "'These Skulls Are Not Enough': The Repatriation of Namibian Human Remains from Berlin to Windhoek in 2011," *Dark Matter: In the Ruins of Imperial Cultures*, November 18, 2013, paragraph 1, http://www.darkmatter101.org/site/2013/11/18/these-skulls-are-not-enough-the-repatriation-of-namibian-human-remains-from-berlin-to-windhoek-in-2011/.

25. Anke Bartels, Lars Eckstein, Nicole Waller, and Dirk Wiemann, "Postcolonial Justice: An Introduction," in *Postcolonial Justice*, edited by Anke Bartels, Lars Eckstein, Nicole Waller, and Dirk Wiemann (Amsterdam: Brill, 2017), 2.

26. Shigwedha, "The Return of Herero and Nama Bones," 199.

27. See Allister Sparks, "Namibia's 'Bastards' Insist on That Term," *The Washington Post*, last modified January 18, 1983, https://www.washingtonpost.com/archive/politics/1983/01/18/namibias-bastards-insist-on-that-term/f2e54cbd-fa9a-40d5-91b2-cf2e66d80be0/; Mary Braid, "We May Be Few but We're Proud to Be Basters," *Independent* [U.K.], last modified August 2, 1998, https://www.independent.co.uk/news/we-may-be-few-but-were-proud-to-be-basters-1169179.html.

28. For examples of how colonizers and Nazis used some of Fischer's work, see Benjamin Madley, "From Africa to Auschwitz: How German South West Africa Incubated Ideas and Methods Adopted and Developed by the Nazis in Eastern Europe," *European History Quarterly* 35, no. 3 (July 2005): 429–64.

29. See Ann Laura Stoler, "Colonial Archives and the Arts of Governance," *Archival Science* 2 (2002): 87–109.

30. Andrew D. Evans, "Race Made Visible: The Transformation of Museum Exhibits in Early-Twentieth-Century German Anthropology," *German Studies Review* 31, no. 1 (February 2008): 87–108.

31. Shigwedha, "The Return of Herero and Nama Bones," 200.

32. Ibid.

33. Neville Melvin Gertze, *Report on the Return of Twenty Human Skulls from Germany to Namibia* (Berlin: Embassy of the Republic of Namibia, 2011), cited in Shigwedha, "The Return of Herero and Nama Bones."

34. A Memorial of the Nama leader, Cornelius Fredericks, has been placed on Shark Island, the site of a Lüderitz concentration camp.

35. See Ruth Schneider, "Don't Mention the G-Word," *Exberliner*, last modified November 23, 2011, http://www.exberliner.com/features/don%27t-mention-the-g-word/.

36. See Edwin Black, "In Germany's Extermination Program for Black Africans, a Template for the Holocaust," *The Times of Israel*, last modified May 5, 2016, https://www.timesofisrael.com/in-germanys-extermination-program-for-black-africans-a-template-for-the-holocaust/.

37. Ibid.

38. Lars Müller, "'We Need to Get Away from a Culture of Denial'?: The German-Herero War in Politics and Textbooks," *Journal of Education Media, Memory, and Society* 5, no. 1 (Spring, 2013): 50–71.

39. Elise Pape, "Postcolonial Debates in Germany—An Overview," *African Sociological Review* 21, no. 2 (2017): 2–14.

40. Lorenzo Veracini, "Decolonizing Settler Colonialism: Kill the Settler in Him and Save the Man," *American Indian Culture and Research Journal* 41, no. 1 (2017): 7.

41. Deutscher Museumsbund, *Guidelines on Dealing with Collections from Colonial Context* (Berlin: German Museum Association, 2018), https://www.museumsbund.de/wp-content/uploads/2018/07/dmb-guidelines-colonial-context.pdf.

42. Eckstein, "Recollecting Bones," 9.

43. Daniel Pelz, "Skulls and Bones: A Dark Secret of German Colonialism," *Deutsche Welle*, last modified April. 6, 2018, https://www.dw.com/en/skulls-and-bones-a-dark-secret-of-german-colonialism/a-43279594.

44. Michael Pickering, "A Helping Hand? Comments on the 'Recommendations for the Care of Human Remains in Museums and Collections' by the Deutscher Museumsbund (German Museums Association)," *H/Soz/Kult*, February 2017, 1–8, 2–3. http://hsozkult.geschichte.hu-berlin.de/index.asp?id=4000&view=pdf&pn=forum&type=diskussione.

45. Ciraj Rassool, "German Museums, Human Remains and the Challenges of Colonial Legacies," *H/Soz/Kult*, February, 2017, 1–8, 7, https://www.hsozkult.de/debate/id/diskussionen-4016.

46. Rassool, "German Museums," 2.

47. Vimalassery, Pegues, and Goldstein, "Introduction: On Colonial Unknowing," paragraph 2.

48. Ursala Wittwer-Backofen, Mareen Kástner, Daniel Möller, Marina Vohberger, Sabine Lutz-Bonengel, and Dieter Speck, "Ambiguous Provenance? Experience with Provenance Analysis of Human Remains from Namibia in the Alexander Ecker Collection," *Anthropologischer Anzeiger* 71, nos. 1–2 (March 2014): 65–86, 65.

49. Lars Eckstein, "Recollecting Bones: The Remains of German-Australian Colonial Entanglements," *Philosophische Fakultät, Universität Potsdam*, 2016, 1–14, 8, https://publishup.uni-potsdam.de/opus4-ubp/frontdoor/deliver/index/docId/41365/file/ppr147.online.pdf.

50. Latour, "From Realpolitik," 5.
51. Ibid.
52. For an insightful discussion of the emotional struggles of German researchers today who have to deal with these Australian Repatriations, see Lars Eckstein, "Recollecting Bones."
53. Larissa Förster and Sarah Fründt. "Human Remains in Museums and Collections: A Critical Engagement with the 'Recommendations' of the German Museums Association (2013), Editorial," *H/Soz/Kult*, February 2017, 2, https://www.hsozkult.de/debate/id/diskussionen-3909.
54. Vimalassery, Pegues and Goldstein, "Introduction: On Colonial Unknowing," paragraphs 22–27.
55. Wittwer-Backofen et al., 67.
56. Ibid., 74.
57. Ibid., 75.
58. Ibid.
59. Ibid., 81.
60. Ibid., 82–83.
61. Ibid., 82.
62. David Olusoga and Caster W. Erichsen, *The Kaiser's Holocaust: Germany's Forgotten Genocide* (2010; London: Farber and Farber, 2011), 224–25.
63. Eckstein, "Recollecting Bones," 9.
64. For a related discussion of colonial debates about genocide see Henry Reynolds, *"An Indelible Stain" The Question of Genocide in Australia's History* (Ringwood, Vic.: Penguin, 2001).
65. Gesine Krüger, "The Restitution of Bones: Memory and DNY Identity," for Politics of Memory, Practices of Remembrance," 2013 *Alltagswoche Fest*, April 17–20, 2013, Hanyang University, Seoul, Korea, 2, https://www.academia.edu/4539235/The_Restitution_of_Bones_Memory_and_DNA_Identity.
66. University of Freiburg staff, "Repatriation of Skulls from Namibia," *University of Freiburg*, last modified March 4, 2014, https://www.pr.uni-freiburg.de/pm/2014/rektorat-zeremonie-ruckfuhrung-04-03-14-pm-english.pdf.
67. Shigwedha, "The Return of Herero and Nama Bones," 211.
68. For an overview of some of these debates in the Netherlands, see Jos Van Beurden, "Decolonisation and Colonial Collections," *Low Countries Historical Review* 133, no. 2 (2018): 66–78.
69. Ciraj Rassool, "Re-Storing the Skeletons of Empire: Return, Reburial, and Rehumanization in Southern Africa," *Journal of Southern African Studies* 41, no. 3 (2015): 653–79, 653.
70. Ibid.
71. Ibid., 653.
72. Ibid., 669.
73. Krüger, "The Restitution of Bones."
74. Claudia Prinz, "A Critical Engagement with the 'Recommendations" of the German Museums Association (2013)," *H/Soz/Kult*, February 2017, 1, https://www.hsozkult.de/journal/id/zeitschriftenausgaben-11267?language=en.
75. Wittwer-Backofen et al., "Ambiguous Provenance?" 65–86.
76. Rassool, "Re-Storing the Skeletons," 653.
77. Ciraj Rassool, "German Museums, Human Remains and the Challenges of Colonial Legacies," *H/Soz/Kult,* February, 2017, 5, https://www.hsozkult.de/debate/id/diskussionen-4016.
78. Ibid., 5–6.
79. For a study of the "practical aspects" of preserving, conserving, and preparing select remains avoids discussions of the ideological issues, see Diana Gabler and Katherina Kepplinger, "Practical Aspects of the Case of Human Remains in Ethnographic Collections: Using the 'Recommendations for the Case of Human Remains in Mu-

seums and Collections' by the German Museums Association" *H/Soz/Kult*, February, 2017. https://www.hsozkult.de/debate/id/diskussionen-3999.

80. Krüger, "The Restitution of Bones," 2.

81. Ibid.

82. Olusoga and Erichsen, *The Kaiser's Holocaust*.

83. Wittwer-Backofen et al., "Ambiguous Provenance," 67.

84. Kenneth F. McCallion et al., Amended Class Action Complaint, *Vekuii Rukoro et al. v. Federal Republic of Germany*, United States District Court, Southern District of New York, Civ. No. 17-0062, February 14, 2018, 79.

85. Krüger, "The Restitution of Bones," 2.

86. Joan M. Schwartz and Terry Cook, "Archives, Records, and Power: The Making of Modern Memory," *Archival Science* 2 (2002): 1–19, 1.

87. Katharina Schramm, "Casts, Bones and DNA: Interrogating the Relationships between Science and Postcolonial Indigeneity in Contemporary South Africa," *Anthropology Southern Africa* 39 (2016): 1–14, 1.

88. Shigwedha, "The Return," 211.

NINE

The 2017 Ovaherero and Nama Reparations Lawsuit

The publicity surrounding the 2011, 2014, and 2018 repatriation of human remains activities helped sustain interest in Namibian reparations cases. Both during and after these image events interdisciplinary scholars were writing about the competing narratives that became a part of the "politics of memory" in Namibia and Germany. As Gabriele Steinhauser noted in July of 2017, these issues were complicated by the "multitude of constituencies" who were arriving on the scene "with their own agendas."[1]

By this time investigative journalists seemed comfortable writing about the actions of Lothar von Trotha, the 1905–1908 concentration camps in German South West Africa, colonial monumentalization,[2] and the plight of impoverished Ovaherero and Nama communities in twenty-first-century Namibia. During periods where so many were talking about restorative justice issues all around the world, the Namibian case was now "testing the limits of historical apologies."[3] In addition to the diplomatic sparring of negotiators from Germany and Namibia, there were "tribal chiefs angry about being excluded from the talks," and German-Namibians were "nervous about their standing in modern-day Namibia."[4]

In order to help unpack some of the argumentative dynamics of the heterogeneous rhetorics that were referenced by Gabriele Steinhauser, I want to begin with a portion of the chapter that contextualizes legal matters for readers by suggesting that critics can discern and identify some of the dominant rhetorical frames that were produced by those who commented on the 2017 Ovaherero and Nama reparations filings.

As usual, the main focus will be on the discursive continuities and ruptures that can be found in the colonial and postcolonial *epistemes* that were formed, maintained, and recirculating during these legal proceedings. I will also be extending the theoretical work of critical indigenous scholars who have argued that those who craft critiques of postcolonial legal regimes need to keep in mind "our locations in the colonial present as we contemplate and work toward the ongoing imperative of decolonization."[5]

CONTEXTUALIZING THE FILINGS OF THE 2017 OVAHERERO AND NAMA REPARATIONS CLAIMS

A critical rhetorical review of some of the legalistic commentaries about Namibian reparations that circulated before the 2017 filings would show that observers usually adopted one of two dominant frames of analysis as they wrote and talked about GSWA affairs and German legal obligations. One rhetorical frame was constitutively created by those who seemed to downplay the extent of German colonial settler violence, and these rhetorical formations represented the views of those who wanted to "remember to forget." For example, some encouraged Namibian activists to let the past stay in the past, and they argued that the Nama or the Ovaherero needed to stop filing lawsuits in places like the International Criminal Court (ICC) or U.S. courts.

In this twenty-first-century variant of multicultural, bi-national rhetorics, former colonial states justified forgetful by arguing that it was in the best interests of all of the parties concerned to concentrate on future Namibian development schemes. Rupert Polenz, one of the German negotiators working with the Namibian government, used a variant of this argumentative stance when he remarked that "for Germany," it did not matter what the "newspapers write," it would be the Namibian government's decision to sue or not sue that would be part of official bilateral negotiations.[6] The Namibian government wasn't suing, so Polenz wasn't worried. In March of 2019 one of the lawyers who represented Germany in the American courts, Jeff Harris, told journalists that his team was "never litigating on the facts or what happened in Namibia in those [GSWA] years."[7] In other words, he was fairly confident that his teams wouldn't ever have to worry about getting to the point in these legal proceedings where they had to worry about debating about the merits of this genocidal case.

Winning in the "court of law" did not, of course, mean that the German litigants could be sure of winning in the "court of public opinion" if they won on jurisdictional grounds so Germany's lawyers and diplomats talked to reporters about what they would be arguing if they ever did discuss the merits of these reparations cases. For example, Germany's defenders usually mentioned the passage of time, the problematic nature of any retrospective application of the 1940s Geneva Convention of Genocide provisions, the supposed problems that came with the labeling of colonial "wars" as genocides, or the need to give credit to the German parliament who had already provided Namibia with hundreds of millions of Euros in development aid.

The groups who helped co-construct this particular regime of truth adopted modernist and scientific rhetorics that made it appear as if Namibia's poverty and stratified economic system—that was still controlled by alliances of Ovambo politicians and representatives of German-speaking white communities in Namibia—had little to do with settler-colonial legacies. Namibians' health and well-being was oftentimes linked to the maintenance of that "special relationship" that existed between Germany and Namibia.

Reparations activists who made cameo appearances in this particular bi-national tale of developmental progress could be configured as antagonistic obstructionists who stood in the path of progress when they placed their own "tribal" concerns in front of more inclusive nationalistic Namibian concerns. The groups who shared these collective beliefs in German innocence rebutted the claims that were coming from Ovaherero and Nama plaintiffs who constantly exuded confidence when they were asked by reporters about court appeals and the ultimate outcome of their lawsuit.

Those who helped craft and reassemble that second major frame—that might be called the postcolonial reparations *dispositif*—were reassembling grids of intelligibility that drew from the reservoirs of arguments that been circulating in elite and public archives since at least the time the Social Democrats had argued so vehemently for "Native" rights in the Reichstag (chapter 3). Purveyors of these reparations arguments attacked the notion that there was any statute of limitations for colonial genocidal acts, and they argued that Germany must pay for having perpetrated the twentieth century's first genocide.

Those who supported the Ovaherero and Nama reparations movement efforts refused to accept the *mythos* of the "good" German colony. Instead of giving the Germans credit for having built places like Windhoek or Lüderitz, or congratulating German speakers for helping to develop Namibia's economy through large agribusinesses, the focus here was on the underdevelopment of Namibia, the lingering disparate power relationships in that country, and the destructive legacy of the GSWA years. As the lawyers for the claimants would explain in one 2017 text, the "Ovaherero and Nama sovereign entities were thereby forced into a much-reduced and limited quasi-sovereign status, which is where they remain under Namibian law, condemned for generations to perpetual and institutional poverty, lack of education, and social and cultural deprivation."[8]

While the German and Namibian negotiators rarely talked to the press about profitable German corporate ventures in Namibia, or the agrarian power of the German-speaking communities living in Namibia, those who supported the Ovaherero and Nama reparations positions opined that something had to be done about politicians who allowed so many indigenous poor to be living alongside relatively affluent descendants of "atrocity" perpetrators.[9]

At the same time, it was the adamant refusal of the German diplomats to allow activists to be involved in bilateral negotiations about Namibian development or genocidal claims that infuriated so many Ovaherero and Nama representatives. These activists considered these exclusionary practices to be postcolonial insults that reminded so many of the attitudes of the GSWA German settlers and soldiers who passed "Native ordinances" to keep Africans in their place.

The activists and scholars who were familiar with Namibian histories and colonial legacies might see clear parallels between colonial arrogance and postcolonial indifference, but to lay audiences on the sidelines—who were not familiar with these imperial histories—the arguments of the German and Namibian negotiators might appear to be rationale, fair, inclusive, and progressive. For critical scholars this provided another example of what Manu Vimalassery, Juliana Hu Pegues, and Alyosha Goldstein were referencing when they argued that "theorizations of settler colonialism" attempted to "secure the terms of reason and reasonableness" in order to "render unintelligible" many indigenous or decolonizing practices.[10]

Those who circulated the arguments that came from the postcolonial reparations frame were adamant that the Ovaherero and Nama needed to be treated as equal global citizens and as autonomous decision makers. For example, when Ida Hoffman heard all of this talk about how the special envoys for Namibia and German were engaged in negotiations about possible trusts or more developmental aid for all Namibians, she responding by arguing that "we do not want what they do for us. . . . We want reparations so we can do exactly what we want for our people and ourselves."[11]

The activists were insistent that they wanted restitution that was specifically framed as "reparations" and not cloaked in the garb of German largesse. This was not supposed to be about charity or bilateral development. Elderly Namibians who wanted to buy back land from German-speaking Namibians did not need to hear about abstract, pet theories of trickle-down economics or the patronizing rhetorics that were coming from empowered German diplomats.

Some activists might ask this: Were the Holocaust survivors treated this way when they sued or reached agreements about reparations? Whether or not the activists were making legitimate moral or legal points when they made these comments, Holocaust reparations analogies have been, and continue to be, a point of contention. Some of the scholars who use variants of continuity or *Sonderweg* theories, who know about these lawsuits, seem hesitant to comment on whether the Nama or Ovaherero activists have a legitimate case that should be based on Holocaust reparations precedents.

That said, a critical review of many of the activist commentaries that mentioned the 2017 filings of the Ovaherero and Nama reparations case in American courts shows that the activists did not shy away from talking about Holocaust precedents. They made comparisons between the "first" genocide of the twentieth century and the Nazi death camps, and they were willing to comment on what they viewed as overt racism. Henning Melber and Reinhart Kössler, writing in 2018, were sad to report that during a period when many thought that their restitutional victories were "near at hand," German diplomats seemed to be backtracking on genocidal acknowledgments.[12] The Ovaherero and the Namibians had supporters who belonged to the Left Party, sections of the Green Party, Social Democrats, Afro-Germans and postcolonial writers, but they entered a "public sphere" where "white supremacy and racism" still served as obstacles for reconciliation.[13]

This type of emotive argumentation from scholars like Melber and Kössler may not resonate with those who want to hear what they view as more formalistic, logical, historical, or legalistic ways of contextualizing reparations claims, but it made complete sense to those who had to watch German dignitaries walk out of rooms during repatriation ceremonies or those who noted how German lawyers refused to answer summons to appear in New York courtrooms.

Given the suasory power of the assimilationist or multicultural framing of these affairs, we can readily understand why some, hearing these *realpolitik* arguments, might relent and go home. Previous lawfare failures in overseas forums (see chapter 7) might have deterred other potential twenty-first-century litigants, but the Ovaherero representatives who lost their previous U.S. lawsuits in American courts from 2001 to 2007 were ready to try again.

This time the Ovaherero were more strategic, and they made sure that the Nama—who could also make a case that they were also nearly annihilated—became co-plaintiffs in a 2017 lawsuit that covered everything from the topic of illegal "taking" of property to the German colonial violations of international law. Together these groups could now talk about restitution for the killing of some one hundred thousand Africans during the GSWA years.

All this officially began in January of 2017, when these plaintiffs filed a lawsuit against the German government for what was called a "campaign" of genocide by German colonial troops. This particular filing added a new wrinkle to all of this lawfare when part of the amended complaint (filed a year later) referenced the exclusion of the plaintiffs from the bilateral negotiations that were taking place between special envoys from German and Namibia. Ken McCallion,[14] the lead attorney for the plaintiffs in this 2017 case, explained to reporters from Reuters that part of the reason that the plaintiffs were suing had to do with the fact that German government representatives had already publicly acknowledged that any settlements that were reached during the bilateral negotiations were not going to include reparations that might aid the victims of that German South West Africa colonial genocide. "There was no assurance," McCallion noted, that "any proposed foreign aid by Germany will actually reach or assist the minority indigenous communities that were directly harmed."[15]

Some German diplomats tried to talk to the media about how some types of development aid could be specifically tailored to the specific needs of the Ovaherero and Nama communities, but many activists still viewed this as a strategic way to fend off efforts to have to pay reparations that could be used to buy back contested lands.

During the early mediated press coverage of the 2017 court filings, one occasionally found mention of the similarities or differences that existed between the needs of Ovambo, Ovaherero, Nama, San, Damara, or "Basters" communities in either Namibia or South Africa. For example, some journalists noted how many of the members on the Namibian negotiating staff who were working with the Germans were coming from Namibian regions *that had not been a part of the "police zone"* during the GSWA years.[16]

So given the existence of these varied ways of conceptualizing colonial violence during the German South Africa years, and these different takes on German aid, how would lawyers who appeared in front of American judges strategically frame the plaintiffs' case in *Rukoro et al. v. Federal Republic of Germany* (2017)?[17]

LAWFARE FRAMING OF OVAHERERO AND NAMA ACTIVIST STANCES IN *RUKORO ET AL. V. FEDERAL REPUBLIC OF GERMANY*

Reinhart Kőssler, writing in 2012, once complained about how Jeremy Sarkin, a South African law professor, was writing histories about the Herero and Nama that seemed to show that Sarkin played the role of an attorney who was trying to persuade the jury,[18] but it is interesting to note how many portions of "facts" sections of legal texts enable lawyers to play the role of legal historians who have to provide narratives for busy judges so that they can see the trajectory of particular redress claims. Six years later Henning Melber and Reinhart Kőssler would argue that the "facts are hardly in question" but the "words are" regarding GSWA matters,[19] but this modernist way of viewing postcolonial lexicons doesn't take into account the rhetorical construction of those facts in legal settings.

The initial complaint in this 2017 Ovaherero/Nama class-action lawsuit sought unspecified amounts of monetary damages for thousands of descendants of the victims, for the "incalculable damages" that were caused by the colonizers living in the Second Reich's German South West Africa.[20] It was perhaps no coincidence that the historical materials that appeared in many of the plaintiffs' texts drew from the work of writers who explicitly or implicitly noted that GSWA affairs were genocidal in nature.

For some observers the 2017 filings by the Ovaherero and Nama provided a unique opportunity to critique some of the older, mainstream Namibian histories while advancing the causes of the reparations activists. Gabriele Steinhauser remarked on how debate "had surged in recent years about whether and how nations should take responsibility and made amends for horrors inflicted generations ago."[21] She treated the Ovaherero and Nama court filings as part and parcel of efforts to redress all sorts of colonial or imperial wrongs. Steinhauser mentioned how Belgians had apologized for Belgium's involvement in the 1961 assassination of Patrice Lumumba, how the French had expressed contrition for what happened in colonial Algeria, and how Japanese representatives had been involved in negotiations that led to the 2015 settlements with South Korean "comfort women" who were paid $9 million in support funds.[22] These synchronic examples of colonial redress illustrated how the Ovaherero and Nama were not the only litigants deploying lawfare in their pursuit of restorative justice.

Many legal experts who reviewed these 2017 Ovaherero and Nama reparations efforts were convinced that the 2013 U.S. court decision in *Kiobel v. Royal Dutch Petroleum Co.*—that had narrows the reach of the Alien Tort Statute to foreign conduct that "touch[es] and concern[s]" the U.S.—might present an impossible barrier to those who were trying to seek justice for matters that happened long ago and involved events that took place thousands of miles away. After all, the plaintiffs were not arguing that U.S. companies had aided the German colonizers in GSWA, nor were they claiming that the U.S. government had been involved in supplying arms to the German colonizers who used their machine guns and artillery at places like Ohamakari/Waterberg.

Most American lawyers might want to ask, How did the "Namibian genocide" [23] touch and concern American interests? There were no shortages of legal observers who were convinced that it had been much easier to file complaints for Holocaust survivors. Kenneth McCallion responded to some of this pessimism when he told reporters that he was fully aware of the *Kiobel* case precedent, but he argued that that the court decision in *Kiobel* still left "open" for U.S. courts the opportunity to assert jurisdiction in genocide cases.[24]

Legal formalists often treat "jurisdiction" as some apolitical topic that has little to do with the "merits" or politicized issues, but some critical scholars have commented on the ideological features of jurisdictional arguments in legal forums. Renisa Mawani noted in 2018:

> In its broadest sense, jurisdiction refers to the inauguration and enunciation of law, "that there is law," and that law speaks on its own behalf, authorizing itself through competing and overlapping legal forms. . . . To be sure, jurisdiction is much more than a territorial concept. In the British Empire, questions of jurisdiction often centered on the racial and legal status of people, populations, and territories, dividing Dominion/colony, native/foreigner, citizen/subject, and slave/free.[25]

American courts would have their own binaries, and their own overlapping legal forms, but this still had everything to do with power, politics, and rhetorical status.

Those who may have agreed with Kenneth McCallion as he talked about the *Kiobel* court precedent were trying to take the position that colonial genocide cases needed to be treated in the same way that courts—since at least the Vietnam War years—had been treating the "modern" genocides. In theory, if the American courts were going to get involved in hearing potential lawsuits about such topics as divestment during the apartheid years, or the Cambodian[26] or Rwandan genocides, then why shouldn't American lawyers have jurisdiction to hear the Ovaherero and Nama claims?

If members of America's judicial system treated the Ovaherero and Nama claims as matters that did not touch or concern U.S. interests, then this would signal that U.S. judges were not going to treat colonial genocide cases in the same ways that they had once treated Holocaust cases or other reparations requests before the *Kiobel* precedent. Germany's lawyers could advantage of the *Kiobel* hurdles, and they could use legal formalistic or positivist arguments about jurisdiction to avoid having to grapple with the emotive nature of the "merits" of the Herero and Nama reparations cases. When Jeff Harris was asked by reporters in 2019 about whether Germany should pay reparations to the Ovaherero or the Nama, he responded that those questions should be answered by members of the Germany embassy in Washington, DC, and not by American judges in New York federal courtrooms.[27] This was an extension of remarks that he made elsewhere regarding the "political question" doctrine.

Some of the very same entanglements of academic colonial histories and public memories that are mentioned by interdisciplinary writers also impact the legal framings of these reparations efforts. To provide just one example of how nation-states can try and dodge some of this lawfare, and can try to extricate themselves from these entanglements, note what happened when German officials first found out about the filing of the Ovaherero and Nam lawsuit in New York District Court. The German Embassy in Windhoek, Namibia, issued a press statement, indicating that Germany—on three separate occasions—had refused to accept the summons and charges related to this case.[28] When legal service was attempted on November 15, 2017 the "Federal Republic of Germany rejected the service of this action—via the U.S. State Department and the

U.S. Embassy-Berlin, because the service of the complaint on a foreign state violates the principle of State Immunity—a core principle of public international law."[29]

Refusing to accept the summons and charges of the Ovaherero and Nama activists thus become one more performative way of demonstrating how the Federal Republic of Germany was not going to view this in the same ways that they viewed the 1952 reparations agreement between West Germany and Israel. Why legitimate the lawfare efforts of those, who in theory, should have appealed to Namibian legislators?

However, when the reparations hearings resumed in January of 2018 state officials in Berlin instructed their lawyers in America that they needed to make a court appearance. One of the claimants, Vekuii Rukoro, was convinced that the apparent Germany change of heart had everything to do with Federal Republic of Germany worries about a possible default judgment. If the Germans had continued to stay away from the American courts during the reparations hearings, this would have meant taking the risk that German publics might hear that some U.S. federal district court judge might find the Federal Republic of Germany to be guilty and accountable for what happened during the GSWA years.[30]

Germany's hiring of lawyers was characterized by the Namibian activists as evidence that they could no longer be ignored. Legal technicalities were not going to stand in the way of having courts of law hear these allegations. Kazenambo Kazenambo, writing for the *Windhoek Observer*, congratulated the Ovaherero and Nama traditional leadership when their case was not kicked out of U.S. courts in early 2018. Kazenambo argued that the very presence of German representatives in the U.S. District Court of the Southern District of New York provided "testimony to the fact that the long arm of justice cannot be escaped by anyone," regardless of whether they were state or non-state actors.[31]

The trajectory of this early pretrial wrangling encouraged many of the Namibian activists to believe that their meritorious case might eventually be presented in front of an American jury. As Vekuii Rukoro watched legal and public reactions to Germany's early rejections of service, he viewed this a sign that the Germans must have realized that they had a weak case that could not hold up in the court of public opinion:

> Germany will try to exhaust all tricks available to it to avoid taking accountability for the genocide it committed against the Namas and Hereros in our country. Hence the unnecessary delaying tactics which are prolonging the inevitable adjudication of our complaint by the court. . . . Germany has every reason to be worried about facing us in court. They can run but they cannot hide. The card they have played is the last card.[32]

Did the Ovaherero and Nama litigants hold the winning hand? Didn't they realize that some of the very same jurisdictional issues that ended the Herero chances of success might resurface during judicial deliberations about the 2017 case?

HOW WERE THE 2017 PLAINTIFF FILINGS ANY DIFFERENT FROM THE PREVIOUS LAWSUITS THAT WERE FILED IN U.S. COURTS?

No doubt the renascent scholarly interest in trying to add the Ovaherero/Nama genocide to the conventional canons of Holocaust and genocide studies has had something to do with the continued filings of legal cases, but this was not the only situational factor that seemed to motivate those who paid millions of dollars to lawyers for putting together these costly cases.[33] These social agents were intent on convincing American judges that they needed to provide declaratory, injunctive, and monetary relief.

In some ways keeping on an eye on these legal cases became a performative act that brought together Ovaherero and Nama communities living in Namibia with many Afro-Germans living in the diaspora. Onlookers in places like Botswana, the United States, South Africa, and Germany could identify with those generations of Africans who were still suffering from the lingering traumas of GSWA genocidal memories. Some of those who were living in the diaspora contributed money to help with the filing of the lawsuits, and others worked on the building of social media platforms and other acts in support of reparations efforts.

Legal wrangling spilled over into public disputation as conversations about reparations were symbolically linked to other forms of redress for colonial wrongdoing. Every time there was a handover of repatriated human remains that were found in German some medical facility, museum, or private collection (2011, 2014, 2018), this triggered calls for more German expressions of contrition, repatriation, reparations, or land redistribution. As Reinhart Kŏssler observed, the "repatriation of skulls in March 2014 and, to a lesser extent, the demolition of the Windhoek Rider monument some two months earlier revealed a concern among activists of southern and central communities" in Namibia that the Namibian government might try to reappropriate "their history" and resituate it within a more nationalistic narrative.[34]

Whether they publicly admitted it or not, many Herero activists who supported the 2017 filings seemed to have realized that it had been a mistake to put together the older 2001 complaints in ways that only focused on Ovaherero, but not Nama, victimage. The new legal filings in U.S. courts were filed by both Nama and Herero representatives, and their supporters now argued in myriad ways that those legalistic choices mirrored the earlier academic treatments of the 1904–1908 war in German South West Africa.

This helped legitimate the activist causes and it helped with the attempted "mainstreaming" of the reparations arguments that were once marginalized when they came from the politicized work of the "East German" Horst Drechsler or the "West German" Helmut Bley (see chapter 6). Academic squabbles over the ontological existence of a genocide, the contentious nature of "continuity" or "*Sonderweg*" claims were temporarily set aside as more vernacular essays were produced by investigative journalists or laypersons who now took for granted many of the features of what was now also called the Namibian genocide.

A host of multidirectional textual materials were circulated in the popular presses that covered the *Rukoro* et al. case, and interested readers of mainstream newspapers or alternative press outlets learned about how those colonial horrors could be connected to the racial sciences of someone like Eugen Fischer, to the decisions of the Nazis to expel Jews and Poles in the "East," or to the death camps in the Holocaust.

This more inclusive way of writing about the "Kaiser's Holocaust" or the "Namibian genocide—that accounted for Nama or other indigenous suffering—proved a type of rhetorical framing that invited many other ethnic communities and cosmopolitans around the world to join the ranks of those who already supported Ovaerero and Nama reparations efforts. This was no longer just the "Herero reparations movement" but rather the type of decolonizing legal case that might open the door for other litigation that could highlight the colonial abuse of others. The San and "Basters" of Namibia might join in the hopes that they, down the road, might also receive reparations for their own descendants' colonial suffering.

This inclusion of the Nama made sense historically and politically, and it meant that this particular evolution in the rhetorical framing of the reparations lawsuits helped secure more local, regional, national, and international support for colonial reparations claims.

These new alliances with the Nama appealed to global social agents who also wanted to become involved in the postcolonial activism. In places like Hamburg and Windhoek and Cape Town and New York City, there were rallies to provide support for the Ovaherero and Nama litigants and the impoverished Namibians who could talk to reporters about their plight.[35] The topic of German speakers ownership of vast tracts of Namibian lands was no longer a taboo subject.

One other significant change in these second reparations lawsuits had to do with the inclusion of American plaintiffs who had ties to Namibia. In one key portion of the complaint one finds this argument:

> Many descendants of the Ovaherero and Nama peoples and lawful claimants as Plaintiff class members have emigrated from Namibia, and now call the United States their home as U.S. Citizens, lawful residents, and patriotic Americans. There are approximately 140 Ovaherero class members in the New York metropolitan area alone, most of whom are members of the Plaintiff Association. Other members of the Classes reside throughout the United States and are active in vari-

> ous organizations dedicated to the preservation of Ovaherero and Nama culture, and educational and outreach programs regarding the Oveherero/Nama genocide.[36]

The use of this type of legal formalism helped establish jurisdictional links between Namibian pasts and American presents as lawyers for the claimants underscored the point that there was American individual and organizational interest in recognizing the Namibian genocide.

Many of the lawyers and claimants who filed the 2017 reparations lawsuits also talked and wrote as if lessons had also been learned about how to argue in front of American judges about jurisdictional questions. The first lawsuits had been filled with helpful materials from the work of Horst Dreschler, Helmut Bley, Jon Bridgman, and Jan-Bart Gewald, but those who wrote those earlier complaints may not have provided enough detailed jurisdictional materials on how any of this could be connected to American interests or concerns.

This time around the lawyers of the claimants made sure that major portions of their briefs, and the declarations of experts that were collected, did a better job of showing how what happened in German South West Africa could be tied to commercial and other ventures in places like New York City. For some this was a futile attempt to show "connections," but for other observers it was argued that this should suffice to at least gain a hearing.

Another important situational factor that made this second filing of reparations cases different from the first Ovaherero filings in 2001 had to do with the formal, and the informal, help that the claimants were receiving from official representatives of the Namibian government.

Namibian vice president Nickey Iyambo issued a statement in early 2018 that indicated that sometime in 2017 the Namibian government had sent Germany a report on the German South West African genocide. Iyambo told members of the press that he trusted that the Federal Republic of Germany would pay serious attention to the position that was outlined in that report.[37] This seemed to suggest that at least some Namibians who occupied positions of power in Namibian political circles viewed the filing of the 2017 claims as more just Ovaherero or Nama "tribalism."

Granted, many writers in mainstream and alternative press outlets were warning readers about the constraints that were posed by notions of sovereign immunity or restricted interpretations of the Alien Tort Statute (ATS), but over time there were growing public support for indigenous activist reparations efforts.

A CRITICAL RHETORICAL ANALYSIS OF THE AMENDED COMPLAINT IN *VERUII RUKORO ET AL. V. GERMAN FEDERAL REPUBLIC*

As noted above, if the 2017 filings of these reparations cases were going to have any chance, then the lawyers for the claimants needed to prepare legal texts that were filled with explanations of how monies, lands, and other real and personal property that were taken from the Ovaherero and Nama in colonial times made their way to the coffers of those living in places like New York City. This accounts for why major sections of the 2018 amended complaint were filled with arguments about applicable U.S. property law and international humanitarian law. This had to be done in skillful ways that conveyed the complaint's master narrative on the near annihilation of the Herero and Nama and explained the German efforts to profit commercially from those atrocities.

As soon as critical scholars or other readers review the specific factual and legal arguments that are outlined in the *Vekuii Rukoro et al. v. German Federal Republic* complaint, they begin to realize that this is a more than a "property" or "takings" case that attempts to build on the judicial successes of earlier Holocaust, American-Japanese internment, or other reparations success stories. This is also a legal case that may have been filed in the New York Southern District Court in 2017 because these filings provided the opportunity to produce what communication scholars call a "condensation symbol," where the ninety-six pages of the amended class action complaint are used to get across broader ideological messages.

Unlike some of the earlier legal texts that began discussions of the genocide of the Nama and Ovaherero by focusing on the words and deeds of Lieutenant General Lothar von Trotha, the 2018 amended complaint did a fine job of outlining some of the institutional, structural, and ideological ways that Kaiser Wilhelm's Second Reich had been complicit in perpetrating what the Federal Public of Germany admitted constituted a genocide.

A review of the "factual allegations" portions of the plaintiffs' amended complaint shows that the plaintiffs' lawyers were going to argue that as soon as Kaiser Wilhelm's Second Reich decided to move away from respecting indigenous land rights and abiding by "protect" treaties, this constituted violations of contemporary international law. These claimants' lawyers used permutations of annihilationist rhetorics as they wrote about how German colonizers before the 1904 war exploited and violated the rights of the Ovaherero and Nama peoples. German soldiers and administrators were characterized as interlopers or "renters" who committed fraud, theft, rape, and murder in ways that precipitated what the plaintiffs' attorneys called "the Ovaherero resistance."[38] This way of framing the beginning of the 1904 violence did not follow the conventional historicizing that begins with Ovaherero social agency, but instead followed the approach of Jan-Bart Gewald, who had suggested during the 1990s that panicking German officers misread affairs in "Hereroland" and acted in ways that forced the hand of peaceful Ovaherero.

The 2018 revised claimants' brief was some ninety-six pages long, and it would be filed by Kenneth McCallion, Professor Richard Weisberg, Thomas Holman, and Yechezkel Rodal. These authors tried to craft a persuasive text that would present American judges and lawyers with plenty of potential answers to the substantive due process and procedural due process questions that had bedeviled those who filed earlier repatriation cases.

All sorts of formalistic rules and principles from torts, property, and international law subfields of law were used to try to establish a *prima facie* legal reparations case that ought to be heard in U.S. federal courts. Portions of the 2018 amended class action complaint discussed the myriad ways that Germany's control over GSWA had led to a genocide, the taking of lands, cattle, personal property, mineral resources, rights of intestacy, and even flesh, skulls, and body parts. One portion of the claimants' brief even claimed that defendant's "takings caused a stagnant birth rate in the Ovaherero and Nama communities," as evidenced by a 1908 article in the *Deutsche Kolonialzeitung* (German Colonial News) that indicated that women and girls had become "sterile from the incessant rape by Defendant's agents who carried venereal diseases."[39]

The lawyers for Veruii Rukoro, Johannes Isaack, and Barnabas Veraa Katuuo also wanted to make sure that they could show how the defendant, the Federal Republic of Germany, had engaged in acts between 1885 and 1909 that had a "direct" effect on the United States.[40] For example, the lawyers for the claimants noted there were hundreds of descendants of the Herero and Nama survivors living in New York.[41] Arguments were advanced about how a New York City museum was involved in the collection of Ovaherero and Nama human remains from German concentration camps, and much was made of the fact that the New York Public library contained one of the rare copies of the infamous 1918 "Blue Book." That horrific story of how Ludwig Cramer flogged the Ovaherero slave Maria (see chapter 4) was now (re)appropriated to provide one of the emotive vignettes in the amended complaint that showed the continued relevance of that infamous Blue Book storytelling.[42]

Critical interpretative communities who read the claimants' complaint will find assertions being made about the *Sonderweg* thesis, as well as arguments about that controversial "continuity" thesis that linked German South West African pasts to Nazi era decision making. For example, on page 5 of this amended complaint, readers will find this familiar narrative:

> Germany's express written policy to exterminate the Ovaherero and Nama indigenous peoples in southwestern Africa during the

> 1904–1908 period was Germany's first genocide of the twentieth century. In many ways, Germany's genocidal policies and practices toward the Ovaherero and Nama peoples, including the use of mass extermination, concentration camps and mistreatment of a targeted population as a "sub-human" group, was a precursor to Germany's later effort to exterminate European Jewry.[43]

These types of rhetorical framings were written as if they represented unassailable facts that were accepted by a consensus of historians and other interdisciplinary scholars when in actuality we have seen how these contentious issues still divide the ranks of thoughtful academics who disagree about various "continuity" theses.

However, as I noted in the first chapters of this this book, all histories, memories, and archives are produced by motivated social actors who try to persuade others through the use of partial, contingent, and indeterminate arguments, and in claimants' amended briefs, to provide a coherent way of making sense out of all of this GSWA violence. This type of narrative framing helped American judges see how previous legal precedents on American reparation payments and Swiss bank accounts cases might have everything to do with Herero and Nama reparations cases. This reduced some of the topical, spatial, and temporal distance that might militate against hearing these colonial cases in the first place.

Some of the claimants wanted to do more than simply allow American justices to infer that these prior reparations cases might set precedents for the Ovaherero and Nama. A more vernacular way of making similar arguments appeared in the public sphere when Vekuii Rukoro told reporters that what "happened to the Jews was only a perfection of what happened (to us)."[44]

This sounded like an echo of what W. E. B. Du Bois had written about the African slave trade and the Holocaust in 1947.[45]

Other portions of the amended complaint seemed to use permutations of arguments that connected the peripheries of empire with German metropole decision making. "A significant portion of the wealth Defendant amassed during its 'colonial experiment, in southwestern Africa," argued these plaintiffs' lawyers, "was derived from its taking of property from the Ovaherero and Nama peoples."[46] These lawyers continued to develop this argument by asserting that while Germany became "one of the wealthiest nations on earth" as a consequence of the defendant's "takings" the plaintiffs "still languish in relative poverty and deprivation."[47]

American judges who were supposed to care about equitable redress might be persuaded to see the unfairness of ignoring colonial atrocities or leaving out the reparations activists from bilateral German-Namibian discussions of these topics. But would any of this resonate with American legal communities?

THE EARLY HEARINGS FOR THE OVAHERERO AND NAMA REPARATIONS CASE BEFORE JUDGE LAURA TAYLOR SWAIN

In late July 2018, U.S. District Court judge Laura Taylor Swain presided over an hour-long meeting where she heard some of the oral arguments that would be presented by both representatives of the Ovaherero and Nama peoples as well as representatives of the German government. A small, but vocal, delegation of Ovaherero and Nama from all around the world congregated and joined the plaintiffs so that they could hear the arguments that would be presented about the one hundred thousand or so Ovaherero and Nama who died between 1904 and 1908 in GSWA.[48] Ngondi Kamatuka, a Namibian-born American of Herero descent, told reporters that all that the aggrieved parties were asking for was "restorative justice for the genocide," and the chance to put before an American jury materials that would help them "weigh the preponderance of the evidence."[49]

The mass media outlets who covered this hearing before Judge Swain made a point of informing their readers about the major legal difficulties that the plaintiffs faced in this second round of reparations cases. This led more than a few observers to ask, Would this judge interpret the U.S. Foreign Sovereign Immunities Act in ways that would help, or hurt, the plaintiff's case?

The plaintiffs' lawyers advanced all sorts of kinds of commercial claims about the nexus that purportedly existed between the United States, Germany, and the old German South West Africa as they tried to find exceptions to the Foreign Sovereign Immunities Act. This had to be done while the plaintiffs' lawyers anticipated problems with other jurisdictional issues.

From a critical rhetorical vantage point, it could be argued that the claimants' lawyers could have sued the "private" corporations who were involved in GSWA affairs as a way of circumventing some of the problems that came from Germany's sovereign immunity, but this may not have satisfied the litigants who wanted to sue "Germany" as the twenty-first-century incarnation of Kaiser Wilhelm's Second Reich.

It seems as though the claimants were intent on having legal critiques of both the activities of the German corporate ventures as well as the Federal Republic of Germany. During the first 2018 reparations hearing before Judge Swain, Kenneth McCallion presented oral versions of some of the written arguments that had appeared in the amended complaint as he talked to the court about how a number of German properties in New York had been purchased with monies obtained from colonial slave labor and the appropriation of indigenous property during the GSWA years. In a fascinating example of the permeable boundaries that existed between public knowledge from journalist sources and more traditional legalistic reasoning, McCallion also used a clever argument about the "sale" of genocide victims' remains to the nearby American Museum of Natural History (AMNH).[50] This was something that had been discussed in many U.S. and international news outlets, and now materials that were found in outlets like the *New Yorker* or the *Washington Post* could be used to argue that German citizens—or the Second Reich—had profited financially from their sale of human remains to Americans.

At this first hearing the lawyers for the Federal Republic of Germany countered by critiquing some of the weakest parts of the plaintiffs' case. Jeffrey Harris, for example, argued that the plaintiffs had not sufficiently demonstrated that a commercial link existed between colonial funds and today's commercial ventures. How, for example, were the claimants' lawyers going to show that specific funds that came from GSWA were actually used to buy property in New York City?

Moreover, Harris argued that the presence of those indigenous skulls at the American Museum of Natural History involved *a private donation* from Felix von Luschan, a German anthropologist.[51] That private agreement, it could be argued, had nothing to do with Kaiser Wilhelm's generals, the Reichstag, or any other public German community or organization.

This type of legalistic wordsmithing bothered some observers who viewed this as a pernicious type of lawfare that stood in the way of Germany's mastering of difficult colonial pasts. "Given that the root cause of the negotiation is nothing less than the first genocide of the twentieth century," opined Jens-Uwe Guettel. "the German government's legalistic stance that such a step would violate the sovereign immunity of the Federal Republic of Germany is both shameful and unconvincing."[52] Guettel went on to argue that Germans should feel obligated to push for "the inclusion of representatives of the victims' descendants in the negotiations."[53] Ruben Carranza, senior expert on reparations for the International Center for Transitional Justice, would tell interviewers in 2019 that while "Germany is avoiding legal responsibility in a U.S. court, it certainly cannot avoid legal responsibility in general—given that it was the occupying colonial power."[54]

These responses to these hearings might have illustrated how many legal pundits supported Ovaherero and Nama reparations efforts, but this did not mean that American judges were going to agree with some of these jurisprudential assessments, or ways of conceptualizing colonial "occupation law." After hearing the arguments from these two teams of lawyers, Judge Swain indicated that it would take some time before she made her final decision regarding the status of this lawsuit.

GLOBAL REACTIONS TO THE FILING OF THE 2017 OVAHERERO AND NAMA REPARATIONS CASE

As soon as mainstream writers, alternative press journalists, and bloggers found out about the filing of the *Rukoro* case, or as soon as they learned about Judge Swain's hearing, they became intrigued by the prospect of seeing descendants of victims of a colonial genocide finally receive compensation from Germany or Germany companies. As Mark Kersten would write just a few days after the filing of the initial court documents:

> While the notion that states have an obligation and responsibility to try to atone for past wrongs isn't in itself particularly controversial, the issue of reparations remains a bit of a minefield. Should reparations be given to individuals, including those who haven't suffered direct violence? Should it be given by governments that weren't directly involved? Or should reparations be given collectively to communities? If so, in what form? What "amount" of reparations is appropriate? Indeed, what counts as enough ? Who gets to decide?[55]

Some were willing to think about the fairness of providing reparations for colonial atrocities, but *realpolitik* issues made it difficult to come up with concrete plans for indigenous reparations for colonial wrongdoing that operationalized key ethical or legal principles.

No doubt many participants in these public debates about the filing of the Ovaherero and Nama reparations case in a New York district court were cognizant of the power dimensions of these filings. Reinhart Kőssler mentioned how in the "context of litigation in the USA" the "genocide in Namibia involved a postcolonial relationship" that was a part of a "much longer time frame," where the "asymmetric relationship" of the litigants is "rooted" in a "colonialism" that is "reproduced" at various levels.[56] Ida Hoffman, who once served as chairperson of the Nama Genocide Committee, provided more pointed commentary. She remarked, "Germans killed our people; they cannot dictate to us how things should be done now, and what we should and should not do."[57]

An even more contentious topic that was occasionally raised in these debates about reparations claims hearings had to do with differences that might have existed between Germany's willingness to compensate Holocaust victims and that nation's unwillingness to pay victims of African colonial genocides. "The only difference," argued Sam Kambazembi, is that the "Jewish are white in color and we are black. . . . The Germans thought they could keep this issue under the carpet and the world would never know about it. But now we have made noise."[58] No wonder that one academic who commented on this legal and public disputation wrote about "communicative silence," "contested and skewed" memoryscapes, and *Verangenheitspolitik* (the politics of the past).[59]

Commentaries about racial difference appear in many African discussions of both legal and moral decision making in colonial and postcolonial contexts, but they rarely appear in other discussions of the moral or legal dimensions of these Ovaherero and Nama reparations claims.

Between 2017 and 2019 many commentators used the 2017 reparations cases as entrée points for discussing past, present, and future problems in Namibian affairs. This lawfare could be used to critique several different types of colonial or (post)colonial wrongs, including those that were experienced during the German colonial years or during the South African apartheid years. For example, Daniel Gross would write an essay for National Public Radio (NPR) that used the story of Mbakumua Hengari as a way of representing the plight of hundreds of thousands of Namibia who were characterized as still suffering from the ravages of the GSWA conflicts. Hengari, a Herero, was said to have grown up on a farm during the 1970s where his family's homestead was "sandy and grassy, a poor fit for staple crops, so he and seven siblings depended on a herd of cattle, sheep and goats.[60] When Daniel Gross asked Hengari to discuss some of the historical roots behind his personal plight, Hengari responded by blaming several generations of systematic racism. Hengari mentioned how the first crises came during the German colonial years, and this then led to a discussion of how the all-white government of South Africa extended some of the colonial policies during the apartheid years. Like many Ovaherero, Hengari had depended on cattle farming for a living, but during the apartheid years those ethnic groups who shared the Otjiherero language—including Hengari's ancestors—were "relocated" to parched lands on the edge of the Kalahari desert.[61]

Some of the "continuity" theses that are disputed in academic circles reappear in vernacular garb as various representatives of indigenous communities talk about these topics in broader rhetorical cultures. As Daniel Gross explains, Hengari "sees a clear line of continuity" connecting the German colonial seizure of cattle from the "nomadic people like the Herero" and the "start of a systematic process perpetuating an environment of poverty."[62] Gross then goes on to quote a Herero lawyer living in Botswana who avers that if it had not been "for the genocide, we would own some pieces of land."[63] Gross told readers of the National Public Radio website that after speaking with dozens of Ovaherero interviewees he kept hearing the same arguments being made about land, the need for reparations like those paid to Holocaust survivors, and the injustice of living in a land that was controlled by German-speaking Namibians.

Given the generational poverty of these regions, and the lack of status quo progress, the Ovaherero argued that it should be the descendants of the victims, and not the nation of Namibia, who should be leading the bilateral negotiations.

Gross would not be the only agent who seemed to care about these larger, structural dimensions of lingering colonial legacies. Some Ovaherero used the filing of the 2017 case as an opportunity for discussing the historical roots of Namibia's economic and political inequities. Nokokure Veii, a member of the Ovaherero Genocide Foundation, explained that she regularly wore traditional dresses for Herero gatherings, like weddings, funerals, and commemorations for fallen Herero chiefs. She complained that the aftereffects of the colonial genocide in GSWA had reduced the Herero "to a mere insignificant minority in the country of our birth," and she mentioned how many of the businesses in Windhoek were still owned by white Namibians.[64]

Sympathetic writers like Daniel Gross thus became social agents who actively intervened in this historicizing and (post)colonial memory work. After listening to several Ovaherero comment on their admiration of the efforts of South Africa's Truth and Reconciliation Commission, the need to alter textbooks, and the legitimacy of litigation, Gross concluded by noting, "The Herero refuse to become a forgotten people. Theirs is a story of patient persistence."[65]

Some of the most intriguing reactions to the filings of the Ovaherero and Nama reparations cases came from African writers outside of Namibia. Mia Swart, writing for South Africa's *Mail and Guardian*, noted some of the similarities that could be found between the Namibian reparations cases and the *Khulumani* "apartheid" case for reparations. Swart also made the point that the filing of the Ovaherero and Nama lawsuit had some "strategic advantages," because it "triggered media attention" and presented a "wake-up call that Germany can no longer ignore the Herero genocide."[66] While some portions of Swart's critique had to do with the legal formalism of these filings, and the judicial hurdles that had to be faced, other parts of her essay pointed out some of the cultural, political, and economic factors that were a part of all of this lawfare:

> Sundays in Swakopmund are deathly quiet. Locals and tourists sit down for a lunch of eisbein or schnitzel in pricey, pristine restaurants. The town is colonial in heart and soul, trading on its German past. White Namibians are reluctant to discuss it—after all, colonial genocide might not be a strong drawcard for tourists. But the recent debate on the Herero genocide of 1904 to 1907 and the fact that the German government has not yet paid reparations to the descendants of the victims may make this town, as well as the rest of privileged Namibia and the German government, wake up. . . . The effects of the genocide are still palpable. . . . White Namibians enjoy a living standard equivalent to those of Scandinavians, whereas the living standard of black Namibians can be compared with that of people in Sierra Leone.[67]

Note how this type of juxtaposing of rich and poor looked very much like the argument that McCallion, Weisberg, Holman, and Rodal had made in their 2018 amended legal complaint.

Some critics who commented on the reparations claims tried to fathom why Germany—given its massive economy—didn't see paying reparations as a chance to advance some of its own strategic communication agendas. Henning Melber, the former chairperson of the Windhoek-based Namibian-German Foundation for Cultural Cooperation, wondered why those who could have seen the "likely material reparation in relation to the size of the German state coffers" didn't view reparations as an "investment in Germany's reputation."[68] This type of intriguing claim may not have taken into account the aphasia, and the other forms of "colonial unknowning," that stood in the way of mastering fraught imperial pasts.

Sometimes those who commented on indigenous reparations efforts proffered their own ways of describing the parallels that could be found between different large-scale administrative murders. A few Ovaherero and Nama interviewees made explicit references to places like Shark Island or the other GSWA camps when they talked about their own lives and those of others living in Namibia. "We live in overcrowded, overgrazed and overpopulated reserves," notes Veraa Katuuo, "modern day concentration camps—while our fertile grazing areas are occupied by the descendants of the perpetrators of the genocide against our descendants."[69] For some, the talk of the concentration camps involved more than the retrieval of partially forgotten GSWA pasts. Namibian lands in the hands of others could be characterized as "rented," stolen," or "occupied."

By 2018, some investigative reporters were writing about the potential social and political fallout that came from the publicity that surrounded these legal filings. Daniel Pelz, a reporter for *Deutsche Welle,* noted that even if the "German government continues to stick to its line or if the Hereros do not get the verdict they hope for the lawsuit has already had some effects."[70]

Some involved in the bilateral negotiations were now mentioning to domestic and international presses some of what was being spent on Namibian projects was directed to the areas that formed the residences of the Ovaherero and the Nama. Ruprecht Polenz, for example, mentioned how some on the German side of the negotiations in 2018 were calling for the formation of a "trust pact," which would include the "idea" to run "projects particularly in the Herero and Nama territorialities in four different areas: vocational training, electricity supply, affordable accommodations and land reform."[71]

Although this was not framed as "reparations," this was a marked improvement over plans that left out the specific needs of impoverished Ovaherero and Nama communities. Reparations activists, however, oftentimes viewed the claims that came from Polenz as just more evidence that German diplomats assumed that they knew what was best for needy indigent communities. Critical indigeneity scholars might consider this to be yet another instance of colonial insistence on "epistemic mastery."[72]

CONCLUSION

It may take years before the Herero and Nama reparations case winds its way through U.S. appellate processes, but there are indications that the plaintiff's legal team has cobbled together a defensible case under trying legal circumstances. At this time, the reparations case is being appealed to the Second Circuit, because on March 6, 2019, Judge Swain handed down a decision that indicated that she was going to grant Germany's motion to dismiss the amended complaint, and that she was going to deny plaintiff's motion for leave to file a supplemental declaration or a second amended complaint. In her 2019 order, Judge Swain acknowledged that the plaintiffs were seeking damages for the Namibian genocide pursuant to the Alien Tort Statute, federal common law, and the law of nations. She noted, however, that she was convinced that Germany was immune from liability under the Foreign Sovereign Immunities Act (FSIA), and she was not persuaded by the claimants' lawyers that they had demonstrated that these Ovaherero and Nama claims fell under the "commercial activity" exception or the "takings exception" to those FSIA immunity provisions.[73] Judge Swain also argued that although the "efforts of scholars and descendants to document and study the genocide are important and laudable, these activities bear no direct and immediate causal connection to Germany's actions in South West Africa and are thus insufficient to give rise to subject matter jurisdiction."[74] Moreover, Judge Swain opined that the plaintiffs had failed to "allege facts sufficient to support their contention that Germany's conduct caused a 'direct effect' in the United States."[75]

Judge Swain's comments seemed to be in response to Kenneth McCallion's efforts to have jurists focus on the broader, governmental, and structural features of the GSWA colonial state that activists believed could be linked to the harms outlined in this particular class action lawsuit. She was not going to buy the claimants' arguments that were being made about how Germany's "bone activities" and the building of Second Reich railways to places like Grootfontein were primarily commercial in nature and provide that "commercial activity exception" to FSIA.[76] As soon as Judge Swain handed down her order, McCallion's team appealed this case to the Second Circuit Court of Appeals.

Responses to Judge Swain's 2019 order were just some of the rhetorical fragments that would elicit public and legal commentary. While some observers of the 2017 Herero and Nama reparations case are interested in talking and writing about how these legal filings might help Namibians over the long term, others point out how this case might impact the filing of other lawsuits. Professor Heike Becker, a professor of anthropology at the University of Western Cape, argued that if the *Rukoro* case "succeeds it will be significant for claims from other genocides committed before the United Nations Convention on the Prevention and Punishment of the Crimes of Genocide was passed."[77]

A few of the claimants who were involved in the filing of this lawsuit seem to hope that these performative acts will force representatives of the Federal Republic of Germany to include activists in future conversations that might take place between Namibian and German delegates. In August of 2018, Vekuii Rukoro told reporters that the Germans, by "trying not to acknowledge the pasts," are continuing to "make serious mistakes regarding present and future policies."[78] Rukoro elaborated by arguing that the "direct descendants" of the victims should not be left out of reparations negotiations or repatriation of remains ceremonies.[79]

Will this 2017 filing of the Ovaherero and Nama lawsuit be remembered as the legal event that paved the way for reparations for colonial genocidal horrors, or will these acts be viewed as futile gestures that have little to do with preservation of "real" genocidal recollections?

NOTES

1. Gabriele Steinhauser, "Germany Confronts the Forgotten Story of Its Other Genocide," *The Wall Street Journal,* last modified July 28, 2017, paragraph 15, https://www.wsj.com/articles/germany-confronts-the-forgotten-story-of-its-other-genocide-1501255028.

2. See, for example, Elke Zuern, "Namibia's Monuments to Genocide," *Dissent,* June 13, 2017, https://www.dissentmagazine.org/blog/namibia-genocide-monuments-reparations-germany.

3. Steinhauser, "Germany Confronts the Forgotten Story," paragraph 3.

4. Ibid.

5. Manu Vimalassery, Juliana Hu Pegues, and Alyosha Goldstein, "Introduction: On Colonial Unknowing," *Theory & Event* 19, no. 4 (2016): paragraph 1, https://muse.jhu.edu/article/633283.

6. Rupert Polenz, quoted in Daniel Pelz, "Namibia Deliberates Suing Germany over Reparations," *Deutsche Welle,* past modified March 21, 2017, paragraph 4, https://www.dw.com/en/namibia-deliberates-suing-germany-over-reparations/a-38044661.

7. Jeff Harris, quoted in Amanda Ottaway, "For Victims of a Little-Known Genocide, A Long Journey to Justice," *Courthouse News Service,* last modified March 20, 2019, paragraph 24, https://www.courthousenews.com/for-victims-of-a-little-known-genocide-a-long-journey-to-justice/.

8. Kenneth McCallion, Richard H. Weisberg, Thomas A. Holman, and Yechezkel Rodal, *Vekuii Rukoro et al. v. Federal Republic of Germany,* Civ. No. 17-0062, Amended Class Action Complaint (New York City: United States District Southern Court, February 14, 2018), 5.

9. Mainstream outlets that discuss these reparations efforts sometimes recirculate some of the photographs and other visualities that once appeared in colonial venues. See, for example, BBC News staff, "Namibia's Reparations and Germany's First Genocide," BBC.com, last modified October 12, 2017, https://www.bbc.com/news/av/world-africa-41596617/namibia-s-reparations-and-germany-s-first-genocide. The interview footage for this BBC visual material was provided by Kate Schoenbach. For an excel-

lent analysis of how some photographs and postcards were used to normalize colonial violence and reduce the distance between Germany and German South West Africa, see Felix Axster, "'[W]ill try to send you the best views from here': Postcards from the Colonial War in Namibia (1904–1908)," in *German Colonialism, Visual Culture and Modern Memory*, edited by Volker M. Langehn (New York: Routledge, 2010), 55–70.

10. Vimalassery, Pegues, and Goldstein, "Introduction: On Colonial Unknowing," paragraphs 1–4.

11. Ida Hoffman, quoted in Al Jazeera staff, "Namibia Tribes Lodge Case against Germany over Genocide," Al Jazeera, last modified March 16, 2017, paragraph 15, https://www.aljazeera.com/news/2017/03/namibia-tribes-lodge-case-germany-genocide-170316162133276.html.

12. Henning Melber and Reinhart Kössler, "Germany is Backpedalling on Calling Its Century-Old Namibian Genocide a Genocide," *Quartz Africa*, last modified January 13, 2018, paragraph 24, https://qz.com/africa/1178317/namibia-genocide-germany-is-trying-to-protect-itself-from-a-widening-legal-liabilities/.

13. Ibid.

14. Kenneth McCallion is an American lawyer who has been involved in several high profile lawfare cases, including ones that involved Jewish Holocaust survivor claimants who sued the French government for what happened in that country between 1940 and 1944. His firm's knowledge of the requirements for torts cases in modern genocidal situations seemed to have helped as his research teams working for the Herero and Nama did their best to ensure that they were prepared for all sorts of procedural and substantive issues.

15. Reuters News staff, "Germany Sued for Damages of 'Forgotten Genocide,' in Namibia," *The Guardian*, last modified January 5, 2017, paragraph 3, https://www.theguardian.com/world/2017/jan/05/germany-sued-forgotten-genocide-namibia-herero-nama; Steinhauser, "Germany Confronts," paragraph 15; Jonathan Stempel, "Germany Is Sued in U.S. over Early-1900s Namibia Slaughter," Reuters, last modified January 5, 2017, https://www.reuters.com/article/us-germany-namibia-genocide-lawsuit-idUSKBN14P25O. For official German reactions to the filing of the Herero/Nama lawsuit in New York courts, see *Die Bundesregierung* staff, "Regierungspressekonferenz vom 6. January 2017," *Die Bundesregierung*, last modified January 6, 2017, https://www.bundesregierung.de/breg-de/aktuelles/pressekonferenzen/regierungspressekonferenz-vom-6-januar-2017-843494.

16. See Elke Zuern, "The Namibian Debate over Germany Reparations," *Africa Is a Country*, July 26, 2017, https://africasacountry.com/2017/07/the-namibian-debate-over-german-reparations.

17. For an abbreviated, but key summary of the arguments that were presented by Vekuii Rukoro and the other claimants, see Judge Laura Taylor Swain, "Opinion and Order," *Vekuii Rukoro et al. v. Federal Republic of Germany*, No. CV 62-LTS (New York: Southern District of New York, 2019).

18. Reinhart Kőssler, "Review Article: Genocide in Namibia: The Holocaust and the Issue of Colonization," *Journal of Southern African Studies* 38, no. 1 (March, 2012): 233–38, 231.

19. Henning Melber and Reinhart Kőssler, "Germany Is Backpedalling," paragraph 10.

20. Reuters News staff, "Germany Sued," paragraph 5.

21. Steinhauser, "German Confronts," paragraph 7.

22. Ibid., paragraph 8–10.

23. See, for example, BBC News staff, "Germany Returns Skulls of Namibian Genocide Victims," BBC News, last modified August 29, 2018, https://www.bbc.com/news/world-africa-45342586.

24. Ken McCallion, quoted in Reuters News staff, "Germany Sued," paragraph 12.

25. Renisa Mawani, *Across Oceans of Law* (Durham: Duke University Press, 2018), 14.

26. See the critique that appears in Hurst Hannum, "International Law and Cambodian Genocide: The Sounds of Silence," *Human Rights Quarterly* 11, no. 1 (February 1989): 82–138.

27. Jeff Harris, quoted in Ottaway, "For Victims of a Little-Known Genocide," paragraphs 24–25.

28. For more on the legal and political implications of these German responses to the summons, see Stefan Talmon, "Suing Germany Over the Genocide in Namibia in U.S. Courts," *German Practice in International Law,* last modified November 23, 2017, https://gpil.jura.uni-bonn.de/2017/11/suing-germany-genocide-namibia-u-s-courts-pitfalls-serving-summons-german-government/.

29. *Agence de Presse Africaine* Staff, "Germany to Challenge Namibian's Genocide Lawsuit," *Agence de Presse Africaine,* last modified January 18, 2018, paragraphs 2–7, http://apanews.net/en/pays/namibie/news/germany-to-challenge-namibians-genocide-lawsuit. For more on Germany's sovereign immunity stance, see *AFP* Staff, Germany Asks U.S. Court to Drop Namibian Genocide Suit," *The Local,* last modified January 26, 2018, https://www.thelocal.de/20180126/germany-asks-us-court-to-drop-namibian-genocide-suit.

30. Vekuii Rukoro, quoted in *Agence de Presse Africane* Staff, "Germany to Challenge," paragraph 16.

31. Kazenambo Kazenambo, "Kazenambo on Genocide Court Case in the USA, *The Windhoek Observer,* last modified February 2, 2018, paragraphs 1–3, https://www.observer.com.na/index.php/opinions/item/9292-kazenambo-on-genocide-court-case-in-the-usa.

32. Vekuii Rukoro, quoted in Talmon, "Suing Germany Over Genocide," paragraph 19.

33. Some of these expenses will be incurred because of the length of these types of proceedings. See Ndapewoshali Shapwanale, "Genocide Case in U.S. Court Likely to Take Long," *The Namibian,* last modified January 9, 2017, https://www.namibian.com.na/159918/archive-read/Genocide-case-in-US-court-likely-to-take-long.

34. Reinhart Kŏssler, "Two Modes of Amnesia: Complexity in Postcolonial Namibia," *Acta Academica* 47, no. 1 (2015): 138–160, 147.

35. See *Hamburg Postkolonial* Staff, "Herero-Genocide Without Apology and Compensation?" *Hamburg Postkolonial,* last modified October 7, 2015, https://hhpostkolonial.wordpress.com/2015/10/07/herero-genocide-without-apology-and-compensation/.

36. McCallion et. al., *Vekuii Rukoro et al., v. Federal Republic of Germany,* Amended Class Action Complaint, 74.

37. *AFP* Staff, "Namibia Demand $30 Billion for German Genocide: Documents," *News* 24, last modified March 18, 2018, https://www.news24.com/Africa/News/namibia-demands-30bn-for-german-genocide-documents-20170318.

38. McCallion et. al., *Vekuii Rukoro et al., v. Federal Republic of Germany,* Amended Class Action Complaint, 26.

39. Ibid., 61.

40. Ibid., 74–77.

41. An intriguing discussion of the views of Ovaherero living in the U.S. and in the diaspora can be found in Elise Pape, "Herero Activists in the United States: Demanding Recognition and Reparation for the First Genocide of the Twentieth Century," *American Institute for Contemporary German Studies, November* 1, 2017, https://www.aicgs.org/publication/herero-activists-in-the-united-states/.

42. McCallion et. al., *Vekuii Rukoro et al., v. Federal Republic of Germany,* Amended Class Action Complaint, 60–61.

43. Ibid., 5.

44. Vekuii Rukoro, quoted in *AFP* Staff, "Namibia Tribes Sue Germany in U.S. Over Colonial-Era Genocide," *Daily Nation,* last modified March 17, 2017, paragraph 17, https://www.nation.co.ke/news/africa/Namibia-tribes-sue-Germany/1066-3853006-28f8aq/index.html.

45. For a rereading of Du Bois, slavery memories, and possible formations of multidirectional memories in place of competitive memories in these remembrances of the slave trade see Michael Rothberg, "W.E.B. DuBois in Warsaw: Holocaust Memory and the Color Line, 1949–1952," *The Yale Journal of Criticism* 14, no. 1 (Spring 2001): 169–189.

46. Ibid., 63.

47. Ibid.

48. Howard Rechavia Taylor, "U.S. Court Hears Case Against Germany Over Namibia Genocide," *Al Jazeera*, last modified July 31, 2018, paragraphs 1–3, https://www.aljazeera.com/news/2018/07/court-hears-case-germany-namibia-genocide-180731201918543.html.

49. Ngondi Kamatuka, quoted in Taylor, "U.S. Court Hears Case," paragraph 4.

50. Ibid., paragraphs 7–8.

51. Taylor, "U.S. Court Hears," paragraphs 8–9.

52. Jens-Uwe Guettel, "The SPD Should Return to Its Anticolonial Roots," *Jacobin*, August, 2018, paragraph 31, https://www.jacobinmag.com/2018/08/spd-namibia-herero-nama-genocide-colonialism.

53. Ibid.

54. Ruben Carranza, quoted in Amanda Ottaway, "For Victims of a Little-Known Genocide," paragraph 30,

55. Mark Kersten, "The 'Forgotten Genocide' That Was the Precursor to the Holocaust," *Justice in Conflict*, last modified January 11, 2017, paragraph 2 (emphasis in original), https://justiceinconflict.org/2017/01/11/the-forgotten-genocide-that-was-a-precursor-to-the-holocaust/.

56. Kőssler, "Two Modes of Amnesia," 149.

57. Ida Hoffman, quoted in Theresia Tijihenuna, "Herero, Nama Amend Genocide Lawsuit," *The Namibian*, last modified February 15, 2018, paragraph 12, https://www.namibian.com.na/174508/archive-read/Herero-Nama-amend-genocide-lawsuit.

58. Sam Kambazembi, quoted in Robbie Grammer, "Germany's Oft-Forgotten Colonial Atrocities in Africa Spark New Lawsuit," *Foreign Policy*, last modified January 6, 2017, paragraph 6, https://foreignpolicy.com/2017/01/06/germanys-oft-forgotten-colonial-atrocities-in-africa-spark-new-lawsuit/.

59. Kőssler, "Two Modes of Amnesia," 138–60.

60. Daniel A. Gross, "Why the Herero of Namibia Are Suing Germany for Reparations," National Public Radio, May 6, 2018, paragraph 1, https://www.npr.org/sections/goatsandsoda/2018/05/06/606379299/why-the-herero-of-namibia-are-suing-germany-for-reparations.

61. Ibid., paragraphs 3–5.

62. Ibid., paragraphs 6–7.

63. Ibid., paragraph 8.

64. Ibid., paragraphs 9–10.

65. Ibid., paragraph 20.

66. Mia Swart, "Herero Make New Claim for Genocide Reparations against Germany," *Mail and Guardian*, last modified January 25, 2017, paragraphs 11–12, https://mg.co.za/article/2017-01-24-herero-make-new-claim-for-genocide-reparations-against-germany.

67. Ibid., paragraphs 1–17.

68. Henning Melber, "Uncovering the 20th Century's First Genocide," *New African* (March, 2017): 26–30, 30.

69. Veraa Katuuo, quoted in Nick Sprenger, Robert G. Rodriguez, and Ngondi A. Kamatuka, "The Ovaherero/Nama Genocide: A Case for an Apology and Reparations," *European Scientific Journal* (June 2017): 120–46, 143.

70. Daniel Pelz, "Pressure Grows on Germany in Legal Battle over Colonial-Era Genocide," *Deutsche Welle*, last modified January 24, 2018, paragraph 4, https://www.dw.com/en/pressure-grows-on-germany-in-legal-battle-over-colonial-era-genocide/a-42267279.

71. Ruprecht Polenz, quoted in Pelz, "Pressure Grows," paragraph 11.

72. Vimalassery, Pegues, and Goldstein, "Introduction: On Colonial Unknowing," paragraph 2.
73. Judge Swain, in "Opinion and Order," 7.
74. Ibid., 10.
75. Ibid., 9.
76. Ibid. 8.
77. Heike Becker, "Namibian Traditional Leaders Haul Germany before U.S. Court in Genocide Test Case," News 24, last modified January 17, 2017, paragraph 4, https://www.news24.com/Africa/News/namibian-traditional-leaders-haul-germany-before-us-court-in-genocide-test-case-20170117.
78. Vekuii Rukoro, quoted in Jakub Lewandowski, "Remains from 'First Genocide of 20th Century' Returned to Namibia," *Newsweek*, August 30, 2018, paragraph 6, https://www.newsweek.com/remains-first-genocide-20th-century-returned-namibia-1097818.
79. Ibid.

TEN

Contemplating the Future of Lawfare in Contests over Namibian Claims for Restorative Justice

Readers need to keep in mind that regardless of how appellate courts after 2019 end up dealing with the *Vekuii Rukoro* case, we are living in litigious (post)colonial times. None of us should be surprised when we hear that all sorts of legal cases are being filed in order to provide redress for those who continue to worry about the lingering legacy of colonial abuses. For example, in 2011 the Hague Court of First Instance was asked to deliver judgment in a civil reparations case that was based on acts of post–World War II colonial violence that were committed in Indonesia between 1945 and 1950.[1] This was a case that was brought by representatives of eight widows whose husbands had been part of a group of 150 "rebels" who had allegedly been killed by the Dutch army at a place called Rawagedeh on December 9, 1947.

These Dutch cases represent only a few of the legal actions that are filed by litigants who seek restitution for colonial wrongdoing, and audiences who become stakeholders in this colonial disputation co-produce all sorts of multidirectional or competitive memories as they argue about this litigation. Turkish inheritors of the lands of the old Ottoman Empire have been asked to pay reparations to Armenians,[2] Moroccans who are descendants of gassing victims during the Rif Wars ask the Spaniards for compensation,[3] and the French have been approached about paying Algerians restitution for what happened during their colonial years.[4] Some have requested that the United States pay the Vietnamese for devastated lives and lands during the old colonial "Indochina wars."[5]

This gets even more complicated if we adopt the stance that some German activists want to take, where they ask for something called

"Völkerverständigung," where "coming to terms" with a "genocide is a matter between peoples and cannot be limited to the governments of Namibia and Germany."[6] German officials respond to these types of arguments by claiming that the only way to overcome the cacophony of diverse opinions about what happened in German South West Africa is by negotiating with a select few representatives who are on the same page, and who are actually empowered to speak for Namibian constituents. These German negotiators do their best to tune out the noise that is coming from investigative journalists or activists who want more than just some expressions of regret that are not tied to any monetary reparations or promises of post-conflict land redistribution in Namibia.

It appears that only the growing power of transcontinental reparations movements can force the hand of those who would rather stand pat and let bygones be bygones. Note the attempts by German diplomats and lawyers, during the initial stages of the 2001 and 2017 U.S. lawsuits, who refused to be served with the summons or complaint, because they fully expected that jurisdictional claims of sovereign immunity would shield them from having to even show up during early hearings. Only worries about potential default judgments finally forced Germany to officially answer the filings of the Ovaherero and Nama lawyers.

Legal experts, transitional justice scholars, and others who keep track of the jurisdictional hurdles that Namibian litigants face in U.S. courts have come up with a host of alternative avenues for restorative justice that might help aggrieved Ovaherero or Nama parties. Ruben Carranza told Amanda Ottaway that these litigants should use a "multi-pronged effort for reparations," that would include the possibility of enlisting domestic support from political leaders and German citizens so that pressure could be brought to bear on those who be producing more "justice-oriented" legislation.[7] William Darity, Jr., a professor of public policy at Duke University, opined that taking these reparations into U.S. courts allowed German decision makers to "evade responsibility and obligation for the compensation."[8] Darity thought that it made little sense for the Ovaherero and Nama to be trying to get redress from an American legal system that already had a history of "shooting down cases for domestic slavery reparations."[9]

In theory, if the German and Namibian elites and publics were some of the key audiences in these reparations debates, then only by winning their hearts and minds could activists decolonize the "colonial unknowing" that I been referencing in the earlier chapters of this book. After all, if the Ovaherero and Nama activists who pay for all of this lawfare are going to continue to write and talk about Holocaust reparation case precedents, then they needed to keep in mind the willingness of many different rhetorical cultures to be a part of those post–World War II restitutional efforts.

If the U.S. jurists were not going to provide restorative justice for African Americans who wanted reparations for domestic slavery, then what hope did foreign litigants have whose lawyers were trying to get to the "merits" of cases that were about the loss of Nama or Ovaherero lands, the "takings" that came from labor abuse, or the rape of indigenous communities during the German South West Africa years? Seeking injunctive and monetary relief in American forums might help with pedagogical consciousness-raising efforts to combat Namibian genocide denialism or revisionism, but will all of this ultimately benefit elderly descendants of the victims of the 1904–1908 Ovaherero/Nama-German War? Can winning lawfare battles thousands of miles away from German metropoles or Namibian shores bring psychic relief to those who feel that they have been injured by lingering colonial or postcolonial sensibilities or grids of intelligibility?

I share the views of many writers who watch these proceedings and who argue that ultimately it will be highly unlikely that the Ovaherero and Nama will ever get their requested injunctive relief or monetary compensation from German defendants. The law firm of McCallion and Associates, LLP, may indeed be able to show that the "facts" indicate that between 1884 and 1915, a "series of expropriative acts were undertaken by Germany" in German South West Africa led to a situation where, "for over 100 years the survivors of genocide and their descendants continued to suffer from political, social, and cultural devastation that they experienced at the hands of the German colonial forces and German authorities."[10] Yet how do some of these scholarly conclusions translate into concrete and efficacious legal settlements or judicial opinions that become entangled in so much aphasiastic reasoning?

Transcontinental supporters of Ovaherero and Nama reparation efforts may argue that these "facts" are incontrovertible and that parallels with Holocaust litigation are undeniable, but for the last eighteen years most American judges have provided clues that they don't agree with some of the historical or legalistic framing of these colonial or imperial incidents. Advocates may complain about legal "technicalities," but lawyers and judges are trained to take seriously jurisdictional issues. Recall how, in March of 2019, Judge Laura Swain failed to find that indigenous colonial suffering during the GSWA years could be linked to specific German conduct that had a "direct effect" in the United States.[11] Those who have no desire to hear these type of cases can use all sorts of legalistic arguments—based on principles having to do with sovereign immunity, "political question" doctrines, statute of limitations, and so on—to rationalize the dismissal of these colonial reparations cases because of lack of jurisdiction.

A few appellate judges in open court or in their written texts may express sympathy when they hear these type of colonial reparations claims, but is highly likely that some of the same jurisdictional arguments that were used to deny the Ovaherero relief in 2001–2007 or the Ovaherero and Nama in 2017–2019 will once again appear in American legal opinions. Formalistic talk of bilateral sovereign immunity agreements, the death of the actual victims of the concentration camps, and the passage of time could provide typical rationales for not getting to the "merits' stages of these reparations cases.

Has all this lawfare been worth the effort if Ovaherero Paramount Chief Vekuii Rukoro and the other litigants gain incremental *international* public support for their moral cause when they lose in the U.S. "court of law"? Should the didactic or pedagogical features of these reparations cases be enough to support the continued filing of these types of cases in American courts? Does this help or hurt what critical indigenous scholars, postcolonial critiques, or critical genocide scholars call decolonization efforts?

In order to help provide tentative answers to those questions, I want to use this final chapter to discuss the future of lawfare in colonial genocide and reparations contexts. I want to outline what I view as six major issues that continue to be of interest to so many as they evaluate the afterlives of the Ovaherero and Nama reparations cases:

1. Has the *best* "legal" or "moral" case been made in front of academic and jurists for Ovaherero and Nama reparations, and was this best case presented in front of U.S. judges during the 2017 and 2018 hearings?
2. Have various types of lawfare served to provide global audiences with those counter-histories or countermemories that have allowed Namibian indigenous communities to have a voice in international courts of "public opinion"?
3. Have any of these legal and public debates about the Namibian "genocide" or the "Kaiser's Holocaust" impacted societal perceptions that Germany has "mastered" colonial pasts? Has all of this helped with the production of multidirectional memories, or have we been left with bitter, competitive memories?
4. Even if we assume that some consciousness-raising came out of the filing of the *Rukoro et al. v. German Federal Republic of Germany* case, has any of this litigation provided tangible evidence of empirical help for aggrieved populations living in Namibia?
5. If U.S. federal courts decline to provide any judicial redress for Ovaherero and Nama litigants, are there any other judicial forms that might provide Namibians with other avenues for filing legal restorative justice claims?
6. Is there any evidence that the proverbial "Pandora's Box" has been opened by these filings of colonial reparations cases?[12]

Let me begin my critiques in this chapter by exploring the question of whether we have seen the strongest U.S. "case" that could possibly be put together by lawyers for the Ovaherero and Nama litigants.

Given the potential historical and contemporary reservoirs of arguments that are available for reparations argumentation could academics, jurists, and others fairly conclude that these litigants put together a strong "case" in U.S. courtrooms between 2017 and 2018?

When, in July of 2015, the president of the Bundestag described the mass crimes committed in Namibia during the early 1900s as "*vőlkermord*"—genocide—it was hoped that this represented the official German government position.[13] However, as Elise Pape noted during the fall of 2018, many were still waiting because the "German government has not official recognized the genocide as such."[14] If this was the case, then what would that recognition entail?

Having already spent more than seventy years dealing with the hauntology and post-conflict Holocaust reparations, it seems as though German officials had a vested interest in arguing that the lawyers for the Ovaherero and Nama in 2017 had failed to construct a *prima facie* legal case that required any detailed responses in either the "court of law" or the "court of public opinion." In adversarial legal systems this obviated the need for any official German defenses or arguments on the "merits" of the case. Was this wordsmithing being used to avoid grappling with moral or social questions that had been raised about German abilities to "master" fraught colonial pasts?

As noted in previous chapters, German diplomats have found all sorts of sophistic ways of dodging questions about reparations, and they can continue to treat German development aid to Namibia as a praxiological substitute for reparations. At the same time, they can individually and collectively let domestic and international journalists know that German officials are not going to be swayed by the arguments that are presented by Namibian activists, members of the press, or postcolonial scholars in Hamburg or Berlin. Kenneth McCallion's legal firm argued there was something telling in the way that Germany dealt with requests for injunctions and court enjoining Germany from excluding the Ovaherero and Nama activists. "German Government officials," the authors of one plaintiff's text averred, "continued to ignore plaintiffs and other representatives of the Ovaherero and Nama peoples—as they had been doing for more than a century."[15] It is very possible that McCallion's insistence that the activists be included is one part of that needed effort to put the "best" case forward? Or are the Namibian negotiators who work with German diplomats the ones who should be representing indigenous or non-indigenous positions on questions regarding the Namibian genocide or reparations?

The act of excluding vocal Ovaherero or Nama activists creates the impression that colonial relational dynamics are still having an influence on the postcolonial ways that German officials treat Afro-Germans or African indigenous communities. It could be argued that in the same way that German judges had once thrown out most cases that were filed by representatives of the Ovaherero or Nama communities during the German South West Africa years, now empowered German officials during the twenty-first century were still marginalizing and belittling the claims of the "other." The past had become prologue.

To be charitable, it could be argued that even if the plaintiffs' lawyers cobbled together an ironclad legal case that met all of the formalistic and positivist American requirements for a successful Alien Tort Act case, there would still be political reasons why the Germans simply could not concede that Namibian reparations payments were warranted. Legitimating talk of reparations payments for colonial wrongdoing might lead to conversations about radical redistribution of Namibian lands owned by German speakers in Namibia. This risked not only having to pay billions of dollars in restitution but it also opened the door for larger conversations about the legitimacy of the titles to land that were held by some twenty-five thousand descendants of "South Westers" living in Namibia.

Granting that the Ovaherero and Nama had put together a convincing legal case would have meant acknowledging that the entire GSWA colony was a part of that "colonial enterprise" that was referenced by Major O'Reilly in his Blue Book texts and by the claimants' attorneys in their amended complaints. Concessions would have to be made that it was not just Lothar von Trotha or a few overzealous soldiers after the battle of Ohamakari/Waterberg who had been involved in the near extermination of some African communities but rather the civil and military authorities who supervised the concentration camps, the owners of shipping lines, the operators of mines, the participants in racist judicial processes, and ordinary citizens who may have shared exterminationist sentiments. Were American judges and lawyers willing to listen to these types of "merit" claims?

Aside from the discussions of sovereign immunity and the passage of time arguments that I mentioned in earlier chapters, one occasionally sees shards of older colonial assimilationist rhetorics in some of the twenty-first-century German diplomatic responses to the press coverage of the filing of the Ovaherero and Nama reparations cases that were filed in the Southern District of New York. Note, for example, how German envoy Ruprecht Polenz responded to reporters who asked him about the potential parallels that might be found between the post–World War II reparations payments to Holocaust survivors and any potential payments for the Namibian genocide. He could have simply mentioned the topic of sovereign immunity and moved on, but that type of response would not have answered the nagging questions regarding the need to redress German colonial wrongdoing. It is intriguing that Polenz implied that some of those who were critiquing bilateral Namibian-German negotiations over colonial wrongdoing were missing the "fact that after World War II, Germany only paid personal reparations to *living individuals* who personally suffered in the concentration camps or were forced to do slave labor."[16] Was Polenz implying that Germany was only legally culpable in cases where there were living plaintiffs? Was he ignoring the other reparations cases that had involved payouts to traumatized members of the second and third generations of relatives of Holocaust victims?

Polenz seemed to imply that the lawyers for the Ovaherero and Nama activists were using the wrong paradigmatic legal arguments and were making a big mistake when they thought that their amended complaints were including the appropriate reparations precedents and the right historical parallels for equitable relief. Since all the actual victims of dispossession, murder, rape, labor exploitation, and so on, were dead, this allowed German diplomats to make legalistic distinctions between the post–World War II Israeli-German reparations agreements and the 2017 Ovaherero and Nama reparations cases.

The use of these types of strategic, temporal, and legalistic arguments meant that envoy Ruprecht Polenz and those who shared his views did not have to give any credence to the scholarly arguments that had been made about the transmission of post-conflict trauma that might psychologically or financially damage members of the "second" and "third" generations.[17]

This type of argumentative frame could also be used to sever the historical connections that were supposed to exist between twenty-first-century poverty in Namibia and "what happened" during the GSWA years. German diplomats could argue that twenty-first-century Ovaherero or Nama poverty was an issue that should concern Namibian governmental officials and not German diplomats or German publics.

In theory, the German government need not worry about having to pay colonial reparations because those who might have had an actionable case were already deceased, and the Ovaherero and Nama litigants were hurting their own case by following the wrong reparations precedents. When a member of the German opposition party in the German Parliament, Niema Movassat of "*Die Linke*" (The Left), heard the types of arguments that came from German diplomats, he opined that the wearing of these types of negotiating blinders had directly contributed to the Namibian decisions to file the reparation cases in New York courts. "It is absurd," Movassat told representatives of one news outlet, "to exclude a certain community from negotiations about a genocide that affected them. It is understandable that the people do not feel [that they are] taken seriously."[18]

Imagine, for a moment, what it would have looked like in the early 1950s if Israeli and Germany officials had tried to make decisions regarding reparations for Holocaust victims without the inclusion of input from members of private groups or the victims themselves who had been active in lobbying for this restitution for many years.

Although some of the arguments that are being used by German envoys and Namibian officials have remained secret during bilateral negotiations, there have been times when Ruprecht Polenz has allowed journalists and publics to get some inkling of the governmentalities and the *epistemes* that are deployed to treat reparations as matters of "social" or "political"—but not "legal" matters. During one 2018 interview, Polenz used variants of familiar lines of legal reasoning when he claimed that there "was no law" during 1904–1908 that could be applied like the "forward-looking" 1948 Genocide Convention. This was a type of critique of retrospective reasoning that has been used in many legal controversies, but in this particular situation Polenz was ignoring the massive number of conventions, German domestic regulations, and international laws that were on the books during the first decade of the twentieth century that were passed in order to prevent the perpetration of "atrocities." Polenz was simply guessing when he predicted that eventually this is what "the New York court will say."[19]

There are no shortages of ironies that would be detected by Third World Approaches to International Law (TWAIL) scholars or critical indigenous researchers or postcolonial scholars who could critique this way of framing justiciable legal cases. Note, for example, how some of Polenz's rhetoric seems to echo some of the arguments that Lothar von Trotha or Chancellor von Bülow or members of the German General Staff made when the Second Reich was accused of violating the provisions of the Berlin Act, Hague Conventions, or the bilateral treaties that were signed with the Ovaherero "nation." When it suited their purposes, and when it helped them acquire at least a third of the Oveherero lands before 1904, the Germans could argue that the Ovaherero had territorial sovereignty and could alienate their land. When they wanted to avoid paying reparations, empowered German leaders could quickly gloss over the topic of indigenous land rights and revert to arguments about how the Ovaherero and Nama were not members of sovereign "nations" who could take advantage of international treaty protections.

Again, as I have argued throughout this book, I am interested in the study of collective epistemic knowledge formations and Ruprecht Polenz is not the only social agent who questions the lawfare stances taken by the Ovaherero and the Nama advocates. Others who hear about some of the particulars of this "reparations case" have expressed ambivalent feelings about these filings. Ewelina U. Ochab, a legal researcher and human rights advocate, seemed to convey some sense of hope in 2018 when she mentioned the precedents that were set when Americans paid reparations to Japanese-American internees and UK officials settled with the Mau Mau claimants over what happened during the colonial years of British rule in Kenya. However, Ochab also noted that sometimes strong objections have been raised against "similar reparations claims" that were promoted by the "Poles trying to claim reparations for the Nazi atrocities committed during W.W.II."[20]

Was Ochab implying that *realpolitik* concerns have something to do with the acceptance or rejection of certain *prima facie* reparations cases? Was she asserting that the Ovaherero and Nama cases were closer to the Mau Mau settlement situations, or was she claiming that these Herero and Nama reparations efforts were like the Polish requests?

As usual, I am only critiquing Ochab's arguments as examples of larger discursive formations and ideological positions that may be hovering around these Ovaherero and Nama reparations requests, and oftentimes a critical review of these critiques of these reparations cases shows that observers often melded together critiques of jurisdictional and merit-type arguments in their analyses of these Namibian reparations cases.

"Best" case analyses should take into account how American audiences rhetorically frame key legislative enactments that have to with jurisdictional matters in these restorative justice claims by "aliens," but that should not end matters. Given the fact that so many formalistic arguments about the nature and scope of the U.S. Tort Claims Act become entangled in political argumentation critical genocide scholars could argue that it is the presence or absence of political will that oftentimes determines how audiences are going to react to the litigation outcomes in these cases. Those who debate about the legitimacy of Holocaust litigation or Ovaherero reparations claims can always defend narrow or broad definitions of sovereign immunity statutes or any other provision. The indeterminate nature of all legal reasoning and texts means that it is the political will, and not the specific wording of any text, that oftentimes determines whether or not someone will have their day in court. If American legislators were sympathetic listeners when they heard Namibian activist complaints, they could always pass enabling legislation that would confer jurisdiction, but the absence of that legislation is telling.

If critical scholars read the complaints, the affidavits, and the other legal texts that have been produced by the lawyers who represented the Ovaherero and Nama claimants in the 2017 case, it appears that these legal social agents have done a fine job of presenting—given the circumstances—the best case that they could that might resonate with U.S. judges as well as the activists and others who are emotionally invested in these reparations debates.

If one studies the archival records and the consequences that attended the filings of the Ovaherero and Nama reparations cases in federal courts, has all this lawfare allowed Namibian indigenous communities to have their say in the "court of public opinion"?

Growing academic interest in exhibits like the *Deutscher Kolonialismus*, international press coverage of apology requests,[21] and the filing of the Ovaherero and Nama suits have helped provide new opportunities for those Namibians who wish to speak out about German South West Africa pasts. A popular slogan that is used on several continents—"not about us without us"—seems like a vernacular version of what postcolonial scholar Gyatri Spivak's had to say about whether the "subaltern can speak."[22] In that famous essay Spivak noted how oftentimes colonizers presumed to speak at, or for, the colonized, and she critiqued those who did not listen to the subalterns who were trying to articulate their own positions on colonizing matters.

During the debates about the filing of the American cases, Ovaherero Paramount Chief Rukoro provided an example of how the legal cases—and German anger at the filing of those cases—was not going to dissuade the Ovaherero or the Nama activists from trying to have their day in court. Rukoro told *The Namibian* that while some Germany negotiators or critics of reparations "put their heads in the sand the ostrich way," the American courts at least provided a forum that allowed his people to have "faith that restorative justice will prevail."[23] With the passage of time Rukoro and his supporters may change their minds about this "faith" in U.S. courts, but for the time being he, and other reparations activists, can hope that the American appellate review process might provide the legal redress that cannot be found in Namibian or German forums.[24]

Legal setbacks have not prevented activist Namibians and those in the diaspora from commenting on the legitimacy of their cause. Ngondi Kamatuka, a Namibian-born American, supported the filing of the 2017 case against Germany, and he argued that all that the Ovaherero were asking for was "restorative justice for the genocide."[25]

Given the polyvalent nature of that ideographic phrase "restorative justice" what was Kamatuka asking for? An official German acknowledge that the "Kaiser's Holocaust" took place? Small amounts of Euros from the Germans that would be distributed to all Oveherero and Nama? A "reparations" trust fund that would support the building of museums or memorials in German and Namibia? Or was Kamatuka asking for tens of billions of Euros so that he, and other claimants, might have the funds that impoverished Ovaherero or Nama needed to buy back lands that were now owned by German-speaking Namibians?

The abstract talk of "restitution" or "restorative justice" may be polysemic, but that does not mean that these words don't gain intersubjective meanings when they are operationalized in concrete situations. Readers need to remember that the monetary figure of $2 billion was requested during the 2001 Ovaherero legal filings in U.S. courts. The German diplomats and lawyers treated all of this as conjectural in nature, since they refused to use the word "reparations" in their characterizations of Namibian "development" aid.

Interviews with some Ovaherero and Nama spokespersons provide us with clues about how these parties interpreted these reparations and lawfare debates. Elise Pape, who kept track of how some Americans of Namibian descent were reacting to the press coverage of the legal hearings, attended several Ovaherero and Nama gatherings where she was able to talk to about sixty of these descendants. She conducted fifteen biographical interviews with Ovaherero men and women of various ages, and during these open-ended interviews she allowed these Ovaherero commentators to voice their opinions without any major prompting.[26] One of her interviewees commented on how Ovaherero activists who followed the legal cases were also petitioning embassies, were protesting when the Namibian president visited the United States, and were working on raising funds for their consciousness-raising about the Namibian genocide.[27]

In the same way that the 1923 reburial of Samuel Maherero helped bring together the remnants who survived the horrors of the German South West Africa settlement years, the communal efforts to "do something" has catalyzed the efforts of those who now form alliances to help educate the rest of us about what happened during colonial times.

Contrast this with the ways that their ancestors were treated in German South West Africa, where indigenous communities were not allowed to pass judgment on whites and where it took the testimony of six or seven Africans to counter the testimony of a single European witness in GSWA trials.[28]

Has the presentation of historical and contemporary academic and activist materials impacted perceptions regarding Germany's "mastering" of colonial pasts?

At this point in time it is difficult for critical genealogists to be able to assess the impact that all of this restitutional rhetoric has had on mainstream opinion in Germany, Namibia, or elsewhere. No doubt many on the left parts of political spectrums oftentimes insist that these discussions show that Germany is "mastering" GSWA and East Africa pasts,[29] but it may be years before critical scholars can track altered power relationships and the impact of these "decolonization" efforts. The continued allure of those "good German" colony master narratives and the ideological power of the "colonial war" *epistemes* should not be underestimated. Twenty-first-century audiences in Canada, the United States, the UK, and Germany want to believe that occasionally "savage wars of peace" had to be fought for the good of colonies. The ubiquitous nature of colonial violence on many continents has made it difficult to document what

George Steinmetz has called the "exceptionally exterminationist" features of German colonization in places like German West Africa.[30]

This reluctance to revisit GSWA genocidal horrors is a part of that "colonial unknowing" that critical indigenous scholars have argued involves more than just collective forgetting or colonial nostalgia. The faith that some Ovaherero and Nama litigants and their supporters have in U.S. jurisdictions can be contrasted with the hermeneutics of suspicion that seems to shadow other vernacular discussions of the German-Namibian negotiations that have been going on for several years. Helin Evrim Sommer, a member Germany's Left Party, noted in 2018 that the "secret bilateral negotiations are not transparent" and were a "farce in a sense."[31] Instead of congratulating German negotiators for having mastered difficult colonial heritages some interviewees talked of "genocide denial." When German Ambassador Christian Schlaga refused to provide his warranted assent to some of the reparations activists' allegations, he complained that he was again the target of "false, slanderous, derogatory and insulting statements."[32] Was he referencing the attacks on his character, or attacks on German historicism? Both?

Some Namibians responded to these types of reactions by arguing that the German governmental officials and their Namibian counterparts needed to openly acknowledge that they may have reached a secret deal whereby reparations would not be on the negotiating table and that the Germany would, in return to bracket out reparations requests, spend more on Namibian developmental aid. German negotiators throughout 2017 and 2018 consistently denied the existence of any secret deals.

Some observers were more optimistic about the future trajectory of GSWA revisionism in German cosmopolitan venues and other European circles. In the city of Hamburg, for example, German Senator Dr. Carsten Brosda, speaking in front of an Ovaherero and Nama delegation who attended the Second Transnational Herero and Nama Congress during the summer of 2018, commented on Hamburg's and Germany's responsibilities for *Schutztruppe* abuses. Senator Brosda, after quoting materials from Social Democrat August Bebel's 1905 speech on how every "tribe" had human rights that needed to be protected, asked for forgiveness and commented on the need for the joint Namibian and German pursuit of reconciliation and remembrance.[33]

Those appropriated parliamentary comments from Bebel provided an example of those archival parchment papers that Michel Foucault had said would be "scratched" over time and time again, that could be taken from the archival regimes of truth and used to produce effective counter-histories or countermemories.

Yet readers need to note how these types of acts of contrition may be the exceptions that prove the rule. Those on the political left in Germany are trying to encourage centrists to join them and speak out about the need to revisit fraught German colonial pasts, but at least for a while, they may be fighting an uphill battle. It takes time before postcolonial viewpoints go mainstream, especially after it took half a century to master difficult Nazi pasts.

Critical scholars could conclude that some progress had been made when German legislators and government representatives were at least willing to mention *"völkermord"* in conversations about the colonial violence carried out during settlement of German South West Africa, but the refusal to negotiate about reparations could be treated as a counter signal that this type of mastering may look nothing like Holocaust remembrance or Shoah restitutional efforts.

Even if we assume that some consciousness-raising came out of the filing of the Rukoro et al. v. German Federal Republic of Germany case (2017), has any of this provided tangible help for elderly Ovaherero and other needy populations living in Namibia?

For some Namibians, the filing of lawsuits has helped legitimate claims that have circulated across generations in some indigenous oral histories,[34] and it has provided psychic and symbolic relief for those who have felt slighted, ignored, and marginalized by the beneficiaries of genocidal practices. Esther Muinjangue perhaps spoke for many Ovaherero when she explained,

> The genocide was always alive in the form of stories and tales narrated through the generations but people didn't always comprehend the nature and scale of the atrocities. The mother of my paternal grandfather was raped by German soldiers, and he is the product of that [rape]. . . . We are not looking for money to line our pockets, the purpose is to restore dignity.[35]

Esther Muinjangue is one of the leading spokespersons for the Ovaherero, and she has visited college campuses, she has appeared in documentaries, and she has often been interviewed by investigative journalists. She is one of the Ovaherero activists who refuses to accept the idea that indigenous claimants can be left out of these bilateral genocidal conversations.

Until the 1990s few Africanists or other scholars had recorded or cited these indigenous oral histories, and in some cases, those who appear to suffer from a variant of what Jacques Derrida would call "archive fever"[36] have often—consciously or unconsciously—valorized the "truths" found in German or British chronicling of GSWA affairs. As critical indigenous scholars like Jodi Byrd and others have noted, the citations and sources that are used in settler colonial studies sometimes dominant historical frames that privilege settler accounts while marginalizing indigenous voices. In the case of GSWA historicizing, there are political and cultural reasons why, for more than a century, more than a few were belittling the truth value of the indigenous oral histories of GSWA affairs. Often presented in African song or verse, some of this indigenous epistemic knowledge looks nothing like other archival materials, and these Ovaherero and Nama or San or "Baster" oral histories have often been treated as unreliable, "secondary," or "anecdotal" types of evidence that could be contrasted with European "primary" archival materials.

The efforts of activists like Esther Muinjangue are helping decolonize these types of twenty-first-century mindsets, and in recent years more and more academics are using multi-modal epistemic methods that combine studies of those indigenous oral histories with provenance, ethnographic, and other types of research.

Including materials from these indigenous histories and public memories in reparations discussions makes it difficult for empowered German or Namibian decision makers to avoid future discussions of Namibian land redistribution. Although the restoration of dignity may be a topic that is raised by many Ovaherero and Nama, we should not forget that other indigenous communities support these reparations cases because they hope, in the long-run, winnable suits might provide the necessary funds that can be used to buy back land in voluntary, or involuntary, transfer of Namibian lands.

As noted above, German diplomats who have no interest in talking about reparations assiduously avoid commenting on the Namibian lands that are owned by German speakers in that country, and they oftentimes don't mention the political power of those whites involved in agribusiness in Namibia. As Tom Bentley astutely noted in 2015,

> Here, then, one can glean a further expediency to Germany's refusal to pay reparations, even beyond crude cost-benefit calculations to the expense of aid. Aid, in contrast to reparations, can be given on German terms. It enables a continued exercising of influence within Namibia and affords unspoken leverage over areas with the German government's interest. Importantly, the emphasis on aid and land reform facilitates the continuation of patterns of land ownership that reflect the inequalities produced in the dispossession of the colonial period.[37]

Critics rarely, if ever, find German diplomats referencing the Namibian lands or agribusinesses that are owned by German-speaking Namibians. Their critiques of the Namibian reparations cases in U.S. federal courts do not drift in directions that would allow for interrogations of old nineteenth-century treaties or the colonial governmental dispossession of so much land. They don't need to bring up these issues—as long as their lawyers in American courtrooms win "jurisdictional" legal battles. When spokespersons for indigenous communities constantly bring up incidents like what happened at the battle of Ohamakari or in the concentration camps like Shark Island, this counters at least some of this aphasia or "colonial unknowing."

If U.S. federal courts decline to provide any judicial redress for Herero and Nama litigants are there any other forms of restorative justice that might be available?

There are some academics, academic journalists, and laypersons who have written about what might happen with some of the Herero and Nama reparations efforts if U.S. legal forums do not provide these claimants with any equitable redress.[38] In 2018 Regina Menachery Paulose and Ronald Gordon Rogo would write about the Namibian reparations efforts and the potential involvement of the International Criminal Court (ICC) or the International Court of Justice (ICJ).[39]

Paulose and Rogo were not the first writers to make these suggestions. During the 1990s several authors wrote about the ICC or the ICJ, and on several occasions supporters of both the Riruako (2001) and the Rukoro (2017) legal filings have hinted that they might try to file cases in The Hague. However, as noted in other portions of this book, formalistic requirements hindered these efforts because the ICJ only "presides over cases involving nation-states."[40] When Riruako talked to Karie Morgan while she was working on her dissertation, he explained that he hadn't actually put the case before the International Court of Justice, but that Germany had. Riruako told Morgan that he knew that as an individual he had no legal standing to try and file that type of case before the ICJ.[41]

Jan-Bart Gewald circulated a different version of this tale when he wrote that at some Herero Day events in Namibia, Riruako declared that the "Herero nation" was going to approach the ICJ to lay a genocide charge against Germany, and this threat set off a chain reaction whereby German researchers felt as if they were forced to investigate the matter. Within days of learning about some of these plans, representatives of the ICJ came out and explained that neither representatives of the Ovaherero nor German officials had actually approached the ICJ.[42]

At first glance one might think that members of the ICC or the ICJ would want to hear these types of human rights cases, but readers have to remember that if one follows some of these organizations' rules, then we need to factor in these litigants lack of "state" status, as well as enforcement difficulties. Even if the ICJ or the ICC ruled in their favor, is there any legal trail of precedents that shows that a nation like Germany has been forced to comply with their decisions, especially in lawsuits involving colonial wrongs?

Those who sympathize with the Ovaherero and Nama litigants—and those who worry about the pragmatism of filing cases in U.S. courts—have discussed everything from having Namibia go to the International Criminal Court to the grudging acceptance of more German development aid. While some in Namibia suggest that this is the time to force major land redistribution without financial reimbursement, those types of strategies are often frowned upon by neoliberal capitalists in Germany, Namibia, and other countries.

Note, for example, the backlash that comes when similar schemes are suggested for radical land redistribution in places like South Africa. Some South African administrators who show an interest in post-conflict resolution and reconciliation that involves radical land redistribution are accused of being the accomplices of people of color who are accused of carrying out "white genocide" on white farmers in South Africa.[43] Old colonial and apartheid wounds are reopened as descendants of Afrikaners and others deploy permutations of victimage narratives that have been around since the time of the British Boer concentration camps.

Regardless of whether the Ovaherero or the Germans actually approached the ICJ, few international law experts have expressed the belief that the ICJ would ever want to hear these types of private cases that were based on colonial matters that happened so long ago.

One alternative approach that has been suggested is that former colonized nations, and aggrieved ethnic communities, accept the formation of commissions of historical inquiry as a form of colonial reparation. Larissa Van Den Herik argued in the *Harvard International Law Journal* that those of us who are living in what Dinah Shelton has called the "world of atonement"[44] need to find constructive ways of thinking about reparations that don't involve the pursuit of lawsuits or financial compensation.[45]

Herik argued that all of the bickering that was witnessed at the 2001 Durban World Conference showed that "claims for historical injustice, including colonialism and slavery," are not easily translated into winnable lawsuits.[46] So if was the case, reasoned Herik, then why not have independent commissions of historical inquiries that can provide "non-legal" forms of "reparatory" justice?[47] She argued that this would allow those on historical committees of inquiry to hear the victims' perspectives, thus providing the type of inclusive processes that the Ovaherero and Nama had been requesting. Moreover, she was convinced that the discussions in these commissions of inquiry could be conducted in productive ways that did not come across as accusatory and functioned liked some "tribunal of history."[48]

While Herik was not asking for the total substitutional replacement of judicial processes, she did see these "independent" committees of inquiry as a way of helping discursively shift the conversations away from a focus on "reparations" and toward "owing" for colonial wrongs.

If, as some Ovaherero and Nama argue, they simply want acknowledgments the formation of these committees of inquiry would be helpful, but if the advocates are really interested in obtaining monetary funds for Namibian land distribution then these committees of inquiry may not be that helpful.

Some in Namibia have also supported the idea that Namibians and Germans need to come together and promote versions of "truth and reconciliation" commissions. For example, during the fall of 2018, Mbakumua Negari noted how South Africans took a "bold step" when they created a truth and reconciliation commission "where people would come vent out and point fingers and, through that process, find a mechanism for trying to level out things."[49] Instead of simply having elite decision makers involved in bilateral diplomatic discussions, a truth and reconciliation commission would provide a type of vernacular forum that would allow the descendants of the GSWA war victims to have their say.

One intriguing alternative to lawfare comes from the private acknowledgments of wrongdoing that might be expressed by the relatives of those who in the past may have been accused of colonial wrongdoing. During 2004, global media outlets told the moving story of what happened when several of Lieutenant General Lothar von Trotha's relatives traveled to the annual public commemoration that is held in Ozombuzovindimba. The von Trotha family members made that journey so that they could join those who were remembering, and commemorating, the victims of the GSWA genocide. At the very site where their ancestor, Lieutenant General Lothar von Trotha, once made fateful proclamations they had this to say:

> We do not intend to play those events down or try to put them in perspective by saying that other European colonial powers had proceeded in the same or similar way. No, in view of the facts, we would like to say the following to the Herero people and to you, one of their highest representatives: we, members of the von Trotha family are ashamed of the terrible events that took place a hundred years ago. We deeply regret what happened to your people . . . [and] the Nama; the cruel unjustified death of tens of thousands of men, women and children.[50]

Contrast this with the massive denialism, or historical revisionism, that I discussed in earlier chapters of this book.

Other possible performative ways of providing some non-legal avenues for redress have to do with changing the names in Germany or Namibia from colonial designations to more contemporary names. In Germany, for instance, street names like Lüderitzstrasse and Peters Allee—places that were named for German colonizers Adolf Lüderitz and Carl Peters—are being replaced with the names like Cornelius-Fredericks-Strasse, so that Afro-Germans, Europeans, and others might commemorative the bravery of a Nama leader who died at Shark Island in one of the camps that was built after the battle of Ohamakari/Waterberg.[51] These types of topographical reformist efforts would appeal to those who could say that this combated denialism or "colonial unknowing." Some of these forms of redress may not appeal to all impoverished

Namibians who want financial restitution, but these smaller gestures might lead to the formation of political alliances that, down the road, might help with the provision of more radical changes.

Yet another avenue for providing some form of redress for colonial wrongs appears in the form of governmental decisions to help with the return of stolen or purchased cultural artefacts from places like Namibia. In 2017 French President Emmanuel Macron made the controversial move of pledging that he would work to return all "stolen" cultural treasures to France's ex-colonies within five years.[52] However, as I noted in chapter 9, many private German institutions are using costly provenance studies to separate "tainted" from untainted human remains that may not be returned to indigenous Namibian communities.

Jürgen Zimmerer, perhaps worried that at least some of these repatriation gestures were being used as substitutes for more radical decolonization efforts, explained to German journalists that Germany's colonial heritage involved much more than simply the return of stolen cultural assets. "It's also about the other colonial-era crimes," he explained, and then he proceeded to list some of those crimes, including the instigation of armed conflicts, the expropriation of lands, and the "genocide in Namibia."[53]

Some might argue that all this talk of repatriation of human remains and legal reparations should pave the way for belated land redistribution in Namibia, but this may be one of the very reasons why it took so long for German officials to openly acknowledge the Namibian genocide. What many empowered decision makers in Namibia and Germany want to avoid is the type of talk of "white genocide" that is now taking place as American President Donald Trump tweets about the murder of South African farmers and the threatened expropriation of farmlands from Afrikaner communities living in post-conflict South Africa.[54]

Is there any evidence that that proverbial "Pandora's Box" has been opened where lawfare has been used, or may be used, in other future legal contests over colonial genocide reparations?

In early chapters of this book, I often mentioned, as an aside, the worries that acknowledgement of colonial genocides in general, or the Ovaherero and Nama "Holocaust" in particular, might pave the way for many other global lawsuits. While some journalists associated renascent interest in these issues with the court filings of the 2001 and 2017 lawsuits, the Namibian grievances need to be placed in much broader "decolonizing" contexts.

Some of the first serious transcontinental discussions of reparations for former colonial wrongs took place at the Durban 2001 World Conference against Racism, Racial Discrimination, Xenophobia, and Related Intolerance.[55] While those who watched this conference argued that Durban provided a wealth of aspirational messages and showed that talk of reparations for imperial wrongs was gaining traction, there were few concrete measures that came out of the Durban conference.

Academic writers who have reviewed the Durban rhetorics, or who followed the trajectory of the twenty-first-century Ovaherero and Nama reparations efforts, have commented on renaissance of interest in reviewing Raphael Lemkin's work and the possibility that expansive readings of genocidal claims might impact future transcontinental talk of restorative justice claims. For example, while audiences before the 1990s focused more of their attention on the "biological" or "physical" genocidal commentaries of Raphael Lemkin, since that time critical genocide scholars and interdisciplinary researchers have been advocating that perhaps it is time to remember that Lemkin was also concerned about "cultural" genocides.

This wordsmithing—that expands the numbers of genocides that might be under investigation—has also attracted the attention of postcolonial scholars in places like Hamburg, Munich, Pretoria, and Lüderitz. Throughout 2018 and early 2019, a host of scholars mulled over the impact that the Ovaherero and Nama cases might have on other potential calls for postcolonial compensation. "This would open up a Pandora's Box in the eyes of other European leaders," argues Henning Melber, because other colonial powers were involved in imperial ventures for much longer periods of time than Germany's three decades of colonial rule.[56] Melber provides a little more detail about the potential impact of an Ovaherero/Nama settlement or court victory: "If Germany would acknowledge claims for direct compensation it would create precedence and open up for claims for all sorts of atrocities during colonial times. The leaders in Paris, Lisbon, London, the Hague and Brussels would not be amused."[57]

This may be why so many former European powers—already worried about the postcolonial dimensions of the "E.U. migration crisis"—are willing to participate in image events where they can express regrets, convey apologies, but adamantly refuse to pay reparations. This allows many in Germany and Europe to adopt the posture of being a "hospitable" place, while staving off calls for costly or traumatic forms of social, political, or legal change.

Readers can appreciate some of this generation's postcolonial reluctance to look inside Pandora's Box. Imagine situations where American lawyers, armed with liberal interpretations of the ATS—as well as the books that have been written about King Léopold's expropriation of ivory, food stuffs, and "red Rubber" out of the "Congo Free State"—filed legal cases against Belgian private corporations based on the Ovaherero and Nama precedents.

The British would not be pleased, because they could potentially be sued on many fronts.

To provide just one of many possible legal scenarios, note how lawyers might be interested in cases that build on historical materials that are now circulating in recent disputes about whether Winston Churchill committed genocide by not rushing to the aid of impoverished residents of Bengal, India, during the 1943 famine.[58] Imagine the consternation of those in the United Kingdom—who have a proud heritage as abolitionists who helped end slave trades and slave practices—would now be asked to pay for the horrors of what happened in what Paul Gilroy has called "the Black Atlantic."[59]

The Palestinians during the centennial of the Balfour Declaration in 2017 were calling for British apologies for their adverse consequences of their mandate system,[60] and those living in places like Ceylon, Greece, or Malaysia could certainly try and put together their own *prima facie* legal cases that followed the lead of the Africans who filed the Nama and Ovaherero lawsuits.

For centuries countless slave ships transported their human cargo to many different continents. In March of 2014, a meeting of the Caribbean Community (CARICOM) decided to approve a 10-point plan of the Caribbean Reparations Commission that would see "reparatory justice" for the victims of "slavery, genocide, and racial apartheid in the Caribbean."[61]

Suppose readers shift their gaze in a slightly different direction and take another critical look at the 1985 Whitaker Report that listed the GSWA atrocity as one of the biggest genocides of the twentieth century. The Whitaker Report argued that that the GSWA atrocity stands alongside "the Ottoman massacre of Armenians in 1915–1916, the Ukrainian pogrom of Jews in 1919, the Tutsi massacre of Hutu in Burundi in 1965 and 1972, the Paraguayan massacre of Ache Indians prior to 1974, the Khmer Rouge massacre in Kampuchea between 1975 and 1978, the contemporary Iranian killings of Baha'is, and the Holocaust."[62] Could lawyers, after a Ovaherero and Nama appellate court victory, use these types of humanitarian reports to set the stage for more colonial or postcolonial lawfare? Or are the facts and circumstances of the GSWA situation unique?

Just a few weeks after the 2017 filings of the Ovaherero and Nama case, journalists working for *Deutsche Welle* asked Jürgen Zimmerer if he thought that other former colonies were going to demand reparations in the future. His response was that it was difficult to predict, but he did admit that some living in former colonies were watching the progress of the Namibian cases in the U.S. federal courts. Moreover, it appears that the British government representatives had admitted to members of the press that they were watching these Namibian developments as well.[63]

That said, some may be tempted to opine that granting the Ovaherero and Nama redress might be achieved without opening legal floodgates. After mentioning these other colonial situations, Zimmerer went on to make the argument that perhaps Namibia was a "special case." During the Germany South West Africa years, he argued, events had transpired that could be documented in ways that made it difficult to deny that genocide had taken place. At the time Zimmerer noted that critics shouldn't object to the alleged belated nature of these filings because of the difficulties of trying to file these cases during the British colonial or apartheid years. There was evidence that neither the administrators for the British mandate system, nor the South African apartheid authorities, would have allowed the Ovaherero to file those types of cases. This is why Zimmerer declared that the Ovaherero and Nama communities were "subjected to the Apartheid system until 1990."[64]

Much could also be made of the fact that representatives of the Ovaherero and Nama communities had been demanding to be included in all types of bilateral talks between German and Namibian negotiators. Scholars like Zimmerer could tell reporters that these parties sought redress in New York courts because they had exhausted all their other remedies. This, Zimmerer argued, is part of the reason why this made this Namibian situation different from what had taken place in Cameroon, Tanzania, and Togo.

However, this was just one academic opinion, and we need to remember how the World Wide Web is filling up with commentaries from bloggers and others who are suggesting that leaders and activists in Tanzania or Cameroon follow the lead of the Namibians. Web access has expanded the nature and scope of transglobal argumentation, and it has allowed both elites and laypersons to be read about Ovaherero and Nama precedents. In Tanzania opposition groups working out of Der es Salaam were reported to have demanded that Tanzanian Foreign Minister Augustine Mahiga ask for reparations from Germany for some of the atrocities that were committed during the German East Africa colonial years.[65]

Activists, scholars, and investigative journalists sometimes argue that what happened in "German East Africa" involved bloody wars that *took more lives* than the Herero and Nama genocide. Some writers, like Abayomi Azikiwe, insist that Tanzania wants compensation for the time when Carl Peters and the German East Africa Company were a part of colonial infrastructures that "imposed a draconian system of land theft, forced labor, economic exploitation and unjust taxation."[66] Azikiwe argued that some seventy-five thousand Tanzanians had died during the Maji Maji rebellion, and that the African Union should back Tanzania's restorative justice claims. After noting that the Ovaherero and Nama were making "similar" demands in Namibia, Azikiwe indicated that Dr. Hussein Mwinyi should work with the National assembly in that country as they pursued an apology and monetary damages for the colonial crimes that were perpetrated in German East Africa between 1905 and 1907.[67]

Some Tanzanians have made other suggestions regarding how best to master difficult pasts in this part of Africa. Mahiga, after meeting with

German Foreign Minister Heiko Mass, argued that although he did want to ask for the return of human remains from German racial science collections, he did not think that demanding reparations was the best solution. Instead, Mahiga talked about the need for restoration of colonial buildings and less expensive demands.[68]

If one needed praxiological proof that some payments of reparations open the door for related demands than one could simply track what happened after the famous 2013 UK settlement with a few thousand Mau Mau litigants. In 2013 some 20 million pounds in costs and compensation had been paid to more than 5,228 Kenyans, but a second suit was brought against the Foreign Office by 44,000 Kenyans who say they also survived the beatings, rapes, tortures, and other abuses that were suffered at the hands of British colonizers during the Kenyan "emergency" years.[69] Simon Myerson, one of the British lawyers for the Mau Mau claimants in this second round of lawfare has argued that part of the motivations behind the filings of these cases have to do with the resentments that were built up by the influx of white farmers who came into Kenya after that region became a colony in 1920. In theory, those who helped the colonial planters build up the area called the Kenyan "white highlands," and these highlanders forced out the native Kikuyu, Embu, and Meru tribes. Myerson points to the fact that by 1948, 1.5 million Kikuyu owned just 2,000 square miles, compared with how some 30,000 British settlers owned 12,000 square miles. This helped radicalize the Kikuyu, and when Sir Evelyn Baring arrived in 1952 as governor, this led to the escalation of violence and contributed to the murder of white settlers and the declarations of a colonial emergency.[70]

The new Mau Mau claimants were said to be suing because there was no real colonial "emergency," and a relatively safe white community carried out abuses in Kenya because they thought that the Mau Mau uprising was caused by communism, hatred of Christianity, or the "perversely evil capabilities of the African mind."[71] Myerson's legal case for the new Mau Mau litigants was thus based on the idea that the British Parliament, after the publicity surrounding the Hola atrocity, had known about some this colonial abuse and yet participated in a "cover-up on an industrial scale."[72]

Note the implicit parallels that are being made between the industrial killing machinery of the Nazis during the Holocaust and the murder of thousands of Mau Mau during the Kenyan "emergency" years. Note also comparisons that could be made between the lawfare talk of the Kenyan "white" highlands and the Namibian lands owned German-speaking Namibians. These are just some of the multidirectional memory possibilities. Given the growing transglobal nature of all of these "decolonizing" efforts that metaphorical "Pandora's Box" may already be open.

CONCLUSION

Readers by now may sense that I am not bothered by the recent attempts to "decolonize" so many historical and contemporary legal and public archives. As I have noted in several parts of this book, I recognize the instrumentalist ways that lawfare is being made to politicize the "rule of law" in many of these Ovaherero and Nama reparations efforts, and yet like many members of TWAIL or postcolonial communities, I recognize the *realpolitik* nature of all empowered legal systems, including those in Germany, Namibia, and the United States. Those who defend the status quo have their own ideological reasons for continuing exclusionary bilateral talks, and for avoiding mention of reparations or radical land redistribution in Namibia.

What troubles me are the differential ways that German public officials are willing to treat the abuses that occurred during the Holocaust years and the German colonial settler periods. After World War II, if West Germans had settled matters by spending only a few tens of millions on reparations to survivors of the Nazi death camps, they would have experienced international backlash. However, when they refuse to negotiate with Ovaherero and Nama activists about restitutional funds that could be paid to those African descendants for historical "takings," this is met with support, or polite silence, by other powers who worry they will be next.

Regardless of whether we frame this as a "political" or "social" or "legal" travesty, it is a mistake to hide the fact that the decolonization that began in the 1960s and continued up until the time of Namibian independence did not result in the handover of vast landholdings by whites in places like Zimbabwe ("the old Rhodesia"), South Africa, or Namibia. Even those German politicians who do acknowledge the ontological existence of the Herero/Nama genocide refuse to take the next step and connect this to

1. the colonization plans of the Nazis for the "resettlement" in the East after the invasion of Poland in 1939;
2. the racial sciences of eugenics carried out by Eugen Fischer and the treatment of Afro-Germans;
3. the "continuity" and "parallels" that can be found the annihilationist and assimilationist sentiments of German settlers and Nazi expansion; or
4. the current condition of impoverished Herero and Nama living today.

The colonial "unknowing" continues, as nations who want to fragment and dissociate these ideas have trouble coming up with the grammars that will allow them to acknowledge colonial genocides while they avoid the legal or moral ramifications of those acknowledgments. If some of the newspapers and other media outlets are right about Germany confronting dark heritages or mastering its difficult pasts, this is not much of a mastering when it is left to private parties and coalitions of dissidents to try and rectify these inequities (see chapter 9).

Given the minority status of the Ovaherero and Nama, who have little representation in the Namibian legislature, we can understand the skepticism of the reparations activists who argue that Germany's grandiose plans for development aid—while well-intentioned—may provide all Namibians with water development projects, more monumentalization, more agribusiness, and more general development aid but very little in the way of tangible benefits for the descendants of the almost one hundred thousand who may have died between 1904 and the time that South Africans invaded the region during World War I.

Having had leaders like Roman Herzog and Helmut Kohl visit Namibia and make trips that are arranged to focus on the needs of the empowered "South westers," it appears unlikely that many Europeans want to see German reparations payments used by indigenous communities to buy land from empowered whites. Note how few of the German officials who talk about repatriation of human remains or the ongoing negotiations with the Namibian negotiators are willing to even mention the power of the tens of thousands of German-speaking Namibians in Namibia today.

Granted, no amount of lawfare can heal some colonial wounds, but even a few attempts at helping ameliorate this situation would be better than having German officials try and explain the differences that exist between Armenian acknowledgments and the Herero/Nama "holocaust" or how the post–World War II Geneva convention provisions can't be retrospectively used to critique GSWA actions. This is a candidate for that agnosia, that study of postcolonial ignorance, that I referenced earlier.

Empowered Germans still seem to be suffering from that lingering aphasia that goes beyond forgetting.[73] If some Germans or Europeans are unwilling to call what happened between 1904 and 1908 a "*vőlkermord,*" then what are they going to call this? A forgotten colonial "war" that looked much like other imperial ventures, a stance that was taken by the German authors of the White Book in 1919? A regrettable "atrocity" that has little to do with Germany's "post-genocidal" age? A politicized topic that brings up false analogies with the "real" genocides like what happened in Rwanda or Srebrenica?

The soldiers who wrote books about their tracking down of the Ovaherero women and children in the veld, and the members of the German General staff who praised the German protection forces' thoroughness, toughness, and courage while they dealt with disease and privation, were living in an honest age that was quite open about how the annihilation of some African "nations" would pave the way for German settler development. So why can't German politicians today *openly admit that they either admire the former colonizers or that they want to protect the power of the German speakers living in Namibia,* who are themselves often torn about what to do about land redistribution in Namibia?

As many followers of Desmond Tutu are fond of arguing, genuine reconciliation can only come after real and substantive confrontations with difficult "truths." At least since the time of Henrik Witbooi and Michael Scott and Horst Drechsler and Helmut Bley, there have been social agents who have been willing to bring up taboo subjects, and now it is up to activists like Esther Muinjangue and Ida Hoffman to carry the torch for social justice redress for aggrieved indigenous communities.

In the future it will be younger generations of scholars, activists, students, diplomats, legislators, and laypersons who will decide if it is indeed time to open up that colonial or imperial "Pandora's Box" and acknowledge both the multidirectional and competitive nature of these fraught pasts.

As a critical rhetorician and a genocide scholar, I realize that in the short term the Ovaherero and Nama may ultimately lose yet another lawsuit in American court rooms, but in the long term the filing of these cases may have awakened many from their dogmatic slumber. Becoming involved in advocacy campaigns that try to change the names of streets that memorialized Carl Peters or other violent colonizers, joining those who ask for the return of all "tainted" human remains, lobbying for the building of memorials for forgotten victims helps. But these activities should supplement—not replace—legalistic efforts to provide reparations and radical land reformation in Namibia.

In sum, even the partial, continent, political, and indeterminate nature of lawfare should not dissuade any of us from recognizing the continued need for more, not less, decolonization efforts. We should not forget the suffering of the tenths of thousands of women and children who faced artillery bombardments and the slaughter of humans and cattle at "battle" of Ohamakari/Waterberg. We have to remember how horrified German soldiers, who had mixed feelings about von Trotha's orders and his proclamations, nevertheless poisoned water holes and cordoned off the desert so that the Ovaherero "nation" had no right to return to a "German" colony. We cannot allow revisionists and denialists to belittle what happened at the five major and small labor camps that led to the deaths of half the detainees while those around them profited from the building of roads, wharfs, towns, and railroads. Nor can we forget the dehumanizing ways that German settlers and colonial administrators passed laws prohibiting "race-mixing," indigenous ownership of major land holdings, or measures that were intended to remind subjugated Africans of their supposedly inferior status.

If the filing of those legal cases in Washington, DC, or New York courts accomplish little else, they will have served as forums that will catalyze the efforts of those who refuse to forget those "heaps of sand" that were found by the British and South Africans in 1915. If the wholesale destruction of the Herero and Nama "nations" or communities did not constitute genocide, then what are future generations going to call this? It is time that global audiences—and not just German communities—acknowledge the genocidal nature of GSWA affairs.

NOTES

1. L. Van den Herik, "Addressing 'Colonial Crimes' through Reparations? Adjudicating Dutch Atrocities Committed in Indonesia," *Journal of International Criminal Justice* 10 (2012): 963–705.
2. George S. Yacoubian, "Financial, Territorial, and Moral Reparations for the 1915 Armenian Massacres," *War Crimes, Genocide, and Crimes against Humanity* 4 (2010): 59–98.
3. *Middle East Monitor* staff, "Spain Falls Short of Apologising for 1920s' Use of Chemical Weapons in Morocco," *Middle East Monitor*, last modified February 18, 2018, https://www.middleeastmonitor.com/20180215-spain-falls-short-of-apologising-for-1920s-use-of-chemical-weapons-in-morocco/.
4. See, for example, BBC staff, "French 'Reparation' for Algerians," BBC News, last modified December 6, 2007, http://news.bbc.co.uk/2/hi/europe/7130307.stm; Robert Fisk, "An Apology from Francois Holland Won't Absolve France of Its Responsibility for Arab Harkis," *Independent*, last modified September 29, 2016, https://www.independent.co.uk/voices/francois-hollande-apology-algerian-war-absolve-france-arab-harkis-a7337166.html.
5. A. J. Langguth, "The Forgotten Debt to Vietnam," *The New York Times*, last modified November 18, 2000, https://www.nytimes.com/2000/11/18/opinion/the-forgotten-debt-to-vietnam.html.
6. Mattias Sköld, "Germany Treading Carefully Regarding Colonial Crimes," *Nordiska Afrikainstitutet*, last modified June 9, 2017, http://nai.uu.se/news/articles/2017/06/09/132653/index.xml.
7. Ruben Carranza quoted in Amanda Ottaway, "For Victims of a Little-Known Genocide, a Long Journey to Justice," *Courthouse News Service*, last modified March 20, 2019, paragraphs 9–10. https://www.courthousenews.com/for-victims-of-a-little-known-genocide-a-long-journey-to-justice/.
8. William Darity, Jr., quoted in Ottaway, "For Victims of a Little-Known Genocide," paragraphs 11–12.
9. Ibid., paragraph 12.
10. McCallion and Associates, "Jurisdiction over the Germany for Violations of International Law in *Rukoro et al. v. Federal Republic of Germany*," 17-cv-00062-LTS (New York: Southern District Court of New York, 2017).
11. *France 24* staff, "New York Court Dismisses Namibia Genocide Compensation Suit," *France 24*, last modified March 7, 2019, https://www.france24.com/en/20190307-new-york-court-dismisses-namibia-genocide-compensation-suit.
12. For earlier examples of worries about this opening of some colonial or imperial "Pandora's Box," see Jeremy Sarkin, *Colonial Genocide and Reparations Claims in the 21st Century* (Westport, Connecticut: Praeger Security International, 2009), 8.
13. Norbert Lammert, "Deutsche ohne Grade: Wer in der Bundesrepublik von Armenier-Genozid Spricht, Darf vom Deutschen Vőlkermord an den Herero und Nama nicht Schweigen," *Zeit*, last modified July 23, 2015, http://www/zeit.de/2015/28/voelkermord-armenier-herero-norbert-lammert.
14. Elise Pape, "Human Remains of Ovaherero and Nama: Transnational Dynamics in Post-Genocidal Restitutions," *Human Remains and Violence* 4, no. 2 (2018): 90–106, 91.

15. McCallion and Associates, "Jurisdiction," 2.

16. Ruprecht Polenz, quoted in Daniel Pelz, "Berlin Unruffled by U.S. Lawsuit on Colonial Era Genocide," *Deutsche Welle*, last modified January 6, 2017, paragraph 13, https://www.dw.com/en/berlin-unruffled-by-us-lawsuit-on-colonial-era-genocide/a-37037313.

17. For a review of some of the reparations arguments that are used by members of the second generation, see Thomas Huber, "Holocaust Compensation Payments and the Global Search for Justice for Victims of Nazi Prosecution," *Australian Journal of Politics and History* 48, no. 1 (2001): 85–101.

18. Niema Movassat, quoted in Pelz, "Berlin Unruffled," paragraphs 14–15.

19. Ruprecht Polenz, quoted in Connelly, "Africans Take Germany to Court," paragraph 16.

20. Ewelina U. Ochab, "The Herero-Nama Genocide: The Story of a Recognized Crime, Apologies Issued and Silence Ever Since," *Forbes*, last modified May 24, 2018, paragraph 5, https://www.forbes.com/sites/ewelinaochab/2018/05/24/the-herero-nama-genocide-the-story-of-a-recognized-crime-apologies-issued-and-silence-ever-since/#e8d26cb6d8c2.

21. See, for example, how some journalists ended up finding out about connections between their own generational family trees and what happened during the GSWA years. See Daniel A. Gross, "A Brutal Genocide in Colonial Africa Finally Gets Its Deserved Recognition," *Smithsonian Magazine*, last modified October 28, 2015, https://www.smithsonianmag.com/history/brutal-genocide-colonial-africa-finally-gets-its-deserved-recognition-180957073/?no-ist.

22. Gayatri Chakravorty Spivak, "Can the Subaltern Speak?" in *Colonial Discourse and Postcolonial Theory: A Reader*, edited by Patrick Williams and Laura Chrisman (New York: Columbia Press, 1993), 66–111.

23. Vekuii Rukoro, quoted in Ndapewoshali Shapwanale, "Nama and Herero Take Germany to Court," *The Namibian*, January 5, 2017, https://www.namibian.com.na/159817/archive-read/Nama-and-Ovaherero-take-Germany-to-court.

24. Ruben Carranza has noted that that the victims "can of course file cases in their own countries courts" but "those courts cannot reach assets in the U.S. or elsewhere and will not have the kind of political impact that a judgment in a country in which judges have a relative degree of independence and enforcement power." Carranza, quoted in Ottaway, "For Victims of a Little-Known Genocide," paragraph 4.

25. Ngondi Kamatuka, quoted in Howard Rechavia Taylor, "U.S. Court Hears Case Against Germany over Namibia Genocide," Al Jazeera, last modified July 31, 2018, paragraph 4, https://www.aljazeera.com/news/2018/07/court-hears-case-germany-namibia-genocide-180731201918543.html.

26. Elise Pape, "Herero Activists in the United States: Demanding Recognition and Reparation for the First Genocide of the Twentieth Century," *The American Institute for Contemporary German Studies* (AICGS), November 1, 1017, https://www.aicgs.org/publication/herero-activists-in-the-united-states/.

27. Ibid., paragraph 9–10.

28. For critiques of that 7–1 witness ratio in GSWA, see Nicole Hahn Rafter, *The Crime of Crimes: Toward a Criminology of Genocide* (New York: New York University Press, 2016).

29. For example, see Jason Burke and Philip Oltermann, "Germany Moves to Atone for 'Forgotten Genocide' in Namibia," *The Guardian*, last modified December 25, 2016, https://www.theguardian.com/world/2016/dec/25/germany-moves-to-atone-for-forgotten-genocide-in-namibia.

30. George Steinmetz, "From 'Native Policy' to Exterminationism: German South West Africa, 1904, in Comparative Perspective," *University of Michigan's Theory and Research in Comparative Social Analysis* (Los Angeles: University of California, 2005), https://escholarship.org/uc/item/11z1k021.

31. Helin Evrim Sommer, quoted in Daniel Pelz, "Namibians Losing Patience over German Slowness to Act on Genocide Claims," *Deutsche Welle*, last modified May 9,

2018, paragraph 1, https://www.dw.com/en/namibians-losing-patience-over-german-slowness-to-act-on-genocide-claims/a-43715135.

32. Christian Schlaga, quoted in Pelz, "Namibians, Losing Patience," paragraph 8.

33. Senator Carsten Brosda, quoted in Kylie Kunguyu, "The Age of European Enlightenment: The City of Hamburg Apologizes for Its Role in African Genocide," *The Southern Times*, June 11, 2018, paragraphs 2–7, https://southerntimesafrica.com/site/news/the-age-of-european-enlightenment-the-city-of-hamburg-apologises-for-its-role-in-african-genocide.

34. See Larissa Förster, *Postkoloniale Erinnerungslandschaften: Wie Deutsche und Herero in Namibia des Kriegs von 1904 gedenken* (Frankfurt am Main: Campus, 2010).

35. Esther Muinjangue, quoted in Andrew Connelly, "Africans Take Germany to Court in New York over 'Forgotten Genocide,'" *USA Today*, last modified July 31, 2018, paragraph 8, https://www.usatoday.com/story/news/world/2018/07/31/africans-take-germany-court-new-york-over-forgotten-genocide/877191002/.

36. Jacques Derrida and Eric Prenowitz, "Archive Fever: A Freudian Impression," *Diacritics* 25, no. 2 (1995): 9–63.

37. Tom Bentley, *Empires of Remorse: Narrative, Postcolonialism and Apologies for Colonial Atrocity* (Abingdon: Oxon: Routledge Press, 2015), 5.

38. See, for example, Rachel Anderson, "Redressing Colonial Genocide under International Law: The Hereros' Case of Action against Germany," *California Law Review* 93, no. 5 (July 2005): 1155–89; Allan D. Cooper, "Reparations for the Herero Genocide: Defining the Limits of International Litigation," *African Affairs* 106, no. 422 (January 2007): 113–26; David Bargueno, "Cash for Genocide?: The Politics of Memory in the Herero Case for Reparations," *Holocaust and Genocide Studies* 26, no. 3 (December, 2012): 394–424; Klaus Bachmann, "Germany's Colonial Policy in German South-West Africa in Light of International Criminal Law," *Journal of Southern African Studies* 43 (2017): 331–47.

39. Regina Menachery Paulose and Ronald Gordon Rogo, "Addressing Colonial Crimes through Reparations: The Mau Mau, Herero and Nama," *State Crime* 7, no. 2 (August 2018): 369–88.

40. Karie L. Morgan, *"To Heal the Wounds": Namibian Ovaherero's Contests over Coming to Terms with the German Colonial Past* (Dissertation: Chapel Hill: University of North Carolina, 2010), 327.

41. Ibid.

42. Jan-Bart Gewald, "Herero Genocide in the Twentieth Century: Politics and Memory," in *Rethinking Resistance: Revolt and Violence in African History*, edited by Jon Abbink, Mirjam de Bruijn, and Klass van Walraven (Boston: Brill, 2003), 279–304, 301; Morgan, "To Heal the Wounds," 327.

43. See James Pogue, "The Myth of White Genocide," *Harper's Magazine*, March, 2019, 43–54.

44. Dinah Shelton, "The World of Atonement: Reparations for Historical Injustices," *Netherlands International Law Review* (2003): 289–325.

45. Larissa Van Den Herik, "Historical Inquiry as a Form of Colonial Reparations," *Harvard International Law Journal* 59, no. 1 (July 2018): 1, http://www.harvardilj.org/wp-content/uploads/Herik-Reparations.pdf.

46. Ibid., 1–2.

47. Ibid., 4.

48. Ibid., 5.

49. Mbakumua Hengari, quoted in Daniel A. Gross, "Why the Herero of Namibia Are Suing Germany for Reparations," National Public Radio, last modified May 6, 2018, paragraph 18, https://www.npr.org/sections/goatsandsoda/2018/05/06/606379299/why-the-herero-of-namibia-are-suing-germany-for-reparations.

50. Von Trotha family, quoted in Sarkin, *Germany's Genocide*, 200; Amy Rivera, *Did the German Actions in the Herero Rebellion of 1904–1908 Constitute Genocide?* (Fort Leavenworth, Kansas: U.S. Army Command and General Staff College, 2008), 106.

51. Gouri Sharma, "Namibia's Long Fight for Justice," *New Internationalist,* last modified August 2, 2018, paragraph 15, https://newint.org/features/web-exclusive/2018/08/02/namibia-germanys-forgotten-genocide.

52. Farah Nayeri, "Return of African Artefacts Sets a Tricky Precedent for Europe's Museums," *New York Times,* last modified November 23, 2018, https://www.nytimes.com/2018/11/27/arts/design/macron-report-restitution-precedent.html.

53. Jürgen Zimmerer, quoted in Daniel Pelz, "Genocide in Namibia: Germany Remains at Odds with Its Colonial Legacy, *Deutsche Welle,* last modified July 30, 2018, paragraph 12, https://www.dw.com/en/genocide-in-namibia-germany-remains-at-odds-with-its-colonial-legacy/a-44887592.

54. James Pogue, "The Myth of White Genocide," *Harper's Magazine,* March, 2019, https://harpers.org/archive/2019/03/the-myth-of-white-genocide-in-south-africa/.

55. M. du Plessis, "Historical Injustice and International Law: An Exploratory Discussion of Reparation for Slavery," *Human Rights Quarterly* 25, no. 3 (2003): 624–59.

56. Henning Melber, quoted in Sköld, "Germany Treading," paragraph 8.

57. Ibid., paragraph 9.

58. Madhusree Mukerjee, *Churchill's Secret War: The British Empire and the Ravaging Of India during World War II* (New York: Basic Books, 2010).

59. Paul Gilroy, *The Black Atlantic: Modernity and Double-Consciousness* (London: Verso, 1993).

60. Sharif Mandhai, "Why Palestine Activists Want a UK Apology for Balfour," Al Jazeera, last modified October 31, 2017, https://www.aljazeera.com/news/2017/10/palestine-activists-uk-apology-balfour-171031054747559.html.

61. Amy Strecker, "Indigenous Land Rights and Caribbean Reparations Discourse," *Leiden International Law* 30 (2017): 629–46. For more on how audiences have responded to some of this activism in Caribbean contexts, see Claudia Rauhut, "Caribbean Activism for Slavery Reparations: An Overview," in *Practices of Resistance in the Caribbean: Narratives, Aesthetics and Politics,* edited by Wiebke Beushausen, Miriam Brandel, Joseph Farquharson, Marius Littschwager, Annika McPherson, and Julia Roth (London: Rutledge, 2018).

62. Whitaker Report, cited in Ewelina U. Ochab, "The Herero-Nama Genocide," paragraph 4.

63. Jürgen Zimmerer, quoted in Daniel Pelz, "After Namibia, Could Other Former German Colonies Demand Reparations?" *Deutsche Welle,* last modified August 2, 2017, paragraphs 1–2. https://www.dw.com/en/after-namibia-could-other-former-german-colonies-demand-reparations/a-39924695.

64. Zimmerer, quoted in Pelz, "After Namibia," paragraph 3.

65. It appears that the Tasmanian ministers, Augustine Mahiga, is rejecting some of these calls. *ENCA* staff, "Tanzanian Minister Rejects German Colonial Compensation Calls," *ENCA,* last modified May 4, 2018, https://www.enca.com/africa/tanzanian-minister-rejects-german-colonial-compensation-calls.

66. Abayomi Azikiwe, "Tanzania Demands Reparations for German Colonial Atrocities," *Pambazuka News,* last modified February 23, 2017, paragraph 1, https://www.pambazuka.org/pan-africanism/tanzania-demands-reparations-german-colonial-atrocities.

67. Ibid., paragraphs 1–4.

68. Ibid.

69. Owen Bowcott, "Mau Mau Rebellion Victims Claim Parliament Was Misled over Torture," *The Guardian,* past modified May 23, 2016, https://www.theguardian.com/world/2016/may/23/mau-mau-rebellion-kenyan-victims-compensation-claim.

70. Simon Myerson, quoted in Bowcott, "Mau Mau Rebellion," paragraphs 4–8.

71. Bowcott, "Mau Mau Rebellion," paragraph 9.

72. Ibid., paragraph 20.

73. For other European examples of scholars who have extended Professor Stoler's work on "colonial aphasia," see Paul Bijl, "Colonial Memory and Forgetting in the Netherlands and Indonesia," *Journal of Genocide Research* 14, no. 3–4 (2012): 441–61.

Bibliography

BOOKS

Adhikari, Mohamed. *The Anatomy of a South African Genocide: The Extermination of the Cape San Peoples*. Cape Town: University of Cape Town Press, 2010.

Anghie, Antony. *Imperialism, Sovereignty and the Making of International Law*. Cambridge, UK: Cambridge University Press, 2005.

Baer, Elizabeth. *The Imperial Gaze: From German Southwest Africa to the Third Reich*. Detroit: Wayne State University Press, 2017.

Balabkins, N. *West German Reparations to Israel*. New Brunswick, N.J.: Rutgers University Press, 1971.

Bayer, Maximilian. *Der Krieg in Südwestafrika*. Berlin, Engelmann, 1905.

Bayer, Maximilian. *Mit dem Hauptquartier in Südwestafrika*. Berlin: Wollenbüttel Melchlor, Historischer Verlag, 1909.

Bentley, Tom. *Empires of Remorse: Narrative, Postcolonialism and Apologies for Colonial Atrocity*. New York: Routledge, 2016.

Bley, Helmut. *South West Africa under German Rule*, translated by Hugh Ridley. Evanston: Northwestern University Press, 1971.

Bridgman, Jon M. *The Revolt of the Herero*. Berkeley: University of California Press, 1981.

Brown, Wendy. *Politics Out of History*. Princeton: Princeton University Press, 2001.

Bruce-Jones, Eddie. *Race in the Shadow of Law: State Violence in Contemporary Europe*. New York: Taylor and Francis, 2017.

Bruwer, J. P. Van S. *South West Afrika: The Disputed Land*. Beperk: Nasionale Boekhandel, 1966.

Ciarlo, David. *Advertising Empire: Race and Visual Culture in Imperial Germany*. Cambridge: Harvard University Press, 2011.

Dove, Karl. *Deutsch-Südwest-Afrika*. Berlin: Wilhelm Süsserott, 1903.

Drechsler, Horst. *Let Us Die Fighting: The Struggle of the Herero and Nama against German Imperialism* (1884–1915). London: Zed Books, 1980.

Drechsler, Horst. *Südwestafrica unter Deutscher Kolonialherrschaft*. Berlin: Akademie-Verlag, 1966.

Emmkett, Tony. *Popular Resisance and the Roots of Nationalism in Namibia, 1915–1966*. Basel: Schlettwein Publishing, 1999.

Epstein, Klaus. *Matthias Erzberg and the Dilemmas of German Democracy*. New York: Howard Fertig, 1959.

Förster, Larissa. *Postkoloniale Erinnerungslandschaften: Wie Deutsche und Herero in Namibia des Kriegs von 1904 gedenken*. New York: Campus Verlag, 2010.

Foucault, Michel. *Surveiller et Punir Naissance de la prison*. Paris: NRF Éditions Gallimard, 1975.

Friedrichsmeyer, Sara, Sara Lennox, and Suzanne Zantop. *The Imperialist Imagination: German Colonialism and Its Legacy*. Ann Arbor: University of Michigan Press, 1998.

Galbraith, John S. *Reluctant Empire*. Berkeley: University of California Press, 1963.

Gewald, Jan-Bart. *Herero Heroes: A Socio-Political History of the Herero of Namibia, 1890–1923*. Athens: Ohio University Press, 1999.

Gibney, Mark, Rhoda E. Howard-Hassmann, Jean-Marc Colcaud, and Niklaus Steiner. *The Age of Apology: Facing Up to the Past*. University of Pennsylvania Press, 2008.

Gilroy, Paul. *The Black Atlantic: Modernity and Double-Consciousness.* London: Verso, 1993.
Goldblatt, Israel. *History of South West Africa.* Capetown: Juta and Company, 1971.
Grimm, Hans. *Volk ohne Raum.* Munich: Albert Langen, 1926.
Huang, Shu-Mei. *Difficult Heritage in Nation Building: South Korea and Post-Conflict Japanese Colonial Occupation Architecture.* New York: Palgrave Macmillan, 2018.
Hull, Isabel V. Hull. *A Scrap of Paper: Breaking and Making International Law during the Great War.* Ithaca: Cornell University Press, 2014.
Hunt, Nancy Rose. *A Nervous State: Violence, Remedies, and Reverie in Colonial Congo.* Durham: Duke University Press, 2016.
Katjavivi, Peter H. *A History of Resistance in Namibia.* Paris: Unesco Press 1988.
King, Richard H., and Dane Stone. *Hannah Arendt and the Uses of History: Imperialism, Nation, Race and Genocide.* New York: Berghahn Books, 2007.
Kössler, Reinhart. *Namibia and Germany: Negotiation the Past.* Windhoek: University of Namibia Press, 2015.
Langbehn, Volker. *German Colonialism, Visual Culture, and Modern Memory.* New York: Routledge, 2010.
Luxemburg, Rosa. *Socialism or Barbarism,* edited by Paul Le Blanc and Helen C. Scott. New York: Pluto Books, 2010.
Mawani, Renisa. *Across Oceans of Law.* Durham: Duke University Press, 2018.
Ngavirue, Zedekia. *Political Parties and Interest Groups in South West Africa (Namibia): A Study of a Plural Society.* Basel: P. Schlettwein Publishing, 1977.
Okupa, Effa. *" Carrying the Sun on Our Backs": Unfolding German Colonialism in Namibia from Caprivi to Kasikili.* Berlin: Lit Verlag, 2006.
Olusoga. David, and Casper W. Erichsen. *The Kaiser's Holocaust: Germany's Forgotten Genocide.* London: Farber & Farber, 2010).
Pool, Gerhardus. *Maharero.* Windhoek: Mibagus, 1990.
Press, Steven. *Rogue Empires: Contracts and Conmen in Europe's Scramble for Africa.* Cambridge: Harvard University Press, 2017.
Reynolds, Henry. *"An Indelible Stain": The Question of Genocide in Australia's History.* Ringwood, Victoria: Penguin, 2001.
Rivera, Amy. *Did the German Actions in the Herero Rebellion of 1904–1908 Constitute Genocide?* Fort Leavenworth, KS: U.S. Army Command and General Staff College, 2008.
Rogin, Michael Paul. *Fathers and Children: Andrew Jackson and the Subjugation of the American Indian.* New York: Alfred A. Knopf, 1975.
Rothberg, Michael. *Multidirectional Memory: Remembering the Holocaust in the Age of Decolonization.* Stanford: Stanford University Press, 2009.
Rust, Conrad. *Krieg und Frieden im Heerolande.* Leipzig: L. A. Kittler, 1905.
Sandler, Willeke. *Empire in the Heimat: Colonialism and Public Culture in the Third Reich.* New York: Oxford University Press, 2018.
Sarkin, Jeremy. *Colonial Genocide and Reparations Claims in the 21 st Century: The Socio-Legal Context of Claims under International Law by the Herero against Germany for Genocide in Namibia, 1904–1908.* Westport, CT: Praeger Security International, 2009.
Sarkin, Jeremy. *Germany's Genocide of the Herero: Kaiser Wilhelm II, His General, His Settlers, His Soldiers.* Cape Town: University of Cape Town Press, 2011.
Schabas, William A. *Genocide in International Law.* Cambridge: Cambridge University Press, 2000.
Schmolek, Wolfe W. *Dream of Empire, German Colonialism, 1919–1945.* New Haven: Yale University Press, 1964.
Schüssler, Wilhelm. *Adolf Lüderitz.* Bremen: Carl Schunemann Verlag, 1936.
Schwabe, Kurt. *Der Krieg in Deutsch-Sudwestafrika, 1904–1906.* Berlin: C. A. Weller, 1907.
Schilling, Britta. *Postcolonial Germany: Memories of Empire in a Decolonized Nation.* New York: Oxford University Press, 2014.

Schnee, Henrich. *German Colonization, Past and Future: The Truth about the German Colonies*. New York: Knopf, 1926.
Short, John Phillip. *Magic Lantern Empire: Colonization and Society in Germany*. Ithaca: Cornell University Press, 2012.
Silvester, Jeremy, and Jan-Bart Gewald (eds). Words *Cannot Be Found: German Colonial Rule in Namibia: An Annotated Reprint of the 1918 Blue Book*. Brill: Leiden, 2003.
Slyomovics, Susan. *How to Accept German Reparations*. Philadelphia: University of Pennsylvania Press, 2014.
Stargardt, Nicholas. *The German Idea of Militarism: Radical and Socialist Critics, 1886–1914*. Cambridge: Cambridge University Press, 1994.
Steer, G. L. *Judgment on German Africa*. Hodder: Stoughton, 1939.
Steinmetz, George. *The Devil's Handwriting: Postcoloniality and the German Colonial State in Qingdao, Samoa, and Southwest Africa*. Chicago: University of Chicago Press, 2009.
Stoler, Ann Laura. *Duress: Imperial Durabilities in Our Times*. Durham: Duke University Press, 2016.
Torpey, John. *Making Whole What Has Been Smashed: On Reparations Politics*. Cambridge: Cambridge, Harvard University Press, 2006.
Townsend, Mary Evelyn. *The Rise and Fall of Germany's Colonial Empire, 1884–1918*. New York, Macmillan Company, 1930.
Troup, Freda. *In Face of Fear: Michael Scott's Challenge to South Africa*. London: Faber & Faber, 1950.
Tutu, Desmond. *No Future without Forgiveness*. New York: Doubleday, 1999.
Vedder, Heinrich. *South West Africa in Early Times: Being the Story of South West Africa Up to the Date of Maherero's Death in 1890*. New York: Oxford University Press, 1938.
von Bülow, Bernhard Fürst. *Denkwurdigkeiten*. Berlin: Verlag-Ullstein, 1934.
von Falkenhausen, Helene. *Ansiederschicksale, Elf Jahre in Deutsch-Südwestafrika 1893–1904*. Berlin: Dietrich Reimer Verlag.
von Rohrbach, Paul. *Deutsche Kolonialwirtschaft:* Berlin-Schöneberg: Buchvert der Hilfe, 1907.
Walker, Henry F. B. *A Doctor's Diary in Damaraland*. London: Edward Arnold, 1917.
Wellington, John H. *South West Africa and Its Human Issues*. Oxford: Oxford University Press, 1967
Wigger, Iris. *The "Black Horror on the Rhine": Intersections of Race, Nation, Gender and Class in the 1920*. London: Macmillan, 2017.
Zimmerer, Jürgen, and Joachim Zeller. *Genocide in German South-West Africa: The Colonial War of 1904–08 in Namibia and Its Aftermath*. Monmouth: Merlin, 2016.

BOOK CHAPTERS

Axster, Felix. ". . . will try to send you the best views from here": Postcards from the Colonial War in Namibia (1904–1908)," in *German Colonialism, Visual Culture, and Modern Memory*, edited by Volker M. Langehn, 55–70. New York: Routledge, 2010.
Bartels, Anke, Lars Eckstein, Nicole Waller, and Dirk Wiemann. "Postcolonial Justice: An Introduction," in *Postcolonial Justice*, edited by Anke Bartels, Lars Eckstein, Nicole Waller, and Dirk Wiemann, 1–20. Amsterdam: Brill, 2017.
Biwa, Memory. "Afterlives of Genocide: Return of Human Bodies from Berlin to Windhoek 2011," in *Memory and Genocide: On What Remains and the Possibility of Representation*, edited by Fazil Maradi, Ralph Buchenhorst, and Maria Six-Hohenbalken, 91–106.New York: Routledge, 2017.
Bonnell, Andrew G. "Social Democrats and Germany's War in South West Africa, 1904–7: The View of the Socialist Press," in *Savage Worlds: German Encounters*

Abroad, 1798–1914, edited by Matthew P. Fitzpatrick and Peter Monteath, 206–29. Manchester: Manchester University Press, 2018, 224.

Comaroff, Jean, and John L. Comaroff. "Law and Disorder in the Postcolony: An Introduction," in *Law and Disorder in the Postcolony*, edited by Jean Comaroff and John L. Comaroff, 1–56. Chicago: University of Chicago Press, 2006.

Gewald, Jan-Bart. "Herero Genocide in the Twentieth Century: Politics and Memory," in *Rethinking Resistance: Revolt and Violence in African History*, edited by Jon Abbink, Mirjam de Bruijin, and Klaas van Walraven, 279–304. Boston: Brill, 2003.

Hinz, Manfred O. "One Hundred Years Later: Germany On Trial in the USA: The Herero Reparations Claim for Genocide," in *Bürgerliche Gessellschaft: Idee und Wirklichkeit*, edited by Manfred Hahn, 375–90. Berlin: Trafo-Verlag, 2004.

Katjavivi, Peter H. "Namibia's Bilateral Relations with Germany: A Critical Relationship," in *Namibia's Foreign Relations: Historical Contexts, Current Dimensions, and Perspectives for the 21st Century*, edited by Anton Bösl, André du Pisani, and Dennis U. Zaire, 135–68. Windhoek: Konrad Adenauer Stiftung, 2014.

Kössler, Reinhart. "Facing Postcolonial Entanglement and the Challenge of Responsibility," in *Reconciliation, Civil Society, and the Politics of Memory*, edited by Birgit Schwelling, 277–312. Bielefeld: Verlag, 2012.

Latour, Bruno. "From Realpolitik to Dingpolitik, or How to Make Things Public," in *Making Things Public: Atmospheres of Democracy*, edited by Bruno Latour and Peter Weibel. 14–44. Cambridge: MIT Press, 2005.

Mégret, Frédéric. "From 'Savages' to 'Unlawful Combatants': A Postcolonial Look at International Law's 'Other,'" in *International Law and Its Others*, edited by Anne Orford. 265–318. Cambridge: Cambridge University Press, 2006.

Moses, A. Dirk. "Chapter 1: Raphael Lemkin, Culture, and the Concept of Genocide," in *The Oxford Handbook of Genocide Studies*, edited by Donald Bloxham and A. Dirk Moses, 19–41. Oxford: Oxford University Press, 2010.

Rauhut, Claudia. "Caribbean Activism for Slavery Reparations: An Overview," in *Practices of Resistance in the Caribbean: Narratives, Aesthetics and Politics*, edited by Wiebke Beushausen, Miriam Brandel, Joseph Farquharson, Marius Littschwager, Annika McPherson, and Julia Roth, 137–50. London: Rutledge, 2016.

Sarkin, Jeremy. "Should Reparations for Massive Human Rights Abuses Perpetrated on African Victims during Colonial Times Be Given?" in *Justice for Victims: Perspectives on Rights, Transitions and Reconciliation*, edited by Inge Vanfraechem, Antony Pemberton, and Felix Mukwiza Ndahinda, 89–104. New York: Routledge, 2014.

Shigwedha, Viho Amukway. "The Return of Herero and Nama Bones from Germany: The Victims' Struggle for Recognition and Recurring Genocide Memories in Namibia," in *Human Remains in Society: Curation and Exhibition in the Aftermath of Genocide and Mass-Violence*, edited by Jean-Marc Dreyfus and Elisabeth Anstett, 197–219. Manchester: Manchester University Press, 2016.

Smith, Hermut Walser. "The Logic of Colonial Violence: Germany in Southwest Africa (1904–1907), The United States in the Philippines (1899–1902)," in *German and American Nationalism: A Comparative Perspective*, edited by Hartmann Lehmann, 205–31. Oxford: Berg, 1999.

Smith, Helmut Walser. "The Talk of Genocide, the Rhetoric of Miscegenation: Notes on Debates in the German Reichstag Concerning Southwest Africa, 1904–1914, in *The Imperialist Imagination: German Colonialism and Its Legacy*, edited by Sara Friedrichsmeyer, Sara Lennox, and Susanne Zantop, 107–24. Ann Arbor: University of Michigan Press, 1998.

Spivak, Gayatri Chakravorty. "Can the Subaltern Speak?" in *Colonial Discourse and Postcolonial Theory: A Reader*, edited by Patrick Williams and Laura Chrisman, 66–111. New York: Columbia Press, 1993.

Twomey, Christina. "Atrocity Narratives and Imperial Rivalry: Britain, Germany and the Treatment of 'Native Races,' 1904–1939" in *Evil, Barbarism and Empire: Britain and Abroad, c. 1830–2000*, edited by T. Crook and B. Taithe, 201–25. London: Palgrave Macmillan, 2011.

Van Der Haagen-Wulff, Monica. "Decloaking Invisibility: Remembering Colonial South-West Africa," in *Postcolonial Justice*, edited by Anke Bartels, Lars Eckstein, and Nicole Waller, 277–94. Leiden: Koninklijke Brill, 2017.

Zimmerer, Jürgen. "Colonial Gnocide: The Herero and Nama War (1904–8) in German South West Africa and Its Significance," in *The Historiography of Genocide*, edited by Dan Stone. 323–43. London: Palgrave Macmillan, 2008.

Zimmerman, Andrew. "Adventures in the Skin Trade: German Anthropology and Colonial Corporeality," in *Worldly Provincialism: German Anthropology in the Age of Empire*, edited by Matti Bunzl and H. Glenn Penny, 156–78. Ann Arbor: University of Michigan Press, 2003.

JOURNAL ARTICLES AND LAW REVIEWS

Adhikari, Mohamed. "'Streams of Blood and Streams of Money': New Perspectives on the Annihilation of the Herero and Nama Peoples of Namibia 1904–1908." *Kronos* 34 (2008): 303–20.

Allen, Jason, and Barbara Ann Hocking. "Unlocking the Alienation: A Comparative Rile for Alien Torts Legislation in Post-Colonial Reparations Claims?" *Human Rights Review* 11, no. 2 (2010): 247–76.

Alnaes, Kristen. "Oral Tradition and Identity: The Herero in Botswana." *Collected Seminar Papers. Institute of Commonwealth Studies* 11 (1981): 15–23.

Anderson, Rachel. "Redressing Colonial Genocide under International Law: The Hereros' Cause of Action against Germany." *California Law Review* 95 (2005): 1155–90.

Bachmann, Klaus. "Germany's Colonial Policy in German South-West Africa in Light of International Criminal Law." *Journal of Southern African Studies* 43 (2017): 331–47.

Balkin, Jack M. "Ideological Drift and the Struggle over Meaning." *Connecticut Law Review* 25 (1993): 869–91.

Bargueño, David. "Cash for Genocide? The Politics of Memory in the Herero Case for Reparations." *Holocaust and Genocide Studies* 26, no. 3 (Winter 2012): 394–424.

Berat, Lynn. "Genocide: The Namibian Case Against Germany." *Pace International Law Review* 5 (1993): 165–210.

Bellia, Jr., Antony J., and Bradford R. Clark. "The Alien Tort Statute and the Law of Nations." *The University of Chicago Law Review* 78, no. 2 (Spring 2011): 445–51.

Beurden, Jos Van. "Decolonisation and Colonial Collections." *Low Countries Historical Review* 133, no. 2 (2018): 66–78.

Bijl, Paul. "Colonial Memory and Forgetting in the Netherlands and Indonesia." *Journal of Genocide Research* 14, no. 3–4 (2012): 441–61.

Bond, Patrick, and Khadja Sharife. "Apartheid Reparations and the Contestation of Corporate Power in Africa," *Review of African Political Economy* 36, no. 119 (March 2009): 115–25.

Botha, Christo. "Internal Colonization and an Oppressed Minority? The Dynamics of Relations Between Germans and Afrikaners against the Background of Constructing a Colonial State in Namibia, 1884–1990." *Journal of Namibian Studies* 2 (2007): 7–50.

Byrd, Jodi A. "'Variations under Domestication': Indigeneity and the Subject of Dispossession." *Social Text* 36, no. 2 (June 2018): 123–41.

Byrd, Jodi A., and Michael Rothberg. "Introduction: Between Subalternity and Indigeneity." *Interventions* 13, no. 1 (2011): 1–12.

Cooper, Allan D. "Reparations for the Herero Genocide: Defining the Limits of International Litigation." *African Affairs* 106, no. 422 (January 2007): 113–26.

Dale, Richard. "Reconfiguring White Ethnic Power in Colonial Africa: The German Community in Namibia, 1923–50." *Nationalism & Ethnic Politics* 7, no. 2 (Summer, 2001): 75–94.

De Prada-Samper, J. M. "The Forgotten Killing Fields: 'San' Genocide and Louis Anthing's Mission to Bushmanland, 1862–1862." *Historia* 57, no. 1 (2012): 172–87.

Dedering, Tilman. "The German-Herero War of 1904: Revisionism of Genocide or Imaginary Historiography?" *Journal of South African Studies* 19, no. 1 (1993): 80–88.

Derrida, Jacques, and Eric Prenowitz, "Archive Fever: A Freudian Impression," *Diacritics* 25, no. 2 (1995): 9–63.

Du Plessis, Max. "Historical Injustice and International Law: An Exploratory Discussion of Reparation for Slavery." *Human Rights Quarterly* 25, no. 3 (2003): 624–59.

Eckl, Andreas. "The Herero Genocide of 1904: Source-Critical and Methodological Considerations." *Journal of Namibian Studies* 3 (2008): 31–61.

Epstein, Klaus. "Erzberger and the German Colonial Scandals, 1905–1910. *English Historical Review* 74 (1959): 637–63.

Evans, Andrew D. "Race Made Visible: The Transformation of Museum Exhibits in Early-Twentieth Century German Anthropology." *German Studies Review* 31, no. 1 (February 2008): 87–108.

Fitzpatrick, Matthew P. "The Pre-History of the Holocaust? The Sonderweg and *Historikstreit* Debates and the Abject Colonial Past." *Central European History* 41, no. 3 (September 2008): 477–503.

Fitzpatrick, Matthew. P. "The Threat of 'Woolly-Haired Grandchildren': Race, the Colonial Family and German Nationalism." *The History of the Family* 14, no. 4 (2009): 356–38.

Gerwarth, Robert, and Stephan Malinowski. "Hannah Arendt's Ghosts: Reflections on the Disputable Path from Windhoek to Auschwitz." *Central European History* 42, no. 2 (June 2009): 279–300.

Gesmar, Haidy. "Resisting Settler-Colonial Property Relations? The WAI 262 Claim and Resort in Aotearoa New Zealand." *Settler Colonial Studies* 3, no. 2 (2013): 230–43.

Gewald, Jan-Bart. "The Road of the Man Called Love and the Sack of Sero: The Herero-German War and the Export of Herero Labour to the South African Rand." *Journal of African History* 40, no. 1 (1999): 21–40.

Goldstein, Alyosha. "The Ground Not Given: Colonial Disposition of Land, Race, and Hunger," *Social Text* 36, no. 2 (June 2018): 83–106.

Hannum, Hurst. "International Law and Cambodian Genocide: The Sounds of Silence." *Human Rights Quarterly* 11, no. 1 (February 1989): 82–138.

Harring, Sidney L. "Germany Reparations to the Herero Nation: An Assertion of Herero Nationhood in the Path of Namibian Development?" *West Virginia Law Review* 104 (2002): 393–417.

Häußler, Matthias. "From Destruction to Extermination: Genocidal Escalation in Germany's War against the Herero, 1904." *Journal of Namibian Studies* 10 (2011): 55–81.

Howard-Hassmann, Rhoda E. "Getting to Reparations: Japanese Americans and African Americans." *Social Forces* 83, no. 2 (December 2004): 823–40.

Imperato, Pascal James. "Review: Differing Perspectives on Mau Mau." *African Studies Review* 48, no. 3 (December 2005): 147–54.

Kauanui, J. Kēhaulani. "Colonialism in Equality: Hawaiian Sovereignty and the Question of U.S. Civil Rights." *South Atlantic Quarterly* 10, No. 4 (Fall 2008): 835–50.

Kelly, Robin. "Poetics of Anticolonialism," *Monthly Review* 51, no. 6 (November 1999): 1–6.

Kössler, Reinhart. "Entangled History and Politics: Negotiating the Past between Namibia and Germany." *Journal of Contemporary African* Studies, 26, no. 3 (July 2008): 313–39.

Kössler, Reinhart. "Imperial skullduggery, Science and the Issue of Provenance and Restitution: The Fact of Namibian Skulls in the Alexander Ecker Collection in Freiburg." *Human Remains and Violence* 4, no. 2 (2018): 27–44.

Kőssler, Reinhart. "Review Article: Genocide in Namibia: The Holocaust and the Issue of Colonization." *Journal of Southern African Studies* 38, no. 1 (March 2012): 233–38.

Kössler, Reinhart. "Review: *Postkoloniale Erinnerungslandschaften: Wie Deutsche und Herero in Namibia des Kriegs von 1904 gedenken*." *Africa Spectrum* 2 (2010): 129–32.

Kössler, Reinhart. "Sjambok or Can? Reading the Blue Book." *Journal of Southern African Studies* 30 (September 2004): 703–8.

Kŏssler, Reinhart. "Two Modes of Amnesia: Complexity in Postcolonial Namibia." *Acta Academica* 47, no. 1 (2015): 138–60.

Krüger, Gesine. "Coming to Terms with the Past." *German Historical Institution Bulletin* 37 (Fall 2005): 45–49.

Kunz, Josef L. "The United Nations Convention on Genocide." *The American Journal of International Law* 43, no. 4 (October 1949): 738–46.

Lange, Felix. "The Dream of a *Völkish* Colonial Empire: International Law and Colonial Law during the National Socialist Era." *London Review of International Law* 5, no. 3 (November 2017): 343–69.

Lau, Brigitte. "Uncertain Certainties: The Herero-German War of 1904." *Mibagus* 2 (1989): 4–5, 8.

Laubscher, L. "Facing the Apartheid Archive, or Archons and Researchers." *South African Journal of Psychology* 40, no. 4 (December, 2010): 370–81.

Lowry, John S. "African Resistance and Central Party Recalcitrance in the Reichstag Colonial Debates of 1905/06." *Central European History* 39 (2006): 244–69.

Lu, Catherine. "Redress and Addressing Colonial Injustice." *Ethics & Global Politics* 11 (2018): 76–80.

Madley, Benjamin. "From Africa to Auschwitz: How German South West Africa Incubated Ideas and Methods Adopted and Developed by the Nazis in Eastern Europe." *European Historical Quarterly* 35, no. 3 (July 2005): 429–64.

Madley, Benjamin. "From Terror to Genocide: Britains Tasmanian Penal Colony and Australia's History Wars." *Journal of British Studies* 47, no. 1 (January 2008): 77–106.

Mamdani Mahmood. "Settler Colonialism: Then and Now." *Critical Inquiry* 41 (Spring 2015): 596–614.

Manoff, Marlene. "Theories of the Archive from Across the Disciplines." *Portal: Libraries and the Academy* 4, no. 1 (January 2004): 9–25.

Masson, J. R. "A Fragment of Colonial History: The Killing of Jakob Marengo." *Journal of Southern African Studies* 21 (1995): 247–56.

Mawani, Renisa. "Law's Archive." *Annual Review of Law and Social Science* 8 (2012): 337–65.

McCallion, Kenneth F., and Robert Murtfeld. "Germany's Responsibility under International Law to Compensate the Ovaherero and Nama Peoples of Namibia for the 1904–1908 Genocide." *Harvard International Law Journal* 59, no. 1. (2018): 1–4.

McDonnel, Michael A., and A. Dirk Moses. "Raphael Lemkin as Historian of Genocide in the Americas." *Journal of Genocide Studies* 7, no. 4 (2005): 501–29.

Melber, Henning. "Genocide Matter-Negotiating a Namibian-German Past in the Present." *Stichproben: Wiener Zeitschrift für kritische Afrikastudien* 17, no. 33 (2017): 1–24.

Melber, Henning. "Namibia: The German Roots of Apartheid." *Race & Class* 27, no. 1 (1985): 63–77.

Morgan, Karie L. "Remembering the Nation-State: Hereros' Pursuit of Restorative Justice." *Time & Society* 21, no. 1 (2012): 21–38.

Müller, Lars. "'We Need to Get Away from a Culture of Denial'?: The German-Herero War in Politics and Textbooks." *Journal of Education Media, Memory, and Society* 5, no. 1 (Spring, 2013): 50–71.

Nelson, Keith L. "The 'Black Horror on the Rhine': Race as a Factor in Post–World War I Diplomacy." *The Journal of Modern History* 42, no. 4 (December 1970): 606–27.

Nielsen, Mads Bomholt. "Selective Memory: British Perceptions of the Herero-Nama Genocide, 1904–1908 and 1918." *Journal of Southern African Studies* 43, no. 2 (February 2017): 315–30.

Niezen, Ronald. "Speaking for the Dead: The Memorial Politics of Genocide in Namibia and Germany." *International Journal of Heritage Studies* 24, no. 5 (2018): 547–67.

O'Donnell, Krista. "Poisonous Women: Sexual Danger, Illicit Violence, and Domestic Work in German Southern Africa, 1904–1915." *Journal of Women's History* 11, no. 3 (Autumn 1999): 32–54.

O'Donnell, Susan, and David Perley. "Toward a Sociology of the Reconciliation of Conflicting Desires." *Canadian Review of Sociology* 53, no. 4 (November 2016): 474–81.

Osiel, Mark J. "Ever Again: Legal Remembrance of Administrative Massacre." *University of Pennsylvania Law Review* 144 (1995): 463–704.

Pape, Elise. "Human Remains of Ovaherero and Nama: Transnational Dynamics in Post-Genocidal Restitutions." *Human Remains and Violence* 4, no. 2 (2018): 90–106.

Pape, Elise. "Postcolonial Debates in Germany—An Overview." *African Sociological Review* 21, no. 2 (2017): 2–14.

Paulose, Regina Menachery, and Ronald Gordon Rogo. "Addressing Colonial Crimes through Reparations: The Mau Mau, Herero and Nama." *State Crime* 7, no. 2 (August 2018): 369–88.

Peltonen, Matti. "From Discourse to '*Dispositif*': Michael Foucault's Two Histories." *Historical Reflections* 30, no. 2 (Summer 2004), 205–19.

Pozen, David E. "Transparency's Ideological Drift." *The Yale Law Journal* 128 (2018): 100–165.

Rassool, Ciraj. "Re-Storing the Skeletons of Empire: Return, Reburial, and Rehumanization in Southern Africa." *Journal of Southern African Studies* 41, no. 3 (2015): 653–79.

Reinders, Robert. "Racism on the Left: E. D. Morel and the 'Black Horror on the Rhine.'" *International Review of Social History* 13 (1968): 1–28.

Rosengarten, Andrea. "'A Most Gruesome Sight': Colonial Warfare, Racial Thought, and the Question of 'Radicalization' during the First World War in German South West Africa." *History: The Journal of the Historical Association* 101, no. 346 (July 2016): 437–47.

Rothberg, Michael. "From Gaza to Warsaw, Mapping Multidirectional Memory," *Criticism* 53, no. 4 (Fall 2011): 523–48.

Sarkin, Jeremy. "Reparations for Historical Human Rights Violation: The International and Historical Dimensions of the Alien Torts Claim Act Genocide Case of the Herero of Namibia." *Human Rights Review* 9, no. 3 (2008): 331–60.

Sarkin, Jeremy, and Carly Fowler. "Reparations for Historical Human Rights Violations: The International Historical Dimensions of the Alien Torts Claim Act Genocide Case of the Herero of Namibia." *Human Rights Review* 9 (2008): 331–60.

Schaller, Dominik J. "Raphael Lemkin's View of European Colonial Rule in Africa: Between Condemnation and Admiration." *Journal of Genocide Research* 7, no. 4 (December 2005): 531–38.

Schramm, Katharina. "Casts, Bones and DNA, Interrogating the Relationship between Science and Postcolonial Indigeneity in Contemporary South Africa." *Anthropology Southern Africa* 39, no. 2 (June 2016): 1–14.

Schwartz, Joan M., and Terry Cook. "Archives, Records, and Power: The Making of Modern Memory." *Archival Science* 2 (2002): 1–19.

Shelton, Dinah. "The World of Atonement: Reparations for Historical Injustices," *Miskolc Journal of International Law* 1, no. 2 (2004): 259–89.

Shenhav, Yehouda. "Beyond 'Instrumental Rationality': Lord Cromer and the Imperial Roots of Eichmann's Bureaucracy." *Journal of Genocide Studies* 15, no. 4 (2013): 379–99.

Shiner, Larry. "Reading Foucault: Anti-Method and the Genealogy of Power Knowledge." *History and Theory* 21, no. 3 (October 1982): 382–98.

Spitzer, Ryan Michael. "The African Holocaust: Should Europe Pay for Reparations to African for Colonialism and Slavery?" *Vanderbilt Journal of Transnational Law* 35 (October 2002): 1313–48.

Sprenger, Nick, Robert G. Rodriguez, and Ngondi A. Kamatuka. "The Ovaherero/Nama Genocide: A Case for an Apology and Reparations." *European Scientific Journal* 13 (June 2017): 120–46.

Steinweis, Alan E. "East Europe and the Notion of the 'Frontier,' in Germany to 1945," *Yearbook of European Studies* 13 (1999): 56–69.

Stoler, Ann Laura. "Colonial Aphasia: Race and Disabled Histories in France." *Public Culture* 23, no. 1 (Winter 2011): 121–56.

Stoler, Ann Laura. "Colonial Archives and the Arts of Governance." *Archival Science* 2 (2002): 87–109.

Stoler, Ann Laura. "On Archiving as Dissensus." *Comparative Studies of South Asia, Africa and the Middle East* 38, no. 1 (2018): 43–56.

Strecker, Amy. "Indigenous Land Rights and Caribbean Reparations Discourse." *Leiden International Law* 30 (2017): 629–46.

Strickland, Rennard. "Genocide-at-Law: An Historic and Contemporary View of the Native American Experience." *University of Kansas Law Review* 34 (Summer 1986): 713–55.

Tamboukou, Maria. "Truth Telling in Foucault and Arendt: *Parrhesia*, the Pariah and Academics in Dark Times." *Journal of Education Policy* 21, no. 6 (2012): 1–17.

Torpey, John. "'Making Whole What Has Been Smashed': Reflections on Reparations." *The Journal of Modern History* 73, no. 2 (June 2001): 333–58.

Van den Herik, L. "Addressing 'Colonial Crimes' through Reparations? Adjudicating Dutch Atrocities Committed in Indonesia." *Journal of International Criminal Justice* 10 (2012): 693–705.

Van Heyningen, Elizabeth. "The South African War as Humanitarian Crisis." *International Review of the Red Cross* 97 (2015): 999–1028.

Veracini, Lorenzo. "Decolonizing Setter Colonialism: Kill the Setter in Him and Save the Man." *American Indian Culture and Research Journal* 41, no. 1 (2017): 1–18.

von Hammerstein, Katharina. "The Herero: Witnessing Germany's 'Other Genocide.'" *Contemporary French and Francophone Studies*, 20, no. 2 (2016): 267–86.

Wallace, Marion. "'Making Tradition': Healing History and Ethnic Identity among Otjiherero-Speakers in Namibia, c. 1850–1950." *Journal of South African Studies* 29, no. 2 (June 2003): 355–372.

Weigend, Guido G. "German Settlement Patters in Namibia." *Geographical Review* 75, no. 2 (April 1985): 156–59.

Werner, Wolfgang. "Playing Soldiers: The Truppenspieler Movement among the Herero of Namibia, 1915–1945." *Journal of South African Studies* 16 (1990): 485–502.

Wilson, George M. "Edward Said on Contrapuntal Reading." *Philosophy and Literature* 18, no. 2 (October 1994): 265–73.

Wittwer-Backofen, Ursala. Mareen Kástner, Daniel Möller, Marina Vohberger, Sabine Lutz-Bonengel, and Dieter Speck. "Ambiguous Provenance? Experience with Provenance Analysis of Human Remains from Namibia in the Alexander Ecker Collection." *Anthropologishcer Anzeiger* 71, nos. 1–2 (March 2014): 65–86.

Yacoubian,George S. "Financial, Territorial, and Moral Reparations for the 1915 Armenian Massacres." *War Crimes, Genocide, & Crimes Against Humanity* 4 (2010): 59–98.

Zimmerer, Jürgen. "Colonialism and the Holocaust—Toward an Archaeology of Genocide." *Development Dialogue* 50 (2008): 95–124.

SELECT MATERIALS FROM THE INTERNET

Buser, Andreas. "German Genocide in Namibia before U.S. Courts." *Võlkerrechtsblog*. January 11, 2017. http://voelkerrechtsblog.org/german-genocide-in-namibia-before-u-s-courts/.

Butler, Judith. "Precarious Life and the Obligations of Cohabitation." *Nobel Museum, Stockholm,* May, 2011. https://www.terada.ca/discourse/wp-content/uploads/2012/06/Butler_Sweden2011.pdf.

Chutel, Lynsey. "The Remains of the Victims of Germany's First Genocide Are in the American Natural History Museum." *Quartz.* September 16, 2017. https://qz.com/africa/1078660/namibia-genocide-natural-history-museum-has-remains-of-victims-of-germanys-genocide-in-africa/.

Eckstein, Lars. "Recollecting Bones: The Remains of German-Australian Colonial Entanglements." *Philosophische Fakultät, Universität Postsdam.* 2016. https://publish-up.uni-potsdam.de/opus4-ubp/frontdoor/deliver/index/docId/41365/file/ppr147.online.pdf.

Erichsen, Casper W. "Shark Island, 1904–1907: A Historical Overview." Namibia Digital Repository . n.d. http://namibia.leadr.msu.edu/items/show/154.

Förster, Larissa, and Sarah Fründt. Human Remains in Museums and Collections: A Critical Engagement with the 'Recommendations' of the German Museums Association (2013), Editorial." *H/Soz/Kult,* February 2017. https://www.hsozkult.de/debate/id/diskussionen-3909.

Guettel, Jens-Uwe. "The SPD Should Return to Its Anticolonial Roots." *The Jacobin Magazine.* August 2018. https://www.jacobinmag.com/2018/08/spd-namibia-herero-nama-genocide-colonialism.

Hamburg Postcolonial Staff, "Herero-Genocide without Apology and Compensation?" *Hamburg Postkolonial.* October 7, 2015. https://hhpostkolonial.wordpress.com/2015/10/07/herero-genocide-without-apology-and-compensation/.

Lammert, Norbert. "Deutsche ohne Grade: Wer in der Bundesrepublik vom Armenier-Genozid Spricht, Darf vom Deutschen Vőlkermord an den Herero und Nama nicht Schweigen. *Zeit,* July 23, 2015. http://www/zeit.de/2015/28/voelkermord-armenier-herero-norbert-lammert.

Pape, Elise. "Herero Activists in the United States: Demanding Recognition and Reparation for the First Genocide of the Twentieth Century." *American Institute for Contemporary German Studies, November* 1, 2017. https://www.aicgs.org/publication/herero-activists-in-the-united-states/.

Pickering, Michael. "A Helping Hand? Comments on the 'Recommendations for the Care of Human Remains in Museums and Collections' by the Deutscher Museumbund (German Museums Association)." *H/Soz/Kult,* February 2017. http://hsozkult.geschichte.hu-berlin.de/index.asp?id=4000&view=pdf&pn=forum&type=diskussione.

Rassool, Ciraj. "German Museums, Human Remains and the Challenges of Colonial Legacies." *H/Soz/Kult,* February, 2017. https://www.hsozkult.de/debate/id/diskussionen-4016.

Sharma, Gouri. "Namibia's Long Fight for Justice," *New Internationalist.* August 2, 2018. https://newint.org/features/web-exclusive/2018/08/02/namibia-germanys-forgotten-genocide.

Skŏld, Mattias. "Germany Treating Carefully Regarding Colonial Crimes." *Nordiska Afrikainstitutet.* June 9, 2017. http://nai.uu.se/news/articles/2017/06/09/132653/index.xml.

Steinmann, Daniel. "Reparations Claimants Leverage German State Property in New York to Establish District Court's Sovereign Jurisdiction." *Namibian Economist.* February 18, 2018. https://economist.com.na/32789/headlines/reparations-claimants-leverage-german-state-property-in-new-york-to-establish-district-courts-sovereign-jurisdiction/.

Steinmetz, George. "From "Native Policy' to Extermination: German Southwest Africa, 1904, in Comparative Perspective." *University of Michigan's Theory and Research in Comparative Social Analysis.* Los Angeles: University of California, 2005. https://escholarship.org/uc/item/11z1k021.

Stephan, Felicia. "The First Genocide of the 20th Century before a Domestic Court." *Vŏlkerrechtsblog*. May 28, 2018. https://voelkerrechtsblog.org/the-first-genocide-of-the-20th-century-before-a-domestic-court/.

Talmon, Stefan. "Suing Germany over the Genocide in Namibia in U.S. Courts." *German Practice in International Law*. November 23, 2017. https://gpil.jura.uni-bonn.de/2017/11/suing-germany-genocide-namibia-u-s-courts-pitfalls-serving-summons-german-government/.

Zuern, Elke. "Namibia's Monuments to Genocide." *Dissent*. June 13, 2017. https://www.dissentmagazine.org/blog/namibia-genocide-monuments-reparations-germany.

GOVERNMENT DOCUMENTS

Alien Tort Claims Act of 1789. Title 28 U.S. Code. Chapter 85. Section 1350.

The German General Staff. *Die Kampfe der deutschen Truppen in Sud- westafrika* . Berlin: E. S. Mittler, 1907.

Gertze, Neville Melvin. *Report on the Return of Twenty Human Skulls from Germany to Namibia*. Berlin: Embassy of the Republic of Namibia, 2011.

Great Britain, *Report on the Natives of South West Africa and Their Treatment by Germany* (London: His Majesty's Stationary Office, 1918.

LEGAL CASES AND LEGAL DOCUMENTS

The Herero People's Reparations Corporation et al., v. Deutsche Bank Ag, et al. Civ. No. 01-01868 (CKK), July 31, 2003. 2003 WL 26119014.

Herero People's Reparations Corporation v. Deutsche Bank. 370 F. 3d 1192, 361 U.S. App. D.C. 468. (D.C. Circuit, 2004).

Herero People's Reparation Corp. v. Deutsche Bank, A.G., 543 U.S. 987, 125 S. Ct. 508, 160 L. Ed. 2d 371 (2004).

Hereros v. Deutsche Afrika-Linien GMBLT & Co. (3rd Cir. 2007).

Goldmann, Matthias. Declaration of Matthias Goldman, *Vekuii Rukoro et al. v. Federal Republic of Germany*, Civ. No. 17-0062, April 24, 2018. https://papers.ssrn.com/sol3/papers.cfm?abstract_id=3169852.

Lockman, Michael J. "Jurisdiction over Germany for Violations of International Law in *Rukoro, et al. v. Federal Republic of Germany*." 17-cv-00062-LTS. New York: Southern District Court of New York, 2017.

McCallion, Kenneth, Richard H. Weisberg, Thomas A. Holman, and Yechezkel Rodal. *Vekuii Rukoro et al. v. Federal Republic of Germany*, Civ. No. 17-0062, Amended Class Action Complaint. New York City: United States District Southern Court, February 14, 2018.

Princz v. Federal Republic of Germany. 26 F. 3d 1166, 1173 (D.C. Cir 1994).

Vekuii Rukoro et al. v. Federal Republic of Germany. U.S. District Court for the Southern District of New York. No. 17 CV 62-LTS. (March 6, 2019).

THESES AND DISSERTATIONS

Biwa, Memory. *"Weaving the Past with Threads of Memory": Narratives and Commemorations of the Colonial War in Southern Namibia*. Cape Town: University of Western Cape, 2012.

Jonker, Leonor. "'More Than Just an Object': A Material Analysis of the Return and Retention of Namibian Skulls from Germany." Master's thesis. Utrecht: Universiteit Utrecht, 2015.

Morgan, Karie L. "To Heal the Wounds": Namibian Ovaherero's Contests over Coming to Terms with the German Colonial Past." Dissertation. Chapel Hill: University of North Carolina, 2010.

Wallenkampf, Arnold Valentin. *The Herero Rebellion in South West Africa, 1904–1906: A Study in German Colonialism*. Dissertation. Los Angeles: University of California, 1969.

Woxland, Max. *Lebensraum in Context: A Challenge to the Southwest Africa to Auschwitz Continuity Thesis*. Waltham, MA: Brandeis University, 2013.

Index

About the Author

Marouf Hasian, Jr. is a full professor in the Department of Communication at the University of Utah. He is the author of more than a 150 journal articles, book chapters, and book reviews. He the author of numerous other books, as well, on such topics as eugenics, law and rhetoric, critical memory studies, the West Africa Ebola crisis, the situation in Gaza, and medical humanitarian issues. He is currently working on several projects related to various national and international claims regarding diverse types of physical and cultural genocides.

www.ingramcontent.com/pod-product-compliance
Ingram Content Group UK Ltd.
Pitfield, Milton Keynes, MK11 3LW, UK
UKHW041126071026
15587UKWH00009B/263

9 781683 931881